PRESENTS

WHAT IF?

Experts' Survival Strategies for Natural Disasters, Urban Threats, and Other Deadly Emergencies

COMPILED BY THE EDITORS OF
OFFGRID MAGAZINE

Published by

Recoil Offgrid Books, an imprint of Caribou Media Group, LLC
5600 W. Grande Market Drive, Suite 100
Appleton, WI 54913
offgridweb.com | gundigest.com

To order books or other products call 920.471.4522 ext.104
or visit us online at gundigeststore.com

DISCLAIMER: Prices and details for items featured in RECOIL are set by the manufacturers and retailers, and are subject to change without notice. Please read all local and federal laws carefully before attempting to purchase any products shown in this guide or building your own firearms. Laws change frequently and, although our text was accurate at the time it was originally published, it may have changed between then and what's currently legal.

ISBN-13: 978-1-951115-79-1

Edited and designed by Recoil Offgrid Staff

Printed in the United States of America

10 9 8 7 6 5 4 3 2 1

CHAPTERS

Natural Disaster

Advice on how to prepare for Mother Nature's worst and the collateral damage that can be both unpredictable and indefinite.

Crime

Learn to thwart some of the most common methods criminals use to target victims and carry out their crimes.

Terrorism

We take a look at tactics historically used by terrorists and mass murderers to wreak havoc on society.

CHAPTERS
(CONTINUED)

Travel

From traveling domestically to internationally, check out how you can survive threatening situations away from home.

Grid Down

Take precautionary measures to sustain yourself when the resources we take for granted become unavailable.

"This is a call to people to understand how much power this magazine is providing to its readership — we shouldn't wait for the storm to come to prepare the umbrella. This book is a treasure for people willing to see that what they are giving us is personal responsibility. And that's empowering."

— Ed Calderon
Edsmanifesto.com

Ed Calderon spent more than a decade working at the forefront of counter-narcotics, organized crime investigation, and public safety in Northern Mexico. He now lives in the US where he travels nationwide, teaching various urban survival skills to law enforcement organizations, military units and private citizens alike, with a hard focus on anti-kidnapping and improvised weapons. The quote above, submitted by him as we finalized the release of this book, is flattering given his unique experience — he has lived a lifestyle of active preparation to ensure his survival in environments filled with imminent threats.

This serves as an excellent example of how preparedness has changed since the birth of the RECOIL OFFGRID brand. When we started in 2013 as a counterpart to our sister publication RECOIL magazine, the term "survival" referred primarily to traditional bushcraft skills. Many people's primary plan was "bugging out" to some other location and roughing it for a little while until the worst blew over. The idea of "prepping" was almost considered an extremist ideology by much of mainstream American culture. Those who took charge over their own well-being were met with derision in the form of self-serving questions like What are you so afraid of?

Many of those same people have, for the last two years, had the answer to their questions delivered to their doorstep in the form of supply shortages, riots, spiking street crime, lockdowns, and the inconsistent, somewhat haphazard rules of pandemic mitigation. This is why we've worked hard over the last several years to diversify our content far beyond that of many survival publications. We include preparedness topics relevant to urban and suburban families who may be faced with any number of emergency situations they won't be able to "bug out" from. Topics such as evasive driving, concealed weapons, urban gardening, and information security — knowledge once dismissed as apocalyptic Hollywood fantasy — have all borne real world applications of one kind or another in very recent history.

While we do aim to entertain as well as inform, we hope you will not dismiss our What If scenarios as apocalyptic prose. Our team has worked hard to draw from news headlines and documented case studies, and called upon established practitioners with relevant expertise, to provide some thought-provoking responses to situations we've not just imagined but seen unfold on our phones and TV screens.

— Tom Marshall
Editor, RECOIL OFFGRID

01

YOU'RE FORCED TO ENDURE A BLIZZARD WITH NO UTILITIES?

By RECOIL OFFGRID Staff
Illustrations by Robert Bruner

Early in 2021, Texas faced record-low temperatures that caused millions to be without power. Think about that for a second. Even in one of the most industrialized nations in the world, Mother Nature dealt a huge (and freezing) blow to commerce and living conditions. As human beings, we've become dangerously over-reliant on our climate-controlled life and amenities. Although this winter storm was a freak occurrence, there's no doubt that its estimated death toll of 230 could've been reduced by better preparation.

Now, imagine yourself stuck in an area with frigid conditions where you must forgo many of the resources you might've stockpiled at home. Whether you live in a locale that could potentially be affected by severe cold during the winter months or you just happen to be vacationing somewhere remote, do you know what it'd take to survive if immediate help from first responders is nowhere in sight and utilities are disabled? How can you use the resources at your disposal to survive plummeting temperatures?

The Scenario

Situation type: Blizzard/power outage
Your Crew: You and two friends
Location: Chandalar Lake, Alaska
Season: Winter
Weather: Snowy/windy; high 4 degrees F, low -10 degrees F

The Setup

You and two friends have been planning an Alaskan hunting trip for several months. You rent a remote hunting lodge in a rural area near Chandalar Lake that's only accessible on foot. Although it's wintertime and you knew the weather would already be brutal, the forecast is anticipating a blizzard. Since it's too late to cancel and get a refund, you decide to roll the dice and make the best of it, hoping the weather will turn around and become more favorable.

After arriving at the airport, you and your friends rent an SUV, stop to buy some food and other provisions, and venture down a long dirt road to a designated parking area before heading out on foot to the lodge. The path up to the parking area is a windy uphill track, which would make getting back down nearly impossible in heavy snow, and you have no idea if the road below is regularly cleared or not. It's inconvenient, but you have to make several trips back to the car in order to carry all your supplies to the lodge. However, you're confident your experience will be a positive one and you have enough food and water to hold you over for the few days you'll be there.

The Complication

You bring a small battery-operated radio to get updates on weather since cell service in this area is practically non-existent. Daylight is also compromised by the fact that sunrise in this part of Alaska typically happens around 11 a.m., with sunset occurring around 2:30 p.m. You settle in for the night with winds picking up and heavy snowfall, hoping that the weather will pass you by. You rise early to trek out to the hunting blinds and wait, but the snowfall is practically at window level now. You and a few friends have to force the door open to push the snowpack back far enough to even get a leg through the door. In other words, your situation is getting grim, and you decide not to risk getting caught in the continuing blizzard by going out to hunt.

The radio is saying the blizzard is one of the worst in the state's history, and it's anticipated to go on for two weeks. Then, the unexpected begins happening. Power at the lodge goes out. The gas system soon freezes over, as does the water, meaning you have nothing to drink except what you brought. There's no heat in the lodge except for an old potbelly stove that you'll have to go procure wood for. The food and water you brought isn't going to last a couple weeks. What do you do? Try to get back to the car, which may be compromised by an impassable road? Attempt to walk until you find help or cell service? Try and wait it out? What's the best course of action for this situation? We asked cold-weather survival expert Jerry Saunders and forester Patrick Diedrich for their takes on the situation.

FORESTER PATRICK DIEDRICH'S APPROACH

Thinking about spending a multi-day trip in an environment as majestic and foreboding as Alaska can be an exhilarating – and perhaps intimidating – proposition. Living in the relative comfort of the lower 48 means that I have access to just about anything I could want, including close proximity to developed communities and their emergency services. As I plan for a hunting trip to one of the most remote locations in North America, knowing in advance that a severe blizzard is on the way, I use one word to guide my planning process: redundancy.

Hunting in freezing temperatures can be tricky in the best of circumstances, and I want to be confident that my friends and I will have an enjoyable trip, regardless of a massive snowstorm on the way. When I come back home, I want to stock my freezer full of freshly harvested game, not to nurse frostbite. I start thinking about the most likely scenarios my friends and I will find ourselves in the middle of and work from there. Out of everything that could possibly happen, at a minimum we'll need several strategies to stay warm, hydrated, and consume enough calories to maintain a healthy metabolism in cold conditions.

Pre-trip planning also includes doing a little research on the behavior of the plants and animals in the region, doing some map reconnaissance and identifying nearby towns or useful natural resources. One of the most important things anyone can do before heading out into the wilderness – whether it's for a few hours or a few days – is to let someone know where you'll be and how long you plan to be there. Before I find myself in a place with no cell reception, I let friends and family know what's going on. Since we're going to an isolated lodge in central Alaska, it may also be a wise decision to reach out to local emergency services, and just let them know where we'll be staying. If they don't hear from us after an extended inclement weather event, they'll know to at least check on us after things have calmed down.

Backcountry Living

After disembarking from the plane in Alaska, the first thing I do is ensure I leave the airport with a 4WD vehicle. The higher the ground clearance the better, in case the snow starts to accumulate on the road on our way there. My own vehicle would have a strong tow strap and some emergency gear, and I'd try to acquire this for the rental. If these items are unavailable, other than giving the vehicle a careful inspection and filling it with a full tank of gas, I'll just have to drive more slowly and be extra cautious while heading to the lodge.

Since it seems like hunting for dinner may not be an option, I'm going to need extra provisions. On the way to the lodge, we stop at the nearest store and load up. High winds and blowing snow almost always result in trees over power lines. No power can render any steps to keep water flowing or heat radiating completely useless. Sure, there's plenty of wood to burn in the surrounding forests, but acquiring firewood is physically intensive. Pair that with working in the cold, and the average adult could potentially burn thousands more calories than they would under normal conditions. This means preparing extra calories, ideally foods high in fat, protein, and sugars. We buy as many extra nuts, canned meats, and snacks like granola or peanut butter as we can reasonably bring with us.

Calories accounted for, we double-check to make sure we have packed everything we'd normally bring on a camping trip, plus a few specialty items for hunting in the snow – sleeping bags rated for freezing temperatures, tarps, and wool blankets to stay warm. Items made of modern wool are a great way to reduce the amount of gear I need to bring and avoid having items out of commission if they get soggy. Redundancy as my mantra, I make sure to pack enough so if anything important gets wet or broken, I have some kind of contingency. Tools for starting a fire, such as lighters and matches are a no-brainer, but having a few extra is better than running out when you need it most. For preparing firewood, we need an ax and a crosscut or bowsaw. Chainsaws are a nice luxury, but they also require fuel, sharpening, and firm footing on the ground – all of which may be unavailable, and too cumbersome to stock up on. Snowshoes and a sled for easily moving a carcass or firewood will also make life much easier.

After triple-checking our supplies and arriving at the parking location, we quickly begin moving our supplies from the vehicle to the lodge. Two of us will make any necessary trips to get all the gear and food up to the lodge, while the third begins looking for more firewood and kindling. Restocking a healthy supply of firewood before leaving a lodge or campsite is considered the pinnacle of proper backcountry etiquette. But, even if we find a good stash of dry wood when we get to the lodge, it'd be prudent to collect as much as we can before the snow starts to really starts to fly in earnest. In this region, it'll most likely be paper birch or sitka spruce that burns with the highest amount of BTUs, and as an additional bonus, the resinous bark of paper birch will light on fire wet or dry. Upon completion of the move-in, we hunker down for the night with flashlights and the emergency radio on standby.

Staying Toasty

Knowing in advance that a winter storm is moving in, waking up to rapidly accumulating snowfall isn't alarming. But losing power and heat changes this outing from a hunting event to a survival situation. Using the final moments of the propane heat to get organized and come up with a plan is critical.

Getting everyone into the same room as the potbellied stove, we systematically seal all drafts with wadded paper, duct tape, or whatever we can find. We'd also need to ensure that the flue on the stove is open, and that the chimney is free of any obstructions or perforations to avoid succumbing to carbon monoxide poisoning. Everyone stacks as much firewood as we can find close enough to the stove that the radiant heat will help dry out any moisture. We then summon our inner children to build a multi-layered living room tent out of some of the tarps and blankets we brought. This is going to be an A-frame-style shelter with the back sealed to the floor and the opening facing the stove. Doing this creates an insulating effect between us and the interior walls, reducing the amount of fire we need to burn to stay reasonably warm.

One of us will always be on fire duty, watching the potbellied stove to ensure the fire is burning continuously. The designated fire attendant will also monitor our emergency radio for any important messages relayed by the National Weather Service. The remaining two people can either catch some shut eye or use any breaks in the weather to go in search of more firewood and food.

If we leave to gather more supplies, we must be careful not to allow too much warm air to escape. Much like an airlock on a spaceship, instead of leaving directly from the stove room, we use an adjacent room to venture outdoors. This may mean having to use a window closer to the ceiling if the snow is too high, or tunneling our way up using the outside wall of the lodge as a guide. Some buildings this far north even have what are called "doors to nowhere" exclusively for this purpose.

If the weather persists much longer than our supply of wood is lasting, we could use the axe and saw to start breaking down any wooden furniture or cabinets to keep the fire from dying. The worst-case scenario would be having to cannibalize the wooden structure of the lodge to a point that using any more material would expose the warm room to the outside. This could be avoided with thorough initial preps and a watchful eye on weather conditions.

Hunting in the Snow

Maybe the storm will not be as terrible as predicted, and we'll get to do what we came for. Waiting comfortably in one place in the cold is an art that's not as easy as it sounds. Wearing multiple layers that I can vent while moving from lodge to blind, and vice versa, will avoid excessive sweat accumulation.

Bringing a day pack will allow room for additional gear or give me a place to store layers to prevent overheating. Additional items to avoid cold injuries and ensure a successful hunt would be a face mask and ski-goggles, hand and boot warmers, trail mix, a thermos, binos, and an emergency fire-starting kit.

Hunting this deep into the backcountry means I will most likely not have to stray too far from the lodge to yield results, and I don't feel like having a satellite phone or some other expensive GPS communication is absolutely necessary. But a reliable compass and a roll of neon flagging will help me get to and from the blind without getting disoriented. If visibility worsens and white-out conditions seem like a possibility, I'll retrace my path and head back immediately.

Nourishment

Having three square meals a day isn't as concerning as staying hydrated. Even if we're unable to hunt, and we run out of our provisions, we'll survive for several weeks if we stay warm and have access to sterile drinking water. A silver lining to this scenario is that we have frozen water in abundance all around us. By keeping that potbellied stove fired up, we can continuously melt snow and boil it to kill any harmful biological contaminants. If there's access to certain evergreen trees, there may even be needles and scales to make tea rich in vitamin C. Our initial preps should help us avoid any serious hunger concerns, but to be safe, we'll ration food by dividing it into as many days as the blizzard is forecasted to last. Eating before trying to go outside to hunt or gather wood may give us just enough energy to perform these tasks without becoming overly fatigued.

Fighting Panic

Keeping spirits high is just as important as warding off the cold and staying hydrated. Having a positive mental attitude has been scientifically proven to help people heal from injuries faster and avoid getting sick. Many of us are not used to the prolonged absence of sensory stimulation, so being isolated in silence can be unnerving. Staying focused on the duties that need to be done instead of dwelling on the dire circumstances is one way to avoid anxiety. Another way could be to come up with games or find something to keep our minds and hands busy, such as working on ways to improve our living situation.

COLD-WEATHER SURVIVAL INSTRUCTOR JERRY SAUNDERS' APPROACH

Rolling the dice on a possible two-week blizzard in Chandalar, Alaska, would be a very calculated decision. I wouldn't even consider attempting a gamble like this unless the plus two that I am bringing are seasoned veterans of the cold as well. If I'm going on a sketchy backcountry adventure, I want several trusted people to know where I am and do as much as they can to get me out, but only if they can do so without compromising their own safety.

In 1991, a Canadian C-130 Hercules crashed just 12 miles from the base it was tasked with resupplying. Due to a severe blizzard, it took the Canadian military over 30 hours to get to the crash site. Many people died due to exposure (-60 degrees F) and many more people willingly put their lives at risk to save them. Being stuck in a cabin for two weeks is an inconvenience — don't turn it into a survival situation for everyone.

Preparation

Comms Plan: If I know a blizzard is coming and there's a possibility of my 72-hour hunting trip turning into a future survival documentary, I'm going to call the lodge owner prior to departing the lower 48 and ask about contingencies and available resources in the area. I'm going to leave my detailed itinerary with my emergency contact and give them explicit instructions to "notify everyone" if I don't call within 24 hours of my planned re-contact time. I may not be in immediate danger, but it's nice to be a blip on more radars than less.

Bring the Right Gear: One of the best pieces of gear you can take with you to an extreme cold-weather environment is a ticket for an extra checked bag. It doesn't matter what I'm already carrying. I use an old G.I. sea bag because it's long enough to hold my larger items and robust enough to keep gear from tearing through. Snowshoes, ax, Silky Big Boy saw, avalanche shovel, large cold-weather boots, and most of my heavy weight down items travel there to pad it. Spend the time beforehand acquiring the proper sizes and clothing for the environment. I'd avoid a travel plan solely based on attempting to rent or purchase these items upon arrival. Remote locations are notorious for having unreliable supply chains and making wrong sizes "work."

Map Study: Print hard copies. Then laminate these hard copies. Everyone gets one, and everyone is clear on basic routes to key items, such as the nearest airport or best medevac route. Even on a sunny day, this is an important lifesaving precaution. Technology is great, but the cold has a nasty habit of draining batteries and with the forecasted blizzard, having low to no reception should come as no surprise.

I like to use www.caltopo.com to print my maps. I can add and remove layers as I see fit, and it has tools to measure distance and mark my route. For a trip with this much risk involved, I definitely want to have magnetic azimuths and distances from the lodge to the hunting blinds and any location that may aid my exit strategy, such as the parking area and the airstrip.

Along with map and compass, I carry a Garmin InReach. This acts as nav and part of my comm plan also, but I don't heavily rely on it.

Dress for Failure: "Tighty whities" have no place in the tundra. I say that because it's funny and it catches your attention, but the infamous tight, white, cotton undergarment is a perfect example of what not to wear. The old adage "cotton kills" is meant to be a stern warning, but not always true. Cotton isn't recommended as an undergarment because it's absorbent and holds the sweat next to your body. Having that moisture in contact with your skin is what robs your body of heat. However, wool and many other synthetics do not absorb the moisture like cotton, but transport it from inside of the clothing to the outside and allow it to evaporate away using your body's natural radiation. That's called "wicking."

Avoid tight-fitting clothing as it can constrict your blood flow. If you're not walking, loosen your boots and when you're on the move, don't over-tighten them.

Dress in layers. The base layer is next to your skin and consists of undergarments if you so choose, and a lightweight wool shirt/pant combo. The mid-weight layer goes over the base layer and usually consists of a quarter-zip fleece and fleece pant combo. On top of that goes the heavy down layer. I have many pieces of down for different levels of warmth, but for blind hunting below zero, I want the heaviest stuff I have. Finally, the environmental layer consists of materials meant to be impervious to rain, wind, and snow, but it should still have zipper vents for when I'm on the move.

Only bring wool socks. Don't skimp here. Wear only one pair unless you buy the next size up. Two pairs in the same size will be too constricting.

A la Carte: Two items I carry in my hunting pack for emergencies are a MSR Windburner personal camp stove and two freeze-dried meals. These are typically compressed as small as possible and wrapped in duct tape for the best storage.

Going into an extreme cold-weather environment, I know that my calorie intake will need to increase from the recommended 2,000 calories a day to somewhere closer to 9,000 calories a day. While on a ski trip into the Arctic, I was eating a pound of butter and six chocolate bars a day, on top of the three meals I was eating already, and I was *still* losing weight. So, buy lots of butter, chocolate, and bacon.

A practice I put in place a long time ago when travelling to remote northern villages is that when doing my planned stop at a grocery store for supplies, on top of everything else I buy, I always make sure to pick up one of those 12-pack boxes of ramen. If I can, I buy the spicy ones — they warm you up faster. For around $6, you can have 12 extra meals, supplement current meals, or just have something to leave behind for the next guy.

Buddy Check: Verify that you have redundancies within your group. Make sure up to the departure date that you're talking and asking each other the tough questions. Did you leave a solid contact plan? Do you have the meds you need? And make sure to know who has allergies to what.

Crisis

Horse and Rider Concept: Imagine for a minute that your brain is a horse. Horses are more quick and powerful than you and I will ever be, but also highly emotional. If you've ever seen an out-of-control horse, you know that's a problem. Now also imagine a small but very rational rider, controlling the horse and not allowing it to run wild. You need to be that rider at this moment.

Priorities of work become very defined at this point. You need to dig out, ensure proper ventilation, stay dry, warm, and fed. You have all that you need at the cabin. At this point, attempting an exit strategy could serve to only further compound the problem.

W.I.N. (What's Important Now?): With utilities out, I'd immediately transition to the woodstove. Dig yourself out of the front door, or if you have to, go out a second story or loft window if available. With bad visibility, I'm going to tether myself to a secure part of the house using paracord or some other secure makeshift leash. If there's a woodstove, there may be a woodpile lying around. This is one of the key things I look for when taking initial inventory at a rental cabin.

IBT (Individual Based Tactics): While I'm working outside, the other two of my group can be inside improving and insulating a new place to sleep. Close what doors you can and hang a covering over open doorways to act as an airlock. I've even used my SOL two-person survival blanket and sewing needles from my survival kit to accomplish this task.

The Last Frontier

If you've never worked with a wood stove, here's a crash course of everything I've learned in the last six years of heating my cabin with only wood.

Cold air is heavy. Start with a relatively clean stove. Make sure all the ports are open — you want it to draw as much oxygen as possible. The initial moments of your fire need to be really intense in order to push the cold air up and out. If it's only snow blocking the stove pipe, it will burn up and through it, but if it's ice, you're going to have to clear it.

Burn it wide open. It might be tempting to try and dampen the fire to make it last longer, but this makes it more prone to smoke and increases the risk of a chimney fire. Who knows when it was cleaned last? Play it safe and burn it to completion. If your room is small, you won't need to keep it going non-stop.

Clean but not too clean. Ash is insulative. You'll need to clean out the stove at some point. Clean out enough to allow sufficient space for the burn, but leave about an inch of ash on the bottom of the stove. Toss the ash outside to help give you traction on the ice and snow.

Gather wood. You need a sled. It's a staple of any northern hunting lodge. You don't really use backpacks in over-the-snow travel, you use a sled to disperse the weight onto the snow behind you. If you can't find one, make it. It'll take about a full-size tree a day. Birch will be your most easily identified tree here. You'll know it by its white bark that peels off like paper. Save the bark because this is some bulletproof tinder. This is why I never travel without my ax and a good saw like the Silky Big Boy. With this saw/ax combo, it takes me roughly two hours to process a tree to ready to burn firewood.

Create a routine. Take turns getting wood, splitting wood, and cleaning the stove. Chores such as this can become a choke point and create discord in the group.

Utilities

With the power out, there's no electricity for the well to draw water. Grab a pot from the kitchen, and pour what water you have in it. "It takes water to make water." By just throwing snow in a pot, you can impart a seriously burnt taste on your water. If it's a large enough pot, it'll just lightly steam all day and put back the moisture in the air that the woodstove will take out.

Be aware that propane is an odorless gas, but has an added chemical called mercaptan. Mercaptan gives it the offensive "rotten egg" smell. If you smell this at any time, you must get out and ventilate immediately. As far as troubleshooting the gas system, here's what I know: Start at the tank, lift the protective cap on the tank, and check the gauge first, so you know if you even have gas. Then, follow the copper line to a regulator – it looks roughly the size of a hamburger and will usually be brown or white. While propane doesn't freeze until it reaches around -44 degrees F, sometimes the regulators can stick or become frozen. If it appears frosted, you may be able to wrap a few of the disposable hand-warmers around it and wrap it with a towel to gently rewarm and insulate it. Don't forget to explore the property. You might find other heating options, such as a propane grill outside, or a Mr. Buddy Heater stored with ice fishing stuff.

Don't Forget the Owner's Closet

Most of the rental properties that I've frequented up north, and I know the ones I take care of for people, all have an "owner's closet." This is a survival situation treasure trove. It's usually stocked with family photos, the water heater, the owner's personal tools, booze, and an emergency cache. Accessing it only requires the SERE Pick Bogota picks that I keep in my Wazoo Cache belt. In the worst case, a mechanical breach and an apology check would probably suffice.

This is a serious inconvenience, a true survival situation, and a sh*tty day all rolled into one. Given recent events in Texas, an extreme cold-weather event isn't just isolated to the far north anymore. Have a plan for your home, make an emergency cache and maintain it. Be prepared and be responsible for your own life. No plan survives first contact, but with enough preparation and training, you'll see the sun on the other side.

While some may entertain the idea of having to trap mice or rodents inside the lodge for food, please consider that many owners utilize rat poison in their rodent control plan. Many of these poisons such as Bromadiolone are very potent and have the ability to cause "secondary poisoning." Such poison is an anticoagulant and can cause you to bleed out internally.

CONCLUSION

Climate control, GPS, and modern plumbing are things most of us will always take for granted until they're taken away. But these are relatively new technologies when compared to the entire span of humanity's existence. Something to always think about when considering a survival situation is that, if humans couldn't live without these amenities, our species would've perished long ago. No matter how deep the snow, how frigid the temperature, or how seemingly insurmountable the odds, we can persist if we attack the situation with unrelenting determination.

These tips and techniques are, of course, applicable to any urban environment that may also be suffering a cold spell. When people are freezing to death in a major metropolis, it should be glaringly obvious that everyone needs to understand how to protect themselves from being deprived of daily conveniences and utilities. Taking winter survival courses from accredited instructors and stocking up on the aforementioned clothing and supplies can go a long way in an emergency. ⁛

02

YOU'RE ATTACKED BY A WILD ANIMAL?

By RECOIL OFFGRID Staff
Illustrations by Robert Bruner

It's a beautiful summer day, so you decide to go for a family hike/picnic in the nearby Cleveland National Forest with your spouse and two children (ages 10 and 7). You've hiked this area before and are relatively familiar with the various hiking paths that lead to scenic areas with natural hot springs, where you plan to stop for a picnic. The hike out and back with a stop for lunch should take about four hours total. You pack plenty of water, an insulated bag full of food, and comfortable clothing before heading out to a trailhead off Ortega Highway between San Juan Capistrano and Lake Elsinore, California.

This area of the Cleveland National Forest is vast, and although you have a cell phone, reception is spotty in many areas, U.S. Forest Service and park ranger presence is limited, and you're at least a 45-minute drive from any hospitals. You're also aware there have been recent mountain lion attacks in the area, so you're conscious of the location of nearby Forest Service fire stations in case something should happen and you end up in desperate need of medical attention.

The Scenario

Situation type: Mountain lion confrontation
Your Crew: You and your family
Location: Southern California/Cleveland National Forest
Season: Summer
Weather: Warm; high 97 degrees F, low 63 degrees F

The Setup

It's early afternoon when you arrive at your destination. You decide to hike through a known, but uncommonly traveled trail that goes to the San Juan Hot Springs, a relatively secluded area. The hike will take you inland by a few miles, but you feel the beauty of the destination is worth the extra effort. After walking for about half an hour, you stop to take a breather and rest your feet.

The Complication

As you gaze around and estimate how much farther you have to travel, suddenly you hear a blood-curdling shriek from your youngest child who had been standing a short distance away. As you turn in that direction, you see a large mountain lion walking off into the brush carrying your child by the neck in its jaws. It climbs an oak tree about 150 yards from where you are and settles on a branch about 7 feet off the ground with your child gasping for air.

In a panic, you reach for your phone to find that it says, "No service." Calling for help from this location isn't an option. What do you do? Should one person run for help while the other attempts to free your child? Will attempting to confront the animal and free your child risk greater trauma or possibly death, making a bad situation worse? If you had a weapon, would it be too risky to use it? What steps can you take to protect your child and escape?

GAME WARDEN JOHN NORES' APPROACH

Having spent the first three of my 28-year California Department of Fish and Wildlife (CDFW) game warden career patrolling this region within the Cleveland National Forest, I'm intimately familiar with mountain lion presence and encounters in western Riverside County and throughout the rest of California. The CDFW reports there are between 4,000 and 6,000 mountain lions residing in California and have verified 17 mountain lion attacks on humans between 1986 and February 2020.

An additional four fatal attacks occurred around the turn of the previous century. Of the modern era's 17 attacks, 3 were fatal, and 8 victims were children under the age of 11. While these statistics are alarming, the relatively low number of attacks over this 34-year period tells us the likelihood of getting attacked by a mountain lion is extremely low, especially given the millions of outdoor recreationalists adventuring throughout mountain lion habitat on a daily basis throughout the Golden State.

Preparation

Adequate first-aid supplies (in both your pack and vehicle) for any outdoor contingency are critical, especially when going into an area known for lion attacks. Trauma gear for gunshots, broken bones, and deep puncture wounds that generate heavy arterial bleeding are a must. The following essential trauma items are always in my pack and vehicle for redundancy to cover any trauma medicine contingency: hemostatic gauze (QuikClot/Celox) pack, at least one Israeli bandage, two C.A.T. tourniquets, 4x4 gauze bandages, and a roll of first-aid adhesive tape. Having these supplies on hand is critical, as is the knowledge to deploy them efficiently and correctly should the need arise. Well before this hike, I've trained the entire family how to use these tools properly and refreshed them again on these skills since we're going into a known lion habitat.

Other essential items in our vehicle are plenty of water; electrolytes and two water purification devices; an emergency space blanket; food (at least two days' worth in the event of an unplanned overnight stay in the backcountry); a fire-starting tool; a sharp multipurpose knife and sharpener; a compact semi-auto pistol with integrated white light and laser combination (chambered in a caliber adequate to stop a wild animal attack with controlled expansion hollow point bullets); an extra pistol magazine; a handheld GPS device with onX Hunt topographical map program installed; a flashlight/headlamp; extra lithium batteries for all the devices carried; sunscreen; a wide brim "boonie" style hat; light jackets; and other layering clothing. I also carry an Iridium satellite phone in my pack for remote backcountry areas without cell coverage.

Food storage in both our vehicle and especially in our backpacks while in the field is of concern in this region not only for mountain lions, but other wild animal species too. Breaking food items down into quart or gallon Ziploc bags significantly dampens, if not eliminates, fresh food smells on the trail.

Remember most wild animals' sense of smell is exponentially better than humans, so eliminating this preventable animal attractant where possible is essential.

Because of recent lion attacks in the region, I've analyzed the topographical maps for the area we're exploring and chose a route on a marked, well-defined, and open trail with good 360-degree visibility surrounding it. While mountain lions can attack anywhere, they're more comfortable and likely to do so in densely wooded areas where they can stalk close to their prey undetected. We'll stick to more wide-open trails on this hike and not make it easy for them to attack. In the event of an attack, we've also identified at least two (primary and secondary) evacuation routes back to our vehicle utilizing open, high-visibility trails where possible.

Since I prefer to carry at least my pistol in austere backcountry areas, our family needs to be familiar with the firearm possession laws in the Cleveland National Forest. Firearms are generally allowed to be possessed on National Forest lands throughout the U.S. only during legal hunting seasons. The exception to this restriction is that those with a concealed carry weapon (CCW) permit may carry their firearm on U.S. Forest Service lands year-round. This hike is happening during a peak summer month when hunting seasons are closed, but fortunately I'm able to carry my pistol under the provisions of my CCW permit. Remember that rules may vary throughout the nation, so be sure to check firearms carry regulations in the area you intend on exploring.

Given confirmed mountain lion presence and reported attacks in our chosen hiking area, we must review measures to prevent an attack from happening in the first place as well as the most effective response if an attack occurs. Prevention starts with the following guidelines: Hike in numbers, as attacks are less likely in a group. Don't let small children wander off the trail unattended. Keep your kids in the middle or front of your group to prevent a cougar ambush from the rear. Avoid areas with freshly killed animals, as cougars often stash their kills to eat later and will defend their meal. Leave the area immediately if you come across cougar kittens – lions will defend their young. Small dogs can attract or invite cougar attacks, so unless you have a large, situationally aware K9 with extensive backcountry experience, it's best to leave them at home.

If encountering a mountain lion, don't run away. Running may trigger an attack. Never turn your back to a lion; maintain constant eye contact with the cougar while making loud noises, yelling, and waving your arms as you deliberately gain distance from the animal.

If the encounter turns into an attack, don't play dead. Fight back using your hands, legs, and anything else that can be used as a weapon. If you carry a firearm and have the proper ammunition, training, experience, and mindset to effectively neutralize an attacking lion, a gun can be a very effective tool to stop an attack. Before using a firearm, however, you must make sure the situation allows for a safe shot (position of animal, safe backstop, crossfire with other people, etc.) before pressing the trigger. Because California mountain lions are protected mammals on both public and private property and can only be dispatched for public safety reasons (verified attack or potential attack) and/or in depredation cases (livestock, pet loss, etc.), be prepared for the investigation that'll ensue if you have to dispatch an attacking lion with your firearm.

While using pepper spray may stop an attack some of the time, I've seen and heard of numerous cases where it didn't. Given this, be ready to use any available defensive weapons like rocks, sticks, knives, and other instruments. Several cougar attacks have been thwarted by striking the animal with improvised weapons including bicycle tire pumps, soda cans, water bottles, and even an entire mountain bike in one notable case. Bottom line, don't give up. Exhaust every defensive tool within reach to survive the attack.

On Site

Identifying mountain lion and other animal tracks and scat along the trail is also critical. These indicators verify if a threat exists and tell us not only how recently, but also how frequently that threat is in our region.

Realizing medical assistance will be a long time in coming, trauma gear is readily accessible in my pack, and I have emergency response numbers (USFS, Cal-Fire, and sheriff's 911 dispatch) preprogrammed in our Iridium satellite phone. For added family protection, I'm first on the trail with my handgun holstered and quickly accessible. Behind me is our 7-year-old daughter, followed by our 10-year-old son with my spouse at the back of the line, also armed with a handgun.

The safest hiking method for preventing a mountain lion attack, this formation also gives us the largest and most deterring presence possible. If we unfortunately come across a lion or other predator along the trail, my family will stay behind me while I cover the animal's approach with my pistol. We'll stay close together, moving around and away from the threat as a unit while waving our arms and yelling at the lion to make the largest and most intimidating presence possible as we gain distance away from the stalking predator.

Crisis

When our youngest child is attacked, dragged off, and pinned between a lion's jaws in the tree above us, we respond quickly and deliberately. With severe puncture wounds to our child's neck, the lion stationary in a tree above us, no cell coverage, and help at least an hour away, it's up to us to save our family.

Keeping our team together and behind me in a safe cover position, my spouse activates the satellite phone to call for help while watching our back for other predators in the area. I move into position for a broadside shot, ensuring our child isn't in the line of fire before engaging the lion with enough shots to the cat's vital zone to stop the threat and force the release of our child. Cougars are thin-skinned animals and having dispatched several public safety/depredation mountain lions throughout my career with my duty pistol, I see these shots neutralize the cat effectively as it drops from the tree.

With the lion and our child on the ground, I ensure the cat is neutralized and begin assessing wounds for severity before starting treatment immediately on my child. She's conscious, yelling in pain, and bleeding from the back of the neck, but fortunately the puncture marks indicate no damage to the spinal cord or carotid artery. I stop the bleeding using a QuikClot gauze pack, 4x4 gauze pads, and a compression wrap, while maintaining spinal precautions. Given the chance of unseen spinal damage or concussion, hiking out to safety isn't an option. We'll need a helicopter evacuation. As I maintain trauma care, airway, shock, and concussion protocol monitoring with our 11-year-old's assistance, my spouse is on the sat phone with a 911 dispatch center giving our exact location through GPS coordinates. She conveys identifiable landmarks around us for an inbound helicopter crew to easily spot. She requests a helicopter that has a medic, hoist, and Stokes litter system aboard to evacuate a non-ambulatory victim quickly – capabilities very few air ships have for these types of emergencies. Following the call, my spouse photographs the scene with her cell phone camera. I monitor our child while maintaining scene security, keeping our family far enough away from the lion carcass and surrounding area to avoid inner perimeter contamination for the pending wildlife attack investigation.

SURVIVAL ADVOCATE ROGUE'S APPROACH

With two small children, the possibility of an animal attack is always on our minds whenever we head out for an adventure. We often hike in mountain lion country, so while we want to have fun on our hike, we're also on high alert. With more and more people getting outdoors and encroaching on nature's territory, predators are taking more chances.

Preparation

Whenever we head out for a hike, we pack the essentials: snacks, water, a small survival kit, a first-aid kit, sunscreen, and bug spray. Both my husband and I each conceal-carry our respective firearms; we also each have a folding knife. In instances where we aren't allowed to carry firearms (like many places in California), we carry bear spray and an air horn, in addition to our knives. Bear spray has been known to deter mountain lions and bears. An air horn has also been known to spook predators. In addition, our Jeep is stocked with a large first-aid kit, food, water, and a ham radio.

Before heading out, I always do some research on the area we're about to explore, which would include researching the local animals. Knowing what's out there will allow me to know what I'm looking for as far as tracks, scat, etc. If I'm unfamiliar with what tracks or scat an animal makes, I'll search for that at the same time. I'll even download pictures onto my phone so I can compare while out in the wild.

When doing research, I also look up self-defense laws, specifically when it comes to animal attacks. In California, the law allows you to defend yourself against a wild animal attack if there's danger of an immediate attack.

On Site

Whether we're in mountain lion country or not, we always tell our children to stay close to us and in turn, we stay close to them. In general, we try to keep our kids in between us, so we always have eyes on them, as well as the surrounding area. Plus, big cats like to come from behind, so we wouldn't want our children to bring up the rear. Of course, because they're children, oftentimes we have to continually remind them and/or guide them back between us as we walk.

If we were to spot a mountain lion early, we'd be as loud as possible – scream, stomp feet, jump up and down, wave arms, and so on. We'd stand our ground and show our dominance. Whatever you do, don't run!

Crisis

Despite our best efforts, there may be times when we stop to rest or inspect a specific area, momentarily letting our guard down. If this were to happen and a mountain lion took the opportunity to attack one of my children, taking action immediately is critical. One parent would remain behind with the other child and attempt to call for help, while the other would move in to rescue the child who's being dragged away by the mountain lion. One parent leaving wouldn't seem prudent in this instance, as the other parent may need assistance with the animal or the wounded child.

Whether or not I knew my child was conscious and aware, I would yell to them to scratch, kick, punch, claw, do whatever they could to hit, hit, and hit some more. Of course, they're afraid and hurt, so they might be unable to do anything at all. However, fighting back is generally key to breaking free from a mountain lion attack.

Reaching for my phone wouldn't be my first priority – my priority is to get my child free and rush them to safety. My adrenaline would be pumping, I'd be scared, angry, and I'd put all that energy into stomping, screaming, being as loud as possible, throwing sticks, throwing my gear, throwing rocks, throwing anything I could get my hands on. I would also use my air horn to scare the animal away. If none of that worked, I'd take the bear spray out and begin to spray it as close to the animal's face as possible. There may be residual bear spray that'd affect my child, but if I don't get my child out of the clutches of the mountain lion, then a little bear spray in the face is the least of our worries.

If nothing worked, I'd attempt to climb the tree to scare off or attack the animal. If I couldn't climb the tree, I'd call my husband over to help boost me up to the mountain lion's level and begin an aggressive attack.

Once the mountain lion releases my child, we'd break out the gauze from our first-aid kit and begin to apply pressure. At the same time, we'd be rushing back to the parking lot/headquarters, all while one of us would continue to attempt to call for help. Our adrenaline would still be pumping so we'd be moving fairly quickly.

If service wasn't available as we continued back to our Jeep, or we simply couldn't reach anyone, as soon as we got to our Jeep, we'd call for help via our ham radio. Even as we reached out via ham, we'd be driving to the nearest facility that could provide medical attention, which may be a ranger's station, hospital, or clinic of any kind. If at any point we were able to reach someone via radio and they couldn't reach us, we'd ask where the nearest facility is to our location so they could direct us. In this situation, time isn't our friend, and we need to find help immediately while continuing to apply pressure to the wound and treating it to the best of our medical knowledge.

Hiking with the family is a lot of fun, but there are also a lot of dangers that we need to be prepared for. Animal attacks may sound unlikely and are statistically rare – some sources say around 160 annually throughout the United States, but those 160 people probably never expected to be attacked, either. With proper research and preparation, anyone can be prepared for the worst-case scenario.

CONCLUSION

People forget that the wilderness is just that, an untamed area of our world where survival of the fittest is the norm, and the natural order of things is for larger animals to prey on smaller ones. As we push further and further into rural areas, the hunt for food can often turn to human victims. No one ever thinks it's their turn, but assume that the hills have eyes and prepare accordingly for animals that have a level of stealth and strength honed by millennia of evolution.

Success and survival in this case, or in any other animal attack scenario starts with comprehensive preparation before going afield. The careful selection of the right gear for the adventure is also critical, and being ready to take appropriate and decisive action when the unthinkable happens is paramount to surviving any animal attack. Know the potential dangers in the outdoor environment you plan to explore, be prepared, never take Mother Nature for granted, and enjoy the journey. ⁘

03

A HOUSE FIRE BREAKS OUT DURING AN ICE STORM?

By RECOIL OFFGRID Staff
Illustrations by Robert Bruner

I wasn't exactly sure what woke me, and I didn't even remember dozing off. A strange scent stung my nose and the cat was acting weirder than normal. The tubby feline was making some very odd noises – peculiar even for that psycho of a cat. I lifted my head, and my groggy mind started to process the information that was streaming into it. That scent was smoke. And the room was far too warm. A jolt of alarm shot through me.

I was fully awake and something was very wrong. There was a haze in the air and a crackling sound coming from the room behind me. I stood up and coughed a bit, then turned around to find the room behind me in flames. *My God*, I thought, *the cabin's on fire! And with the ice-covered roads, there's no way the fire trucks can get to us.*

This installment of RECOIL OFFGRID's *What If?* marks a change in the formula. It's an alteration that many readers have requested, and we hope that everyone will see it as an upgrade. Rather than recounting a fictional tale about fictitious characters, we've been asked to explain what we would personally do if we found ourselves in the given survival situation. From preparation to the execution of skills and survival tactics, we'll be sharing our own plans and reactions to the upcoming survival scenarios. We hope you find this feature to be an enjoyable read, and we hope it provides you with even more valuable information than it did before.

The Scenario

Situation type: Short-term survival
Your Crew: You and your fiancé, Candy
Location: Acadia National Park, Maine
Season: Winter
Weather: Cloudy; high 32 degrees F, low 13 degrees F

The Setup

Your goal is to turn this Christmas vacation into the most romantic marriage proposal ever. After a roughly one-hour drive from your hometown of Bangor, you make it on December 20 to a gorgeous lakefront cabin in Acadia National Park that you booked through Airbnb. With no one but Candy's cat tagging along, you've planned an unforgettable weeklong getaway that'll climax with you surprising her with a 1-carat diamond ring on Christmas morning.

The Complication

On the fifth morning, Christmas Eve, darker clouds roll in. Then, the freezing rain starts to fall – water droplets that freeze upon contact and cover everything with sheets of ice. Hours later, the lights go out. Total blackout. You check your smartphone for an update, but data and reception are almost nonexistent. Fortunately, you find a battery-powered radio and turn it on. Reports confirm a massive ice storm has moved in, and authorities urge people to stay indoors. Realizing you'll have to hunker in place indefinitely, you start up the fireplace and try to assuage Candy's fears.

After she finally falls asleep, you light a candle so you can find a place to secretly set up a GoPro camera to record your marriage proposal the next morning. Exhausted, you end up nodding off at the kitchen table. You wake up at some point later to Candy's cat making all manner of strange sounds. You find that the candle you lit has tumbled over and the flame has spread from the polypropylene floor rug to the Christmas tree, the drapes, and the couch in the living room. A quarter of the cabin is in flames and filling up with thick smoke!

The New Plan: If you were at home, you'd call 911 and grab your fire extinguisher. But you're at a rented cabin, you have no idea if there's an extinguisher, there's no mobile phone reception, and the steps and sidewalk outside look like a skating rink (let alone the roadways!). So how do you deal with the fire? And if you're successful, how do you vent the house, survive the power outage, and endure the rapidly dropping temps?

FIRE AND RESCUE EXPERT SCOTT FINAZZO'S APPROACH

Prep

If we were to be honest, it's safe to say the majority of people — preppers included — would not bring much in the area of "supplies" to a romantic getaway. Even though there are some who would bring survival provisions, if there's any chance for success, the focus on packing would more likely be comfort and romance.

So, let's assume that not much was brought in terms of survival gear. But, like any good traveler, I did a little bit of homework on the cabin, the weather forecast, and the surrounding area. Acadia National Park is a secluded but popular island destination. Visitors can expect mountains, miles of shoreline, and plenty of wildlife scenery. Any supplies brought from home would likely be a basic survival kit kept in the car (food, water, knife, rope, first aid, flashlights, etc.) and items for warmth: blankets and fire starters.

Knowing that sketchy weather is in the forecast, I'd ensure the car is as full of fuel as possible when we arrive and contains the aforementioned basic survival kit. Anyone who has endured any type of dangerous weather knows that running out of fuel, when it's desperately needed, is a stressful and potentially deadly scenario.

On Site

Hotels have specific requirements that are dictated by municipal life safety codes such as working smoke detectors, sprinklers, and posted egress paths. Airbnb is different. Their policy is that the homeowner shall meet all local safety requirements, meaning they'll vary from location to location.

Being safety-minded, any time I stay at a rental, I identify the presence and location of a few things: smoke detector(s), carbon monoxide detector, fire extinguisher(s), and utility (gas, electric, water) shutoffs. I also check egress paths, determining the safest ways out of each room, particularly any rooms above the first floor. I would also make sure the egress paths are clear. Being startled in the middle of the night by an emergent situation and needing to quickly leave a structure can be greatly hampered by clutter between you and an exit. These steps take only a few minutes and equip me with peace of mind and a few critical emergency plans.

My girlfriend and I would discuss the importance of staying together. Because of the ominous weather forecast and the potential isolation, neither of us should wander away from the cabin alone for any reason. We'd agree to keep cell phones charged and turned off, but near us at all times. No one wants social media notifications distracting them from a romantic getaway. But, in the event of an emergency, a cell phone can be invaluable, and I consider it part of my vacation and emergency preparations.

I also believe it's important to keep car keys, shoes, and a flashlight nearby when I sleep. Any type of unexpected event can occur overnight (fire, tornado, earthquake) and you will be at a serious disadvantage if you're barefoot and cannot see. And if you need your vehicle to escape or to use as shelter, digging through pant pockets isn't feasible when there's an imminent threat.

We'd also establish a meeting place. If we become separated for any reason, there should be a mutually agreed-upon location where we'd meet. I'd say the cabin itself is a meeting place, but if something were to happen to the cabin, we'd determine a nearby landmark (a distinct tree, rock, a boat dock, etc.) to reconvene at.

Crisis

The first and foremost priority in any emergency is life safety. In the fire service we have *Incident Priorities*: 1. Life Safety, 2. Incident Stabilization, and 3. Property Conservation. Human life should always be the most important consideration in any crisis. The order may change, but the priorities don't. For example, one may stabilize the incident in order to achieve life safety. In the case of our cabin fire, the most important factor is our lives. Getting out is a priority. Regardless of the perilous weather outside, it's a far better environment than the firestorm building inside.

The absolute first thing that must be done is to wake my girlfriend. She should grab her shoes and flashlight while I locate the cat. Hand her the cat and car keys. Instruct her to go get in the car, start it for warmth, and call 911. Even if we have "no service," network providers must transmit emergency calls, whether we use their network or not. So, there's a chance. If possible, she should back the car a safe distance away from the house. In icy conditions, that may not be possible, but as long as the car isn't inside the structure, it's the safest alternative. Pet owners never like this next statement, but if I can't quickly and easily locate the cat, it'll be left to fend for itself for the time being. The good news is that pets have instinctive survival skills, and, at the very least, will attempt to rescue themselves. As soon as I direct her to the door, it's critical that I turn my attention to the fire.

Based on over 20 years in the fire service I'll tell you that a nonprofessional extinguishing a fire of moderate size or greater is nearly impossible. It requires quick action, a good understanding of fire, and more than a little luck. First, a little bit about fire.

There are four factors necessary for fire to exist: oxygen, fuel, heat, and a chemical reaction. Without getting into too much chemistry, heat is applied to a fuel (wood, paper, cotton, plastic, etc.), which causes it to release vapor. The oxygen in air acts as an oxidizer allowing the fuel to burn and the chemical reaction brings them all together. By removing any one of these factors, fire cannot exist. So I'll need to eliminate at least one of those elements.

A common theory is that fire doubles in size every 30 seconds. Obviously this will depend on several factors, but the bottom line is the fire in our cabin is large and getting larger. I also know that fire is only part of the problem. It's releasing superheated deadly gases, such as carbon monoxide and hydrogen cyanide, which can instantly be lethal.

If the fire hasn't broken out the window near the burning drapes, smoke will be filling the cabin. I need to act fast! The window may soon rupture, which will allow some heat and smoke to escape (good), but will also feed the fire. The cool, ambient air will likely bank the smoke down, and, depending on wind direction, could blow it right toward me (bad).

There isn't enough accessible water to fight a fire of this size. For the sake of this scenario, let's assume a fire extinguisher isn't available. I need to reduce the fire to a manageable size. I grab a blanket, preferably a heavy one, and squeeze one end together like I'm holding a club. I beat it against the leading edge of the fire. *Remember the fire tetrahedron (seen right)? This action removes the necessary oxygen.*

Making sure I hit the fire firmly helps to avoid creating a counterproductive fan effect. The fire won't fully extinguish until I get to the seat of it, but snuffing out the leading edge will buy critical time. I should be very cautious to not draw the products of combustion back toward me as I draw back the blanket.

If I act quickly enough and some things go my way, I can reduce the fire to a point where water can be utilized. Then, a sink sprayer (if it'll reach) would be a great tool, or pots/buckets of water from the sink can be employed to finish the job. Applying water to the seat of the fire will aid in rapid extinguishment, and then I can continue to apply water to any embers or smoldering objects.

Once the fire is out, ventilation is critical. I must get the poisonous gases created by the fire out of the house. The best way is to determine wind direction and open windows and doors at opposite ends of the cabin, in the direction of the wind, creating a flow path through the cabin. This will let cold air in, but that is an unfortunate necessity. Without proper ventilation, carbon monoxide (odorless, colorless, tasteless) can accumulate in fatal concentrations. Finally, I'll locate the electrical panel and ensure the breakers associated with the affected parts of the cabin are turned off.

The best chance for success in this scenario lies in the preparation and taking some basic fire safety precautions. At all times, particularly when you're snowed-in and utilizing open flames for heat or ambiance, extreme caution and care must be taken. The flame must be in a safe location and monitored. When we're finished with the fire, it must be fully extinguished and the firewood, candle, cigarette butts, etc., left in a non-combustible container or area.

This scenario combines several extremely dangerous situations occurring simultaneously. The ice storm is a major factor until the fire occurs, then becomes secondary. I'm forced to prioritize. When a fire develops, regardless of the ambient conditions, it must be dealt with as quickly as possible. The reality is that when there's as much fire as in our scenario, it'll be extremely difficult to overcome. Heat is measured in British Thermal Units (BTUs), and as the fire grows exponentially, the BTUs become so great that they're difficult or impossible to overcome with the tools at our disposal. But considering all the factors, I have no choice. My life and the life of my girlfriend (and her cat) depend on it. I must be prepared and act quickly.

SURVIVAL EXPERT TIM MACWELCH'S APPROACH

Prep

Do Your Homework: Before travelling anywhere new, I like to study the area, research the accommodations, and try to uncover anything else that might be relevant. A paper map of the area is an excellent resource to acquire and study. I can even bring it with me, and it works whether there's power or not. I make note of important sites, like police and fire stations, and even jot down extra information on the map, like non-emergency phone numbers for local police, fire, and rescue squads.

The map can be used to determine multiple ways in and out of the area, too. And if I want to place information on the map that I don't want others to see, I'll use a UV marker. An ultraviolet (UV) marker is a pen whose marks are transparent under normal lighting, but glow under an ultraviolet light. These markers can be purchased online or in specialty shops. To then read the invisible writing, I use a "pet stain finder" light, which is a little battery-powered UV flashlight commonly available in pet stores.

Check The Weather: This part of preparation is vital, since it can help me plan the gear I'll bring and make decisions on my course of action. I probably wouldn't find myself in a predicament as severe as the one depicted here. I check the weather forecasts often, particularly during the winter. When any hint of ice is mentioned, I go home and stay there. Ice storms are fairly predictable events, and we wouldn't have gone to a remote cabin in the northeast – we'd have gone home. But let's say that the weather guessers got it wrong. They might have predicted snow, and I would certainly view a little snow as nice backdrop for an amorous getaway.

Bring the Supplies: For a weeklong winter vacation in a private cabin, I'd bring enough supplies to last more for than a week, just in case we had to stay longer. This is in addition to my normal vehicle supplies. I like to treat each of my family's vehicles as a rolling warehouse of survival supplies. There's always extra food in there, along with a full-sized fire extinguisher, a first aid kit with commonly used OTC meds, an assortment of handtools, and a solar charger for my mobile phone. On top of that, for the stay I'd bring plastic bins filled with the following:

> Food (both fresh and shelf stable)
> Water (bottled water, 16-ounce bottles for easy rationing)
> Lighting (non-flame preferred, LED flashlights can run for days on one set of batteries)
> Batteries
> Extra winter clothing and outerwear
> A battery-powered mobile phone charger, or a car charger if the vehicle stays nearby

While On Site

Once I reach the cabin with my lady and her feline friend, we'd naturally take a look around inside and outside of the cabin, checking out the amenities and the features. I'd pull the vehicle close and unload all of our things. As we settle in, the food would go in the kitchen, the flashlight would go on the nightstand, and the fire extinguisher would come out of the vehicle and go into the same room as the fireplace (but not right next to it).

In the given scenario, a big emphasis of mine would be the firewood supply. Not only useful for a romantic fire, that firewood represents a source of backup winter heat (also a backup light source and a way to cook food). I'd make sure we had an ample supply, and that it was covered to stay dry.

After settling into the cabin, we'd check the weather periodically to stay aware of changing conditions. When the phones stop working and the power goes out, we'd use a radio to stay informed (even if we had to sit in the vehicle periodically to listen to the car radio).

Crisis

Holy crap, the cabin's on fire! Once I spot the fire, the first thing I'd do is yell for Candy and try to get to her. Ideally, she'd wake up, yell back, and be able to crawl out of the cabin with me — toting her cat and at least one of our mobile phones. But I'd have to be prepared to drag her out of the structure, if she had lost consciousness. Why drag her? Because I can crawl while dragging her — keeping both of our faces in the clearer, cooler air by the floor. If I scooped her up and carried her, we'd both be breathing more smoke. Once outside, we'd use the vehicle for shelter, continuing to try 911 on our phones and running the engine for warmth.

But what if we were dropped off at the cabin, and there was no vehicle or any neighboring cabins for shelter? Then we may have no choice but to deal with the fire ourselves. There may be a fleeting moment when we could stop a small fire with a handheld extinguisher (or even a kitchen sink sprayer). Everyone should know how to use a modern fire extinguisher and which type to have. Class A extinguishers are the most practical for household fires, as they put out fires involving paper, plastics, cloth, wood, and rubber. Spray the extinguishing dust at the base of the fire, sweeping back and forth — this would be done after you've called 911. Again, you'd only try to act as your own firefighter if the fire is small with minimal smoke. Make sure you check the gauge on your extinguisher seasonally to make sure the pressure needle is in the "green."

In the event that we had successfully killed the fire, but had no vehicle or any other place to get out of the ice storm, we would have to vent the smoke and fumes from the cabin. Despite the frigid temps outside, every window and door would need to be opened, and we'd need to stay out of the dwelling for as long as we could, ideally several hours. During this time, the burned materials could be removed to lessen the smell and the fumes in the cabin. The rug, drapes, charred Christmas tree, and burned couch cushions would have to go. The smoke and invisible gases of a house fire are very dangerous to breathe, and these would need to be fully vented before occupancy is resumed. Of course, this "open house" would remove all warmth from the cabin, and with the power out too, running a fireplace or woodstove would be the only practical option for warmth (unless we had cold-weather sleeping bags).

Jump forward to Christmas morning, after a frightening evening with little sleep, warmth, or holiday cheer — we'd have to wait for the salt trucks to hit the community before we could get out of the cabin and head for home. This could be hours, or days, depending on the severity of the storm. Thankfully, we'd have a fire for warmth and cooking, with plenty of food to eat since I always overpack.

CONCLUSION

Sorry extremists — no volcanoes, pandemics, or zombies in this edition of *What If?*, just a very dangerous and disturbingly common emergency — a house fire. We did, in RECOIL OFFGRID style, however, make the situation a little trickier. With the added complications of the ice storm, the power failure, the impassible roads, useless phones, and the remote location of the cabin, the basic house fire protocol of "get outside and call 911" doesn't seem as clear cut.

Since every emergency is different, you'd have to weigh the pros and cons of fleeing a dwelling or playing firefighter if you're caught in a house fire during dangerous weather conditions. When a fire breaks out under normal conditions, get out and stay out unless it's a very small fire that you know you can extinguish. Of course, every home should have smoke detectors with fresh batteries to assist in early fire detection.

Furthermore, every house that uses combustion-based heating (fire places, wood stoves, oil furnaces, and gas heat) should also have a carbon monoxide detector. And just be careful folks! Frayed holiday lights and deep fryer cooking can spark a raging fire inside your home while frigid conditions exist outside. We hope that this *What If?* scenario reminds you to heed all fire prevention warnings during this winter season. Stay safe and happy holidays!

04

YOU'RE CAUGHT IN A TORNADO?

Story By Tim MacWelch
Illustrations by Jordan Lance

As the fat raindrops pounded against the windshield, it grew harder and harder to see the dim red taillights of the vehicle ahead. I was clear-headed and wide awake, but the whole scene had the feeling of a foggy dream – the kind in which everything moved at half speed, except for my mind.

The rain lessened, and as the visibility cleared a bit, my son spotted a massive twister attached to the cloud bank. Like a serpent, it writhed and slithered through the air. Where it touched the ground, it was wreathed in a ring of debris. As we watched in shock, it started to grow wider. It looked like the finger of God, wiping man's creation off the surface of his creation. And I felt certain we were in its path, and that it was coming to wipe us off the map.

For this installment of *What If?* we ask, "What if you're caught on the open road with your child as a huge tornado forms nearby?" Even if you're not a parent, this scenario should still hit home for each of us.

The Scenario

Situation type: Natural disaster
Your Crew: You and your son, Bobby
Location: Tulsa, Oklahoma
Season: Autumn
Weather: Cloudy and unusually warm, 85 degrees F

The Setup

As a history teacher in your late 40s, you're driving your 15-year-old son, Bobby, to his baseball game across town. Unfortunately, you're running late. During rush hour. While your '99 Dodge Durango might be getting long in the tooth, it fortunately still hauls ass when needed. Plus, there's plenty of room for Bobby's catcher's equipment to sit alongside your vehicle's emergency kit.

The Complication

You've just gotten onto U.S. Route 64 when you notice the gray clouds have gotten pretty dark, dropping thick droplets of rain. By the time you merge onto Interstate 244, the rain is so intense that visibility has dropped dramatically. Except for a few knuckleheads, everyone has slowed down. You look at the clock on the dashboard and curse. At this pace, you're gonna be late. Just as the rain lets up, Bobby calls for you, his voice unusually high for a kid who hit puberty several years before: "Dad! Look!" You turn just in time to see a tornado forming off to your right. You can't tell how far away it is, but it looks huge.

The New Plan

If you were at home, you'd head for the basement. If you were at work, you'd head to the nearest designated storm shelter, most likely the local school's storm-resistant gymnasium. But on the open freeway? If the tornado suddenly turns toward you, you might only have seconds to find lower ground, a difficult proposition in a moving vehicle on a concrete expressway with retaining walls on both sides. Will you stop and abandon your vehicle? Or try to outrun this twister?

SURVIVAL EXPERT TIM MACWELCH'S APPROACH

I've seen tornadoes before, but that didn't lessen the impact of seeing one so large and so close to me and my child. Three instincts battled for the attention of my conscious mind: fight, flight, and sheer panic. Of course, I wanted to flee, to get my son as far away from harm as I could. But in the traffic and with the low visibility, I knew that the chances of getting away swiftly and safely were growing slimmer by the minute. As the traffic ground to a halt, I wondered if we should try to drive on the shoulder of the freeway to outrun the storm. Then I considered what would happen when someone else veered out of the lane in front of us to try the same escape route? The likelihood of a collision took that emergency move off the table.

With traffic now at a virtual standstill, we really only had two choices. Stay in the vehicle, hoping it would offer enough protection should the twister head our way, or get out of the vehicle to seek lower ground.

"Bobby, grab all of your catcher's gear while I grab the emergency kit," I told him, trying to hide the panic in my voice, "and get ready to run!"

Through Bobby's rain streaked passenger window, I looked in the direction of the tornado, desperately hoping it was shrinking or retreating. Instead, it appeared a bit larger and a little closer. Enough was enough. I put the Durango in park, and Bobby fumbled with his baseball equipment trying to gather it in one armload. I stepped out of the vehicle and went around to the back to grab the emergency kit. The wind ripped at my clothing and the raindrops stung as they hit my skin.

Climbing back in the driver seat, I slammed the door and looked at the twister again. Still larger, and the roar of it could now be heard inside the Dodge. Like a freight train from hell, bearing down upon the halted line of traffic. Bobby was ready to jump out of his skin. As I stepped out of the SUV, the howling wind was almost loud enough to hurt my ears. I urged Bobby to join me, and he slowly opened his door.

What happened next was the reason I didn't take the Durango down the highway shoulder. Out of nowhere, a vehicle came hurtling down the side of the road. It clipped the open door, and the force spun the Durango. Looking like a limp rag doll, I saw Bobby flung from the vehicle, landing hard on his shoulder against the wet pavement. He cried out in pain, and in the short time it took me to reach him, the hit-and-run driver had vanished.

The wind grew louder still, as I scooped up my son's gear, the emergency kit, and hauled him to his feet. As we fled the road, I yelled at every car I passed, "Get out! Lie down in the drainage ditch!"

Finding the roadside drainage ditch was easy; we virtually fell into it. We were lower than the road, as well as the surrounding land. Thankfully, there hadn't been enough rain to completely fill the ditch with water. Only a small cold rivulet of muddy water streamed through the excavation. I placed Bobby's helmet on his head. As my son cradled his injured arm, I held him tightly and placed the catcher's chest pad over both our heads.

The cold stream of water flowed against our skin as we lay in the open trench, the best shelter we could find. I yelled, "Close your eyes, son!" The tornado was nearly on top of us. With our eyes slammed tight, we couldn't see the tiny bits of debris that were sailing past us, but we could feel them scratching and penetrating skin. Bobby cried out, and I screamed in response. The wind seemed to blow the sound right back down my throat. Seconds passed, each one feeling like an hour. When I thought I could take no more, the wind slowed and the deafening roar quieted.

A moment later, the noise of the wind diminished to that of a rushing river. Things quieted as the twister dissipated, until all noise ceased. Bleeding from dozens of cuts and splinters, I lifted the padding and looked around. Just as suddenly as it appeared in the nearby field, the tornado vanished from sight.

But it had left its mark, one that the survivors would never forget. The scene could only be described as complete devastation. Vehicles were tumbled like the abandoned toys of some giant toddler. Debris from fences and buildings was strewn all around. Our Durango was barely recognizable, lying upside down on its crushed cabin – 50 feet away from the highway. As I helped Bobby to his feet, the quiet was haunting. The stillness was only broken by the sporadic moans of the injured.

We dropped the catcher's padding, and Bobby took off his helmet. We then walked, still holding onto each other, toward the nearest victim. I opened my vehicle emergency kit, and pulled out the first-aid kit. It was a young man, not much older than Bobby; he had a slice on his scalp that was bleeding freely. As I bound his wound, I remarked that he was lucky to be alive. He looked up at me, with an indescribable expression. The teen said, "Luck had nothing to do with it." He pointed to a car with a fence board piecing the windshield, buried into the driver seat.

"That's my car," he quietly stated. "I was going to stay in there, but I followed you instead."

DISASTER PREP CONSULTANT JIM COBB'S APPROACH

We'd merged on to eastbound I-244, and it was like driving directly into a waterfall. Bobby, bless his heart, had been talking nonstop about the new girl in chemistry class, but held his tongue when he saw how hard it was coming down. He knew dad needed to concentrate on the road. Traffic slowed to a crawl and was nearly bumper to bumper in the center and right lanes. The left lane was fairly empty, save for the typical speed demons with less sense than God gave a turnip.

Just as we crossed under Memorial Drive, the rain seemed to lessen a bit. I hadn't even finished my sigh of relief when Bobby yelled, "Dad! Look!" Off to the southeast, we could see what looked almost like a finger beginning to reach down from the clouds. This was a big, fat middle finger telling me that our plans for the baseball game were about to take a hard right into Screwedville.

I hate to admit this, but I just sat there, transfixed by the sight of an actual funnel cloud. I'm an Okie, born and raised, but had never actually seen one up close and personal, believe it or not. It was my son who snapped me out of it: "Dad, what do we do?"

Tornadoes generally move from southwest to northeast, due to the rotational winds. However, that's by no means a rule set in stone. There have been enough reported and verified anomalies that I knew there was no way I could be certain where this thing was headed. I also couldn't get a good read on distance. I felt as though it were maybe a mile away, but we were in kind of a gully on the east side of the Memorial Drive overpass, so I couldn't see exactly where the funnel was going to touch down.

I had three options: I could try to get around the traffic ahead of me and get as far away as I could as quickly as possible, I could sit tight in the SUV and hope for the best, or I could bail and head for shelter.

"Dad, let's get under the bridge," Bobby suggested. "That should give us some protection."

"No way, buddy. Bad idea. All an overpass does is create a potential wind tunnel and puts us in more danger. We're going to get the hell out of here." With that, I spun the wheel to the left and started to cut across to the exit ramp onto Memorial Drive. I knew that tornadoes moved about 30 to 40 mph on average, and I hoped I could outrun it. I'd driven Memorial Drive countless times and knew there were a ton of side streets just north of where we were. I figured I could dump off the interstate and take some of those side streets back to the west to at least get away from the area.

Just as I was getting into the exit lane — *wham*! One of those aforementioned idiots slammed into us. He hit just ahead of my driver-side front tire and spun us around about 180 degrees. Suddenly, we were facing west and looking at dozens of headlights. My side of the Durango was sitting a little lower than it had been before, and I knew without looking that we were dead in the water. Flat tire at a minimum, probably worse. The guy who hit us just kept on going.

I jumped out of the SUV and looked toward where I'd seen the tornado last. It was either growing or heading our way, possibly both. "Bobby! C'mon, we have to get out of here!" I ran to the back of the Durango and grabbed my small EDC shoulder bag.

As I ran around the SUV and opened Bobby's door, I saw he was holding his right arm. He groaned, "Dad, my shoulder hurts." He'd been holding onto the "oh, crap" handle above the door when we were hit. Bobby was cradling his arm, holding it tight to his body. We had zero time for me to do any sort of injury assessment. We needed to boogie.

I knew there was a McDonald's restaurant immediately to the south of our location. Just about all restaurants, including fast food joints, have walk-in coolers. That was about the best I could hope for in terms of an emergency shelter right now. But we needed to get to it first.

I looped my EDC bag over my shoulder and slung it across my body. I then tore off my belt and put it over Bobby's left shoulder and brought it around in front of him, cinching it tight and trapping his right arm. He winced; I knew it hurt like a bastard, but there wasn't much else we could do at the moment.

I've always felt people spend far too much time on their cell phones, either updating social media, playing games, or sending text messages. For once, though, I was grateful that someone had come up with the idea of including a camera on phones. Traffic was now at a complete standstill as just about every driver had gotten out of their vehicle to take photos of the tornado.

Bobby and I got across the road as quickly as we could and lurched our way up the concrete embankment. Even with an injured shoulder he beat me to the top of the hill. We darted around a wooden fence and ran across the parking lot as storm sirens blared. The tornado loomed for what seemed like mere yards away as we yanked the door open and ran inside.

The manager was already in the process of directing people into the kitchen; we followed suit. There were about eight of us total, and we all made our way into the cooler. I stacked a few boxes on the floor and sat Bobby down.

As might be expected, we lost power and thus lights right after we got into the cooler. I pulled one of my LED flashlights from my EDC bag and used it to take a look at Bobby's shoulder. He'd wrenched it pretty good, but it didn't look dislocated. I draped a bag of frozen fries over his shoulder to help with the pain and swelling until we could get it looked at by a doctor or EMT.

We could all hear the wind howling outside as the tornado passed by. Everybody jumped when we heard a window smash. Once the noise outside quieted down, we made our way out of the cooler. The smashing we'd heard was the result of a mailbox from a neighboring business taking flight into one of the restaurant's windows. Other than Bobby, no one appeared injured. I always keep at least two lights in my EDC bag. One high-end, and another cheap enough that I can lend out or give away. I gave that one to the manager as he couldn't find the one that was supposed to be under the counter.

I called 911 and was surprised at how quickly a rescue squad arrived to take a look at Bobby. I had already called my wife, and she arrived at about the same time as the EMTs. I could see from the parking lot that traffic had started moving on I-244, and there was no way I was going to play *Frogger* to get back.

CONCLUSION

Though many assume tornados only occur in the Great Plains, twisters have been documented in every state in the USA and on every continent, except Antarctica. They can happen day or night and almost anywhere cold air meets subtropical air. Living in areas prone to these meteorological marauders, means you need to be able to make the right decisions with only a moment's notice. It's always smart to keep an ear on the radio, an eye on live local TV, or set up notifications on your smartphone to receive tornado alerts during stormy weather.

And if you're outdoors during the day, you should stay alert for thick clouds with rotation underneath. Tornados themselves are sometimes invisible in dry air and without accumulated debris, so you can also watch for spinning dust or debris at ground level during a storm. This is the sign of a tornado that hasn't picked up any material yet. And during both the day and night, you can listen for the common sound made by a tornado – a continuing rumble that sounds like a train (rather than a rumble that dissipates, like thunder).

Finally, you may see bright flashes of light on the ground level near a storm (especially at night). These flashes are the wind snapping power lines. If any of this is on your radar, seek shelter *immediately*. Get to a sturdy building or structure, or an inner room in your home. Get away from windows and other openings. Taking refuge in a storm cellar is best, while cowering in a trailer is the worst. The lightweight construction and air void underneath trailers, mobile homes, and small modular homes mean they're easily flipped – chew toys for a ravenous storm.

And if you're caught in the open without shelter, lie in a ditch and do your best to protect your head. It's not the wind that kills people, but the debris carried by it. ⠿

05

YOU'RE TRAPPED BY A MAJOR FLOOD THAT THREATENS TO DROWN YOU AND THOSE AROUND YOU?

By Tim MacWelch

Illustrations by Sarah Watanabe-Rocco

I knew I wasn't supposed to text and drive, especially while I was on the clock delivering packages. But I was on the open road and my wife had already texted me five times in the past two minutes. It must be urgent, I thought. I'll just see what she needs. Thank God I looked up from the phone when I did. There hadn't been a lot of cars on the road at that time of day, but there were brake lights and vehicles stopped right in front of me.

I slammed on the brakes hard and nearly struck the SUV in front of me before coming to a screeching halt. Before I could finish the cursing, I looked beyond the SUV and saw the reason it had stopped. There was muddy water rushing over the roadway — lots of it. And as I sat there stunned by this unexpected sight, I watched the top of the guardrail disappear under the murky surge. The water was rising!

For this edition of "What If?" we're asking, what if a massive river flood engulfed your path in a blink of an eye? And to see how this story would play out among different experts, *OG* asked three different survival writers to tell you their tale.

In this installment, we have Erik Lund, a federal law enforcement agent with a bevy of tactical and survival experience. We also have Ryan Lee Price, a freelance journalist and outdoors enthusiast who has contributed to the SHTF column in our sister publication, *RECOIL*. Finally, I'll be telling you a story too. I have been a professional survival instructor for the past 20 years, and have written multiple best-selling books on survival.

This is what it would be like to be a modern-day Noah, minus the bombproof ark full of delicious animals.

The Scenario

Situation type: Flood
Your Crew: Just you
Location: St. Louis, Missouri
Season: Spring (mid April)
Weather: Raining, 68 degrees F

The Setup

You're a delivery driver for an international courier service (think UPS) in your early 30s. Little do you know that the warm temperatures and excessive rain of the past two weeks have melted this past winter's snow pack faster than expected, elevating the Missouri River. While driving on a highway along your usual route, you come around a bend to find a low-lying part of the road blanketed by floodwater — and it's rising fast.

The Complication

The rush of floodwater causes other drivers to freeze out of panic. You know you can't drive through the water; you don't want to stall your engine or, worse yet, have the water sweep your van away and kill you. And you're certainly not going to sit there like the others and hope the water stops before it gets to you. But there are cars behind you and you can't exactly reverse your way to freedom. Do you bust a U-turn? Stay in your van and search for supplies or tools to help you? Or do you bail on your van and go on foot ... even though there are no tall buildings in sight? Just as you decide to make your move, you realize the SUV stopped in front of you contains a young mother and three kids of grade-school age. You certainly can't leave them to stall out or drown. What do you do?

AVERAGE JOE RYAN LEE PRICE'S APPROACH

Rain is just rain, right? I always brought my poncho when the weather turned sour, and I kept some all-purpose boots in a bag behind my seat along with some other stuff – some bottled water and a few granola bars. But I wasn't thinking of ponchos or granola bars or the rain or anything else – except my next stop – that is, until I came around the bend to see that New Halls Ferry Road where it meets Douglas Road seemed to disappear under a torrent of rushing water. It was like someone opened the floodgates.

I slammed on the brakes and nearly rear-ended a cream-colored SUV already hood-deep in the river and getting immersed in the rising tide. Two cars ahead of the SUV were swamped in the middle of the flood. Inside, shadows moved in a panic.

I threw the truck into reverse only to hear the muffled screech of slick tires on wet roads and the sickening sound of metal crunching metal behind me. It looked like I wasn't going anywhere anytime soon.

Brown eddies of water swirled and stormed across the road, and carried upon the rapids were tree branches, debris, and trash along with it. The water surged closer, and one of the cars in the middle of the flood gently lifted up and slid across the road, slowly rolling onto its roof and under the mucky water. The other swamped car began to move too. The water was only a few inches below the windowsills, when a man in a business suit clamored out of the window and attempted to make his way onto the roof. It happened so fast. His foot slipped, plunging the lower part of his body into the water; his arms clawed at the roof of his car, and only for a small second, the struggling grimace of terror twisted across his face.

Then he was just gone. No bubbles. No yelling for help. No sign of him at all.

Screams came from the SUV, and the water wasn't stopping. It was well past time to leave, but I couldn't. These trucks are 24-feet long and made to drive in straight lines; they don't exactly turn on a dime. I'd have to do a 30-point U-turn to get this rig pointed the other way on this small road. Plus, the three-car pileup presented quite an obstacle I couldn't just plow through – not with a fully loaded truck and a 215hp engine. I was stuck and could only hope the river crests before it reaches me. The SUV wasn't so lucky.

The window of the SUV rolled down and a woman's head jutted out into the rain. She was waving her arms wildly and yelling to be heard over the rushing water and rain. I threw on my poncho, slid open the door, and stepped into the shin-deep water, sloshing the 20 steps to her window. She was frantic, lost, hysterical, saying said she was on her way to Bridgeton and took the wrong road and didn't know where she was. The SUV's engine was flooded and wouldn't start. There were three kids with her, none looked older than 5.

She asked me if I saw the guy get swept away. Of course I did! *And we're next*, I thought. "What do we do?" she pleaded, looking to me. Her kids were perched on their seats, either panicked or crying.

"You've got to get out of there," I said without thinking. "Come with me. Leave everything."

She handed me a Hello Kitty umbrella like she wanted me to open it for her kids. I threw it into the water. Useless. The kids piled out through the windows, and between the two of us, we carried them back to my truck. They were safe in the back, but it wouldn't do us any good if we couldn't get away from the rising flood. I kept a couple of packing blankets for fragile cargo, and they wrapped themselves in them. Behind my truck, one car had already turned around and left, while the people from the other two were pushing one of the wrecked cars from the road. I joined them in the rain.

The front end of the red car was completely caved in, and the force of the collision had spun the silver car sideways across the road. Its engine belched steam through the downpour. It wasn't going anywhere under its own power and was difficult to push into the grassy shoulder that was nearly underwater.

"This water is still rising," I shouted to the other two drivers over the din of the rain. "Once these cars are out of the way, we can take my truck!"

The second car was easier to move. The water level near the truck was up to my thighs, and, out into the middle of the swelling river, only the rear of the SUV could be seen poking up from the torrid waters. It was difficult to walk in the rushing river without holding on to something, but the three of us joined the woman and her kids in the back of the truck.

The water had reached the top of my hood, but I knew these Cummins diesels could take a beating. I turned the key and … nothing. Click and nothing. It wouldn't start. My heart sank. I tried a third time, and the engine roared to life. As water poured in and around my feet, I stabbed the gas pedal, and we lurched rearward and out of the surging flood. All was saved with only moments to spare.

Just as the woman and I shared a small smile thanks to our good fortune, a grumbling thunder filled our ears. The woman's eyes grew wide as I looked at her. She screamed and pointed just as a wall of water slammed into the left side of the truck. Everything jolted sideways. Boxes, paper, and people were flung around the cargo area, and everything began to spill out a gaping tear in the thin sheetmetal side of the truck. Gurgling screams and the crashing of debris drowned out all sounds. Freezing water surrounded me, and darkness filled my eyes.

I was swept from the truck, as if yanked through the sliding door by the hand of God and pitched into the thrashing waters. The lumbering truck tumbled under the whitecaps, hemorrhaging cardboard boxes, and parcels, while I was tossed farther downstream, alone. The two men. The three kids. The woman. All gone.

I was roughly carried down the swelling torrent like a pinball, but I was able to have enough wherewithal to put my feet forward in the classic white-water rapids position. The water, as it swelled over the undulating landscape, dragged me under and spun me around time and again. I bounced off of debris in the flood, boxes full of who knows what, and was caught up on fences and trees, but always torn free.

If I had time, I could make a life preserver from my pants, but instead I clamored for anything that would float. Of the boxes tumbling through the flood with me, I was able to tuck one under each arm to keep me upright.

Water filled my lungs, and I coughed and sputtered. Light, dark, air, water … Dead ahead was a small house or a barn. It was taking the brunt of the flood, but most of it was still standing. My truck had already careened off its side and spun around behind it, and I was approaching quickly.

A small stand of trees loomed large in front of me, part of a small spit of high ground. I reached for them, kicking my feet in the rapids to edge closer. I strained my arm, my fingernails digging into the bark. The water thundered past me as I shimmied up the drenched embankment. I took off my belt and tied myself to the tree. How long could I hold on here, and what had happened to everyone else? Was this the end?

FEDERAL AGENT ERIK LUND'S APPROACH

The rear tires locked up at the same time I felt the seatbelt tighten across my chest. My truck was rapidly bleeding off speed, but it was going to be close. The SUV in front of me had come to a complete stop. I got on the brakes quick enough, but would there be enough real estate between us to prevent a collision? The truck shuddered and skidded, audibly protesting the demands I had put on the brakes. Packages broke free from their shelves and started flying into the cab. I felt something smash into my calf, but I didn't notice any pain.

As fast as it had started, the shuddering subsided as the truck came to a stop. I looked at the SUV just a few feet in front of me and noticed three wide-eyed children looking at me. I smiled at them and gave them a thumbs-up. The youngest one smiled at my gesture and hid her face in the seat. Looking up from the SUV, the smile on my face quickly disappeared. The reason for the sudden stop became readily apparent. Mother Nature had decided this part of the highway would make an excellent location for a new river and she wasn't wasting any time filling it up.

At the current rate of flooding, the rising waters would be to my truck in minutes. My gaze was broken when I noticed the woman from the SUV in front of me get out and look around. I got down out of my truck and walked to her. She was looking at the growing river as I walked up to her, "When do you think it'll stop?" she said. I looked her directly in her eyes and said, "It's not! And if we don't leave right now, we are going to get swept away!"

A look of disbelief came across her face as a pickup truck blasted by us barreling toward the flooding river. The truck slowed slightly as it entered the rushing water. Just as it looked like the truck was about to make it across, the rear of the truck suddenly swung around with the current. The river was flowing too fast and as soon as the truck tires lost traction, it was over. Circling out of control, the rushing water soon flipped the truck with the driver still inside. I watched, hoping to see a head pop to the surface, but it never did.

I looked back to the woman and grabbed her arm asking her name. She responded. "Look, Christy. We have to get out of here right now. This entire area is a flood plain and will be underwater very soon. Get in your car and follow my truck across the median."

Christy seemed to now comprehend the gravity of the situation and nodded her head in agreement. As I turned to get back into my truck, Christy said, "Oh my God, your leg is bleeding!" I looked down at my calf and sure enough, there was a long gash across it and blood was running down my leg. I guess that package hit me harder than I thought. "Don't worry about me," I said, heading back to my truck. "Get in your car and follow me across."

A quick look at the gash confirmed that it would need a few stitches, but that would have to wait. I needed to get the bleeding stopped quickly for now. I grabbed my sling bag and pulled out my travel medical kit. I opened a package of gauze and wiped away the blood. Keeping pressure on the wound, I grabbed a small bottle of hydrogen peroxide and poured it down into the wound. It would kill anything in the wound, including some of the good skin. It wasn't an ideal solution, but it was a quick clean.

I wiped away the foaming blood and fluids and grabbed a small tube of superglue from the kit. I liberally coated both sides of the wound and squeezed them together. After maintaining pressure for a few seconds, the wound was closed. I was careful to leave just a corner of the wound unsealed to allow the wound to seep fluid. I repacked my kit back into my sling bag and looked up. Christy was ready to go, but it was already too late.

The flowing river had already started to flow up the grass median separating the highway. I would never get the truck across without getting stuck. I only had one option left.

Climbing out of the truck, I threw on my sling bag while running up to Christy's car. I opened her door and said, "Grab whatever you need and get the children. We have to run." I helped the children out of the car and picked up the youngest one. Christy screamed, "Where do we go?" I pointed to an 18-wheel tractor trailer, "Run to the truck!" The quick 50-yard run to the truck seemed to take forever. Getting to the cab, the truck driver climbed down from the cab and said, "Get in."

In between my heavy breaths I asked him how much weight he was hauling. He responded that he was fully loaded, 78,000 pounds. *Perfect! The weight of the truck will help keep it from drifting away in the current*, I thought. I told the driver that we needed to get onto the top of the trailer. It sits up higher than the cab of the truck and it'll be easier to spot us when the rescuers arrive. He agreed and started climbing onto the top of the trailer.

Climbing up onto the trailer, all eyes seemed to be on me. Everyone was safely on top of the trailer and I finally had a moment to mentally catch my breath. I looked toward the river to survey the scene and froze in astonishment. The flooding had already reached Christy's SUV and its roof was barely visible. Water was flowing into the open side of my truck, flooding the storage area. Christy walked up and touched my arm, breaking my gaze on the horizon. "Thank you," she said. I smiled back sheepishly and walked over to the truck driver who introduced himself as Karl.

I asked Karl if he had any blankets in the truck as it would be dark soon and it was sure to get colder. Karl agreed and I helped him retrieve them from the cab of the truck. When we got back onto the trailer with the blankets, Christy told us she had called 911 and that the locals were aware of the flooding and were sending help. All of us settled down and watched the sun slowly set, while the river continued to rise and sweep away everything in its path.

Shortly after darkness had fallen, the emergency lights from the first responders could be seen off in the distance, but they weren't getting any closer. I peered over the edge of the truck. The flooding was up over the tires of the tractor trailer. *There's only one way they can reach us now*, I thought. I grabbed my sling bag and pulled out two glow-in-the-dark chem-sticks. I gave one each to Christy and Karl: "Tie the string to the sticks and when I tell you, activate the lights and swing them in circles over your heads." I pulled out my EDC flashlight and started scanning the dark sky.

About 30 minutes later, I heard the muffled sound I was expecting. "OK, activate the lights and start swinging them," I told Christy and Karl. I turned and located the navigation lights of the helicopter. I pointed my flashlight in its direction and activated the strobe function. Instantly the helicopter turned directly toward us. As it got close, the powerful searchlight activated and illuminated our entire area. I turned back to Christy and Karl with a smile and said, "They've got us now." Looking down at Christy's children I asked, "Who wants to go for a ride in a helicopter?" All three hands shot into the air instantly accompanied by big smiles. Yep, me too.

SURVIVAL EXPERT TIM MACWELCH'S APPROACH

My first thought was the same as everyone's first thought when faced with a crisis. How do "I" get out of this? I wasn't thinking about the other drivers around me, or any passengers they may have. My first thought was selfish, and just about me. It was human nature I suppose, but as I looked around I wasn't proud of my knee-jerk response. There were lots of people around me, stopped and stuck in their vehicles too.

I thought of making a U-turn and driving down the side of the road, but I had nowhere to maneuver my big delivery van. I looked out my window and saw that the water had reached my tires. I tried calling 911 many times, but the call wouldn't go through. I set the phone on my dash and looked out my windows to see if there was anything I could spot that would help me. That's when I saw the little girl looking at me through the rear window of the SUV in front of me. I could see her shaking. As I thought *I have to do something*, I felt a sudden cold wet feeling on my feet. The water was coming inside my van.

I had reached the point where I had to do something. But I wasn't the only one. I noticed that the driver of a pickup truck to my left was growing very agitated. He was clearly angry, pounding his fists on the steering wheel and moving his mouth as if shouting. I couldn't hear his words over the sound of the water or through the glass, but clearly he had reached his breaking point. He pulled out of the fast lane to cut in front of the last vehicle before the moving water. He then pulled forward into the water. The idiot was trying to drive through it!

He made it a few car lengths out into the muddy torrent, but when the water was halfway up his doors — the truck's bed lurched sideways and then the rest of the vehicle followed it downstream. As it slid off the roadway, the driver tried to emerge from the window. But with the window open, the water rushed in and the truck sank completely. In a matter of seconds, the vehicle and its brash driver were simply gone. Wherever he was trying to go in such a hurry, it cost him his life.

Then I heard a sound from outside, over the water's roar. It was a high-pitched sound in front of me. I realized it was the children screaming.

I couldn't leave that family to the same fate as the impatient driver, and time was not on my side. I opened the van door and stood up to survey the scene behind me. Numerous tractor trailers were stopped on the road behind us. There was no way they could turn around. The cars and trucks that tried to turn around in the rain-soaked median were hopelessly mired in the muddy riverine soil. I could also see that there was no higher ground or climbable trees nearby, and the flood waters were quickly filling the several square miles around us.

In the distance behind me, I saw a tractor trailer with a flatbed. I decided that would be my high ground. The water was still rising, so it was past time to move. I took off my webbing belt, one of my everyday-carry items and tied a slip knot in each end. Then I trudged through the knee-deep water to the family in front of me. As I reached the driver, I could tell that she and her kids were at their wits' end. At first, she didn't roll down the window, she just looked at me. Through the glass I called, "I'm here to help you!" This finally spurred her into action.

She rolled down her window and asked what I was going to do, as if still suspicious of my intent. I told her that I would take her and the kids to higher ground. With that, she was out of the car. I told her that I would carry the smallest child, a terrified little girl with braids in her hair. And that the other two kids would be tethered with my belt and we'd both hold onto that. I asked the older boy and girl to give me their hands and I secured the belt tightly around their wrists. Then I hoisted the little girl onto my back and we began to trudge through the water. The mother and I both held tightly to the center of the belt, and each kid clung to the ends of the belt. The little one held me as tightly as she could, nearly choking me until I asked her to move her arms down a bit.

The water was at my knees and the children's waists. As it flowed past us, I felt small things hitting me. No doubt, they were bits of debris, sticks, and other junk stirred up by the water. After a few minutes, we had reached the tractor trailer I had seen, a flatbed covered in lumber. I had to smile a little. It was brand-new, soaking-wet, pressure-treated wood – some of the heaviest lumber on the market. We might as well be climbing up onto a boulder. I helped the mom and kids onto the stack, and some nearby drivers who caught on quick to this idea.

Once all the nearby flood refugees were atop the lumber pile, I finally felt my breathing return to normal. This load of lumber wasn't going anywhere, unless the water got really high. I put that nasty thought out of my head and helped another man to climb up onto the top of the lumber stack. It was the truck driver, the steward of our improvised high ground. His unlikely passengers and I thanked him profusely for not kicking us off his load. He graciously accepted our thanks and told us that he had done another good deed.

Before leaving the cab of his truck, he had reached the state police on the CB. He had informed them of the situation and given them an idea of the large number of people in harm's way. They said that help would be on its way very soon. I didn't know what kind of help they could give to evacuate scores of people on short notice, but it was the best news I had heard all day. The minutes ticked by and the water rose further, lifting cars and even my delivery van, then sweeping them into the current.

I began to look at my watch and wonder when this would end. As the bed of the trailer was finally covered by water, I heard a pulsing sound in the distance. It was a helicopter, and there were several specks in the sky behind it, more helicopters! I knew they couldn't see us, they were too far away, but instinct took over. I began to wave my hands, and so did most of my new friends.

CONCLUSION

Virtually every ancient culture told stories of world-ending floods. They scribed these frightening tales into clay tablets and chiseled them into stone. This was clearly a global fear to our ancestors, and flooding remains a global threat today. Fast-moving water that is only a few inches deep can knock a person off their feet and drag them to their death in deeper water. And a wall of deeper water can knock down homes and leave heavy vehicles bobbing like corks on a wave.

While we need water to live, it can ironically be the death of us as well. Whether you live in a flood-prone area, or not, it's vital to know that you should never try to drive through a waterlogged road or walk through flowing floodwaters. And if the authorities make emergency announcements about flooding in your area, you'd damn well better listen. ::

06

A DEVASTATING EARTHQUAKE RIPS APART YOUR CITY?

By Tim MacWelch

Illustrations by Sarah Watanabe-Rocco

As the fake yellow boat bobs on its underwater track, you're surprised by the rumbling that you feel just as you take a seat next to your daughter and son-in-law. Must be the ride, you think, as you can barely contain your excitement of having mechanical dinosaurs pop out at you. But as the other passengers sit down in the rows behind you, you have a sense that something is wrong with this Jurassic Park ride. Very wrong. The mild trembling increases to bone-rattling vibrations. Soon the typical screams of delight and surprise you've been hearing all day at Universal Studios change to shrieks of genuine fear.

As the first cracks appear in the nearby concrete, your mind finally assembles the pieces – this is an earthquake! The shaking magnifies, almost throwing you from the boat. The roof over the waiting area begins to come apart, raining down faux logs and thatches upon the amusement park-goers. Then the ground starts to open up...

In this edition of "What If?" we wonder what would happen if the "Big One" finally hits a city like Los Angeles and your family is caught in a massive earthquake. If the San Andreas fault line finally produces a series of devastating tremors, it'll affect millions of Southern California residents in different ways across dozens, if not hundreds, of miles, so no one survival strategy would work best for everyone. So, in an OFFGRID first, we asked a trio of writers to each take on a different scenario affected by the same natural disaster.

First is Patrick McCarthy – a freelance journalist, lifelong outdoor enthusiast, and frequent OFFGRID contributor – who has been tasked to assume the persona of a financial hot shot working in downtown Los Angeles when the quake hits. Next up is Erik Lund – a federal law enforcement agent with a vast array of tactical and survival expertise – who tackles what it'd be like to be an off-duty police officer stuck in a sea of cars on the Pacific Coast Highway. And myself, I have been a survival instructor for the past 20 years, and am the author of a new book on survival and emergency preparedness, *How To Survive Anything* (yes, even earthquakes). I'm handling the hypothetical scenario in the opening of this article. These are our stories of rising above the rubble.

AVERAGE JOE: PATRICK MCCARTHY'S APPROACH

The Scenario

Situation type: An 8.9-magnitude earthquake
Your Crew: You, your executive assistant, and an office full of coworkers
Location: Downtown Los Angeles
Season: Late summer
Weather: Highs in the 90s F

The Setup

You're a single 40-year-old financial hot shot with an even hotter girlfriend. You work in one of the huge office towers in downtown Los Angeles and live in

Pacific Palisades. You work with Natalie, your 55-year-old executive assistant, and about 15 other people in your immediate department.

The Complication

It's a blisteringly hot day in late August. You're in the office finishing up the workday when an 8.9-magnitude earthquake rocks not just downtown Los Angeles, but the entire Southern California area. It rips up concrete, topples buildings, ruptures gas lines, and shuts down electricity. Fortunately, your office tower is still standing thanks to the seismic design in the building's foundation, but inside it looks like a bomb has gone off. Shattered glass. Broken ceiling and walls. Toppled tables and shelves. People are screaming, if they're not on the floor covered in debris. And you wake up to find yourself lying on the ground, blood dripping from your forehead and Natalie crouching over you, trying to help.

My highly structured life was thrown into chaos. The day started out normally. I got up at 5:30, went for a run, made a smoothie, and got ready for work. I'd planned on going with Jess to that Italian place tonight, so I decided to take the Porsche. I showed up at the office around 7, and as I got off the elevator, Natalie greeted me with the morning's agenda and iced Americano. After checking my email and giving the portfolio a onceover, the morning dissolved into consultation calls and spreadsheets.

Suddenly, a distant rumble forced me to pause my call mid-sentence. Within seconds, the rumble had become a deafening roar, and the floor started pitching and rolling like some deranged amusement park ride. I managed to duck under my desk as light fixtures shattered to the floor nearby. That was the last thing I remember before blacking out.

I came to with Natalie leaning over me, frantically asking, "Are you OK?!" She had pulled me from underneath my collapsed desk, unconscious. Apparently part of the rafters had come down right on top of me, but the thick mahogany desk shielded my body from most of the impact. (It better have – I spent nearly 10 grand on that thing.) However, my head was bleeding profusely, and I knew I need to put some pressure on it immediately. Other than a few cuts and scratches, Natalie was unscathed. She grabbed the first-aid kit from my closet and helped me wrap the wound in gauze and tape. Holding my palm to my head to slow the blood flow, I cautiously stood up to survey the damage.

My corner office was a wreck. Toppled bookshelves, smashed flat-screen, ceiling tiles and concrete chunks littered the floor. I felt uneven ridges beneath the carpet, indicating the building's structure might have been compromised – we had to get out of here before the inevitable aftershocks. Natalie and I stumbled out of my office to find yet more damage. The cubicles were in ruins, and the roof on the far side of the room had partially collapsed. Fortunately, it looked like everyone else in the office has already left – how long was I knocked out?

Before heading for the emergency exit, I remembered the get-home bag I stashed in my office. Its contents were pretty basic, but had enough supplies to last the day. I also pulled out the .38 revolver I secretly kept locked in the office. Memories of the 1992 riots never truly faded from my mind.

With the bag over my shoulder and the revolver in my pocket, Natalie and I started making our way down the dimly lit emergency stairway. After descending four of the 12 floors, an aftershock hit. Natalie and I leaned into the corner as dust rained down. We could hear the building's structure groaning and cracking around us, but miraculously it held. Once the oscillations subsided, we continued down to the lobby. Incredibly, the massive chandelier still dangled in the atrium's center, swaying lazily back and forth like a pendulum. We stuck close to the wall and clambered over debris, finally stepping onto the street through the gaping hole where a thick glass pane once was.

Basketball-sized chunks of rubble were strewn along the sidewalk, and Wilshire Boulevard's asphalt was rippled and cracked as far as I could see in both directions. Hundreds of businesspeople congregated in the streets, some slumped over on the curb staring into their useless cell phones, others wandering aimlessly in shock. Knowing that another aftershock might be coming, we needed to get away from the multi-story buildings as soon as possible. I also told Natalie that I needed to find Jess at her law office just a few miles away; Natalie agreed. Our building's attached parking structure had completely collapsed – I guessed that didn't bode well for the Porsche – so we proceeded on foot.

After marching about four blocks, we were hit with another aftershock. We weren't far from an aging 13-story building when I noticed it starting to buckle – it was coming down! Natalie and I ducked into an alley on our right just as the structure crumbled, sending down an avalanche of concrete and sending up a dust cloud. I quickly grabbed two dust masks and two safety goggles from my get-home bag. I'd seen buildings collapse on the news, and we didn't want that choking gray cloud of debris lining our lungs or getting in our eyes. Donning the masks, we moved on through the haze that enveloped the street.

After it cleared, I noticed that my head wound was only oozing a bit. The last place I wanted to go during this pandemonium was a hospital.

Five more blocks passed, and things hadn't gotten any better. I wondered how much of the state was affected? We approached the towering law office Jess works at to find it still standing. Sure, all the glass was shattered, but the structure was virtually undamaged – apparently there was something to that new earthquake-resistant construction after all. I recognized one of Jess's coworkers out front, and she pointed me in her direction. Thank God, she was OK! After giving Jess a monstrous hug and a kiss, I discussed with her and Natalie what to do next. We decided to head for MacArthur Park down the street. At least it would get us away from these crumbling buildings and into some open space.

The park was crowded, and it appeared that LAPD had set up a makeshift aid station on one corner. I heard one of the officers say that the epicenter was in Pasadena, about 10 miles away. If it was this bad here, I couldn't even imagine what it must have been like there. We headed for the other end of the park, found some shade, and finally sat down. My bag had enough water and protein bars to last until morning, and I still had the .38 revolver, so at least we could stay here in relative safety until we found a way to get back home.

Having lived in California my whole life, the idea of a "Big One" on the San Andreas fault was talked about ad nauseam. TV newscasters said it was inevitable, and Hollywood made movies about it, but it always seemed like one big running joke ... "Sure, the weather here is great and all, but you never know when we're going to break off and fall into the Pacific!" I'll tell you one thing: I'm not laughing now.

FEDERAL AGENT ERIK LUND'S APPROACH

The Scenario

Situation type: An 8.9-magnitude earthquake
Your Crew: Just you
Location: Seal Beach, California (30 miles south of Los Angeles)
Season: Late summer
Weather: Highs in the 90s F

The Setup

You're a 35-year-old male who works as an officer for the Los Angeles Police Department, but you live about 30 miles south in Seal Beach, Orange County (partly so you don't live in the jurisdiction you work in, but mostly because it's beautiful and, as a surfer, you enjoy living along the coast).

The Complication

While driving on the Pacific Coast Highway (PCH), the "Big One" rocks not just Seal Beach, but the entire Southern California area. It rips up concrete, topples buildings, ruptures gas lines, and shuts down electricity. People are screaming if they're not crushed under rubble. Traffic is ground to a halt as everyone figures out what's happening.

It didn't hit me at first. Mentally, that is. Driving a vehicle on the highway during an earthquake was definitely a strange experience and one that took a few moments to register. Driving south on PCH and watching an entire mountainside of land and road disintegrate and fall into the Pacific Ocean was my first clue that things just got serious. I slammed on my brakes and narrowly stopped in time before running off a newly formed cliff; those in front of me weren't so fortunate. Once the violent shaking stopped, I jumped out of my truck to take a look at what I just witnessed. How do you process an entire section of highway just disappearing into the ocean? I wanted to go right to the edge and look over, to see what's left and to see if I could help, but it was just too dangerous. My whole concept of terra firma had just been radically redefined, and I wasn't about to let the earth swallow me too if I could help it.

I scrambled back to my truck, thinking about my options. Aftershocks were to be expected with an earthquake this severe. I needed to get off of what's left of PCH right away before more sections of road crumbled beneath me. Then I needed to plan my next steps.

Dozens of people were wandering around, trying to make calls or send texts, but it was pointless. The entire communications grid had either been destroyed or was totally overloaded with calls. Nothing was getting through for a long time. Just then a text alert tone on my phone snapped me back to reality. It was an automated text message from the Emergency Operations Center (EOC), which maintains a separate satellite communications system for emergency responders. It informed me that the Los Angeles Police Department's disaster response emergency plan was now in effect and all personnel were to report to their duty stations as soon as practically possible. The last part always struck me as funny — "as soon as practically possible." How was anything possible now? After almost 14 years as an LAPD officer, I thought I'd seen most everything there was to see, but this was just surreal. Still, I confirmed receipt of the message. *At least someone would know I'm alive since I responded,* I hoped. Now, it was time to get out of here and find my way to the EOC field station.

But I paused. *I needed to be certain,* my conscious spoke up. *I couldn't leave anyone down there.* I jumped into the Ford Raptor and eased it forward as close to the edge of the crumbling pavement as I dared. Leaving the truck running, I went to the bed of the pickup and pulled out a 50-foot tow strap. I looped the strap around my waist and attached it to the front strap hook on the truck. Two young guys wandered up and asked me what was happening. I told them I was with the LAPD and that we needed to check to see if anyone was alive down there. Surprisingly, they offered to help.

I quickly told them the plan: "I'm going to crawl to the edge and see if I can see anything down below. If the edge gives way and I fall down, grab the strap and pull me up. If you can't, then slowly back up the truck and it will pull me up." They nodded in agreement. I noticed more people starting to wander up to watch the show.

Confident the strap was secured to my truck and, more importantly, to me, I crawled on my hands and knees toward the edge. As I got within a few feet of the edge, I transitioned to a low crawl, chest to the asphalt. Peering over the edge, I saw nothing — no vehicles, no people. Anything that was on the highway was now crushed under a mountainside of dirt and in the ocean. I offered a silent prayer and worked my way back from the edge. After a few feet, I stood and went back to the truck. By now, a small crowd of about 15 people had gathered around my truck as word has quickly spread that I was a cop. One of the young men asked if I saw anything. I could feel the entire group looking at me. Subtly, I shook my head, "Nothing." The solemnness of the moment caught everyone. The look in everyone's eyes expressed the exact same thought: *That could have been me.*

From the back of the group, in an almost imperceptible low voice, came the question everyone was thinking, "What do we do now?" I took a breath. "OK, people," I said in my most calm yet authoritative voice. "Let's get in our vehicles and slowly head back up the highway. We'll try to work our way back until you can get a clear route to your homes." As the crowd slowly dispersed, a voice in the back shouts, "We can't!"

A woman cut through the group to get to me as the others stopped to listen to her: "About a half mile back, around the bend, the same thing happened. I saw the road in my rearview mirror fall into the ocean. A huge section is gone. We're trapped here." I asked her if she was certain. "Positive," she responded. A murmur of panic spread through the crowd. *F*ck me! How the hell am I supposed to get to the EOC field station now?* I think while trying to maintain my calm exterior. The shaking ground quickly snapped me out of my thoughts. "Aftershock!" someone shouted. The ground rolled and wobbled violently. Another section of road, the same section I was just looking over, disappeared down into the ocean! Everyone tried to maintain their footing under the violent shaking. The aftershock lasted just 15 seconds, but it felt like an eternity. And the damage and the implications were crystal clear. This area was not safe and we need to move – now! The big question was how?

I yelled for everyone to listen up. The group settled down and looked at me. "We need to leave this area immediately!" I said. "How many of you have four-wheel-drive rigs?" Three hands go up. "OK, we're going to drive right up over that small embankment and start driving inland away from the highway," I commanded. "I don't care whose land it is or what's in front of us. We're getting out of here. Take only what you need from your cars and get into the trucks. Children inside the cabs, the rest of you climb into the beds if you need more room. We're not leaving anyone so squeeze in tight."

Five minutes later, and the three other loaded trucks lined up behind my Raptor, ready to leave. I had several small children and a woman named Carmen inside my truck. I looked at the kids and asked, "Who's ready for an adventure!" In unison, they yelled, "We are!" I looked at Carmen, and she let a little smile slip out from behind her nervous expression. "Let's roll," I said with a smile. I eased the truck up the grassy embankment and started driving inland, away from the newly formed coastline.

Unsure of what other destruction I might encounter, I figured I was hours away from getting to L.A. to report for duty. But at least I was fighting my way to safety and helping some folks along the way. I was keeping my fingers crossed that there would still be an EOC field station when I got there.

SURVIVAL EXPERT TIM MACWELCH'S APPROACH

The Scenario

Situation type: An 8.9-magnitude earthquake

Your Crew: You, your wife, your daughter, your son-in-law, and your granddaughter

Location: Universal Studios Hollywood (9 miles north of Los Angeles)

Season: Late summer

Weather: Highs in the 90s F

The Setup

Hailing from Ohio, you're a 55-year-old who's on vacation with his wife (Joanne), your 25-year-old daughter (Natalie), your 26-year-old son-in-law (George), and your 1-year-old granddaughter (Dorothy).

The Complication

You're boarding the Jurassic Park ride along with your daughter and son-in-law. Disappointingly, your wife Joanne is too faint-of-heart to go on this ride, so she volunteers to wait just outside the ride entrance with your 1-year-old grand-daughter. Just as you're allowed to board one of the ride's "boats," the mega quake rocks not just the theme park, but the entire Southern California area. Chaos erupts, as people aren't sure what to do or where to go next. You look to your left and find your son-in-law's toes and left sandal crushed by a metal pole.

When the quake finally stopped, I couldn't ignore the pain of being tossed about like a rag doll. But looking over at my son-in-law, I know he was in a bad place. His face was pale. He was gritting his teeth and looking downward. I followed his gaze and was shocked to see the small pool of blood and piece of metal pinning his left foot to the floor panel of the ride. A support pole holding up the roofing for the nearby waiting area had fallen partially onto the boat – and on George's foot. I pulled up on the pole, but it wouldn't budge. Natalie was still seated between us, immobile and in shock. Fearful that the piping had pierced George's foot, I tried again. The pole moved a little. Frustrated, I looked around for help, but the ride attendants and fellow park-goers were all in varying states of pain and distress.

We needed to help ourselves. I looked at Natalie. "I need you to focus!" I told her. "You need to help me lift this up and off." I told George to lift, too. With six hands gripping the metal pipe, we hoisted the pole, and George slides his foot free. The wound looks awful and is now bleeding profusely. This can be dangerous for him, but a huge aftershock could be fatal for all of us. We have to bind George's foot, find the rest of the family, and get to open ground where no more debris could fall on us.

I knew we had to get George mobile. I'd never been particularly fond of the fellow, but he had been a good husband and father so far. Seeing him put on a brave face for my daughter gave me a newfound respect for him. He said to go ahead and find Joanne and the baby, but I refused – we would stick together. I used one of Natalie's extra shirts as a dressing for George's foot. Then, with George in between us, Natalie and I lifted him. We began to hobble forward. The going was rough for us. The smooth walkways of the park were now jagged, broken chunks of asphalt and concrete. The path was littered with the dead, dying, and injured, who were having the time of their lives mere minutes ago. As our trio staggered toward the place where we last parted with Joanne, the sight of the injured children hit me the hardest. The crying and screaming of the young was almost deafening.

It seemed to be taking hours to traverse the 50 yards or so to where my wife and granddaughter had been waiting, but I was sure it was only a few minutes. A strong wave of nausea sickened me when I saw the bench where they had been sitting crushed beneath a fallen palm tree. But they weren't there. They were missing, but at least we still had hope.

I called my wife with my mobile phone, but the lines were jammed, no doubt by tens of thousands, if not hundreds of thousands of people desperately calling to check on friends and family. I tried several more times, only to hear to maddening beeping that indicated the system was swamped I remembered that data might work more reliably than voice calls during disasters so I tried texting her as well. *Where would she go with the baby? She would have tried to get to us*, I thought. And then I heard the crying. A different cry that sounded familiar. And as I turned toward it, I saw my scratched and dirty wife emerging from the bushes next to the path — baby Dorothy in her arms, squalling and struggling to get free, reaching for her mother and father. The quake had knocked my wife off her feet several times, and the final time she ended up stumbling over a downed trash can and landing in the bushes. The reunion of parents and children would have been touching at any other time, but we were all just numb from the weight of the tragedy.

With the group together again, we weighed our responsibilities and our needs. George's foot hadn't stopped bleeding, and he needed proper dressings immediately. We stopped at every nearby souvenir shop and information desk, hoping the park officials would have emergency services set up. But they were all swamped with people more severely injured than George.

Then my wife reminded me about the medical kit in the car that we always traveled with. There was food and water in there as well. The only problem was that the parking lot was clear across the other side of the park. After a quick discussion, we decided that we couldn't rely on the park's overwhelmed paramedics and security guards. We had to fight our way to the car. So, we began our slow trek through the rubble and the chaos. On her last fall, my wife hurt her hip, so her movement was as slow as George's. Natalie had to hold the baby in one arm while supporting her husband on the other side.

Fortunately, we must have had a guardian angel watching over us, because a voice called out: "Hurry! Hop on." I turned to find a park attendant driving up in an electric vehicle. Thanking him profusely, I helped get George and Joanne into the back of his maintenance cart. I told him we needed to get to the parking lot to get our medical supplies in our car.

Without saying much, he floored the pedal. Under any other circumstances, I would have been frustrated by the cart's measly top speed of 15 mph, but today I was more than grateful to be able to wheel around the pandemonium. He got us as far as the park entrance before dropping us off. "There's still a lot more people back there who need my help," our guardian angel said before speeding off.

The multi-level parking structure had collapsed and the sight of the adjacent parking lot was hardly a relief. It was if some giant toddler had strewn his toy cars around in a frustrated fit. Some vehicles were untouched and neatly sitting in their rows, while others slid off upheaved sections of earth and pavement and pancaked into other cars. Still more vehicles were nose down in deep crevasses. Thankfully the sign post near our parking spot was still standing, and we quickly found our car. The right side was pinned by the neighboring vehicle, but the left side was clear. I fished out my keys and opened the hot car. We lowered the windows, opened the two free doors, and blasted the A/C to cool the interior.

My wife, a retired nurse, pulled out the medical bag and went to work on George's foot. She cleaned the wound and dressed his injury. As she worked, we listened to the news on the car radio: "…an 8.9 earthquake has leveled homes and businesses throughout the county and nearby areas." I changed the station, hoping for news that wasn't so obvious: "Stay in your homes and be prepared for multiple aftershocks…"

When my wife finished with George, she looked at me with a peculiar expression. She looked ashamed. The words "survivor's guilt" flickered in my mind for a moment, but I didn't have time to explore the thought. "We have to help the others," she said matter-of-factly, the way she does when she's stating not asking. "I know," I replied. We set up George, Natalie, and the baby as comfortably as we could at the car. And with the threat of aftershocks and God knows what else still in my mind, my dedicated wife and her reluctant husband hauled the medical bag and went back into the park.

CONCLUSION

Although this story is a work of fiction, an earthquake of this magnitude is a real possibility. An 9.0 off-shore earthquake shook Japan on March 11, 2011, creating a 30-foot-tall tsunami and taking the lives of over 15,000 people. This natural disaster also created a technological disaster, when the Fukushima power plant was destroyed and subsequently released radiation into the air and the sea water.

Less severe, but closer to our story, 60 lives were lost in the Northridge, California, earthquake of 1994, which was a mere 6.7 on the Richter scale. Have no doubt that an 8.9-magnitude quake in a densely populated area would be a disaster the likes of which we've not seen in modern times. And while there's no way to predict exactly what the future holds, it's a safe bet that natural disasters like this will continue to happen, just as they've happened since the birth of this planet. For those living in an earthquake-prone area, take steps to ensure your family's survival. Stock up on supplies that will support you in the aftermath of the disaster. Keep some supplies at home, at work, and in your vehicle. Make plans for your family's actions during a quake. Have a rally point in case you're separated and the phones are out.

Above all, take this threat seriously. You don't have to move or become a shut-in — just be aware that a disaster like this can happen at any time. And while no one can stop a tremor from happening, anyone can take steps to be better prepared in the event of an earthquake. ::

07

YOUR PRIVACY HAS BEEN COMPROMISED BY INTERNET DOXING?

By RECOIL OFFGRID Staff
Illustrations by Joe Oesterle

George Orwell was right — invasion of our private lives is becoming a greater threat with each passing decade. Even if it's not being used by Big Brother's totalitarian regime, our sensitive information is increasingly accessible to unscrupulous corporations, cybercriminals, and anonymous strangers who know where to look. According to Wikipedia, "Doxing or doxxing is the act of publicly revealing previously private personal information about an individual or organization, usually through the Internet." It's an increasingly common act of intimidation and an exposure meant to enable complete strangers to actively engage in harming you.

In 2012, an interactive map was posted online showing the names and addresses of New York handgun permit holders in Westchester and Rockland counties. Was this freedom of the press or potentially endangering people? Whether those gun owners like it or not, their info is now exposed, even if the post is deleted.

The list of similar situations goes on. From the dentist who shot Cecil the Lion, the Ashley Madison data breach, or celebrities Tweeting out the home addresses of people they don't like, one thing is for certain — the more information you have online, the greater the risk of it being used against you. If you were part of a group that's becoming increasingly stigmatized — and you may already be without knowing it — how can you protect yourself from the prying eyes of the outrage culture zealots who mean to harm you?

The Scenario

Situation type: You're being doxed
Your Crew: You, your wife, and your children
Location: Your hometown
Season: Autumn
Weather: Normal

The Setup

Imagine you attended a city council meeting to express your concern about the side effects of a growing homeless population in your area. You plan to voice concern for your family's safety after witnessing an increase in drug sales, sexual assaults, and public defecation. This meeting is packed with people on both sides of the issue. Some activists who attended this meeting did so in an effort to retaliate against residents who were speaking out against the homeless problem. While attending, they photographed attendees, got names and addresses off the sign-in list, and used public social media posts and press photos to identify the key participants in the meeting.

Also, an online petition appearing to solicit residents to push for legislation that imposes tougher penalties against homelessness had recently been started. By the time the petition had reached several thousand signatures, including your own, it was determined that everyone who'd signed up had been catfished. The fake petition was actually started by a self-proclaimed social justice blog that published all the names, addresses, phone numbers, and personal info for the world to see. The blogger didn't openly condone violence, but encouraged his followers to go "have a conversation" with everyone on the list to teach them the error of their ways.

The Complication

Now hostile notes are being left in your mailbox, harassing calls and texts from blocked numbers are coming in, and you genuinely fear that the reprisals will become physical. How can you protect yourself against open-source information collection, harden your digital footprint, and mitigate risk without abandoning technology altogether? We asked tactical trainer Katheryn Basso and financial industry expert Dennis Santiago to weigh in with their recommendations on how to stay safe when revenge-driven people are targeting you based on what they can find on the internet.

TACTICAL TRAINER KATHERYN BASSO'S APPROACH

I used to take a lackadaisical approach to my internet and phone habits. I kept my location services on 24/7, connected Google to everything, and handed out my personal data and contact information to any account that needed it. After all, I had nothing to hide. In fact, I figured if something were to happen to me, maybe it would help the police locate me. Unfortunately, in today's divisive climate where your beliefs, hobbies, or actions may offend the wrong person, limiting your internet footprint is vital to privacy and safety.

As memberships and access to even the most mundane interests become digital, the threat of your information falling into the wrong hands increases. Your hacker could be a 13-year-old boy just testing his latest Kali Linux skills, a highly sophisticated cybercriminal who makes a living off blackmail and extortion, or a violent person looking to harm you. This anonymity makes it difficult to identify and prosecute the perpetrator – you may never know who is committing a crime against you, or why they're doing it.

You may be surprised how much of your information is already available to the public, just waiting to be used against you in some hateful campaign. However, it's not too late. With some dedicated work, you can increase your privacy and lessen doxing damage before it occurs.

Preparation

Let's first call out the biggest issue: I gave my true name and real address to an unverified online petition. Let's say I wasn't thinking straight and slipped up. That's fair; it happens. In this particular situation, I assumed the petition going around was for government purposes: gather enough signatures of actual residents to push for legislation change. Most of these online petitions require personal information (full name and address) they ensure will remain "safe" within their site. In order to properly arm myself from doxing, I need to change my thinking. I need to assume a data breach will occur at some point with every online site.

I'm sure you think that's extreme, but I was in the military during the Office of Personnel Management breach. If 4.2-million current, former, and prospective federal employees' background information can be stolen, how secure do you think your information is at the local coffee shop? Is that free coffee for joining their mailing list really worth it?

One free and easy way to see if your email address and/or phone number were part of a breach is to check them at HaveIBeenPwned.com.

Unfortunately, in today's age of connectedness, digital marketing, and data analytics, most businesses and sites require a name, email address, and/or phone number to access member-only benefits. So, how can I live in today's age of loyalty points, travel rewards, and grocery shopping discounts while also remaining as safe and secure as possible? I should assume I'll be exposed, then take a few general security steps to mitigate the breach.

1. Remove my information from data aggregates: Third-party data mining companies have been collecting my publicly accessible information since I got my driver's license. This includes addresses, phone numbers, email addresses, known associates, etc. The good news is I can request they remove my personal data from these sites. This is a long and tedious task, but I know it's worth it to gain control over my security. Check out Michael Bazzell's IntelTechniques. com for a helpful list of data-removal options.

2. Opt for a credit freeze: Putting a freeze on your credit prevents identity thieves from attempting to open new accounts (i.e. credit cards and loans) in your name. A credit freeze doesn't prevent you from using your current accounts. You can unfreeze your credit at any time, and it's absolutely free. Freeze your credit at each of the three main credit bureaus.

3. Use various junk email addresses: I use multiple email addresses for my junk email – those accounts that require an email address for access. I rarely check these accounts since I know they'll be sold to third-party companies for marketing. Since these accounts are usually part of breaches and aren't tied to important accounts, any follow-on phishing attempts are easily spotted.

4. Create strong passwords: Most of these breaches include email and passwords. I use a secure password manager that creates strong passwords for my accounts. If you asked me what my password was for any given account, I wouldn't be able to tell you without going into my password manager. I highly recommend you use unique passwords for each account and update them every 60 to 90 days.

5. Use a VPN: A Virtual Private Network secures your connection by creating an encrypted tunnel between your device and the website you're visiting. This not only prevents hackers from intercepting your data, but it also masks your Internet Protocol (IP) address so your activities cannot be traced back to you. Compare VPNs before you purchase; they are *not* all created equal.

6. Use VOIP phone numbers: My phone is constantly talking to cellular base stations that could be used to triangulate my location. While these services are restricted to authorized personnel – like law enforcement and bounty hunters – they aren't 100-percent safe from the human factor (disgruntled employees, assistants wanting to make extra cash, or hackers). Google numbers or paid Voice-Over-Internet-Protocol numbers provide an extra layer of security between yourself and nefarious individuals. I hand out a VOIP number when required to provide full contact information. And if one of these numbers gets compromised, I can easily switch VOIP numbers without the hassle of changing my true number.

7. Encourage security habits with family and friends: Those closest to you tend to be your weakest link when it comes to securing your privacy. Again, most people don't think about their own physical security when they're safely behind their phone or computer screens. While social media has provided us a way to connect, it's also a treasure trove of open-source information that can lead people to your location. How much you restrict on social media is a personal choice – I know many people who refuse to have accounts. However, you can't always control your friends and family. I tend to have a 24- to 72-hour rule with social media; I upload pictures one to three days after an event. My friends or family, however, may upload a picture of us immediately. There's not much you can do except avoid pictures or ask them politely to wait or remove the image. Encouraging your friends and family to follow your privacy habits may not always be easy, but it's worth the conversation.

8. Encourage security habits with your neighbors: While the same privacy-minded habits can and should be pushed with neighbors, physical security habits are just as important. After a few scary incidents here, an active neighborhood watch, security cameras and trail cams have proliferated through the community. Deterrence is important to maintain physical security, especially if one of our addresses is posted online for nefarious purposes.

Crisis

Now that I've taken certain privacy precautions, let's return to the scenario. My name and address have been released online. All that work was easily compromised by one single mistake, yet my preparation has prevented a bigger disaster. Yes, they know my address, but my emails, accounts, credit, and passwords *should* still be safe. So, what are the next steps?

1) Get the police involved. Take a screenshot and report this to the police. Most states have some form of anti-harassment/anti-stalking laws that cover doxing situations. Do note, even if they're able to take the site down, it doesn't prevent the wrong people from obtaining my contact information. It's out there now; it can be continually republished as long as there's still a will to create harm. Thus, I'd request extra police presence; ask them to drive by my house as part of their rounds. Again, deterrence is important. Due to limited staffing, this may or may not be possible, but I can ask. Since I have security cameras, any physical trespassing will be caught on tape. I can provide this to the police as well to assist in their investigation.

2) Change my number. Luckily, I provided a VOIP number that can easily be changed. If, for some reason, my real number was leaked, I'd cancel that plan, get another phone, and start using a different VOIP number. Get clean first.

3) Become physically secure. Depending on the level of threats, I'd have to decide whether to stay at my residence, leave my house temporarily, or permanently move. This is a huge decision based solely on the danger and my willingness to accept risk. Often with these doxing situations, threats subside once the perpetrators move on to their next cause.

I, like most people, have Googled myself. Now that I'm writing in true name and taking part in interviews, I am becoming more exposed in the public sphere. I've chosen a level of security that fits my goals and lifestyle: I want to exist, but not necessarily be found. The steps outlined above are a few basic privacy measures that'll assist you in living safer in a digital age; they are by no means all encompassing, nor will they set you up for extreme privacy.

FINANCIAL INDUSTRY EXPERT DENNIS SANTIAGO'S APPROACH

You wake up to a nightmare. Out of the blue your privacy has been stripped away. It's all because you said something, wrote something, or participated in an action that you believed was moral and ethical. You expressed your opinion like a free person in America has the right to do, but an organization of strangers didn't like it.

And now you're asking yourself three questions: *What could I have done to avoid this? How do I make this end? What needs to change so it doesn't happen to others?* We'll break that down, but first a little insight to let you know what you're up against. This is vile, asymmetric warfare.

For instance, you're probably aware of the term "Facebook jail," a sort of purgatory for your residual self-image in the matrix of the internet. Anything you say on social media can result in anonymous complaints being filed against you. Your accounts become increasingly restricted, if not hacked and vandalized. You don't wind up there by accident. Somewhere out there, strangers are accusing you of being a witch, turning in complaints, and asking the algorithms, moderators, and reviewers of the web to burn you at the proverbial stake.

That harassment also follows you to your workplace. The barrage of phone calls and emails affects you there too. Like the complainants on social media, this army of strangers are demanding you be fired. The company you work for goes into a panic because they're in the headlines for all the wrong reasons. In some cases, your career may tumble out of control or come to an end.

Politically outspoken people who exercise their 1st Amendment right to free speech are particular targets of this sort of harassment. Doxing doesn't care who it hurts. It can be for any cause. In this age of the tiniest thing triggering nuclear retaliation, you could've said you didn't like wearing a mask. On the internet, someone will be angry enough to take offense; and where there's one, there'll be many more. And some of them will be vicious.

What could I have done to avoid this?

The first thing to realize is that doxing is a very personal version of psychological warfare. It's very much an antisocial and cowardly act by one human against another. If it's done to you, the people engaging in it are actual enemies. They're seeking to exploit your vulnerabilities to intimidate you. They're out to silence you by whatever means they can. What you need to do is minimize your target profile.

The second thing to realize is that there's no such thing as anonymity on the internet. Many people use pseudonyms. Such a practice almost always eventually gets you into trouble. It's fun to come up with a catchy name for yourself and immerse into a role-playing persona with the anonymity of a pen name. You express thoughts standing on a soapbox from inside what feels like a cocoon of anonymity. This makes people brave, sometimes enough to take extreme edges of the argument. This is all but guaranteed to raise the ire of those who hold opposite views.

Before the internet, it was difficult for these opposing parties to find each other in the real world. Conflicts were avoided simply because the pairs of volatile personalities would never meet in real life.

With the internet, that barrier to interaction is gone. Billions of people can have access to every musing you express on the medium. And if they don't like you, they'll take note of you, not because of who you are, but because of the ideas you represent. Ideas they hate. When doxing perpetrators attack, they're hoping the revelation of secret identity will be enough to silence the target. Avoiding an attack in the first place requires you manage your vulnerability.

First, consider not being anonymous in the first place. Being yourself in the universe of debate means there's nothing hidden to expose. It's taking the high ground with your opinions. Revealing who you are when you open your mouth forces you to heighten your awareness of the consequences of what you say. They can't expose what's already in the open.

Second, curate who you interact with. Engaging in politics with strangers is a dangerous thing we humans do to each other. Online, remember to trust no one. Do your homework and check out every person who tries to come into your orbit.

Did that person actually say they believe that anyone who's hesitant to be vaccinated should be "compelled" to do so or be banned from participating in any social activity? Did you see that person comment to someone else that they actively report persons they don't agree with politically to the social media platform's anonymous complaint utility?

Situational awareness is something most people interested in their survival and happiness should practice. Detecting persons with dangerous antisocial traits who act on those impulses is one of those recognize-from-afar things. It's OK to mute friends who've become hyperactivated by spending time in too many echo chambers. I now do that at the onset of political election cycles. It's better for preserving friendships based on enjoying what's common and tolerating what isn't.

When I detect people who are truly dangerous, I just block them. I use the harshest protective tool available on the platform, and make sure I can't see them and they can't see me. The technical term for that in electronic warfare is "interrupting the firing solution sequence." It's really hard to click on the report-this-post option on a social media platform if that person can't see the post in the first place.

I'm not saying entirely avoid people who have colorful personalities, or those who have differences of opinion. That's silly. Our ability to live within a culture of independent citizens depends on our ability to tolerate each other. You're just trying to winnow the psychos, which is a prudent thing to do as far as I'm concerned.

Third, take the time to realize that every action you take is self-revealing, like a walk through a minefield. It's important to know who's real, who's a fake personality, and what's an artificial intelligence robot (those can now emulate humans very well indeed). They're out there on the internet. You'll run into them if you actively discuss current events and politics. They aren't there to discuss things. They're there to trigger to you discuss things and demonstrate subject matter affinity that they can sell as marketing data to other companies on the internet.

It also could be as simple as ad revenue being the motivator – every digital news bureau and all their clickbait-packaged stories are all about making that top-line fraction of a penny each time they get someone like you to look. On the internet, the money has always been about the commercials, the ads that get served along with the stories. If you choose to involve yourself publicly in these issues, it's important to stay aware of this. When you post or repost a story, meme, or article, you're revealing a piece of research information about yourself. Hundreds of algorithms go to work on that information a microsecond after you click "send."

Fourth, curate yourself responsibly. There's a concept of how you comport yourself in public and in private that's important to manage when interacting with the world on subjects that can trigger other people to take offense. My advice here is that what you say in public should always be measured. How you ponder the extreme ends of the spectrum of possibilities should always be private. What position you finally come up with should be a balance between emotion and reason. It's good to take the time to research your opinion to see where it falls in the spectrum of society. Too many people think the privacy of what they type into a keyboard while alone late at night is profound, and then the sun rises in the East. Don't be that guy.

Fifth, don't fall into the trap of trying to be the most popular person in the room. There's a macabre thrill that comes along with seeing what you've said explode virally into thousands, or even millions, of likes. It can be addicting to chase popularity. The internet beguiles with tales of riches for people who have turned the corner curating themselves into a money-making operation. But for a person selling nothing but their opinions, it tends to be a chase that ends in anguish. Eventually you'll fly too close to the sun and your wings will melt. The most important people in a room have an aura that's easy to spot. They're just quietly there. They aren't the ones jumping up and down yelling, "Look at me!" You don't have to be one of them either.

How do I make this end?

In this case, whether you did or did not abide by the vulnerability management things listed above, you got doxed anyway. Now what? You're in crisis mode. First, start limiting the damage. Change all your passwords and screen names. Review all your contacts and cull anyone overtly hostile. You just hit a moment on the internet where it's better to have a few trusted friends than thousands of acquaintances. In the worst case, suspend your accounts, if there's an option to do so.

Second, if the harassment becomes physical, don't ignore it. Put up "no trespassing" signs at your property boundary. If it's bad enough, change your phone number. Get a new email address. Put up multiple high-definition cameras and record everyone that comes to your doorstep. If you can, add additional cameras that record the license plates of cars coming and going. Do this until the hoopla passes. Then, you can consider going back to normality.

Third, deal with the consequence effects of being doxed. If you were using a pseudonym to hide your identity to participate while throwing flaming bombs yourself, you may now have a price to pay in the real world for having done so. That's a risk you took. That's a price you must be prepared to pay. I haven't found anyone who's done this and never had to face the day it blows up in their face. Karma. It's real. Back to my advice, "Don't be that guy." But if it did happen, I have another piece of advice that's seen me through many trying times, "Sometimes the only way to win is to lose gracefully." That may be what you need to do. For your family's sake, do what you need to do.

What needs to change so it doesn't happen to others?

The thing about doxing is that your attackers are also ones hiding in the shadows of anonymity. I believe that's the beginning from where society needs to mount a counterattack. Current laws and abuse reporting policies tend to protect the anonymity of whistle blowers. The problem is that these protections apply even when the whistle blowers are actually malicious witch hunters.

It's not like the social media companies don't have records of who made the complaints against you. Users' emails and IP addresses are retained, and the presumed anonymity of the accusers can be pierced if malice is revealed. Artificial intelligence algorithms to test for maliciousness and abusive reports can be designed. Tech companies can scrub the internet to halt a viral contagion from propagating, or to manage a political war, as we saw in 2020. The problem is that none of these systems are being used to protect the maliciously accused from frivolous attack, particularly when it comes to real-time solutions that follow the principle of innocent until proven guilty. In corporate America, risk management is designed around the exact opposite principle – the accused is in the wrong until cleared. The technologists and the legal departments that advise them should probably be pushed to get those principles into a better balance.

It's not that these detectors are hard to make either. Patterns of abuse tracking are certainly part of determining whether to put a user into virtual "jail." Why not use patterns of abuse analysis to detect serial abusers of other people's right to have an opinion? It's similar to the process of hunting pedophiles online. It's time to stop enabling abuses by the witch hunters.

To be sure, such an abuse-catching system would find bad behavior across the entire spectrum of opinion in America. The internet's technology and legal framework design enables the problem. But is it so bad that everyone will have to learn to behave and be more civil while exercising the 1st Amendment?

CONCLUSION

Anyone can be doxed. Even if you avoid social media, use a VPN, two-factor authentication, firewall, and password manager to hold each unique password for each unique secure email account from a non-attributable computer or phone, you can't control the human factor. This isn't just a cyber issue – it's a life issue. And if you plan on getting involved in your community, your children's school fundraiser, or your work's outreach program, there's a chance your information, such as a picture of your face and contact information, could be released to the public. That's a part of the world we now live in.

However, taking precautionary steps to limit exposure could prevent an event like this from becoming a nightmare. Security isn't always convenient; it's not always easy. But considering the alternative, it's worth it. You choose – the life of an antisocial mountain hermit or existing in the real world with certain inconvenient steps to ensure privacy. ⠶

08

YOUR NEIGHBORHOOD IS ATTACKED BY AN ANGRY MOB?

By RECOIL OFFGRID Staff
Illustrations by Robert Bruner

Unfortunately, we live in an era where some groups who claim to be warriors for tolerance and justice show their true colors by being intolerant toward anyone who isn't completely accepting of their rhetoric and actions. You might just be enjoying a dinner out with friends and, without provocation, you're confronted by a crowd of angry activists demanding you immediately show your allegiance to their cause. If you refuse, you may be verbally accosted or attacked. It seems that the notion of agreeing to disagree is lost on many, and their insistence on forced ideological compliance through violence reveals what lengths they'll go to in order to push their agenda.

We often see this on the news and quickly go back to eating our dinner, while thinking to ourselves *I'm glad that's not happening where I am.* But what if it was right at your front door? It's nearly impossible to reason with an angry mob that's intent on acting as your judge, jury, and – in the worst-case scenario – executioner. If a group of protestors hell-bent on making their point at the expense of the safety and property of others came to your neighborhood, are you prepared to deal with it?

Mark and Patricia McCloskey in St. Louis clearly felt the intruders who broke into their gated community were hostile and put their lives in jeopardy. Their decision to demonstrate they were armed to discourage any threats to their home and safety has now culminated in a cascade of legal troubles that are far from over. Given the reality that brandishing firearms could result in felony charges even when you feel threatened, we asked law enforcement officer Chad McBroom and attorney Jason Squires to weigh in with their expertise on what they would do if confronted with a similar situation.

The Scenario

Situation type: Angry mob in your neighborhood
Your Crew: You, your pregnant wife, and 10-year-old daughter
Location: Everett, Washington
Season: Winter
Weather: 50 degrees F, low of 41 degrees F

The Setup

Protests by activist groups and random provocateurs are being seen all over the country in response to an increasingly contentious political climate. While many have remained peaceful, some have escalated into full-on riots, looting, and assaults on average passersby who were in the wrong place at the wrong time or just trying to protect their businesses or homes. You live in a safe, upper middle-class neighborhood on a cul-de-sac in a Seattle suburb. Your two-story house has a decent-sized front yard, a two-car garage, and gated side-yard entrance.

Your home isn't dangerously close to any of the recent civil unrest concentrated primarily in the metro area. However, the recent trend has been for many of these protests to fan further and further out toward neighborhoods on the outskirts of downtown, both open and gated, to accost residents. When you return home from work on a Friday evening to your 10-year-old daughter and pregnant wife, you again hear on the radio that protestors are moving through the streets, but this time they're reported to be within a few blocks of your home.

The Complication

Within half an hour of your arrival at home, you begin hearing commotion outside. A crowd has formed and begins hurling bottles, rocks, and other debris at the homes. Since you're in a cul-de-sac, it's hard to determine if they'll remain there or keep moving after they feel they've made their point. Most of the crowd is masked; some are wielding blunt-force weapons such as baseball bats, and you think at least a few might be carrying firearms as well. Since it's getting dark, it's too difficult to determine what other weapons they have.

Your neighbor across the street, a retired police officer, comes out of his house while leaving the door open and his wife in the doorway. He begins shouting at the crowd to disperse and leave the area. You can tell he isn't armed. As he approaches the protestors at the edge of his yard, he takes a sudden punch to the jaw and falls to the ground limp. Some of the other protestors charge the house and push his wife inside. Many in the crowd cheer, but you feel your heart sink into your stomach.

Could this escalate to other home invasions, including yours, and require lethal force? You frantically call 9-1-1 and explain the situation, but due to civil unrest in other parts of the city going on simultaneously, the dispatcher cannot give you any assurances on how quickly law enforcement may arrive. For now, you're on your own. What do you do?

COMBATIVES EXPERT CHAD MCBROOM'S APPROACH

Preparation

When people who are driven by a social or political agenda become violent, they'll typically focus their rage against those they believe to be supporters of the injustices they're rallied against. Keeping my home sterile of any political campaign signs that might make my home a target for those with dissenting views would be my first point of preparation. Likewise, the vehicles associated with my home need to be as sterile as possible. Many of us are proud of our family and our beliefs and like to display that pride to the world around us, but that can make us vulnerable. A stick figure family says how many people and pets live in the house. An NRA sticker says you likely have firearms in your home. An honor sticker says where your kids go to school. A parking permit in the window says where you work. These are things that not only give away personal information, but may even make us targets.

Disinformation can be an effective tool as well. If I knew a crowd was heading my direction, I'd consider displaying messages that'd be considered supportive of the cause in hopes the mob might decide to avoid harassing someone they think is a sympathizer. I've seen this tactic successfully used to an extent by local businesses trying keep their storefronts from being destroyed by rioters.

To the extent possible, I'd keep all vehicles inside the garage to not only limit the potential for property damage, but also to shield them from protestors and make them accessible to me and my family should we need to evacuate. With the random protests that have been taking place, I'd keep all vehicles topped off with fuel and park them facing outward to make a quick exit more feasible.

Since protests and riots have been random and without a logical pattern, I'd find it necessary to keep extra nonperishable goods stocked in the pantry should scarcity set in due to restricted movement or property damage. This would also ensure that we have plenty of food should we need to shelter in place for an extended period.

I'd have a bug-out bag readily accessible should we need to hit the road. The items I'd include in the bag would be three MREs, several bottles of water, an SBR or rifle-caliber pistol, extra magazines with ammunition, trauma kit, a lighter, solar power pack and cell phone charger, two flashlights, chemlights, four space blankets, a few energy bars, lockpick kit, 550 cord, and duct tape.

Knowing that anarchist types like playing with fire, I'd have two fully charged fire extinguishers inside the home, one upstairs and one downstairs. I'd also remove any fabric window dressing that could easily catch fire should pyrotechnics be thrown through my windows.

From a legal standpoint, I'd make sure I was up to speed on the state and local laws governing the use of deadly force, especially as it relates to home intruders and the protection of property. I'd also make a call to my home insurance provider to make sure my coverage was up to date to cover any newly acquired assets since my last policy review.

On Site

With an angry crowd already formed and displaying violent behavior outside my home, I wouldn't attempt to flee via vehicle. Being situated in a cul-de-sac places us in a situation where the crowd has nowhere to advance but toward us. Attempting to leave in a vehicle would only place my family out in the open where we'd likely be trapped in the middle of the mob with nowhere to run.

My first course of action would be to turn off all the lights inside the house and get everyone away from the windows and positioned toward the interior of the house. Having the inside dark may convince the protestors that no one is home to harass. It also makes it difficult for outsiders to see inside, while the exterior lights and streetlights make it easier for me to see what's going on outside.

Next, call 9-1-1 to notify the authorities and keep them on the phone to produce a detailed audio record of the events. Hearing the genuine fear in the voice of the caller and chaos of the situation might be just what a jury needs to rule in your favor should your actions be tried in court.

I'd then arm my wife with a shotgun and a sidearm and grab my own pistol, AR-15 rifle, and plate carrier I keep in the bedroom closet. With my wife protecting the kids, I'd take up a defensive position at one of the upstairs windows where I could observe the crowd as well as my neighbor's house.

I'd also set up a camera to record as much as possible to protect myself legally and maybe help send some of these bastards that just assaulted my neighbor to prison. The security camera I have located at the front of my house will record action from the ground level.

As the situation progresses and the possibility of facing a home invasion increases, I'd have my wife and kids fortify the front door by placing our large kitchen table behind it. While it won't stop a crowd this size from gaining entry, it'll slow them down and give us time to respond.

In addition to the possibility of a home invasion, the other major threats are fire and gunfire from outside. With the doors and windows creating choke points that make an invading mob easier to deal with, these two threats might pose the greatest dangers. Keeping the family away from exterior walls and windows will enhance their safety. I'd also instruct them to stay low to the ground and place hard furniture like wooden desks between them and the walls to add a layer of ballistic protection.

While we continue to enhance our defenses, I'll have my wife get on the phone and try to contact some friends or family who are relatively close-by to begin forming an evacuation plan should we decide to flee the crowd on foot. Monitoring local news broadcasts may give us an aerial view of the situation that can help us determine the best escape route. Barring any known obstructions, our most likely escape route will initially be over the back wall through to the next street.

Crisis

As I observe the crowd, I'm looking for nonverbal cues that'll indicate an imminent attack. I'm looking for instigators to display gestures indicating direction. Pointing toward individuals can communicate specific instructions being given. Pointing or gesturing toward my house or a neighbor's house can communicate the objective of actions being directed.

The Washington Criminal Code says homicide is justifiable when committed either: (1) "In the lawful defense of the slayer, or his or her husband, wife, parent, child, brother, or sister, or of any other person in his or her presence or company, when there is reasonable ground to apprehend a design on the part of the person slain to commit a felony or to do some great personal injury to the slayer or to any such person, and there is imminent danger of such design being accomplished;" or "(2) In the actual resistance of an attempt to commit a felony upon the slayer, in his or her presence, or upon or in a dwelling, or other place of abode, in which he or she is." Furthermore, the law states, "there is no duty to retreat when a person is assaulted in a place where he or she has a right to be."

Dealing with a large and potentially violent group of protesters can be a touchy subject when it comes to the legal ramifications. While the sheer numbers can be intimidating, setting foot on your property only constitutes a misdemeanor trespassing violation. There must be reasonable grounds to believe there's an imminent danger of serious bodily harm or death before deadly force can be legally justified.

Given the fact that I just witnessed members of the crowd physically assault my neighbor and force their way into their home with his wife, I have an articulable reason to believe that the members of the crowd approaching my own home have the same intentions. I haven't seen the neighbor's wife run out of the house since the crowd forced their way inside, which suggests she may have been brutally assaulted or is being held captive by the intruders.

My plan at this point is simple. With our ability to retreat being non-existent, our safest course of action is to hole up inside the house and address whatever threat presents itself. We're now under the threat of serious bodily harm or death, so I tell my wife to let loose some OO buckshot on anyone who forces their way through the front door.

While continuing to occupy my high ground position from the upstairs window, I'm looking to address any imminent threat against my family. If I see a gun or pyro device directed toward my home, I will use deadly force. Hopefully, the mob will decide to move their party elsewhere, but hope isn't a strategy.

ATTORNEY JASON SQUIRES' APPROACH

Preparation

Every household should have basic supplies for any disruption in service. What is service? This can be a disruption in power, water, or essential governmental services like police and/or fire department. In my home, I keep three weeks of food and water as a basic level of preparation. Stop and think how much water a family of four requires for three weeks of survival. The answer: a lot. Water is approximately eight pounds per gallon and a family of four can easily use five gallons every other day. That's a 55-gallon drum of water, and very few people have such a cache in their home.

Second, I always have three weeks of food. I find that food is easier because Meals Ready to Eat (MREs) are a fantastic source of emergency calories. Remember, each person will use, at a minimum, one bag a day. That's a case every three days (12 meals per case with a family of four). That amounts to seven cases of MREs, which are more sensitive than people commonly understand. The average military MRE has a shelf life of three years. That shelf life can be extended to five or more if the MREs are kept in a temperature-sensitive environment.

I'll add that in a hostile political environment, items like fire suppression are also key to protecting you and yours. I place fire suppression as an essential part of preparation. If an angry mob appears, fire is a very significant danger. As such, I have a multitude of fire-suppression tools like extinguishers (one for every room), fire blankets, and masks for smoke. At this stage your supply cache is getting quite immense — 55 gallons of water, seven cases of MREs, fire extinguishers, and other resources have nearly filled one room of an average house. This is a must for any "shelter-in-place" crisis. In addition, each family member requires clothing to deal with temperature and precipitation. I'd add that sturdy footwear is critical. I wouldn't want my daughter running in her flip-flops.

As far as firearms, I have the usual assortment of AR-15s, tactical shotguns, and pistols. I have completed enough formal training to declare myself competent in their use and operation. Notice I didn't say that I show up at a range once a year and shoot a paper target 25 meters away and call it "good." I've spent the time and money to learn under some of the best instructors in the industry. A person doesn't need to chase a Tier One operator around to obtain such proficiency, but a structured tactical class with a competent and a highly regarded instructor is a must. Remember the three "T's" of survival: training, training, and training.

When discussing preparation for home defense, I take things to another level. I have security cameras around the property and flood lighting. These items are a must even without a calamity.

Next step, I equip my home with security gates at every entrance. These are iron gates secured with a deadbolt lock that provide an added layer of protection. In times of domestic turbulence, a strong door is a must. I'd also add that political signage can be a target for people who disagree with you. Normally, this can result in a neighbor upset at your political point of view. However, in a mob situation, a party or candidate sign can make you a target. I have security screens on each window. I have a sturdy vehicle, always a four-wheel-drive, to provide a quick exit if the situation necessitates a speedy departure.

Lastly, for preparation, I have a $5 million personal liability umbrella (PLUP). A PLUP is a very inexpensive insurance policy that instantly adds $5 million to home and auto policies. At around $200 per year, a PLUP can significantly protect from civil lawsuits. Check the policy for any exclusions for Intentional Acts. Do not purchase a policy that doesn't protect you from a use-of-force situation.

Crisis

Before anything else, remember the old idiom: "Discretion is the better part of valor." It's one of a million such quotable notables that Americans are fed on a daily basis, but this one is key. Simply put, thinking logically and avoiding trouble is the most effective weapon in any crisis. Use your brain. If something looks bad, move. Leave. Get to a safe location before trouble starts.

It's Friday night in Seattle, and you come home to your lovely, pregnant wife and 10-year-old daughter. This isn't exactly a crack "fire-team." Soon after you arrive, trouble starts.

You hear loud noises and something like a megaphone. There are chants and screaming, and it's getting louder. This problem is coming to you. You must act. What can I do to protect myself and my family? There's nothing more important than protecting you and yours. Your neighbors are secondary considerations, let's be honest. Do what you can to assist, but you and yours must come first.

Your retired law enforcement neighbor decides to confront the protestors. Why? In all of known history, does the mob disperse at one man's presence? No, of course not. The mob attacks the single man, hitting him about the head. Can you assist? No, not legally. Some jurisdictions allow you to defend someone else (third-party defense) under certain circumstances. But, the prudent thing is to call 9-1-1 and secure your home rather than stumbling into the fray alone.

If there's a lull, you can break cover and run to assist your retired neighbor. But, absolutely do not run to confront the mob with a firearm -- this poses a risk of serious legal exposure. Aggravated assault is generally defined as "the intentional or reckless placing of another person in a reasonable apprehension of an imminent deadly attack upon their person." Does pointing a weapon at a rioter constitute an aggravated assault? Yes. And, in some jurisdictions you may be charged with a prison mandatory offense. People hate to hear that legal protections are so fragile. But this is the reality in our current legislative environment.

There are currently no known protections for mob actions. Each individual in the mob is given their own legal protections. You might hear: "I was only filming this for social media when he pointed a gun at me!" We as defenders see the mob as its own entity. Each rioter is a tentacle of the same monster. However, the law does not share our view. Each person must be using or threatening deadly force at you to even potentially justify an armed response. So, keep all of this in mind before leaving your home with a weapon. As a defense attorney for 21 years, I fear a politically motivated prosecution more than any mob.

Your Home

This is where the analysis takes a different turn. No matter what, you should protect yourself and your family from any harm. An angry mob throwing incendiary bombs at your house is a completely different analysis than your neighbor suffering a beating. When, and if, a mob is attempting to enter a home, residents within are almost commanded to protect themselves and their family. Remember, the closer the assault to where you lay your head on a pillow, generally, the more legal protections you'll have in a self-defense situation. Please know that confronting an angry mob with an exposed firearm in front of your house will likely result in you being charged with a crime. However, repelling a deadly attack inside your home is a completely different situation that wouldn't likely result in prosecution.

I'd have fire suppression gear staged everywhere and repel an attack with my fortifications like iron gates, deadbolt locks, or sandbags against walls. Currently, Amazon sells 1,000 sandbags for $299. To avoid criminal prosecution, one must call for help. Call 9-1-1 multiple times if necessary. There'll be an electronic record even if help doesn't arrive. Express fear knowing the 9-1-1 calls are recorded. It's not the time to appear stoic. Ingress into your yard and incursion into your home are different things. Protecting your tool shed isn't the same as protecting your pregnant wife or 10-year-old daughter. Rely upon your defenses when protecting property. Rely upon heavy, sturdy gates and locks. Your security cameras will record the calamity on the property, and your insurance can replace it afterward.

Most jurisdictions don't allow the defense of property the same as the defense of the interior of the home. When it comes to the family, protect them, but be smart. Use the minimal force necessary to protect yourself. I handle cases where people use the "threat display" — *Go away! I have a gun and I'm in my front yard!* Why would someone do this? Avoid the mob as best you can, and hope the police show up. This sounds cowardly to many, but there aren't currently many legal justifications/protections outside the home that insulate people from criminal prosecution. We need better legal protections for citizens who defend themselves against mobs, but those protections don't exist yet.

CONCLUSION

Circle back to the idiom, "Discretion is the better part of valor." If there's trouble in your area, go stay with Uncle Fred until things calm down. Riots are becoming commonplace, regrettably. When possible, protect your family by putting distance between yourselves and any threat. In instances when this is impossible, shelter in place and protect your family with the minimal force necessary to repel any attack inside your residence. Fortify your defenses, stay indoors, don't confront the mob, and you'll improve your odds of avoiding costly criminal prosecution. Some might call you a coward for avoiding conflict, but it's better than facing decades in prison at the hands of an activist judge and unsympathetic jury.

Getting trapped at home by an unruly and potentially violent group of politically motivated protestors is one of the most difficult scenarios one might face in today's era of civil unrest. The volume of people and chaotic nature poses many logistical and use-of-force challenges.

Minimize your target signature and prepare for both immediate evacuation and long-term hold-out. Do everything in your power to avoid a violent confrontation, but if it becomes unavoidable, be ready to fight back efficiently with lethal force. ⁘

09

YOU BECOME A TARGET OF TARGET OF ROAD RAGE?

By RECOIL OFFGRID Staff
Illustrations by Cassandra Dale

James Madison once sagely conveyed, "If men were angels, no government would be necessary." Had Madison ever driven a car on a gridlocked freeway he'd likely have concluded the same about the necessity of this article. Neither men nor women are angels. When behind the wheel of a 4,000-pound rolling ego-inflator, they sometimes become quite the opposite.

According to a 2019 survey of Americans by The Zebra, an insurance comparison website, 82 percent of respondents admitted to having road rage or driving aggressively at least once in the last year. Further, 42 percent claimed they yelled or cursed at fellow drivers. Thirty-eight percent indicated they used obscene gestures toward others on the road. That's a lot of anger, but unless these signs of frustration escalate, they're relatively harmless. Our primary concern is what happens when yelling and honking goes too far.

The 2019 survey also reports that 7 percent of respondents got out of their vehicle to verbally confront a fellow driver. Six percent threw objects. Another 6 percent got into a physical fight. Astonishingly, 5 percent admitted to intentionally ramming a car, and another 5 percent admitted to forcing someone off the road.

In 2006, 80 fatal crashes were directly related to road rage incidents. In 2015, that number exploded to 467. That's a 500 percent increase in less than a decade. In 2016, the National Highway Traffic Safety Administration reported that the U.S. averaged at least one deadly road-rage-related incident per day.

Extreme forms of road rage are still rare, but have the potential to be incredibly dangerous, which is why they need to be within our spectrum of preparedness. Road rage can easily be confused with aggressive driving, but the two are distinct, both contextually and legally. Aggressive driving can simply be the a-hole not letting you merge or someone speeding past you at 90 mph. Road rage differs, especially as the law is concerned, because it demonstrates violent intent toward another.

You might have experienced it yourself or know someone who has. We put our panelists in a potential road rage situation to see how they'd react. Security specialist Mel Ward has been involved in at least half a dozen incidents with several involving drivers exiting their vehicles. Off-road driving instructor Muggs McCoy has leveraged his military and law enforcement background to teach students tactical mobility in a variety of dangerous situations.

We know road rage happens, and we know what it is. Let's look at a few ways to deal with it, lest that deranged person start seeing red and decide you need to be the recipient of their anger because you were in the wrong place at the wrong time.

The Scenario

Situation type: Road Rage, Pursuit
Your Crew: You, your spouse, and your children
Location: North Carolina, I-95 Northbound headed toward Virginia
Season: Summer
Weather: 93 degrees F, but feels like 108 degrees F

The Setup

Buckling the last of your children into their car seats, you and your spouse begin a 250-mile journey to Virginia to visit some Civil War battlefields. Things are serene as green countryside whips past your windows, the young ones playing on tablets while your teenagers argue about teenager things. Leaving behind farms and fields, you make your way onto a major artery of the East Coast and start the trip in earnest, looking forward to exploring some of the nation's history.

The Complication

As you merge onto I-95 Northbound, you notice the pickup truck driver next to you in the left-hand lane is irate and gesturing at you wildly to pull over. Clearly, he feels your merge forced him out of the right-hand lane and into the left lane in an unexpected fashion. Having signaled and merged at highway speed, you tell yourself this guy probably just wasn't paying attention and was simply surprised. Everyone on the road these days has their heads buried in their phones and only seem to occasionally acknowledge the road conditions around them. This guy will just have to deal with it. You accelerate to put some distance between yourself and the angry driver and ask your wife where the closest Starbucks is.

Suddenly the pickup is back, this time 6 inches from your driver's side door as he veers at you repeatedly, trying to force you to the shoulder. He's so close you can see the veins in his neck bulging above the tattered collar of his dingy T-shirt. This isn't a little guy. He's big. He's pissed. And he's not willing to let this perceived infraction go. What do you do? Pull over and talk to him? Have your wife call the police while dodging his Mad Max routine? What can you do to get out of this spot without anyone getting hurt?

PROTECTIVE SPECIALIST MEL WARD'S APPROACH

No matter what, do not pull over and do not get out of the car. Ensure your doors are locked if they aren't already, and have a passenger call 9-1-1. This is just for starters. I drive for a living in parts of the world where the only difference between this scenario and mine is if this happened at work, I know the guy wants to hurt me. In the U.S., I'm only reasonably certain he wants to hurt me. For me, this means there's no difference, so I treat them the same.

Maintain highway speed. Don't try to lose the guy by flooring it, and don't change lanes like the *Fast & Furious*. I wouldn't recommend slowing down either. This might reduce the chance of a high-speed accident, but this could also allow the guy to get in front of you, cut you off, and force you to stop. We don't want to stop.

Your spouse needs to give the police an exact location and heading: "We're northbound on I-95 passing Exit 88." They also need to give a solid vehicle description and tag: "White GMC pickup. Plate number 123XYZ." Give them any additional requested information, but make sure you use the words "road rage" as that's a legal term and immediately sets the context of the situation. If possible, have a passenger record the entire episode on their phone to present evidence of your actions as well as his. If you have a dashcam – particularly one that's rear-facing – that's additional documentation you can use (see Issue 18 of our sister magazine CONCEALMENT for an overview of dashcams and their features).

At work, I absolutely will not stop no matter what, unless the vehicle is disabled. I'd do the same thing in the States. Some might suggest driving to a public place – if he's in pursuit and follows you there and you stop, you're going to have a confrontation, and you're not driving an armored sedan like I am. We solve this problem by not having that confrontation.

I'd stay on the highway and not exit. If you exit, or decide to head to a gas station, or the police station, or anywhere off the highway, you're going to first come to a stop sign, red light, or encounter local traffic or something else that'll bring you to a stop before your intended destination.

If the guy is really serious, he's going to get out the moment you're forced to stop and approach your door. I've seen it happen at work, and I've seen it stateside. If this happens, all that's between your family and this enraged behemoth is some thin auto glass. You're too vulnerable in this scenario, so do what you can to avoid it.

By staying on the highway, this guy will literally have to commit to ramming you off the road. He might try. But he also might not be willing to bang up his truck. If you can persist long enough, he also might cool off a bit and give up. Further, there's a good chance every other vehicle in the vicinity is witnessing this and also calling 9-1-1 on your behalf, so be sure to stay cool and drive defensively.

You need to stay focused on the road. Use your peripheral to track this dude in your battle computer, but also have your spouse or passengers give you updates on what he's doing. By focusing on the road you'll have better command of your vehicle and environment, and you'll be able to avoid getting into the usual back-and-forth, "F you!" "No! F YOU!" in these types of situations. You're way better off ignoring this guy – aside from what he's doing with his vehicle – because you won't be feeding his rage-furnace with whatever hand gestures you come up with.

Preparation

You need to have a firearm and have with you whatever permits are required by your state, as well as those of any state you're passing through. Also, be aware that certain counties or cities you travel through could have further restrictions governing the possession and concealment of firearms in a motor vehicle that differ from the state. Study up before you travel.

Have a trauma kit – not just a first-aid kit – accessible inside the vehicle's interior, not in the trunk. I'm talking about at least four C-A-T tourniquets, six rolls of Kerlix gauze, and four or more occlusive dressings. You'll also want several packets of a hemostatic agent, four rolls of ACE wrap bandages, and four trauma dressings.

The most vulnerable parts of your vehicle are the windows and windshields. Short of paying big bucks for "bulletproof" glass, it's possible to harden these weak areas by using a product like Scotchshield from 3M. You'll need to do some research in your area, but an automotive center or window tint shop can install this for you. Basically, it's a window tint that helps keep the auto glass together even when shattered. I've seen demonstration videos online of a treated window taking several hits from a rock before weakening to the point where access to the vehicle's interior is possible.

Crisis

What if we're forced off the road or otherwise come to a stop due to traffic or something unforeseen?

Well, this is going to suck, because your vehicle isn't a rolling saferoom like mine is at work. Make sure your doors are locked, and don't get out. We want everyone to stay inside the vehicle and only "crack seal" in the direst of circumstances. By staying locked inside, you're forcing the aggressor to make an overt attempt at entry, which, stateside, is another legal and physical threshold this guy has to cross. If he's not willing to smash your windows, all he can do is yell at you through the glass until the cops arrive or the road ahead clears enough to let you continue leaving him in the dust.

If he does try to come through that window by smashing it, then I shouldn't need to tell you what to do. You need to protect yourself and your family. If that guy reaches through the window, or opens an unlocked door and starts grabbing people, it's game on. If you've prepared, it'll also be game over for the aggressor. Defend yourself and your family and re-notify 9-1-1 that you've engaged in self-defense against a violent aggressor who attempted to break into your vehicle and request police and emergency medical services.

I'd continue to cover the aggressor from inside the vehicle until the police arrive unless it becomes absolutely necessary to exit. If you do need to exit the vehicle, ensure the aggressor is down, he's alone, and the scene is safe to do so. Check your mirrors and have your passengers scan 360 degrees for any additional threats. You've made it this far. You don't want to hop out of your seat and get hit by another car or be engaged by a passenger riding with the aggressor you never saw.

If you do get out, it's up to you to render aid to the attacker. I wouldn't. If he's wounded, it's possible he attacks you again while you're trying to help him. Again, this is why I recommend staying in the vehicle. You can articulate all this to the police when they arrive: You stayed inside your vehicle the entire time while the threat consistently came after you and your family. You did everything you could to avoid him by never leaving your vehicle until you had to, or until the police on scene told you to.

OFF-ROAD DRIVING INSTRUCTOR MUGGS MCCOY'S APPROACH

2020 has been quite the year. Wildfires, locust swarms, economic crisis, earthquakes, murder hornets, social unrest, hurricanes … oh yeah, and a global pandemic. Needless to say, it's been a very taxing year on our mental health. It seems each day brings a new cellphone video of someone losing their mind over an innocuous situation. Mental strain from culminating events seems to have pushed many past their limit. Something as simple as driving your car can quickly turn into a life-or-death situation when patience gets tested and emotion takes over. Road rage often has more to do with anger management than criminal intent. Knowing how to act and react will provide the greatest opportunity to keep you and your family safe.

Preparation

Many assume they have little control when a road-rage incident occurs — after all, you're in a metal deathtrap traveling 75 mph down the highway. But let's back up and take a look at what we can manage. First, you're in control of your own and your family's training and preparation. Before I even get into the car that day, I know I've already performed mental exercises with my family. Mental exercises involve working through various scenarios of "What If" to help our brains make quick decisions during a real conflict. The last thing I want is to freeze when faced with a threat. Discussing options of various forms of fight or flight with my family gives me confidence they, too, will act. These exercises can be practiced alone or with your family at any time. I typically use road trips or dinnertime to discuss scenarios with my family. It's important to note — how I react to a situation is often very different than how my spouse or child reacts. When discussing options, I always take into consideration their training and physical capabilities. Like most things, the decisions we make are situation dependent.

I also carry basic items on myself and in my car that support my needs for various circumstances and conditions. I have a knife and a pistol on my person as part of my everyday carry; in my vehicle, I have pepper spray and a collapsible baton. Now, these are only to be used in specific, immediate threat of life, last-option cases. However, just knowing I have worst-case scenario protection accessible allows me to process the force continuum scale in a methodical way. Again, mental exercises are imperative in these situations in order to keep your family safe while also staying within the rules of law.

Above all else, I'm in control of myself. If I'm calm, then I know my family will remain calm. If I remain level-headed, I'll find openings to de-escalate the conflict. If I can de-escalate the conflict, everyone remains safe.

On Site

Now in the vehicle, there are things you can do to set yourself up for success to avoid conflict. One of the easiest ways to avoid confrontations is to prevent an encounter. Don't be a distracted driver by texting, flipping through Yelp, or talking on the phone. There are many safety features one can enable to ensure you keep your eyes on the road and your hands on the steering wheel. For example, connect your phone to Bluetooth in the car; use a GPS on your dashboard or through your vehicle's display screen; make it a family policy that the passenger is the only one to fiddle with music, maps, or answer phone calls. I use an auxiliary cable to connect my phone to the car so I can make or take phone calls through the stereo. My wife is responsible for both navigation and restaurant selection. My job as the driver is to get myself and family from point A to point B in a safe manner. That's it. This means I drive defensively — I look out for other drivers who aren't paying attention and predict what they could potentially do (e.g. drift in my lane, run a stoplight, rear-end me at an intersection). I keep a safe following distance, stay out of drivers' blind spots, and give myself time to react to others' mistakes.

If I'm an undistracted driver, I can observe when a situation is escalating. Initial warning signs of road rage include indications of impatience: darting back and forth between lanes, inching around vehicles, using the shoulder illegally, etc. Usually, this is followed by drivers throwing their hands in the air, pounding the steering wheel in frustration, tailgating, horn honking, and the prize-winning display of the middle finger.

This behavior is most often found in heavy traffic. Commutes with impatient people are a recipe for road rage. If possible, I adjust my schedule around stressful times such as rush-hour traffic, the start and finish of three-day weekends, or events that bring masses of people together on the road. If I cannot avoid traffic, I ensure I provide myself plenty of time to get to my final destination and listen to something that makes the trip enjoyable. Part of being a defensive driver isn't overreacting if I get cut off or must yield to another driver's stupidity. Remember, this isn't an ego contest; nothing good will come out of losing your temper.

Crisis

No road rage behaviors should be ignored. You must keep an eye on dangerous, erratic drivers so you can be prepared to react. That doesn't mean make matters worse by escalating the tension with your own poor behavior. Rather, attempt to distance yourself from the driver either by slowing down or changing lanes. Don't speed up. Don't turn a dangerous situation into a worse one by breaking the speed limit and "challenging" your threat to give chase.

In this particular road-rage situation, the moment the guy veers his pickup at my vehicle, I'm asking my wife to call 9-1-1 on my phone and use hers to find the closest police or fire station. Since my phone is connected through my vehicle, I can keep both hands on the wheel, keep my eyes between the road and threat, and still voice to the police what's occurring. They can either provide me directions from there or dispatch an officer to my location. Meanwhile, my wife will be looking for a safe, preferably official place to navigate me to. Exiting the highway will either deter the driver from pursuing me, or enable him to follow me to a location where everyone can safely hash things out. My job at this point is to keep my vehicle under control. I'd slow down; I'd be careful of overcorrecting as I avoid his attempts to force me off the road. This repeated action of staying slow and steady hopefully will de-escalate the driver and make him feel like he "won" the confrontation. Yet the entire time, I'm on the phone with the police, letting them know on record what's occurring and where I'm located. No matter how this conflict ends or how the driver shares his perception of your wrongdoing when police arrive, I want to make sure my voice is on record as the defensive driver attempting to de-escalate.

That being said, if he's able to veer me onto the shoulder before the police arrive, I have a few options. If we're both stopped on the side of the road, I'm going to take advantage of my greatest asset — my vehicle. My car has four metal sides, four tires, and a roof for protection. This means I can stay safely in my vehicle, doors locked, windows rolled up, on the phone with the police waiting for an officer to arrive. The man could exit his truck and scream all he wants — as long as I don't meet him toe-to-toe, the only damage is my traumatized family. However, this opens the possibility of him directing a weapon at me, my car, or my family. It's higher risk because there are many unknowns.

Another option: Once we both stop, and he exits his truck, I'm going to back up and drive away. Since I maintained control of my vehicle the entire time, I know it's still in good working order. My goal is to delay long enough for the police to reach us or create enough space for me to safely exit the highway. Getting out of the car to confront this man when I have an opportunity to stay in and drive away is a huge mistake for multiple reasons. One, because I'm a concealed carry instructor and holder, I know any use of deadly force when I had other options (i.e. driving away) doesn't meet the threshold of the use of force continuum. Two, depending on what's said in our exchange, or what this man perceives I did that prompted his aggressive behavior, my claim as an "innocent party" could come into question. Additionally, talking to an irate and dangerous man will do nothing to de-escalate the situation. More likely, the conflict will lead to a fistfight or use of weapons. I'm taking an unnecessary risk to myself and my family facing him person-to-person. Using my vehicle to my advantage will help me control the situation and keep everyone safe.

Road rage involves a lot of ego. Surviving road rage involves controlling your own. It's safe to say, road rage incidents are more likely caused by uncontrolled temper than criminal intent. Anything you can do to de-escalate the situation will benefit all parties involved. As a responsible citizen of the world, focusing on what you can control, preparing yourself and your family for possible conflict, and keeping a cool head throughout all situations will enable you to survive emotional events.

CONCLUSION

You can see how ugly this scenario can get. This is why you shouldn't get off the highway or out of the vehicle unless absolutely forced to do so. All of the road rage incidents I've personally been involved with either resulted in the aggressor eventually losing interest, or one of the two parties remaining inside the vehicle and the other being unwilling to smash the windshield to further the engagement.

If you get caught up in the emotion of the incident, whether it's the one described above or another take on it, and go toe-to-toe with some yahoo on the side of the road, who is looking after your family? Is the guy alone or does he have three other guys in the truck with him? Does a third-party decide to pull over and try to intervene, and now you're throwing hands with two guys instead of one? Where's your spouse again? What are the kids doing? How complicit are you going to look on the video recorded by a bystander who showed up halfway through the confrontation?

Prepare for best and worst-case scenarios, but call the police, keep moving, and do everything you can to stay in the car and avoid the confrontation. ⁘

10

YOU'RE CONFRONTED BY SOMEONE IMPERSONATING A LAW ENFORCEMENT OFFICER?

By RECOIL OFFGRID Staff
Illustrations by Lonny Chant

Many of you who are regular readers of RECOIL OFFGRID know the tactical landscape quite well by now. You could easily procure clothing and equipment of various contexts to persuade the uninformed that you have scepters of authority and special privileges. In fact, if you read "The Crimson Perception" in Issue 35, you'd have a working knowledge of how, combined with a convincing story, you could easily fool many into thinking your disguise was the real deal.

What if someone used this trickery for nefarious means and attempted to pull you over in what looked like an actual squad car or law enforcement motorcycle? Their badge and clothing might appear official. How would you know if it's an actual police officer or an imposter? What are your rights to verify credentials or refuse to comply if you think your life's in danger? How far can you go without being charged with resisting arrest if you're wrong? In this edition of *What If*, we've asked attorney Jason Squires and former law enforcement officer Hana Bilodeau to weigh in on what your options are if you think you're being spoofed.

The Scenario

Situation type: Confrontation with someone you suspect is impersonating a police officer

Your Crew: You

Location: Your hometown

Season: Summer

Weather: Clear; high 98 degrees F, low 68 degrees F

The Setup

For years, the news has reported situations where people have been pulled over by individuals impersonating law enforcement officers. Sometimes it's merely a self-righteous vigilante attempting to issue phony parking tickets. Unfortunately, there are other situations where someone has procured a car or motorcycle with law-enforcement-oriented features, badges, and duty gear, then confronted an individual under the pretense that they've committed a crime. In these rare situations, the imposter has often been a deranged individual using the guise of law enforcement to abduct, rob, or kill their unsuspecting victims.

The Complication

After a Friday night out with friends, you're driving home after midnight when you notice you're being tailgated. You can see it's a solid-color American sedan with dark paint, a visible push bar, and a spotlight on the A-pillar. You think you may have been slightly over the speed limit, but you haven't been drinking, so you're only mildly fearful that you've broken any laws. Suddenly, you see red/blue flashing lights flicker on inside the windshield and grille of the car behind you. You're driving through an industrial section of town where there are no open businesses, foot traffic, or other vehicles around. You think this may be an unmarked squad car, but are suspicious since you can't see the exempt symbol on the plate or any other markings. You're apprehensive about pulling over in this area, so you attempt to buy time by driving under the speed limit for a few more blocks.

When you refuse to pull over right away, the tailing car blips a siren, turns its spotlight on the back of your car, and uses the loudspeaker to command you to pull over immediately. You're still not positive it's a cop, but stop ASAP because you don't want to get charged with evading. You pull over in a secluded part of this industrial area, and a man gets out with what looks like typical duty clothes: tactical pants, duty belt, radio, button-up shirt, holstered pistol, and boots. He asks you to roll down the window, shines a flashlight in your face, says he suspects you've been drinking, and asks for you to provide him your license and registration. You comply, and he goes back to his car, mutters inaudibly into a hand mic connected to the radio on his belt, and returns to your vehicle. He then asks you to get out of the car so he can conduct a field sobriety test.

As you're not convinced this is legit, you ask for the officer's credentials. He quickly flashes a generic-looking badge. You continue to question his credentials and ask him to call a supervisor, but he says that's not possible right now. He becomes increasingly irritated, and says you'll go to jail if you resist his orders. You remain suspicious, but consent to the test since you haven't been drinking. After performing the tests by following his pen with your eyes, reciting the alphabet backward, and walking a straight line, the officer tells you to turn around and put your hands behind your back, then audibly gets out a pair of cuffs. What are you entitled to demand in order to protect yourself from unlawful incarceration from someone who may be masquerading as a police officer? Do you attempt to flee or fight at that point if there's any doubt in your mind? Do you wait to use a hidden cuff key to escape later on if it becomes clear you're dealing with an imposter?

FORMER FEDERAL OFFICER HANA BILODEAU'S APPROACH

Every now and then we hear a news broadcast about a report of an individual impersonating a police officer, followed by speculation as to why someone would do such a thing. We'll never know what makes these criminals tick, but one thing we do know is that a person who is posing as a police officer is doing so to gain some sort of power over someone else, innately putting that person at risk.

Preparation

Living with a defensive mindset requires preparing for the unknown. Scenario-based training is the best way to determine whether or not you're mentally and physically prepared for a situation where your life or safety may be compromised. Designate a couple minutes a day where you can mentally run through a scenario to figure out where you may be vulnerable. While out for your nightly jog, ask yourself a couple of questions. *If someone were to attack me at this moment, what would I do to protect myself?* As you're driving to work and stopped at a light, ask yourself, *if someone were to attempt to carjack me at this moment, how would I survive?* While wandering through the mall with your family, ask yourself, *if an active shooter event were to transpire, how would I get myself and my family to safety?* If the answers to these simple hypothetical scenarios leave you questioning your safety, you now know you have to make alterations to your day-to-day routines to better equip yourself should your safety be compromised. Now that we've started turning the wheels on our mental preparation, let's move back to the scenario at hand.

Step 1. Research: Do some research on your geographical area. Who has jurisdiction in the city and towns you frequent? Is it the sheriff's office, state police, local police, or federal law enforcement? Once you have the answer to that question, do a simple online search of the residing department's badge and patch, which is typically openly displayed on their daily uniform. Become familiar with what the badge and patch looks like for each of the entities that represents the jurisdiction in which you reside. Researching the badge and patch versus the uniform of the entity is advisable because most departments have multiple units, and each unit's uniforms may be different based on their job assignment.

For instance: duty uniform, dress uniform, detail uniform, summer uniform, winter uniform, bike unit, motorcycle unit, plain-clothes unit, and the list goes on. One thing remains the same across the board: Each department has a patch representing the entity. This patch is either proudly displayed on each shoulder of their uniform shirt or just one of the shoulders on the issued uniforms. Each officer is issued a department ID card and badge with a badge number. These are widely used as a means of primary identification. It's common policy that the officer is required to carry each of these items with them when on duty.

Step 2. Know your rights: Although each state and municipality will have differing and unique laws and procedures regarding traffic stops, it's important to know that there are certain rights at the federal level that are common across the United States.

The "plain view doctrine" prohibits law enforcement officers from investigating inside a vehicle or anything else outside of plain view without a warrant. You don't have to answer an officer's questions during a stop, although this may be frustrating for the officer. In most cases, you're only required to provide license, registration, and insurance information if applicable.

Step 3. Practice your verbal cues: Questioning your safety doesn't need to come across as combative or confrontational, especially if the person you're dealing with is actually a law enforcement official. The job of a police officer is very difficult. The reasons they do things at times may not be readily understandable for the average person; most likely they're acting in a manner to protect themselves and others. Be sure to practice verbal and physical restraint even if you feel agitated. Hopefully, this will allow you and the person of authority to come to a common ground.

On Site

You've properly prepared your defensive mindset, and you've identified that the vehicle, area of stop, and officer all appear suspicious. Let's take a look at how to safely mitigate this uncomfortable situation.

When the officer approaches, only roll the window down enough to pass your personal effects out to the "officer." If you don't see proper identifiers — name tag, badge, badge number, or department patch, politely address the officer: "Good evening sir/ma'am. I didn't see a name badge, what is your name? What department do you work for?" You can even bring up the elephant in the room. "This is a rural area, and I've never seen an unmarked cruiser like that. I didn't see identifiers on your uniform. What department do you work for?"

The hairs on the back of your neck are still standing. If you have cell service, the next step would be to call into the department and request a second unit or a supervisor to respond to your location to confirm the identity of the officer. If you don't have cell service, when the officer returns with your personal documents, in a respectful manner while maintaining your safety inside your vehicle, explain to the officer that you don't feel comfortable with the circumstances of this traffic stop. Request the officer have an additional unit or supervisor car dispatched to the area for your safety. Remember, you're not obligated to exit the vehicle at this point if you believe your safety is a risk.

Every jurisdiction will either have additional officers on duty or a mutual aid agreement with surrounding towns or the state. Be persistent and respectful in your request for an additional unit, stating that you will comply with every lawful order once the officer's identity is confirmed and an additional unit arrives. Remind the officer you're not resisting his/her commands and that, no matter the time frame, you'll patiently wait in your vehicle for the second unit to identify the initiating officer. Once that occurs, you'll fully comply with what is being asked of you.

Crisis

The pressure is now on. Even though you're politely and respectfully communicating with the officer, he/she is now agitated and threatening additional charges and/or physically removing you from your motor vehicle. What steps should you take now that things seem to be taking a turn for the worse?

Stay strong: Continue to calmly and respectfully request that the officer have a secondary unit respond to the traffic stop to identify him/her as an active LEO and witness the traffic stop. If the officer doesn't have appropriate identifiers on their person, such as a department ID, badge, and badge number, they're most likely breaking one or more of the department's policies. Most departments have a policy stating that when an officer is working in an official capacity, they have the duty to appropriately identify themselves to the individuals at hand to get them to comply with the lawful order.

Even with the impending threat of additional charges, if it's proven that the individual is actually an officer, you'll have your time to answer to any additional charges and explain that your behavior was to ensure your safety.

Repeat No. 1: Stay strong. Listen to your gut. If something doesn't feel right, it's probably not right. Escalating your demeanor to meet the level of another never ends well. Remain calm and strong in your request for proper identification and a witnessing unit for the remainder of your interaction with the officer.

The best advice I can give when it comes to personal safety scenarios is: "Get comfortable with the uncomfortable." The average person will never feel comfortable when faced with having to disobey a person of authority. If you're acutely aware of your surroundings and do your diligence to keep up to date on what your local/state municipalities offer for modes of safety, you'll know if something isn't right. If an officer is behaving in a manner that makes you feel uncomfortable, you definitely should err on the side of caution until your suspicions are either confirmed or refuted. It's an officer's job to keep you and the public at large safe. In doing so, they must make sure your rights and needs are met during their interaction with you, no matter how egregious of an offense you may or may not have committed. Not everyone puts your safety at the forefront, which is why it's even more important for you to stay aware, trained, and diligent in your endeavors of survival.

ATTORNEY JASON SQUIRES' APPROACH

Preps

In my vehicle, I have my driver's license, registration, and proof of insurance. I keep all the information up to date and contained in a single folder. I don't want to fumble for documents and give an officer the impression I'm confused or possibly impaired. I also have my cell phone with a full charge. I have absolutely no contraband in my vehicle and keep it orderly and tidy. I want to convey that I'm organized and lucid during any encounter, especially after midnight on a weekend.

I've consulted with an attorney regarding what exactly "reasonable suspicion" means in layman's terms. This is the minimum standard by which a law enforcement officer is allowed to initiate a traffic stop. The officer under this standard must ask themselves, "Do I have a reasonable suspicion that a violation of the law has been committed?" Notice the law doesn't require reasonable suspicion that a crime has occurred. So, the vehicle code is a completely acceptable reason to initiate a traffic stop. What's the vehicle code? It's the annoying set of laws or city ordinances that describe exactly how you must make a left-hand turn, maintain functioning lights, and so on. I always make sure my vehicle has all exterior lights functional, and I always wear my seatbelt. This is good preparation to avoid unnecessary law enforcement encounters. So, if I get a crack in the windshield, I must get it fixed to be compliant with these laws.

I keep a functioning flashlight in the car with fresh batteries. The glove compartment is free of clutter and has the flashlight and registration and current proof of insurance in an envelope. My license is in my wallet. I have tools to fix flats, and my wallet contains multiple forms of proof to establish my identity. I have debit cards, credit cards, gym membership, etc. Law enforcement can be somewhat suspicious when a person only possesses a driver's license and no other form of identification. I also carry a firearm, as is legal in my state (Arizona).

The Stop

The car travels unusually close to my rear bumper. In previous law enforcement encounters, the officer didn't follow so closely. I'm immediately concerned and suspicious because if I made an abrupt stop, this person would hit me. It makes sense that a true police officer would maintain a safe distance. This person, maybe an officer, isn't being safe – that's a red flag.

The emergency lights are activated. Damn. I see blue and red light emanating from his front grille. This tells me I'm not dealing with a normal police cruiser, and I begin to wonder whether this person is really a member of law enforcement. I notice that the lights don't flicker or pulsate the way normal law enforcement lights in my area do. And the lights I'm seeing are very different. However, I notice the large push bumper, like squad cars sometimes have for traffic patrol. So, I'm seeing an undercover police car that looks just like a normal police car without the normal markings – another red flag.

I want to pull over, but I'm concerned. This is a bad part of town. I've noticed red flags and I'm suspicious. I realize that law enforcement has the power to stop cars and detain individuals. I certainly don't want to be charged with a crime merely because I have concerns. I slowly proceed as far as I can to attempt to get to a well-lit, well-traveled road or intersection. If it's not available, I know I have to stop. The approach suggests law enforcement, so as a law-abiding individual I must comply.

The person gets out of the vehicle and approaches my car from the rear. It's at this time that I look for overt signs of personal security. Meaning: I'm expecting the officer to shine his flashlight into the rear compartment to make sure there are no threats hidden inside. I expect the officer to position himself at the B-pillar (the spot where the driver's seatbelt retracts into). Officers usually stand there initially to protect themselves from an armed assailant trying to swing a weapon around at them. This position allows them to immediately back up, putting the driver in the position of shooting over his shoulder. Unfortunately, this person does none of the things I expect him to. He walks right up to the car and turns and faces me near my driver-side mirror. He's looking back at his car and looking around for some reason. He keeps his flashlight directly in my eyes to distract me. I notice he has the usual uniform that can be purchased at any surplus store.

This person asks me strange questions, like does anyone know you're out here this evening? He asks for my license and never really looks at it. He appears to have a radio on the belt, and not the lapel-mic most have. I see no body camera on his person even though most agencies now require body-worn cameras. At this point I'm in a precarious position. If I follow the law, I might possibly endanger myself because I'm not sure he's a police officer. So, I ask, "Are you really a police officer?" This enrages him. He's more aggressive at being challenged. I ask to speak to a supervisor. He says there isn't one available without making a single radio request. I have my firearm in my car, but I know better than to ever pull a firearm on a police officer or even a would-be police officer. My brain and my accelerator are my weapon, not my pistol.

The person orders me out of the vehicle. He didn't go back to his patrol car and run my name like almost all officers do right away. For all he knows, I'm Ted Bundy. This is an extreme red flag. For their own safety, real officers need to know if I'm wanted in Kansas for murder, for example. They usually go back to the car and run my name to make sure there are no outstanding wanted notices or warrants anywhere in the nation.

He again orders me out of the car. I ask again for him to call for a supervisor. He says in a much louder tone, "Out of the car, now!" He's definitely escalating the encounter. I say: "Officer, I don't believe you are a true member of law enforcement, and I need proof you are who you claim to be." He quickly flips a badge that I couldn't read. I state again, "I need to have a supervisor here immediately, and I will wait patiently for the supervisor to arrive." I notice there's no backup present either – red flag.

Failure to obey a lawful order is a crime. Unlawful flight from a pursuing law enforcement officer is a crime. Resisting arrest is a crime. Being alive is not a crime. As a human you might have to balance these competing concepts with your survival. If you're truly afraid and your fear is reasonable and articulated, you wouldn't likely be charged with a crime. However, you'd better start laying the foundation for a defense by calling 911.

If the person made you believe – truly believe – that he's not a member of law enforcement, and you believed that your life was in danger, you could argue that you had no choice but to flee and immediately dial 911.

"911. What is your emergency?"

"Please help me, please send help. There's a man pretending to be law enforcement who just tried to abduct me. I am Jason Squires, I live at this address, and I'm heading eastbound on XYZ Street or wherever you direct me to find true law enforcement officers. I'm not running from the law. I'm running *to* the law for help. Please help."

What if the person was a cop and you just sped away? You might be charged. There's never a consequence-free option in this world. And pulling away from law enforcement will bring down the hammer. However, the 911 call you made will certainly help minimize your exposure. Calling your buddy before 911? You're going to be in trouble. Calling 911, which is nearly always recorded, begins a new problem, and a sergeant will almost certainly be ordered to arrive. In fact, 911 will likely direct you somewhere and tell you to wait until a marked unit arrives, and by unit, I mean several units.

At that time, you'd better explain all the reasons why you felt like he was there to kill you pretending to be a cop. If you clearly and calmly describe all indicators that he was not a police officer, you might even get what we call in the industry a "street acquittal." However, there are aggravators like speeding away and not doing everything 911 says. Don't be the guy who says, "I was scared and went home." That guy is going away. Don't say, "I don't trust any member of law enforcement, so I ran to my girlfriend's house." That person's also going away. Remember, run *to* the law, not *away from* the law.

Let's envision a place where you don't have cell signal. The suspected imposter chose this area specifically because it's a cellular dead spot. There are so many different examples of how this could occur. I might slowly (I said *slowly*) drive until I find a signal and immediately call for 911. I would calmly state that a person appears to be pretending to be law enforcement and give my name and information.

We cede tremendous power to law enforcement. Bad guys occasionally take advantage of the power law enforcement has over motorists. Retired patrol cars and motorcycles can be cloned to look like current law enforcement vehicles. Bad guys can use this approach to apprehend unsuspecting members of our communities. I will add that females possess great latitude when it comes to articulating fear. No, they're not weaker. However, a woman claiming she's afraid is more likely to be believed than a male counterpart.

Finally

Police officers must identify themselves. They must divulge their badge numbers. Officers must ask for supervisors if requested, or at a minimum backup officers. 911 is the most powerful tool to bring the real good guys to your location. A bad guy won't wait for them to show up. Asking to proceed to a more lighted area or commercial parking lot is reasonable. Expressing fear is appropriate under some circumstances. For example: "Sir, your car doesn't look like law enforcement and you have refused to provide a supervisor or additional units, I fear for my safety and I've called 911." If the officer gets aggressive, wait until the good guys get there and be prepared to explain every single detail as to why you didn't believe he was law enforcement. And lastly, always protect yourself from bad guys by using your brain. If it doesn't seem right, call 911 immediately.

CONCLUSION

We've probably all heard about situations like this in the news or have seen YouTube videos of someone impersonating a law enforcement officer. While some are comical, others are much more nefarious. Kenneth Bianchi, also known as the "Hillside Strangler," along with his cousin Angelo Buono, impersonated police officers using fake badges to lure women into complying with their commands during their crime spree. Remember, it's not a crime to ask questions when something doesn't pass the proverbial smell test.

Earlier this year, the shooting in Nova Scotia involved a gunman dressed as a member of the Royal Canadian Mounted Police who also drove a fake police car. Obtaining a used squad car or modifying one to have certain features that look similar to a legitimate unmarked squad car is easier than you might think, and to a certain extent it's perfectly legal. Take some time to do an internet search on impersonating law enforcement and you'll see how frequently this crime takes place. Know your rights, be cautiously cooperative, and stack the odds in your favor by having evidence recorded via a dashcam. ⠿

11

YOU'RE FACING AN ASSAULT IN A PARKING STRUCTURE?

By RECOIL OFFGRID Staff
Photos by Jordan Lance

The university is predictably quiet tonight, being a Friday night. One by one, students pack up as the time draws nearer for the library to close. Staff make the rounds at 10 to midnight, letting the remaining students know they'd be closing soon and to finish up what they're doing. You shut off your laptop, pack up the books you had scattered about the table, and take a long sigh, wondering how difficult your upcoming midterms will be. Normally you wouldn't be on campus quite this late, but you're behind on your assignments and feel you have precious little time left to complete your work before you leave for spring break.

You say goodnight to the staff member who kindly holds the door open for you as you walk out the front door of the library. You head to the parking structure where you left your car, on the other side of the campus. You don't like the idea of having to walk clear across the campus so late at night, but it was one of those days where parking was limited and you didn't have time between classes to go back and move your car to a closer location like you often do.

After a brisk walk, you climb up the staircase to the third floor of the parking structure, approaching another parked car with tinted windows just sitting there idling. You find it a bit peculiar, but figure it's another student, probably busy talking on the phone before they head out. Instead of hearing the car pull away as you pass it, it curiously shuts off. You then hear the sound of the door closing and footsteps walking away from it. The purposeful-sounding footsteps are getting louder and definitely those of a man. This is somewhat discomforting, but since you already rounded the corner to where your car is parked, you can't see who it is.

Your car is now in your line of sight, but a strange man who looks a bit too old and disheveled to be a student takes notice of you, as if he's been waiting for someone. You feel the hair on your neck stand up as he walks toward you, all the while the steps behind you are getting louder. The man in front of you stares right at you and asks in a gravelly voice, "I'm sorry, my phone died. Can you tell me uh ... what time it is?"

The steps behind you get closer and you turn around to see a military-aged male in a hoodie with his hands hidden inside his front pockets. He stops when he sees you notice him. As you turn back around to the man asking the time, he shifts his gaze and now tries to force a smile that looks about as honest as a $3 bill. There's no other noticeable activity or students that you can see or hear. It's near midnight, and you feel like you may be getting prospected for a violent crime. You begin to shake a little, as this is the kind of stuff you hear about happening to other people on TV. What do you do?

The Scenario

Situation type: Possible mugging, rape, or murder
Your Crew: You
Location: Local state university
Season: Spring
Weather: Clear; high 78 degrees F, low 66 degrees F

The Setup

You're a student working on your graduate degree at a local university. Recently, there have been a few muggings and even a murder on campus. You often study late at the campus library, which is open until midnight, and frequently have to walk to your car across campus to a parking structure or another lot that's quite far from the library. The campus has an explicit no-weapons policy and forbids firearms, claiming that its 24-hour campus security presence is sufficient to keep students and staff safe. You're concerned with this recent string of incidents, especially since you often walk to your car alone and have rarely seen security officers patrolling the area.

The Complication

On a Friday night, you leave as the library closes at midnight and walk across to the parking structure. You ascend to the third floor where your car is parked, noticing that the structure is practically empty. As you head to your car, you pass a vehicle that's parked about 50 yards from your car and idling. The windows are tinted so you can't see inside, but you find it peculiar that it's just sitting there running. You chalk it up to possibly being another student getting ready to leave.

As you approach your car, a middle-aged male walks in your direction. Meanwhile, you hear the car you just passed turn off its engine and the door open and close. As the man in front nears you, he asks if you have the time. You look down at your watch and let him know that it's just past midnight. You hear something behind you, realizing there's another male, perhaps a little younger, approximately 30 yards behind you. The male asking for the time is now only about 20 feet in front of you. Are you being set up for a mugging, physical or sexual assault, or potential murder? Or are these just two other students or staff who mean you no harm? You begin to sense that something is wrong, and the odds of coincidence are dropping fast. There are blue emergency call boxes in the parking structure that connect you directly with campus security, but one of the individuals is between you and the stairs to the closest call box, which is one level below you. What do you do?

TACTICAL TRAINER KATHERYN BASSO'S APPROACH

A college campus is ripe for criminal behavior due to its plethora of easy targets — inebriated partiers, late-night scholars, and young, naive adults recently released into the world. Whether or not criminal behavior has recently increased on my campus, as a woman, I'm always aware of the potential for conflict. Before my first day of class, I do my due diligence to familiarize myself with the local area — location of police stations and hospitals, crime rates, and gang activity — as well as campus protocol and safety measures, such as the location of campus security guards and call boxes, and phone numbers for security escorts or emergency services. The more prepared I am prior to an emergency, the less likely I'll freeze if a crisis ever occurs.

Let's make a few assumptions before we get into this scenario. One, I have to stay at the library until it closes. Whether that's because I need access to a special collection that cannot be checked out, or my roommate makes too much noise for me to concentrate — whatever the reason, I need to stay at the library until midnight. Otherwise, I'd rather study at home and avoid the potential threat. Assumption two: I couldn't get a security escort that night. I'd definitely request an escort, if available. I don't care how tough you are, what your skill level is, or how badass you think you are. One security guard with a radio and pistol significantly increases your chances of avoiding criminal behavior. Swallow your pride or impatience and make smart choices.

With that being said, let's walk through the escalation of conflict in this scenario: avoidance, resistance, and combat.

Preparation: Conflict Avoidance

The only fight I'm 100-percent guaranteed to win is the one I'll never have. Setting myself up to avoid conflict will be my best shot at getting home safely. Criminals tend to choose easy targets — individuals buried in their phones, unaware of their surroundings, or hindered in their movement due to age, injury, or footwear. They'll choose someone they think they can overpower or outnumber; they'll attack in areas where they have the least chance of getting caught. There are a number of choices I can make on campus to make myself a hard target and increase the odds of avoiding conflict:

Parking: It's probably a universal rule on all college campuses that parking is never convenient nor in excess. Let's assume that I'll always have to park in an inconvenient spot far from my intended destination. As I drive through a parking garage, I'll look for a parking spot closest to security features, listed in order of preference: cameras and lights, elevators and stairwells, and emergency call boxes. Again, the intent is to make myself a hard target. Even if I'm the last vehicle in a structure, a criminal is less likely to attack me if he's being recorded on camera and illuminated under lights. If I can't find a spot close to lights or cameras, I want to be close to an egress route. And finally, a call box. I list a call box last because it'd be quicker and safer to use my phone as I'm running to safety than to stop and expose myself to danger as I wait by a call box.

The Walk: So, I've parked my car under well-illuminated lights right next to that bubble camera the campus security installed after the many protests from students concerned about their safety. I have no idea if the camera works, but hey, neither does the bad guy. Now, I have to find my way to the library. I'll choose a route that has as many people as possible — avoid shortcuts through alleys or under bridges, overgrown shrubbery, camera blind spots, Professor Jenning's Botanical Garden, and so on. You know, all the places students like to meet up in the middle of the night for dirty deeds. Those are the places to avoid. Instead, walk on a well-lit and frequented path past camera towers and call boxes. Again, a call box isn't an ideal stop if something goes bad, but it can be a good deterrent. As I'm walking in the early evening, I take notice of my surroundings. What are my danger points — the unavoidable spots I must pass where an attack would be, most likely due to a camera blindspot, broken lightpost, or blind corner? Are there any new structures that could conceal someone? I also look at the people along the way. Who are they? How are they dressed? Who are they with? Where does their interest lie? Are they walking with a purpose or out for a stroll? Identifying the baseline for this walk will help me identify an anomaly later.

The Equalizer: I get it – the policy is no weapons on campus. However, that doesn't mean I can't carry something to defend myself. Weapons are usually defined as a firearm, knife of a certain blade length, or baton. That leaves several sprays, alarms, and self-defense keychains that'll still provide protection against an attacker. In case even these items aren't allowed on campus, I'd choose to carry one in a nondescript or concealed form factor. Whichever I choose, I need to make sure I've practiced using it. The last thing I want is my attacker using my personal protection device against me. I'd carry the following:

Personal Alarms: I'd use a personal alarm more for audible stunning than in hopes of alerting someone of my predicament. Nowadays, people are so used to car alarms that they tend to ignore rather than run to these noises. However, unleashing it up against an attacker's ear may give you an opportunity to get away.

Spray: Mace, powered by the phenacyl chloride (CN) chemical, is an irritant that utilizes pain to subdue its target. However, it's often ineffective against animals and assailants under the influence or mentally disturbed. Therefore, I'd carry pepper spray; its main ingredient is oleoresin capsicum (OC). OC spray is an inflammatory agent that dilates the capillaries in your eyes and causes your mucous membranes to swell, resulting in temporary blindness, coughing, and choking. Some now squirt out foam to reduce spray back.

The Library: Once I'm at the library, I'd maintain my situational awareness. Is anyone lurking around? Is anyone too interested in what I'm doing and where I'm going? Is anyone waiting for me to leave? If so, I'd take this opportunity to inform the appropriate authorities.

On Site: Conflict Resistance

Situational awareness is the ability to identify a threat before it can harm you or your family. There's a fine line between paranoia and preparation. Being observant of your surroundings doesn't mean working yourself into an anxiety-induced suspicion that everyone is out to get you. The point is not to be complacent.

Observe: It's now midnight, and I'm walking back to my car. My head is up; I'm walking with a purpose. My phone is in my pocket; I'm not listening to music. I'm using my eyes, ears, and nose to be aware of my surroundings. Do I see people lurking? Can I hear someone's footsteps behind me? Can I smell cologne? My keys are in my hand so I don't have to fiddle with my bag to find them and because they hold both my personal alarm and my OC spray. Again, it's not about being paranoid, it's about being prepared.

Orient: Since I'm aware of my surroundings, I'll be able to identify an anomaly – an event that doesn't conform to my pre-established baseline. Let's say I previously established that the baseline for this part of campus involves students or faculty walking with a purpose to or from other buildings; it's not an area where people congregate or sit and study by themselves. Since it's a warm spring day, they're in shorts and T-shirts. They have bags to carry their books or papers. They walk alone or in small groups from class. Their interest is focused on the path that leads to their destination or in conversation. With spring break approaching, most are relaxed, showing no signs of stress.

Decide and Act: If I see someone lingering by himself along a side of a building or beneath a tree, with layers of clothes on and no backpack or bag, this would be an anomaly. It doesn't necessarily mean he's a threat, but it does mean he doesn't fit into the baseline. He may be someone trying to find a place to do drugs or meet up with his forbidden love interest. But he should still garner my attention and action. I'd have to determine if I should maintain my current course, alter my path toward the dorms or coffee shop that I know would still be open, or call the police. As long as his interest didn't remain on me and he didn't follow me, I'd likely choose to continue to my vehicle.

Crisis: Combat

In this scenario, I'm on the parking garage level of my car and missed my opportunity to alter my path away from the guy walking toward me and the creepy, idling car. I also messed up by looking down at my watch to check the time, so I'll want to regain observation of the potential threat as soon as possible. As I find myself between two men, I'll have to make a quick assessment of the man in front of me while also listening for the footsteps of the man behind me to determine if he's a threat.

I'd look for signs of the front man's fight or flight response: flushed or pale face, shaking hands, increased respiration rate. I'll look at his hands: Are they holding something? Are they hiding something? I'll listen for the man behind me. Are his footsteps getting farther away or closer? Is his pace quickening or staying the same? If the men show no signs of threat, I'll continue to my car and drive away. However, if I deem them a threat, I'll prep my OC spray and verbally tell them both to get back while I maneuver to their side where I can see both assailants.

This is the turning point. If my assessment was wrong, the two men should back up, perhaps call me crazy, and leave the vicinity. I'd rather be called crazy and stay alive than avoid feeling presumptuous and end up dead. If my assessment was correct, however, it's time for 110-percent violence. If the two men lunge toward me, I'll do everything I can to neutralize the threat, with a combination of OC spray and physical violence. Humans have three very vulnerable targets and only two hands to cover them, so I'll look to strike their eyes, throat, or groin. Once contained, I'll seek cover and protection: If I'm close to my car, I'll get in and drive away, calling 9-1-1 in the process. If the men are between me and my car and the stairwell is close, I'll make a run for it. My adrenaline will be spiked at this point, so I won't be able to rely on my dexterity. But I can have my Google assistant call for help as I head toward a more populated area.

Conclusion

After an attack or assault, people tend to play Monday-morning quarterback with the victim: Why did you go out at that time of night? Why did you park that far away? Why did you put yourself in a dangerous situation? In a perfect world, we'd only need to accomplish tasks in broad daylight with a police officer watching over us on every corner. Allowing fear of a potential attack to dictate our schedules is no way to live. However, making yourself a hard target – being prepared and situationally aware – greatly increases your likelihood of survival not just in this scenario, but at any point where you're alone or with vulnerable companions.

DISASTER MANAGEMENT SPECIALIST NILA RHOADES' APPROACH

Preparation: When dealing with potential attackers, one has to remember that mindset is critical. Good situational awareness can mitigate many different types of situations. In preparation for a potential attacker, I'd first familiarize myself with my campus' weapons policy. While a "no firearms allowed" policy is usually a given, especially on college campuses, carrying a pepper spray, mace, stun gun, or Taser might be acceptable or a gray area in the policies – in which asking forgiveness might be better than asking for permission. That's a risk versus reward trade-off that must be weighed heavily. Some may find it to be worthwhile to carry a concealed firearm, some may not. For some, it'd depend on the potential consequences, both legally and with the school.

If I can't bring my firearm on my person, I'll always have a knife. Granted, this is considered a weapon, but it can be hidden deep in my pockets or bag to avoid detection. Frankly, it's much easier to conceal a knife than a firearm. I normally carry an Emerson Hattin, not only because that's what I own, but because it's easy to open and will give me a fighting chance against an attacker. The unfortunate side effect of edged weapons is that the threat must be within arm's distance of me, which is always much closer than I'd like. I also always carry a good flashlight. My personal preference is a TerraLux TT5 which has a strobe option, but SureFire makes amazing lights too. This would allow me to not only light my path to my vehicle but also aid in threat identification. I could also strobe them if they get too close, which would hopefully make them reassess their life choices. Many flashlights also have a strike bezel if you need to defend yourself physically.

When I go anywhere after dark, I always park close, as close to the door as possible. Otherwise, I look for a parking spot next to a light. Being on campus and paying good money for a graduate degree, I have absolutely no qualms with asking the campus security for an escort to my vehicle. That's their job – to ensure the safety of the students. Parking near a security camera wouldn't particularly interest me. Security cameras, unless they're being monitored constantly and adequately, only help to identify the suspect, not prevent the crime. Since security is provided by the college, I'd have to assume that they have limited staff and may be poorly trained. My own experience with campus security supports the mindset that I'm essentially on my own. However, larger campuses may have their own police department, or a local police department may have a unit attached to the campus as their security. While that's always preferred over rent-a-cops with batons, they have to be near me during an incident to be useful.

An officer in a uniform escorting me to my vehicle would make me a much harder target than walking to my vehicle alone, especially after dark, at such a late hour.

Given that there has been a string of recent incidents, especially a murder, on the campus that I'm attending, I wouldn't go anywhere on campus alone. It's not worth the risk until the suspect is apprehended. I'd either ask a friend to hang out with me while I was studying, or not go to campus to study at all. With Google Scholar and all of the other digital resources available, studying at home is a viable option. It may not be a long-term solution for the semester, but it'll work for a while until there's a change in threat levels on campus. If studying on campus is a necessity, then I'll secure my bag to my person, hold my flashlight in my non-dominant hand, and place my dominant hand on my knife in my pocket. Think the cowboy "thumb-tucked-in-their-pocket" look. This will allow me to have quick access to my knife, which will flip open as I pull it out of my pocket. Lastly, I'll keep my car keys clipped to a belt loop on the front of my pants. Thus, they'll be accessible while approaching my car, but also somewhat tethered to me.

The Complication: Any vehicle that's running for more than a minute or two presents a cause for concern. A male simply walking toward me wouldn't (and shouldn't) set off any internal alarms just yet. With graduate programs on campus, the age of the student is hard to pinpoint. Many grad students (including me) go back to school many years after finishing up their bachelor's degree. Therefore, threat identification will have to wait a few more moments until he plays out his next move. Thus, presenting yourself as a hard target is always paramount. A portion of that is carrying yourself with purpose and free of distractions. That includes phones, earbuds, books, and random things in your hands that can't be used to fend off an attacker — that's what bags are for.

I'm a firm believer that your gut feeling (we refer to it as Spidey-sense in my house) is right 99 percent of the time. When something feels off, it probably is. One of the biggest non-violent threat mitigation techniques is to look them in the eye and say a friendly "hello." Bad guys don't want to be noticed or acknowledged. In our individualist society, where many of us are so easily distracted by our phones, it's easy to see why some attacks happen. When someone approaching my direction looks a little sketchy, I acknowledge them and say "hi," perhaps even making a mundane comment about the weather.

This lets them know that I'm aware of them, I see them, and I'm not scared of talking to a stranger. Now this is where my OODA loop will start kicking into a higher gear. OODA stands for observe, orient, decide, and act. It's an older training framework, but it's still very useful because that's just now our brains operate.

If the situation still continues to escalate, I have a few options. First, always trust your gut. If I feel like I'm in danger, I'll run as far and as fast as I can until I reach some kind of help. Wearing sensible shoes is always a good idea, but don't be afraid to ditch your footwear if it makes you a faster runner. Honestly,

I hate shoes and often wear flip-flops, so abandoning them is a realistic option if a threat presents itself to me.

The FBI's Run, Hide, Fight protocol can be useful in situations as well. However, my only realistic option on this college campus is to run. Fighting could be an option, but I'm outnumbered and underpowered to take on two males. Hiding wouldn't work in this scenario as it's a parking garage, an empty one at that. There aren't many places to hide.

When the man nears me and asks for the time, I give an approximation. There's no need to take my eyes off the potential threat to look at my watch. As I do this, I can try to increase the distance between the threat and me as I continue to my vehicle. At this point I have a few options. With one man 20 feet ahead of me and another 30 yards behind me, my first option is to exit the situation as quickly as possible. There are other directions that I could run should the man ahead of me present himself as a threat. If he continues on his intersecting path, I would position my bag in front of me so I could essentially feed it to him and run like the wind. Nothing in that bag is worth my life.

A few years ago, the FBI published a list of pre-attack indicators, physical behaviors exhibited by suspects before they attempt to commit a crime. It provides some valuable insight into human behavior, but also into the males in this scenario: clenching their hands; erratic eye blinks; target glances; fighting stance; hesitation; flanking; following; removing clothing; yelling; pressing forearms against their side; twitchy, googly, or inappropriately looking at the target.

Search for *A Study of Pre-Attack Behaviors of Active Shooters in the United States Between 2000 and 2013* in order to review it in more depth. The study focuses on active shooters, but is fairly indicative of various types of attackers.

Since one of the two men is exhibiting behavior that would align with the FBI's pre-attack indicators, I have to make the logical assumption that I'm in danger. If I'm wrong, then I'll eat crow later. But again, it's after midnight and nothing good ever happens after dark.

At this juncture I'm left with two different scenarios. The first is that the man really just wants to know the time, is meeting up with the man behind me, and they will go about their business. The second is that the man in front of me is meant to distract me while the man behind me attempts to grab me. After I tell the first what time it is, and he still closes in on me, I have to make a decision. There's no need to invade someone's personal space in an empty parking garage. If he got within 10 feet I'd start strobing him with my flashlight and yelling my biggest-big-girl voice, "Stop! Get back! I feel threatened! I have a weapon!"

At this point, I'd feel comfortable and confident pulling my knife out of my pocket. I can legally articulate being afraid for my life and feeling threatened. The laws in each state vary on this point so make sure you have a solid understanding of this concept. With my hands full, I wouldn't be able to pull out my cell phone to call for help just yet. Most importantly, I need my defensive tools in my hands until I feel that I'm no longer in danger. One would hope that they realize that I'm not an easy target and leave; if not, then I'd feed them my book bag and run like Usain Bolt somewhere safe. This could be my vehicle if I could get it unlocked in a timely manner, but again my hands are full of defensive tools — a car with keyless entry could be very handy. If I can get in my car and the bad guys are far enough back or are running the other way, then that's my first priority. The important thing to note about vehicles is that they're 2-ton defensive tools as much as they're a means of escape. If the men are too close to me, then I'll run as far and as fast as I can and pray that I can find campus security or other people to aid in my defense. The key to this whole scenario is being situationally aware enough to not let the men get so close that you can't make a run for it.

This is a very challenging scenario due to the prohibition on carrying a firearm or weapon on campus. Some people are die-hard rule followers, and that's OK. It all depends on how you assess the risk versus reward. There are still some non-weapon options for campuses that would allow you to defend yourself without technically breaking the rules:

- ❱ Get a roll of quarters and cover it with tape, essentially shellacking it. Throw it in the bottom of a tube sock, tie or rubber band the top, and you have a giant monkey fist. If anyone asks, it's emergency pay phone/taxi money and random dirty laundry.
- ❱ A cable bike lock. No bike required. Carrying a bike lock on campus looks normal, and swinging the combo lock at someone's face could give you time and opportunity to make a quick exit.
- ❱ A pen with a metal shaft, like those made by Zebra. If you encounter an attacker take the pointy end and aim for an eye, preferably, or other soft tissue.

The best thing you can do is avoid going anywhere after dark alone, especially when there are potential threats near campus. Buddy team movements don't mean you're scared; you're simply being realistic about the threats around you. Or just study from home, where you can be legally armed.

CONCLUSION

Gun-free zones, such as college campuses, are target-rich environments for criminals and predators. But that doesn't mean you have to be a soft target. With proper mindset, preparation, situational awareness, tactics, and an appropriate amount of caution, you can stack the deck in your favor as much as possible.

Our protagonist in this scenario found herself in a bit of a pickle, facing a potentially deadly threat. Our SMEs outlined a number of options and actions for her to attempt to extricate herself. But the most important piece of advice is to do your best to minimize the odds of facing such dangerous situations. Many of the recommendations along these lines require real commitment and discipline — but isn't your own well-being worth the investment? And despite your best efforts, you may not always be able to avoid potential conflicts. Thus, you need to be prepared for that as well.

The mindset, strategies, and tactics described in this article are just as applicable off-campus as they are on-campus, and while armed or unarmed. So, take them to heart and make yourself a hard target. ▌▌

12

YOU'VE STUMBLED UPON A POTENTIAL HOME BURGLARY?

By Tim MacWelch
Illustrations by Joe Oesterle

Even if you're not usually absent-minded, you've probably felt the momentary confusion of arriving at home only to find a light was left on. You thought you'd turned it off before you left, but did you just have a brain fart and forget? Did your spouse or one of the kids leave it on? These common oversights can often make your skin crawl for a few moments as you wonder if someone was inside while you were gone. Coming home to an open front door, however, is a more concerning sign that something or someone has been there. You're incredibly vigilant about locking everything up before you leave, but here comes that eerie feeling again. Did you screw up and forget to lock it this time, or are you about to walk in on an intruder?

You swallow and step back to see if you notice anything else out of place. You think about calling out "Hello?" for a second, but hesitate since you could potentially be alerting an uninvited (and possibly armed) guest to your presence. You'd hoped this would be a simple house-sitting gig for a friend, but you may now have stumbled upon a burglary in progress. What do you do?

The Scenario

Situation type: Possible burglary
Your Crew: You
Location: Your friend's house
Season: Winter
Weather: Snowy and windy; high 38, degrees F, low 12 degrees F

The Setup

A wealthy friend of yours has gone out of town for the holidays and left their house in your care while they're on vacation visiting relatives. You agreed to check on it every day until they return (except Christmas) to feed the cat, make sure the heater hasn't broken down, collect mail and any packages that've arrived, and perform a general inspection to make sure nothing is out of order. Your friend has told you that they've been the victim of porch pirates more than once, so this being the holiday season, the potential for theft is higher.

The house is a bit secluded, and up a winding mountain road with no neighbors in the immediate line of sight or within earshot of any potential disturbances. It's also a three-story house that's over 5,000 square feet with numerous rooms, but you'll only need to be in the kitchen and living room area while you're there. The house has an alarm system that provides armed security response, but times in the past that the alarm has been tripped have yielded a slow response from the company ... if any.

Your friend will only be gone for a few days, so you plan on a handful of routine visits until they return. You're also told that the only others who have access to the house are the security company who has the alarm code, but no key, and the housekeeper, who has both. You're also told the housekeeper will not be visiting while the family is away, and that they're practically a member of the family, having worked for them for the last 20 years with no incidents.

You're also told there is a hide-a-key in what looks like a rock near the front porch. Although you have your own key for the visit, and you don't know exactly what the rock looks like, the family made mention that it doesn't look like the other rocks in the vicinity, so it should be easy to spot if you need to gain access. You've also been given a login to watch security footage of the house from your phone, using the cameras installed around the perimeter.

The Complication

It's Christmas Eve and nearing dusk. You decide to make one last pass of the house before coming back in a couple days since there'll be no mail delivery tomorrow. You can leave the cat some extra food to hold it over through Christmas day. As you arrive, you can see what looks like fresh tracks in the snow, but you attribute it to a few last-minute deliveries or the mail carrier. You've arrived a little earlier than normal to get this finished before moving on to your own holiday arrangements, but you begin to notice some things that concern you. As you go to collect the mail from the mailbox, you find it empty and wonder if the mail carrier hasn't arrived yet or had nothing to deliver. There are also no packages in their usual place by the front door – you were certain that some would arrive today. Maybe the delivery is running late as well? You also notice that the light in the upstairs bedroom is off. You know that light in particular is on a timer and wonder if it hasn't kicked on yet because you're here earlier than normal.

As you approach the front door, you see that it's slightly ajar. Did you forget to lock it and the wind managed to blow it open? Is someone here? The blinking red light on the alarm panel shows that the alarm has been activated and that alone makes the hair on the back of your neck stand up. You look around frantically for something that looks like the hide-a-key rock you were told about, but you don't see anything that resembles the description you were given. Did someone manage to find it and get inside? Did the housekeeper show up unexpectedly to drop something off for the family? You decide to investigate further, but feel hesitant since you haven't explored the house in its entirety and don't know the layout.

Your cell phone reception up here is spotty and dropped calls have happened to you here before. The house also doesn't have a landline that you're aware of. You walk into the kitchen and see nothing that looks out of order. As you swing back to head toward the front door, there's a noticeable "thump" upstairs. Is this a burglar? Is it the cat? Is it someone else who has a key to the house you weren't told about? If someone is there, who are they and what do they want? Should you call the police or the security company and wait for their arrival? Either way, it's unlikely that they'll respond quickly given your remote location – if you can get through to anyone at all. Should you attempt to clear the house and risk coming face-to-face with an armed intruder? Should you run to your car to go get help?

FIREARMS INSTRUCTOR SHEENA GREEN'S APPROACH

Preparation

When I've been asked to house-sit in the past, whether my friends knew it or not, they usually provided me with a general baseline about their environment. Routines such as *the neighbor is a home-body and goes out for a morning walk around 7:30, trash is picked up on Mondays; mail gets delivered in the afternoon, sometimes the girl down the street rides her bike over to see if our kids can play on Saturdays* are things that have been relayed to me. While seemingly trivial, those are notes to keep and compare during visits to the house.

Extra questions I could ask if the information wasn't already volunteered would be: *Have you had any issues with crime other than the porch pirates? Are there any weirdos or stray animals in the neighborhood I need to look out for? Has anything serious been posted in your neighborhood Facebook group recently (besides people mistaking cars backfiring for gunshots)?*

Making sure I understand the security system and how it works would be at the top of my list. I wouldn't want to trouble my friend with a call from the security company if I didn't disarm the system in time. This would prompt a few more questions: *What is the notification process if I don't disarm the system in time? Does it alert your family in addition to the security company? Have you ever had law enforcement show up to a tripped alarm? Do you know what the response time was?*

To avoid being mistaken for a burglar, I'd suggest my friend make a contact list for me to keep of family/friends/neighbors who have been made aware of my responsibility to care for the cat and property. This also makes me feel more at ease knowing I have people I can contact who are more familiar with the house in case there's some sort of mishap.

My cell phone gets crappy reception in real life, so something I do when visiting friends is ask for the Wi-Fi password and connect when I'm there. Having the Wi-Fi password sent via a text and saved to your notes on your phone as a backup is helpful as well.

Something I recommend everyone do regardless of the amount of risk in your daily life is set up your SOS and emergency contacts on your smartphone. Depending on the phone brand and operating system, how the SOS is activated could be different, so make sure you're familiar with your own. It's also helpful to know how to dial 911 from the lock screen, so you won't have to fumble with the keypad when seconds count.

Knowing I needed to go to a secluded home where emergency response times could be lengthy, I'd ask someone to accompany me every time I planned to check on the house. Even if the person I ask is not someone who carries a firearm, a second person is always better than being alone. I'd ask my friend to wait in the driver seat with the vehicle running and have their cell phone at the ready in case we need to make a quick exit.

Because of my crappy phone reception, frequency of travel, and preferring to work from a secure internet connection, one option I've explored is the Solis X by SkyRoam. It's a portable Wi-Fi hotspot and has a built-in camera.

On Site

Thanks to the info relayed to me by my friends, I already have the sneaking suspicion that something is a little off and would spend more time observing the scene and outside of the house. If there are tire tracks in the snow, did anyone get out of the vehicle? How many pairs of footprints are there? Where do they lead? Do the tracks look like someone was dropped off? Does it look like the vehicle came and went with no one getting out? The information that I can glean from those questions may sway my actions to either play it safe and review security footage or go ahead and approach the house.

Upon finding the door ajar, now I know I've got a problem, which instantly starts a swirl of thoughts and decisions to make. The first one is going to be whether or not someone is on the other side. The second one is trying to decide to peek around the door or hurry up and go back to the car. Then, at some point, a random reminder for the reason for the visit, "Oh sh*t, did the cat escape?"

Even though I can legally carry a firearm, I'd choose to go back to the car, lock the doors, and tell my friend what I saw. From the safety of the locked car, positioned in a safer distance from the house, I'd have my friend call the police on speakerphone while I pull up surveillance footage and wait for law enforcement to arrive.

Crisis

Knowing our own skills, capabilities, and limits can keep us safe, so I'm not even going to entertain the idea of clearing the house. It's not something I have sought out training for and the idea of me, an armed civilian clearing a 5,000-square-foot house I don't know the layout of is outside the realm of reasonable actions for me.

It's not safe to assume that burglars are non-violent, and therefore caution should be exercised if found face-to-face with the intruder. The training I've received over the years to prepare myself for violent encounters will come into play if and when that story unfolds.

By choosing not to enter the home, as evidenced on the security cameras and my friend as a witness, I save myself a whole lot of legal headache and blame. If burglars had, in fact, ransacked the house and left before we arrived, most of the scene would be untouched and untampered. Hopefully this would make it easier for police to do their job in finding clues and catching the bad guy(s).

COMBATIVES EXPERT CHAD MCBROOM'S APPROACH

Preparation

Area Orientation: The first part of my preparation phase for this type of scenario would be to have my friend give me a detailed tour of the house and property. I'd want to know the locations of all the exterior doors and any other large opening that might serve as an entry or exit point. I'd also note the locations of all security system triggers, such as door and window sensors, glass-break sensors, and motion detectors, as well as the locations of all interior and exterior cameras. Having access to the cameras via my cell phone will allow me to check in and around the house to have the greatest situational awareness prior to entering. It'll also help in identifying any intruders and thieves if a situation does arise.

I'd also want to know if there's a safe room in the house, where it's located, and what supplies are there. Although I plan on having my own equipment on my person, it's good to know where I might be able to find additional supplies. If there's a well-planned safe room inside the house, it'll likely have an alternate form of communication, such as a reliable cell phone or landline separate from the main line.

Establish a Baseline: Next, I'd establish a baseline of the house and surrounding area. What are the normal traffic patterns? What are the local norms? Are there any identified criminal enterprises operating in the area? What's the typical law enforcement response to crime in this area? What are the local habitual areas (public gathering places) and natural lines of drift (shortcuts)? What's the baseline atmosphere ("feeling") of the area?

I'd take a second walk-through of the interior and exterior of the house by myself to eliminate all distractions and observe the lay of the land. What are the natural and manmade obstacles (terrain, walls, fences, cameras, etc.) that would divert or funnel human traffic trying to enter the property surreptitiously? I'd also identify the hide-a-key rock to see where and how it's currently oriented.

Having this established baseline will allow me to identify any anomalies that present themselves when I go to check on the house. An atmospheric shift, disturbance of the area, a vehicle out of place, items moved from their normal location, or a housekeeper's vehicle parked outside at an odd hour are examples of detectable anomalies that could indicate potential danger upon arriving at the residence.

Personal Preparation: My personal equipment would consist of my normal EDC, to include a concealed handgun, knife, flashlight, and cell phone. My phone would have my friend's phone number, the number for the local police department and security monitoring company, and the numbers of any nearby friends or neighbors that might serve as emergency contacts should a situation arise. My secondary communications plan would be my friend's landline if there's one, and the identified safe-room communications would be my contingent communications plan. My emergency communications plan would be to drive to the nearest neighbor or convenience store to use their phone.

When checking on the house, I'd place a phone call to my wife to let her know my location and arrival time so she'd know if I was on site longer than reasonable. She'd know to call and check on me if I was there longer than normal, and to contact the authorities if I didn't answer or return her call within a reasonable amount of time.

On Site

Prior to approaching the house, I'd follow my established protocols that I would've followed with each prior visit. This would include remotely reviewing the security footage and checking to see if any alarms have been triggered using the alarm system app.

During my drive in, I'd be looking for any baseline anomalies. Are there any vehicles that appear to be out of place? A vehicle and driver looking out of place could be an indication of potential criminal activity in the general area. Are the local residents engaged in their normal activities? People will often intentionally or unknowingly respond to their "gut" and change their routine when there's a predator hunting in the area. Are there any law-enforcement vehicles patrolling the area? A police presence might act as a deterrent or cause a perpetrator to change their *modus operandi* on the fly.

Upon arriving at the house, I'd look for other anomalies around the premises. Are there any rocks or vegetation that have been recently disturbed? Are there any footprints or tire tracks in the snow? Are there any lights on or off inside the house that shouldn't be? Have the window coverings been disturbed?

After discovering the front door is ajar and the hide-a-key rock is missing, and assuming my review of the security footage prior to my approach didn't reveal the presence of any intruders, I'd assess the situation to determine the best course of action. The blinking red light on the alarm panel indicating the alarm has been activated rules out the likelihood that the housekeeper is making an unscheduled visit, since she would've disarmed the system using the alarm code.

Given there were no alarm indications or intruders on the video feed prior to my final approach of the house – otherwise I wouldn't be at the front door – the most innocuous scenario at this point is that I had somehow left the front door unsecured and the wind dislodged the door just prior to my arrival. The most dangerous scenario is that an intruder had made entry just prior to my arrival. I'll treat this situation as though it were the latter until I can prove it was the former.

Crisis

My immediate priority is to find a position of cover and concealment while I complete some administrative tasks. If I'm able to get a cellular or Wi-Fi signal with my cell phone, I'll review the security camera footage from the time I last checked it to the present. If I'm able to see any intruders on the video feed, I will be sure to download the video and take screenshots of the perpetrators for later identification. I'd also immediately call 911, report the incident, and wait for law enforcement to arrive.

If I review the video footage and don't see any indication of a break-in, I'd place a call to my wife to inform her of the situation. Based on the information I've gathered to this point, I believe my best course of action is to clear the house myself, as there's no additional evidence of any intruders.

After entering the house and seeing nothing out of order in the kitchen, the likelihood that I screwed up and forgot to secure the door during my previous visit is looking more and more plausible, until I hear the "thump" upstairs. At that point, I'd call 911 and report a possible break-in. Maybe it's the cat falling off the bed, but I'm not taking any chances.

Although I have the legal right to be on the premises and no duty to retreat in my state, the only other people in the house, if any, are the bad guys. If there were innocent people in the house, then my priority would be to ensure their safety and clear the house, but since there are none, there's no reason for me to remain inside the house, and doing so would place me at a tactical disadvantage. My best option at this point would be to vacate the house and observe the front door from a safe distance to see if anyone leaves the house while I wait for the police to arrive.

If I do see anyone leave the house, I'll record as many details as I can (height, weight, sex, clothing, identifying marks, physical impairments, etc.) to give to the police. I didn't see a vehicle parked nearby, so they must have walked in or been dropped off by a getaway vehicle. I'd be watching to see which route they take when they leave the house, if they're carrying anything, if a vehicle picks them up, and their direction of travel.

Taking this approach to this situation is the best way to ensure my own safety. There's nothing in my friend's house worth dying for, especially not the cat. It's possible that police have already been alerted by the alarm company, so they might show up at any moment. Staying outside is the best way to prevent being mistaken for a burglar when they arrive, and to avoid implicating myself in what may be a crime in progress.

CONCLUSION

The entire purpose of this column is to get you, the reader, to think about what you'd do if you were in this situation. It requires some self-awareness and honesty about how you'd be willing to deal with certain situations that have a huge question mark. There are probably individuals out there who'd feel totally comfortable clearing a 5,000-square-foot house alone, but even though you've accepted the responsibility of overseeing and caring for a friend's home and cat, possessions (including dearly beloved pets) are not a higher priority than your own life.

With all the little red flags triggering concerns outside the home, this is one situation where you should be keenly aware of the potential problems that could occur before walking through the door and into an unknown situation. Whether it's your own house or a friend's house that you've been asked to watch while they're out town, clearing a house with a potential threat is a huge risk. If the lives of innocents are at stake, it may be justifiable, but it's unwise to put your life on the line for replaceable possessions. Establishing baselines through observation and orientation and looking for anomalies is the best way to stay in front of a dangerous situation. Avoidance is always the best defense. ⁂

13

YOU'RE LURED INTO A ROADSIDE HOLDUP, ABDUCTION, OR WORSE?

By Tim MacWelch
Illustrations by Cassandra Dale

With your friendliest smile, you walked up to the stranded motorist and said, "Hello sir, can I give you a hand?" From the headlights of your own vehicle, you could see him well enough in the darkness. His expression seemed to be one of relief. He pumped your handshake hard and offered his prolific thanks for your help. Instinctively, you profiled the stranger and checked your surroundings. He wasn't dressed like a country boy (even though you were in a rural area), and you could see numerous tattoos peeking out from his shirt collar and sleeves. A few spider webs and skulls ran across the man's visible skin. No big deal, you reasoned to yourself. Plenty of people have tattoos these days, you thought. But little red flags kept popping up.

His urban clothing style just didn't match with the pastoral area you were traveling through. So what if his apparel seems odd, you rationalized, maybe that's just the new style. As you considered the whole scene again, you realized that there wasn't a rear license plate on the car either, and the other stranded motorist accompanying this man was a rather rough-looking young woman sitting in the disabled car. Still focused on your good deed and with your spouse waiting in your car, you took a gander under the hood as the young woman got out of the distressed vehicle to "stretch her legs."

After some amicable chitchat with the man, you decided to try jumper cables. As you turned back to your vehicle for your tool kit, the man's demeanor changed abruptly. He blocked your path and gave you a sharp shove backward. That's when you spotted the rough woman near the front of your car – and in the bright headlights, the flash of shiny metal called your attention to her hand. As soon as you realized that the object she held was a knife, your skin started to crawl, and you felt sick to your stomach. Before you could take another step toward the knife-wielding woman and your unsuspecting spouse, the man drew a small revolver and aimed it at your face. His thumb pulled the hammer back, and a malevolent grin spread from ear to ear. He had you and your spouse right where he wanted.

In this chapter of RECOIL OFFGRID's "What If?" column, we see that the most ordinary situation can flip on its head and become a deadly set of circumstances. To challenge our judgment, the editors have played against our natural instinct to help other stranded motorists and taken us down a dark road where no good deed goes unpunished. We'll look at some of situational awareness skills and safety strategies you'd need when dealing with potential predators on the roadside. And maybe we'll all think twice about stopping to help people after dark. Con games come in all shapes and sizes, and so do the bad guys.

The Scenario

Situation type: Roadside breakdown
Your Crew: You and your spouse
Location: Highway at night in an area only marginally familiar to you
Season: Summertime

Weather: Clear; high 90 degrees F daytime, low 72 degrees F at night

The Setup

You and your spouse spent the weekend visiting friends out of town. Your friends live several hundred miles from your home, but both of you were able to take a day off from work. So you drove two-and-a-half hours on Friday evening to crash for a few days of grilling and catching up. You spent the weekend laughing at the same jokes and telling the same stories you always do, downing cocktails and burgers. You meant to get on the road first thing Monday morning. But gossiping with old friends was too much fun, and it's now 10 p.m. on Monday night. You and your spouse are cruising down a two-lane state road that winds through mile after mile of open country, dotted with the occasional one-horse town. You're about halfway home, at least an hour from either your friends' or your home. All your favorite radio stations are mostly static, and cell reception is a measly and inconsistent one bar for both of you.

The Complication

On a particularly lonely stretch of road, you see a single vehicle on the side of the highway. Its hazard lights are blinking, and the hood is up. As you get closer, you slow down, noticing a man leaning against the passenger side of the vehicle staring at his phone. Your spouse suggests that perhaps you should stop and offer assistance. You know this situation presents a potential threat. But your significant other reminds you that this is rural country and people tend to be more neighborly out here and, while your concern is legitimate, you might be overreacting in this case. Your spouse then asks what good it is to keep your trunk stocked with medical supplies, food, water, and tools if you can't "pay it forward" and do a good turn for somebody who's having a much worse night than you are.

Maybe your better half is right. You've had a great weekend. You're relaxed. The night is cool and quiet, but summertime highs were certainly high earlier this afternoon. Who knows how long that poor guy has been stranded. Besides, it never hurts to have a few extra karma points in the bank. So you pull off the road, leaving at least a car length when you park behind the broken-down vehicle. You ask your spouse to stay in the car while you get out and approach the man. You notice a woman sitting in the passenger seat. After introducing yourself and offering help, the man pockets his phone and thanks you profusely. He guides you to the open hood and starts gesturing at the engine and talking vaguely about some mysterious noise before the car "just died." You've changed flat tires and oil in your day, but you're no mechanic.

While the two of you talk about possible causes, the woman in the passenger seat gets out and begins walking toward your vehicle. Your attention shifts to her, and to your spouse, but the man continues to harangue you. Except now he starts to ask where you're coming from and going to, and how far from home you are. You gently guide the conversation back to the problem at hand, offering to break out the jumper cables and give that a try. When you turn to head back toward your car, the man stands directly in front of you and shoves you back a step. Over his shoulder, you see his female companion slash your front right tire. You turn your attention back to the man, who is now holding a small pistol. The woman is leaning into the window of your own car, her head and arms inside the vehicle. Somewhere in your mind it registers that both right side tires are now flat. You're not sure exactly what's going on, but those karma points you were hoping for seem to be on the wrong side of the board in this situation.

COMBATIVES EXPERT CHAD MCBROOM'S APPROACH

Preparation

Vehicle & Gear Check: Having lived in rural areas most of my adult life, I've grown quite accustomed to the dangers of traveling underdeveloped state highways with little infrastructure. Before leaving our friend's house, I would make sure the car is topped off with fuel and do a pre-flight inspection to make sure the fluids are at appropriate levels, and the spare tire is inflated.

I'd also do a thorough gear check to make sure all the emergency items we brought with us are still in the vehicle. This would include a TCCC-enhanced medical kit, bottled water, lightweight cold-weather gear, emergency foil blankets, a lockout kit (i.e. lock picks, door shims, etc.), flashlight, spare gun magazines, and a portable charging pack with appropriate phone cables. I'd also do a self-pat-down to make sure I had my standard EDC equipment, including knives, firearm, wallet, cell phone, and flashlight.

Route Check: In a day and age when our cell phones are always by our sides, we tend to rely on them a little too much when it comes to communication and navigation – and not enough when it comes to investigation.

Bad cell service can ruin your day when you're dependent on your phone to navigate an unfamiliar area. When I know I'll be operating in an area where cellular and, more importantly, data service is spotty, I'll download the area maps onto my phone's navigation app. GPS coverage is usually decent even when you can't hit a cell tower, so having the maps stored will allow me to navigate without phone service. As a backup, I always like to have a physical map of the area. Even though I'm probably familiar with the route, I want to have it in case I have to change course.

A little bit of internet investigation will tell me if there have been any recent crime patterns or notable criminal events near the area I'm traveling. I'm looking for identifiable patterns that may indicate any specific types of threats, aside from the random criminal activity. I'm also looking to identify any stretch of highway that may be more accident-prone than others so we can exercise additional caution along those sections.

Gut Check: I believe I have a certain moral obligation and civic duty to help those in distress. I also realize the unfortunate reality is that there are predators among us who will play the role of a wounded animal to lure their prey into striking distance. I try to listen to my gut when it comes to helping others in distress. Our brains can take in a lot more information than we can process. That "funny feeling" we get about a situation is usually our brain sending warning signals based on observations that we just haven't had the time to process.

On Site

I look at every situation to consider which scenarios are the most likely and the most dangerous. In this case, the most likely scenario is a stranded motorist who has broken down on a desolate stretch of highway, has no phone service, and is in need of assistance. The most dangerous scenario is a staged breakdown to lure in a victim for an ambush. Thinking this way keeps me on my toes and helps me to remember to keep my guard up and look for anomalies that may indicate the latter.

Since we decided to stop and render aid to this couple, I want to place my own vehicle in a position that maximizes my reactionary gap, offers the best protection from other vehicles, and provides the most amount of cover for me and my wife. For this reason, I park my car two car lengths behind and offset so the left side of the stranded vehicle aligns with the center of my car. I turn the wheels to the left, facing the road, to add additional cover and ensure that my vehicle will tend to move away from the scene in the event another motorist strikes my car from the rear. This also preps my car for a fast withdrawal if necessary.

I switch my headlights to high beams to light up the area and create a wall of illumination that will conceal activity inside our vehicle. Before getting out to approach the stranded vehicle, I do another self pat-down and check my phone for service. Then, I get out and have my wife move to the driver's seat. I want her to be able to haul ass out of there if things go sideways, a plan I quickly discuss before leaving her behind. Using my headlights to my advantage, I walk outside the cone of light to avoid backlighting myself and mask my movement.

As I approach, I'm looking for cues that might indicate whether this is a legitimate breakdown or a ruse. Does he have a flat? Is the radiator steaming? Are there any signs that this car is disabled? What about signs to the contrary? Is the car running? A running engine would not only be a contraindication, but would suggest the occupants are planning a quick getaway. How about the lights? The driver might choose to leave the lights on so they can be seen at night, but this also tells me the battery has some juice, so I might be a little suspicious if the occupants tell me their battery is dead.

I'm also looking at body language. I've already observed anomalies. I just checked the cell coverage and there's no signal here, so why is this guy staring at his cell phone? Why is he standing outside, leaning against the door, while the female occupant sits inside the car? That's two anomalies right there.

I stop about 4 feet away to maintain a reactionary gap and begin talking to the man, keeping my hands in a natural, non-threatening position at sternum height. My hands are in a position where I can defend, strike, or go to a weapon quickly and efficiently, without appearing aggressive or defensive.

I spot a third anomaly when the passenger gets out and walks toward my vehicle. Normal behavior would be for her to converse with the person rendering assistance. The presence of three anomalies tells me something is off-kilter, and I begin gearing toward the most dangerous course of action.

Crisis

The overt actions taken by the two seemingly stranded motorists confirm that we're now in a "most dangerous" scenario. The act of placing himself between me and my wife while his partner slashes our tires indicates they're using a divide-and-conquer strategy. It also tells me they've planned and rehearsed their assault, because he knows exactly what she's doing.

At this point, the thought that this is just a mugging or robbery never enters my mind. This is more sinister. A staged breakdown to lure us in, a rehearsed plan, disabling our means of evacuation, and the display of deadly weapons are indicators that these people wish to kill us at worst, or take us hostage at best. My decision would be to counter deadly force with deadly force.

I now have two armed threats to address. One is standing in front of me holding a gun; the other is outside my wife's car door holding a knife. I'm hoping my wife was alert enough to identify the threat, but hope isn't a strategy, so I must assume she's unaware of the danger in front of her.

The man shoves me back, which means he's within contact distance. My response is to use a pinning check to direct his gun offline, grabbing around the slide (or cylinder if it's a revolver) to prevent the gun from cycling when he fires. As I perform this action, I simultaneously torque my hips in the opposite direction to hollow my body out. This helps get me out of the line of fire while moving my gun side away from the threat and allowing me to draw my pistol.

I engage the threat from a body-index position. Knowing my wife is downrange, I angle my muzzle downward. As I break contact, I move offline toward my vehicle to close the distance between me and the second threat and get a better angle for selective targeting on the first.

I expect at this point that my wife is engaging the woman, using the car door to knock her off balance. As I address the female assailant, I assess her response. Has she lost her will to fight? Do I need to scale down my level of force? What comes next will depend on her.

Once the situation is under control, I check myself for holes, check my wife, and render medical aid as necessary. I also take this time to re-kit in case these two weren't working alone. I have my wife call 911 if she can get a signal. If not, we'll have to rely on a Good Samaritan of our own to contact the authorities and relay our location.

Never take things at face value. When approaching any situation, ask yourself: What's the most likely scenario, and what's the most dangerous scenario? Then, look for baseline anomalies in human behavior. Following this approach will put you in a proactive state where you can make sound decisions before SHTF and quick decisions when it does.

SURVIVAL EXPERT TIM MACWELCH'S APPROACH

Preparation

One of the most common Biblical concepts to seep into pop culture is the story of the Good Samaritan. Most people understand what a Good Samaritan does, but not everybody knows the original story and context. This tale was first told by Jesus and is included in the Bible in the Gospel of Luke. In short, two supposedly righteous men pass right by a traveler who was beaten, naked, and left for dead on the roadside. A third man comes along, the Samaritan (a follower from different branch of Judaism, who didn't get along with people of the local faith), who helps the poor man. The meaning of the story is that we should help those in need, regardless of our personal differences and preconceived notions. That's a tall order, but it's the task we're handed.

To be a true "Good Samaritan," we're asked to intervene in situations that don't directly affect us. If we fail to act when we could have acted, we may be in more than just a moral or ethical quagmire. We may be going against our very faith. And if you do decide to help, many countries have "Good Samaritan Laws," which prevent a rescuer from being successfully sued if something went wrong as they attempted to help a victim. So in at least one respect, both religious and legal doctrines are in favor of us trying to help those in distress.

Now, let's define "help" in its different forms. There are some ways to help someone in legitimate need without putting yourself at much risk. For example, I'd consider calling a tow truck for this hypothetical young couple, once we reach an area with mobile signal. I might even pay for it, if I was feeling particularly generous. And I wouldn't hesitate to notify local law enforcement, once we reach an area with signal. Everyone should have the non-emergency number for their local law enforcement in their wallet. All of this calling can be done without interacting with the people in question, but maybe that's not the kind of help they needed? Time may be an issue. Maybe one of the stranded motorists needed medical help (which I'm trained and equipped to provide, and you should be too). Someone could die in the time it'd take for you to find phone signal, explain the situation and location to the authorities, and for the first responders to get on the scene. The kind of help they need may only be served in person, and it may be needed now – later may be too late.

So before I pulled over to offer assistance, my first consideration would be whether I'm ready, willing, and able to help. On any given day, I carry a four-way tire iron, a small air compressor, jumper cables, a serous first-aid kit, flares, road triangles, and many other things to help myself and those in need. And if I'm ready, willing, and able to help, then my next question would be whether it's safe to help or not. If cars are whizzing by on the highway, am I likely to get hit by stopping and getting out of my vehicle? If there isn't a soul on the road, am I about to be in some real-life horror movie? These things would certainly be in my head. I could mitigate the traffic threat by pulling as far off the busy highway as possible (without getting stuck in a ditch) and using the vehicle hazard flashers, flares, and reflective signs to reduce the risk of someone plowing into me at 70 mph. Or on the dark and lonesome highway, I could look at the people and the surroundings as I drove by slowly, then circle back if they looked legit (and after notifying the local PD or sheriff's department). We could even pull up beside them and talk through the glass (without fully rolling down the windows or unlocking the doors). Ultimately, I'd have to trust my situational awareness.

In your preparation for scenarios like this, you should take the time to study the legal means of self-defense in your locality. If concealed carry of a firearm is legal in your area, take the time to get a permit (if necessary) and train frequently. Practice drawing it from concealment while standing, while holding a flashlight, and even while seated. Keep practicing to improve your ability to draw quickly. Mix it up by practicing some support-hand flashlight strikes, then drawing your CCW. And since darkness follows day like clockwork, consider adding a tactical light to your handgun.

Our final consideration for preparation is gear. Aside from your normal vehicle tools, first-aid supplies and other vehicular preparedness gear (like food, water, space blankets, etc.), you'll want to have a quality flashlight. There's nothing wrong with carrying a big Maglite. Stuffed with four C cell batteries, it's both a flashlight and a formidable baton for striking. Or you could go with a high-intensity tactical light to blind a potential adversary. Look for one that has crenellations (square teeth). These allow the impact of a small flashlight to deliver pain like a hit from a larger, heavier flashlight.

On Site

Continuing with our scenario, if I decided to help this forlorn and out-of-place couple, my first action is to park in the safest spot. As the location allows, I'd park behind the stranded car and create a good space between my vehicle and theirs, at least three car lengths. I'd also put our vehicle on the road shoulder, but without risking a loss of mobility or control in a ditch, mud, wet grass, or loose gravel. In short, we'd look before we park. I would then turn the dome light off, so it didn't come on when the vehicle doors open. This would keep any bad guys from knowing the number or location of the people in my vehicle. If possible, I'd have my spouse move into the driver seat, without getting out of the vehicle. In any case, I'd want them in the driver seat with the engine running, windows up, and the doors locked. My spouse would then be my "overwatch" for this roadside rescue. From the rear position, my spouse would be able to keep an eye on things at the broken-down vehicle, as well as behind our vehicle and to the sides of it. I'd leave my spouse with instructions to do three quick taps on the horn or flash the high beams three times if anything seems out of the ordinary, and to stay in the car no matter what happens. Before leaving I'd remind them of my love, and I'd remind them that our vehicle is a 1-ton weapon, easily capable of running over bad guys. They need to be mentally and physically ready to drive the vehicle into a person or the other vehicle, if things take a bad turn.

Approaching the stranded car, I certainly don't want to look like a predator myself, especially if the young couple needs legitimate help. For example, I wouldn't approach the scene with my gun drawn. I'd keep the flashlight in my left hand (to free up my dominant firing hand) and watch the motorist's hands and body language. I'd also keep an eye out for any bulges under his clothing that might indicate a hidden weapon. I'd try to keep the strangers in sight, if possible, and not let them get in between me and my vehicle. We don't need to be shy if things start to feel wrong. It's OK to tell them flat-out to stay where you can see them and to find out more about them. It's more important to be safe than to worry about being rude.

Not being a mechanic, I probably wouldn't be able to mechanically assess a vehicle on the roadside (especially in the dark), so it would be hard to determine whether the "breakdown" was deliberately staged. I'd just have to watch the people, study their demeanor, and listen for holes in their story.

Crisis

There's a gun in my face. It should never have gotten this far, but as the threat emerges in this situation, I'm not going to comply or become a victim — I'll defend myself, even if it's through lethal force. There's no compliance here. Why not? Because there's a big difference between a crime of opportunity (like mugging people for wallets and purses, or carjacking random motorists) versus this deliberately staged ambush. Sketchy mister motorist and his skid row princess probably aren't planning to carjack us since she just slashed two of my tires. So maybe they just want our money, or maybe their friends are hiding in the bushes and they're going to chop us up for black-market organs. We don't know, and I'm not going to find out.

If my spouse saw my hands go up, I'd hope to receive a useful distraction (like horn honking or light flashing). But I could make my own distraction too. I'd just need to say something like "Wow, your bitch just got stabbed with her own knife!" In the two seconds he looked away, I'd draw my weapon and fire. Then, I'd check my surroundings, and kick the revolver away from the fallen man. After locating the woman and engaging her, I'd demand that she drop the knife. Compliance equals life for her. Moving into the roadway a little for better visibility, I'd back toward my own vehicle (to avoid being blinded by my own headlights), and I'd check on my spouse (without taking my eyes off the woman).

Now it's time for the long and messy wrap-up. Without mobile phone signal, and with our vehicle disabled, we'd have to take their car (if it worked) or drive on two flats. But so many questions arise. Do I render first aid to the man that I shot in self-defense? If I didn't have to shoot the woman, do I use some kind of restraints on her? Do I stuff her in the trunk of one of the cars? If there's an escape latch inside the trunk, that's a useless method to confine her. It may also cross a legal line that changes our situation. The local laws may side with her for unlawful imprisonment if she's locked in a vehicle. As I said, it's a mess. Most likely, we'd have to leave the scene of a crime to get help. By heading toward the nearest town and watching our phones along the way for a signal, we'd call 911 when we could and inform law enforcement. We'd use GPS, intersections, road mile markers, or the length of time travelled to convey the location to the authorities. Finally, we could head toward the nearest police station or sheriff department to explain what happened and make our statements.

CONCLUSION

We've all seen broken-down cars on the side of the highway, and most us have probably been stranded by a disabled car at some point ourselves. Being stranded is part of our mobile lifestyle. And while more than 99 percent of distressed motorists are truly in need, bad guys feigning the need for help alongside a highway is as old as the concept of the highway itself. Unfortunately, we don't often hear about motorists and hitchhikers being lured into traps and ultimately robbed, raped, or murdered as front-page news until it reaches pathological, serial killer status. Do a few web searches for stranded motorists being kidnapped or killed, and you'll see it happens more frequently than you might think.

From the earliest days of these thoroughfares, "highwaymen" or "road agents" robbed travelers in remote areas and then disappeared with the loot. Little has changed over the centuries, and although very rare, it still takes place today. Roads can provide a natural funnel, directing the unsuspecting quarry right into a trap. Add the bait of the "poor young couple" to the trap, and it's a damn-near-irresistible ploy to catch a soft-hearted do-gooder. And while we're not suggesting you avoid helping beleaguered motorists ever again, we can remind you that there are many ways to help. You don't need to stop on that dark and lonely road. You can simply call the local police non-emergency line. They can check it out and offer help if it's truly needed, and you've still done your good deed to render assistance. ⠶

14

YOU AND YOUR FAMILY ARE THREATENED BY A STALKER?

By Tim MacWelch
Illustrations by Joe Oesterle

There they stood, right on the sidewalk, just on the edge of your yard. You wondered how long they'd been standing there in the approaching dusk. It was bad enough that you made this unwelcomed discovery. You wondered what your spouse or kids would've thought if they had happened to spot your former companion standing out there. They just stood there, looking over the exterior of your home.

That was creepy enough, but then your eyes met theirs. In that instant, a coldness washed over your body. You felt an eerie connection – like predator and prey, and you were the prey in this exchange. This person you thought was part of your past was now standing there staring at you in the present, right through the window of your own home. They smiled faintly at you, but there was no hint of a smile in their eyes. Those empty eyes. That was the part that bothered you the most. It was like no one was home inside the person you once knew. Your "ex" stood there motionless, wearing a smile that was a false as a cheap rubber mask, hiding their real identity and hiding their intentions.

For this installment of RECOIL OFFGRID's "What If?" column, there are no fanatical terrorists, savage animals, or extreme landscapes to challenge our skills and our wits. The editors have given us a far more subtle yet equally disturbing scenario – what if we were stalked by a crazed former love interest? This unsettling situation brings many issues into question. How could we defend ourselves and our family against someone with maligned intentions? And how could the law help us? During this unnerving "What If?" we'll take a look at some of the strategies for personal security and several actions you can legally take to deal with an unhinged person.

The Scenario

Situation type: Ongoing stalking from an ex
Your Crew: You, your spouse, and two children
Location: Your hometown
Season: Spring
Weather: Clear; high 78 degrees F, low 58 degrees F

The Setup

You've been on social media for several years, and with it, your friends list and exposure has grown. Eventually you receive a friend request from an ex you dated in your early 20s who found you on a mutual friend's list. The relationship didn't end on the greatest of terms back then, and you can see that they live within a half hour of where you currently reside. You know they may be able to get an idea, from the photos you and your friends have posted, of where you work and the neighborhood you live in. Although you're somewhat hesitant at first, you decide there's no harm in accepting their friend request to your profile, which is usually private and only visible if someone is added to your friends list. You think that enough time has passed, and whatever happened is water under the bridge.

The Complication

Approximately a month into your acceptance of your ex's friend request, things start to go sideways. You look at their profile and are concerned by a lot of their posts, which exude an emotionally unstable, desperate tone, with a lot of provocative pictures, many of which are sent privately to you. They're constantly private messaging you to go have lunch with them to reminisce, catch up, and hang out more often. You politely decline on the grounds that your spouse wouldn't approve, and you don't think it's a good idea, but you wish them well and are glad they seem to be doing OK. Unfortunately, your attempts to be diplomatic aren't met with the same kind of friendliness you'd hoped for. They don't go away, but instead they escalate their persistence to disturbing and dangerous levels.

Eventually, your ex starts posting old pictures of you and them together, tagging you, and saying that you were abusive to them physically, verbally, and sexually, and that you're trying to rekindle their interest and have an affair with them. Needless to say, it doesn't take long for their friends to chime in and start bad-mouthing you, echoing the accusations. You know your own personal friends know you well enough to dismiss this as jealousy and nonsense, but you're still worried about colleagues and others possibly looking at this differently and taking it too seriously. Rather than dignify any of this with a response, you decide to block them from any and all accounts they previously had access to.

Unfortunately, the blocking on social media only seems to exacerbate the problem. You start receiving calls on your cell phone and home phone from a blocked number making threats to you and your family. How the heck did they get your number? You're unsure how they got it and who is making these threats, since you haven't talked to your ex directly and can't tell if it's their voice. You hope this will just go away, but you start to consider filing a restraining order. You're concerned, however, that this will only provoke additional complications. You see a certain car driving by your house repeatedly, and eventually your 6-year-old daughter says a stranger approached them after school, showed a picture of you, and offered a ride home. This has gone far enough. What do you do to protect yourself and your family from this ongoing, and worsening, harassment? Your life is beginning to mirror *Fatal Attraction*.

FORMER FEDERAL OFFICER HANA BILODEAU'S APPROACH

I've realized in the evolution of social realms that there are things I have to conform to in order to reach my full potential. Social media is one of those things. My profile is set to public, as my account is used for marketing. Aware of the risks when opening my profile, I still chose to keep it as a public platform. The only personal information I provide on my profile is my name, job title, and email address. I acknowledge the risks associated with not having privacy controls attached to the profile, but in order to have the marketing reach, it was a decision I went into prepared.

When posting content, I always follow a few simple rules: I don't post personal content, only content relating to outreach as an influencer; I always keep the location tab turned off; and I'm mindful to the content that's posted — no sexually explicit photos or inciting verbiage. I'm constantly reminding my family that what you post on the internet is there forever. There are some risk factors that we have to accept in exchange for the benefits of the internet and being searchable is one of them. When I post, I do so about fairly generic things, never giving my opinion or diving into political topics. I do this for two reasons: my opinion is mine and I choose not to entice negative interactions, and I've also learned that if negative interactions occur, it's very easy to block and report those with keyboard courage.

If you experience hostile interactions that persist after blocking said profiles, you can contact the social media outlet to file a formal report. If the online harassment is more aggressive and contains actual threats or concerning behavior, a report should also be filed with the local authorities of the city/town you were in when you received the threat. Be sure to take a screen shot or save the content and profile from which the message was sent. If possible, gather the IP address of the user. If the situation rises to the level where you need to track someone down and take legal action against their online activity, it may be helpful to provide authorities with their IP address. The IP address can help identify the offender's general location.

There are limitations to what is made public — you'll not be able to locate or identify this person, their home, or office. Most devices use dynamic IPs that change frequently, so it's also difficult to tie an IP to a specific computer or mobile device. However, there is an exception — if an individual has participated in illegal activities, then a law enforcement agency can get a court order for the IP address and submit it to the internet service provider to request the customer's information. You can also potentially grab an IP address through messaging applications as well:

"For Facebook users: It is possible to find an IP Address using the Facebook messenger/chat application. Using the command prompt tool (for Windows users) or the utility tool (for Mac users) and the netstat function, you can easily trace someone's IP address on this social media platform. You must first establish a connection with the user — this should be an open connection; therefore, the built-in Facebook chat system is the best option to use. Open a new chat window with the user and ensure that they're online. Once you've opened a chat window, keep it open, and then proceed to open the Command Prompt tool or Utility tool depending on your OS.

Once you've opened this tool, simply type in "netstat -an" and press enter. Providing that you have an active connection with the end user, their IP address should then appear after a short period of time. Before executing this command, ensure that you've closed any other windows and browser sessions as other IP addresses could be returned also that could be confusing.

By obtaining the IP address, you can then do as you wish with it and even report it to Facebook if you feel that the user requires a ban or disciplinary action."
Source: www.hotspotshield.com.

If messaging through your phone: Your mobile phone uses an IP address every time you engage someone through a messaging app, such as WhatsApp and Viber. Messaging app usage is growing incredibly fast. Your IP address is invisible to the person you message, but if-and-when you click on a link in a message, the website you sent it to has access to your IP address. Source: https://whatismy-ipaddress.com/get-ip.

Even though I may have covered my bases as best I can, sometimes the online threat is someone you know. Let's say approximately one month ago I was contacted by an ex who I dated in my early 20s. Surely water under the bridge and harmless to accept a friend request, right? If I immediately recognized the communication was inappropriate and left feeling uneasy by the little contact we'd had, I'd start by researching my ex through social media and via internet search tools to see if any red flags come up. If I noted posts on social medial that confirmed my suspicion of a potentially unstable individual, I'd share my findings with my spouse. After conferring with him, we'd continue to monitor the situation, feeling that further intervention may entice or infuriate him.

If things drastically escalated, it'd leave me and my family with no choice but to seek police intervention. In preparation of documenting everything with the police, I'd gather copies of all the online interactions, including social media and messaging. I'd also download my mobile phone records to confirm incoming phone calls. I'd start by filing a police report. Once it was filed, I'd ask for an emergency restraining order, seeking no further contact. An emergency restraining order can be filed as long as the petitioner was a domestic partner at one time. Police intervention is only the beginning. A restraining order is just a piece of paper asking for no contact – it's not a guaranteed safeguard from an individual who believes they're above the law. Because my initial actions may trigger additional threatening behavior, there are still a number of things to do to keep myself and my family safe.

Home Safety

I'd call a family meeting to openly discuss the threat to the family, making sure that everyone understood the gravity of the situation. We'd establish a safety plan for my spouse, me, and our children. We have a home security system and motion-sensor lighting, but adding cameras to the exterior and perimeter of the home would provide us some additional layers of safety. The family would utilize the buddy system, ensuring there were no gaps where a single member of the household might find themselves alone until the threat is dispelled.

Workplace Safety

Requesting a private meeting with my direct supervisor to tell him about the threat, making sure he is fully aware of the severity and recent escalation of behavior, would also be a smart move to document the situation and raise awareness to protect myself and fellow employees. Making sure that building security personnel are also aware of the risk would be another recommended action. Tell a close friend at work what's happening and ask him/her to buddy up with you while walking to and from the parking lot.

School Safety

In anticipation of a possible stalker who could've gleaned enough info from your social media profile that'd lead to a confrontation with your children when you're not present, call a meeting with your children's teachers, principal, and school resource officer. Bring them a copy of the police report and restraining order, and explain the situation, asking for their help in protecting the children while they're under school supervision. Have an entry and exit plan to the school to ensure the children are only coming and going with an approved family member. If your child is involved in afterschool activities, make sure the staff knows about the potential threat to the family and that the only persons permitted to pick up and drop off the children are you and your husband, unless otherwise specified by the two of you.

Personal Safety

I'd also reaffirm my personal defense plan. I have a concealed carry license and choose to carry a firearm when feasible. Unfortunately, there are places I can't legally carry, such as work and my children's school. Because of this, I need to make sure I have a plan in place for the gaps in my safety plan. This could include freshening up on my defensive shooting skills by jumping in a class, finding a trainer in hand-to-hand combat, and making an appointment with a counselor for a mental health check – having a threat invade your personal space can be very taxing on you mentally.

Unfortunately, the behavior of others isn't something we can control, but we can control how we respond to it. Being hyper-vigilant about personal security as well as online security is now more important than ever. The click of a mouse is a decision that takes seconds, but could catastrophically affect you and your family's lives as you know it. If you could predict the future and see that allowing an outsider access to a seemingly innocent social media page could potentially change your life as you know it, would you still do it? Most wouldn't. When it comes to posting, less is more, especially when it comes to inviting prying eyes with maligned intentions.

SURVIVAL EXPERT TIM MACWELCH'S APPROACH

Preparation

Being constantly bombarded by opposing political views, hateful comments, and general nonsense every time we log onto social media, most of us (hopefully) develop a thicker skin by routinely observing this kind of online activity. Our exposure should prepare us for a certain amount of social media harassment. But if it went beyond the normal trolling and turned very personal, I'd have no problem shutting that noise down. Seriously, I'd close down all my accounts and revel in the spare time I just freed up. But I know, for some of you, this is unthinkable or just not possible.

Do your homework to decide if continuing on social media in the face of personal harassment is worth it. Look into the details of that social media platform and take advantage of any preventive measures regarding functionality, filters, and general use.

Of course, you can't control every time someone mentions your name online, but you can provide less fuel for the fire. Limit the invasion of your privacy by limiting your output. For example, stop posting publicly on Facebook. Choose the option to only post for known friends or customize the list of people who get your posts. Posting "I'm out of town for such and such event" publicly tells anyone who cares to look (both on and off Facebook) that your home is wide open for prowling, burglary, and vandalizing.

For those who crave a little more security in their lives, but still want to share everything they're doing publicly, don't post things as they happen. Go with the #latergram approach and give yourself a social media delay. Save that cool picture of your dinner plate for tomorrow morning (when you're not at that restaurant anymore), and post your vacation pics after you return (not while you're gone). This keeps strangers and troublemakers from knowing where you are at all times.

Another preventative step is to be more selective about the people you friend or follow on social media. Most of us often click without really looking in the quest to have a broader reach online. Do your research on the people who want to associate with you. Check them and their friends out before you add them to your friends list. If you see things that make you uncomfortable about their posts or profile, it's best to keep your distance and not associate with them.

On Site

Let's say that I was as careful as I could be regarding the information available about me via social media and online in general, but someone started vilifying me through Facebook. I might ignore or engage, depending on the nature of the posts, and try not to let it get under my skin. From the first threat, I'd take this issue very seriously and deal with it swiftly, but not by replying with an equally threatening response or some snarky remark to prove how brave I am. I'd use one of the best legal weapons that I could wield as a victim of harassment – documentation.

If you're taking the "high road," you have to expect harassment to be resolved through legal channels and the best way to solidify your standing is with proof. Document everything they say and do. Take a picture of every threatening text message. Get a screenshot of every nasty Facebook post (since they can delete the post on their end). Make note of the time and duration of every harassing phone call you receive, recording them if possible. Each and every time you encounter this person, tell them to leave you alone and document the interaction. With tangible evidence to show a judge, you'll have a better chance of getting a conviction or obtaining an order of protection if things escalate to that point.

In addition to documenting each nasty interaction, you could also begin a little research on the person who has begun threatening you. In the case of our scenario, being stalked by an ex, you already know who they are – but see what else can you discover. You don't have to hire a private eye, but a background check or online search could tell you a little more about the current state of the person you thought you knew so well.

One big issue with stalking charges is laws are vastly different between jurisdictions. Your situation (and outcome) may be very different if your stalker is outside of the state where you live, or even outside of the country. Talking to an attorney can let you know what laws are being broken, if any, and legal counsel can give you the information you'll need if you have to take the "next steps" with local law enforcement.

Hopefully, things don't go so far that you need to see a judge. If the abuse is only occurring on a social site like Instagram or Facebook, read through the site rules and notify the site owners about abusive comments. Due to frequency of online abuse these days, a number of social media sites have to provide a way to block individuals. If enough complaints are logged, the social media site can either lock the person's profile or ban their IP from visiting the site. Even if the harassment happens outside of the social site, but points back to it, the site owners will likely be on your side – they don't want to be involved in a dispute or lawsuit, and they don't want to receive bad press.

Crisis

Unfortunately, having someone thrown in Facebook jail is not the solution to every situation. It may just push them over the edge. When the harassment is persistent or includes the threat of violence, it's time to contact law enforcement. But here's another problem – cyber bullying and online stalking are relatively new issues as far as lawmakers are concerned. Many states don't yet have laws with clear-cut definitions on what constitutes these issues. When the laws aren't in place, it can be hard for law enforcement and attorneys to stand up for the victims. Plenty of jurisdictions are considering the enactment of laws that regulate online harassment, but most legislation moves at a snail's pace – if it moves forward at all. Talk to your lawyer about the orders of protection that are available in your home area.

If law enforcement in your jurisdiction is powerless to help with the type of online harassment you're receiving, or your stalker just won't go away, there's a way the law can help – civil action. Depending on the documentation you have, you may be able to build a civil case against your stalker. If their comments and actions interfere with your business relationships, you may have a viable case. If your stalker is spreading lies in print somewhere, you could possibly go after them for libel (damaging someone's reputation by writing false-hoods). You could even run the "infliction of emotional distress" angle.

In any case, an attorney would be the best resource for information on the most appropriate course of action in your jurisdiction. You may even be able to go after the social media site for not removing slanderous videos and libelous posts. These entities will likely have deeper pockets than your stalker, making it possible for you to get your legal fees back (and then some). But don't expect a "win" overnight. Legal battles can drag on for years. Filing lawsuits and deal-ing with courts can be almost as scary as your unrelenting harasser, but you're within your rights to protect yourself and your family in these uncomfortable (and even dangerous) circumstances.

So let's say you got that restraining order; what happens when the restrain-ing order doesn't work? When the online threats escalate to unwelcomed notes placed around your property, "hang-up" or harassing phone calls day and night, or suspicious behavior around your home and family (e.g. spying on your home or approaching your child in public), how can we handle that? Now we're away from the cyber issues and getting into criminal activity that the lo-cal police can address. Again, document everything! Don't touch that threat-ening note on your car, or your slashed tires — that's evidence and you don't want to contaminate it. Call your local law enforcement and get them on scene.

Now, what if you encounter the stalker yourself, or your family runs into them, out on the street? When they're in a public place, that's not against the law. I'd simply leave without engaging the person. If they try to communicate with you or your family members in a negative way, leave and document it and see if you can accumulate witnesses. If they come onto your property, that's trespassing and you might just win that round (with proof). If I were faced with an escalating situation at home, I'd definitely add extra security precautions around the house. If I didn't already have an alarm system, I'd get one. And you'd better believe it would be a system with video cameras. I'd also beef up the door and window locks, and make sure everything is secure before going to bed each night.

And what if offline harassment starts to encompass workplace stalking? Tell your employer about your situation. Your stalker may attempt to file complaints against your work or get you in trouble at your workplace. Once notified, your bosses can keep an eye out for anything odd, such as mysteri-ous workplace complaints against you. Sure, it's embarrassing, but you'll need your staff in the loop for your own safety and theirs. Pride won't shield you from someone looking to ruin your life.

What if your stalker made an anonymous report to Child Protective Services that you (and/or your spouse) were sexually abusing your kids? Your kids would be taken away from you within the hour. Or what if your stalker called 911 from a payphone and said you were making bombs in your home and you planned to use them tonight? Can you say "Hello, SWAT team?" Or what if your ex simply burned your house down? The bitter truth is that you can't always predict how far it will go. Assume this person may be psychopathic and there are no limits to their violent compulsions. Collect enough evidence to get your "ex" locked away if possible, and try to reassemble your life with a mindset of personal security.

CONCLUSION

Mental health is a serious matter that everyone should work to educate themselves about. Can we determine if someone we're only moderately familiar with is going through a mental health crisis, if they're lonely, heartbroken, or simply an evil person who finds fulfillment in persistently inflicting harm on you and your family? It can be hard for even professional mental health workers to make that distinction without thorough evaluation. Are most of us in the position to make that diagnosis through a computer and try to help them or rationalize with insanity? Not likely.

It's important to seek professional help when dealing with an individual who is either inside or outside your personal circle and now projecting their compulsions on you. Talk to authorities, document everything, take photos, let local law enforcement collect any evidence, and keep your friends, family, and coworkers in the loop. There's a broad spectrum between actions of a scorned ex and a sociopath, but across that span, the unwelcomed behaviors of these individuals can have a lasting impact on you and those around you. Don't wait for things to go from bad to worse. Reach out for help as soon as you recognize there's a problem.

And remember, we got by for many years just fine without social media before it became a source of human interaction. There's no harm in shutting it down if you think it'd make you safer. Continuing to dabble in vanity-driven posts but expecting complete protection of your privacy at the same time isn't realistic. There's no solution for bad judgment except changing the behavior that's provoking the problem. ⁛

15

YOU AWAKEN TO A KIDNAPPING, ABDUCTION, OR WORSE?

By John Schwartze
Illustrations by Cassandra Dale

You're in that state between waking and dreaming, where you're not quite sure if what you heard was imagined or not. It's approximately 3 in the morning, and someone just entered your room. Since you're spending the night at your friend Paula's house, perhaps she's looking for something. But at this hour? This doesn't make sense. As you open your eyes and the blurriness fades away, you hear something that sounds strangely like duct tape being unrolled. Your heart rate begins to race as you realize whoever is in the room with you isn't Paula at all. It's someone who shouldn't be in the house.

As you turn your head to get a better look at the situation, the stranger realizes you're beginning to wake up. The man immediately jumps on top of you and covers your mouth with his hand. In a low, threatening voice he growls, "Shut up! Make a sound and you're dead!" Overcome with the immediate shock of what's happening, you fear for not only your life, but Paula's as well.

You're turned over on your stomach, your mouth and eyes are covered with tape, and your wrists are bound behind your back. You have a knife in your purse, only a few feet away from you. If only you could reach it, you'd have a better chance at escaping your unknown assailant. Whatever their intentions are, you're not sure at this point. You adjust your breathing to try to dampen the feelings of panic and think clearly about how to free yourself. You may only have a few minutes to live – or maybe they just want to immobilize you so they can rob the place. There's no way to be sure at this point. Every decision you make could determine whether you survive or not.

In this issue's *What If?* column, we look at a topic that's often in the back of people's minds – an aggressive home intruder with unknown intentions that could be kidnapping, abduction, or worse. While we often see these incidents reported in the media, we find that they're accompanied by little, if any, information about what you can do if ever faced with a similar situation to improve your odds of survival. We plan to change that here, with feedback from two of our writers on what they'd do to sway the given scenario in their favor. We asked Morgan Rogue of RoguePreparedness.com and firearms instructor Sheena Green to offer guidance to help you think through some possible ways to turn victimization into victory.

The Scenario

Situation type: A friend's house
Your Crew: You and your friend Paula
Location: Your hometown
Season: Winter
Weather: Rainy; high 47 degrees F, low 39 degrees F

The Setup

It's a Friday night, and you drive over to your friend Paula's new house to deliver a housewarming gift and catch up on things. Paula tells you she just recently rented out her detached guesthouse in the back to a male colleague at her work, but that he isn't currently home. She asks you if you can spend the night since she's not sure when he's coming back. Paula's husband is also out of town, and her new tenant has lately been bringing over a bunch of male friends who stay up past midnight partying. As a result, she's thinking about evicting him. You've known Paula for years and trust her judgment as far as roommate selection, so you can understand her concern. As you've spent many a late night talking with Paula over the years, you decide to spend the night in her guest room, located next to Paula's room, so she feels a bit safer.

The Complication

You awaken on your stomach in the middle of the night to the sound of tape being unwrapped. As you try to roll over, someone hops over you and pushes one of their knees into your back with great force, wrapping a length of tape around your eyes and head. The attacker says if you shout or try to escape, he'll kill you. He then proceeds to bind your wrists tightly together behind your back with duct tape. At this point, you don't know if this is the roommate Paula mentioned, one of his friends, or a random intruder. You don't know if he's alone or if there are multiple accomplices in the house. You also don't know if this person has a weapon, what their motive is, or if Paula is even still alive.

Through a gap in the tape and outside light peering through the window, you can make out certain features about your assailant in the reflection of a large mirror on the closet door. You can't yet see a weapon in his hands, but that doesn't mean he doesn't have one. Also, the intruder isn't wearing a mask. They're also the only other person in the room at this point. You see your purse right where you left it, about 3 feet from you. It contains a folding knife. Your cell phone is still charging on the nightstand next to you and is within arm's reach — or would be, if your hands weren't bound. Your legs aren't yet bound. What do you do? Scream for help? Use social engineering to talk your way out of it? Remain compliant and hope it influences him to spare you? Try to discreetly break your restraints and escape? Fight your way out?

SURVIVAL ADVOCATE "ROGUE'S" APPROACH

Prep

If I had a friend who was worried about her troublesome tenant and his friends, I'd want to do everything I could to protect her. Before settling down, I'd text or call a friend or relative and let them know where I'd be for the night. Initially, I'd ask Paula to give me a rundown on this tenant, his general behavior and the behavior of his friends, their comings and goings, where they work, what they do, etc. I'd also ask if she'd had any confrontations with them before, if it involved the police, or if they'd ever been inside her home. Knowing the layout of her home would give them a good understanding of how to break into it. This info would help me understand the tenant's present disposition toward

Paula, how big a threat he may pose, and if it's been documented. The more I know, the better.

I carry a firearm and a knife on me at all times. Assuming a reader might not have a firearm or be licensed to carry one, I'll also address defense techniques that could be used either way. I also carry a cross-body purse that contains odds and ends for everyday and emergency use. Since I'm sleeping over at Paula's, my knife and firearm would remain inside my purse while we slept. I also usually carry a dog tag-sized lock-picking set as well as a dog tag-sized folding knife from Grim Survival. They attach to the inside of my pants via a retractable keychain with a carabiner. They're very discreet, and can be easily retrieved or worn in pajamas if needed.

I'm pretty much always alert and wary of becoming a victim due to an attack or sexual assault, so I always strive to learn new skills to protect myself and others. I study Krav Maga because it teaches real-world defense techniques, such as how to push someone off if you're on the ground and they're sitting on top of you, how to get out of a bear hug from either behind or in front, or what to do if your hair is pulled. Practicing these skills over and over is essential to muscle memory and proficiency.

We must also have a strong mind. Being attacked is a stressful, gut-wrenching experience. If we have the will to survive, then our chances of survival increase dramatically. Another way to strengthen our mind is to plan out solutions to hypothetical scenarios. I do this by envisioning steps I could take to survive various situations that might happen whenever I'm out and about. The more I think about ways to survive something, the more confident I feel.

On Site

Paula's house has no alarm system and it's unfamiliar to me, so I'd check the windows and doors, making sure all locks work and everything is secure. A chain lock can be broken or taken off very easily from the outside; deadbolts and a kick plate are more secure and should be used if possible. Putting a wooden rod in the track of the sliding glass door or window also increases security. Although she may not have some of these items, I'd suggest she invest in these types of reinforcements; perhaps some could be improvised the night I stayed over.

I'd also check the backyard gate for a lock and ensure nothing nearby could be used to climb over, such as a garbage can. The tenant would presumably have a key to an outside gate, but it'd still be one more way to thwart any other intruders. I'd keep the porch, patio, and kitchen lights on — illuminating the interior gives the impression that someone is home and may still be awake. Someone still awake and able to quickly dial 911 could discourage a home invader looking for the low-hanging fruit of people who aren't home or could be taken by surprise.

Since Paula has every right to be worried, I'd reassure her and recommend she lock her bedroom door (if possible) and try to get some sleep. It might sound extreme, but I'd also tell her to place a chair or some other heavy obstruction against her bedroom door on the inside to further impede an intruder and possibly buy some time to react. I'd tell her that if she hears any suspicious noises to immediately grab her phone, listen for any further noises, and be ready to call 911 if she feels unsafe.

As I head to bed, I'd keep my phone within arm's reach, ideally on a wireless charger so that I can easily retrieve it without having to fumble around with charging cables. I'd also keep my purse within reach on the floor next to the bed. Since the door to my guest room doesn't lock, I'd have to figure out a way to not only block a possible intruder, but also to wake up if someone were trying to enter. If nothing better were available, I could also place a chair against the doorknob on the inside.

Crisis

Let's assume for this situation that some of these additional security measures weren't possible or failed for some reason. Waking up to someone tying my hands behind my back and telling me he'll kill me would lead me to believe that the assailant likely has a weapon or perhaps plans to strangle me. Whether his threats are empty or not, I'd have to think quickly.

My legs aren't bound yet, and I've learned how to break out of duct tape, even with my hands tied behind my back. Assuming he'd have to change positions and release his knee from my back at some point, I wouldn't say a word or scream, but instead just wait. I have no idea if anyone would even hear my screams, so screaming would be useless at this point.

The moment he releases his knee from my back, I'd roll to the opposite side of the bed so that I could fall to the floor, sit up, and quickly lunge my hands up as far as they'll go and forcefully drop them back down again to attempt to break the duct tape. By rolling away from my attacker, it gives me a few moments to work on getting out of the tape. If I couldn't break the tape with the first thrust down, I would try to slip my legs through my arms. While this can be difficult and takes practice, it can be done.

This would all happen quickly, but I'd be banking on the possibility that my attacker would be caught off-guard by my sudden actions and wouldn't react right away. I'd pull the duct tape up enough to see clearly as soon as I freed my hands. If he wrapped his arms around me from behind to try to subdue me once again, I would attempt to lift my arms up and break free from his grip, turn, and punch him in the groin — a good spot to hit, whether you're fighting a male or female.

If I couldn't break free from his hold with this technique, I could also simply bend down a bit and attack the groin, step on his feet, kick him in the shins, legs, or whatever your limbs I can reach — attacking some area of his body is better than doing nothing. I would try to jump over the bed to access my phone or purse to retrieve my firearm or knife.

If he grabbed my leg and tried to pull me back, with my other leg, I would kick his arm, face, or whatever my free leg could reach. I could also possibly use the sheets to cover his head and disorient him. If I couldn't retrieve my knife or firearm fast enough, I'd be reaching for and throwing whatever I could at him to slow him down. Anything can be an improvised weapon and could potentially put him on the defensive.

I may have to scratch, claw, and bite my way out of his grasp to reach my weapon and cell phone. I could also use the small dog tag folding knife I'd kept in my pants to defend myself and buy enough time to get to the other side of the bed to retrieve a more effective weapon.

If I were able to reach my firearm, I would tell him to lie on the ground as I kept my gun on him and called 911. If he didn't comply with my orders, this is where it gets tricky. If he runs away, I may not have to use my firearm. If he's fleeing, then in the eyes of the law, he may no longer be considered a threat. If I were to shoot at a fleeing assailant, even with what just happened, I could go to prison. The specifics will depend on the laws in your jurisdiction, so be sure to research and understand them. However, I would keep my gun at the ready and the phone line open, then go check on Paula. On the other hand, if he continued to attack me or tried to take my weapon, I may have to use deadly force to protect myself.

Ideally, after confirming whether Paula is safe or not, I'd remain on the call with the 911 operator until the police arrive. When they get there, they don't know the situation or if I'm really the bad guy — all they know is that I have a gun. I'd tell them that I'm a concealed carry holder and do my best to comply with what they're asking and work out the details later, such as if I need a lawyer. Simply being handcuffed doesn't forfeit your right to speak with a lawyer. Gather your thoughts and remain compliant, but answering questions should be done in the presence of an attorney. [Editor's note: see "Aftermath" in Issue 1 of our sister publication CONCEALMENT for post self-defense shooting legalities.]

Whether you're scared for your life in your own home or just walking down the street to work, you should always take every precaution necessary to avoid being a victim. We don't always have security guards or police nearby when we need it most, so we must be responsible for our own safety.

FIREARMS INSTRUCTOR SHEENA GREEN'S APPROACH

Prep

Even though I hadn't stayed at Paula's new home before, could there be a way to become familiar with the layout without even setting foot in it? Possibly. Using social media, I'd look to see if Paula had shared any photos like many excited new homeowners do. Since she recently purchased the house, there might also be a listing with more details on a real estate site. I'd use Google Maps and to see what the outside of her house and the neighborhood looks like to make sure I went to the right place. It'd be worth noting how close the neighbors are and what the terrain is like immediately surrounding Paula's house.

The news about her tenant and his late-night guests would be an instant red flag. If he were to come home and bring his friends to drink and party, the possibility of having mind-altered strangers in close proximity to where we'll be sleeping wouldn't sit well with me. Avoiding a bad situation is impossible if it descends upon me while I'm peacefully dreaming.

Upon awakening to the fragility of life years ago, I resolved to take at least one self-defense class a year in addition to firearms training. To supplement the classes, I listen to audiobooks with self-protection themes to fortify my mind and prepare myself mentally.

If I didn't know about her tenant situation prior to arriving, there wouldn't be much extra preparation before my visit, outside of my normal EDC. For the purpose of this article, I'll address the situation with the tools presented earlier and examples from training I've taken.

On Site

Asking for a tour of the home would help supplement any impressions of the house's layout I saw online and enable me to start planning ways to increase our security. Planning escape routes to nearest exits, knowing which second story windows can be used as exits, or hunkering down behind a sturdy, locked door with a cell phone are all options that should be considered.

If needed, barricade or block a flimsy exit door with furniture or a doorstop to slow down an intruder before retiring to bed. Since I'm with my friend, I'd want to test it and be sure the furniture or chair I used won't give way.

A folding knife in a purse on the other side of the room is worthless. I'd need quick access, staged within arm's reach and not folded if possible. Paula should have some type of tool or self-defense implement by her bed as well.

I'd suggest that we have a slumber party/movie night in the living room. We could leave lights on in adjacent rooms and have more space to move to other weapons or exits. We could also turn ordinary objects into weapons if needed: scissors, screwdrivers, bookends, fireplace tools, you get the idea.

Implementing emergency plans with friends, family, or trusted neighbors is imperative. Agree to keep cell phones next to the bed and call 911 at the first sign of trouble. Stay on the line with 911 while heading to a designated safe room. Identifying a location down the street to flee to together or meet up at is also a good idea. Make sure it's a well-lit location with access to help and preferably security cameras as well.

Making a preemptive phone call to the local PD on their non-emergency line is one of the easiest things to do. Inform them of the tenant who parties frequently and, since Paula's husband is out of town, request a patrol car to make a few trips over the course of the night if possible.

Crisis

The automatic bodily response to being startled awake is disorientation coupled with accelerated heart rate and breathing. The mind races, as it quickly has to process all the sensory inputs to produce an appropriate response. Slipping into panic mode can shut down decision-making capabilities. Slow your breathing to force the brain to match it and clear your mind.

Any fear that was suppressed by confusion will come forward. Reject fear paralysis by addressing it, resolving to survive, and winning the fight. Adding self-talk into stressful situations when there's loss of control will also help prevent panicking. Breathe. Calm. Listen. Think. What's my best option?

He said that if I made a sound or tried to escape he'd kill me. If murder was his only motive, he could have done it already. This means he has other intentions; my initial thought is rape.

In this scenario, being pinned on my stomach with my hands behind my back, there isn't much I can do except for one move called VINE: straighten the legs and lock them at the ankles while engaging the glutes, hamstrings, and quads. This will seal up the legs and tuck the tailbone. I'm banking that he'll try to pry my legs apart with both hands. We all laughed at the Thighmaster, but this is a good reason to dust off the one in the basement.

He won't be able to get what he wants, and he'll have to roll me over. It may seem more vulnerable by giving him access to my breasts and mouth, but it's a better defensive position and I can use it to gain more control over the situation.

An escape technique while having the hands and arms bound with duct tape is to keep the forearms and hand muscles tense and engaged while the tape is being applied to create wiggle room inside the duct tape once they relax. Application techniques for duct tape and placement are variables that'll determine escape techniques – some are more difficult than others. A more experienced criminal may be better at it than a novice.

If he rolls me on my back to try to pry my legs apart from the front, I probably have a limited amount of time before he increases force to get what he wants. I would try to quickly work my hands while they are underneath my body so he can't see what I'm doing, hopefully freeing one hand from the other.

Smelling his alcohol-laden breath, hearing him huff and puff, and feeling his hands on me, I'd use my senses to locate where his head is. If I know where his head is, I can determine where his eyes are. Even though he sloppily placed duct tape over my own eyes, once my hand is free, I can and will drive my fingers into his face without hesitation. The ideal targets are his eyes. Make the first strike count! Unless he's really out of his mind, his hands should move to his face upon successfully redirecting his external priority (you) to an internal priority (his face).

As soon I make contact with one hand, the other one would rip the duct tape off my eyes. Plant one leg into the bed and use the other to kick him as hard as possible to create some distance. The situation will determine what target areas are available when the time comes. Once you've created some space, grab your phone and purse if within reach and GTFO.

Unfortunately, we must also look at this scenario from the opposite outcome. What if I couldn't get my hands free? What if instead of continuing the attempt to pry my legs open he hit me with a lamp from the nightstand, and I momentarily broke my VINE and passed out?

If I was unsuccessful at keeping him off me, I may lose control over the situation, but there's one thing I do still have control over – my internal situation, my own mind. The mind is always our most valuable weapon.

Rather than withdrawing from the situation and checking out, I can choose to study parts about him that'll help me identify him in the future so he can be caught and locked away. What did he smell like? Did he have long hair or short hair? What's his body size compared to mine? Could I feel the texture of his clothes to determine what he was wearing? If I could get the duct tape off my eyes, I'd want to note any distinctive marks on his face and body, tattoos, piercings, etc. And, while it makes me uncomfortable even writing it, I'd look at the color of his eyes.

The second best weapon in this situation is your voice. While he said no shouting, he didn't say no talking. This is where skills in social engineering can buy time to plan the next move. I'd try to sit up and, as I'm moving, ask politely if it's OK to sit up while reassuring him that I won't run away. It's a false promise, but as long as he doesn't say no and push me back down, I'll be in a position to try to slide my hands underneath then straight up my front to remove the tape from my eyes. More possibilities to fight or run can happen from here.

CONCLUSION

This *What If?* scenario is designed to get you thinking about your own personal safety. While we may or may not travel without a firearm or fixed blade on our person, this article specifically addresses the tools in the setup. Undeniably, there are many variables in such a crisis that we simply don't have space to address here, but the idea is to get you thinking ahead of time to help reinforce the overarching principle of this publication – preparation. The best bet is learning ways to prevent this situation from happening at all. Steve Tarani addresses this in his book titled, *Prefense: The 90% Advantage*.

The more things we can do to prevent an attack from happening, the more we decrease the chances of it happening. Educate yourself: take classes on martial arts, escape and evasion, and situational awareness. The article *Vanishing Act* in the previous issue of this magazine (#29) addresses some of the ways to prepare yourself for a kidnapping scenario. Read about self-defense, join a gym, and find like-minded friends to train with. The opportunities are out there; you just have to find them and commit to learning. You're your own first line of defense.

If you're a woman reading this, find a class where you can literally manhandle some dudes so you know what it feels like to fight someone bigger than you. You may be surprised at how strong you actually are, or you may be surprised that you aren't as strong as you thought. Either way, you'll learn about the areas you need to improve. So, why wait until the last minute to figure it out? We're all responsible for our own safety, and the best way to stop the world's victimizers is to stand up to them. ⁑

16

YOUR VEHICLE IS ATTACKED BY AN ANGRY MOB?

By Tim MacWelch

Illustrations by Ruben Juarez

"What's this protest about?" my wife absentmindedly asked as she thumbed through Facebook on her phone. "More president hating or something about vegetable rights this time?" she mocked. The ride to our son Johnny's game was taking longer than expected, and we were all getting frustrated with the slow pace. Earlier in the day, I had heard something on the radio about protests, and as the vehicles ground to a halt, the uncharacteristic evening traffic started to make sense.

People with poster board signs, many with covered faces, began to fill the spaces between the idling cars. Some of the more energetic protesters started to jump onto car hoods and hurl objects at the gridlocked motorists. Then I saw it, a few cars ahead of us. Several men crowded around a car, and the driver surged forward. Many voices cried out loudly as the vehicle sped away. The first of the cries sounded like pain, and the following ones had a tone of anger and surprise. Someone had just been injured.

The protesters then began to lash out at the remaining vehicles, smashing windows and even pulling a woman out of her car! This was getting ugly quick. My knuckles turned white as I gripped the steering wheel hard, and all I could think was how the hell I was going to protect my family from this.

For this episode of RECOIL OFFGRID's "What If?" column, the editors have created a situation to place a family in the proverbial crosshairs of a group of protestors who turn violent and take out their aggression on passing motorists. Here we'll discuss some possible methods to handle these circumstances, and walk you through preps, plans, and decisions to consider if you find yourself in a similar situation. While we won't hijack a garbage truck to "scoop and compact" our way through these marching marauders — we'll present some options that just might keep you out of harm's way.

The Scenario

Situation type: Traveling to a ball game
Your Crew: You, your wife, and son
Location: Los Angeles, California
Season: Summer
Weather: Clear; high 97 degrees F, low 79 degrees F

The Setup

There has been a recent string of protests in areas of downtown Los Angeles you often travel through, but you have no idea how long it'll last or where exactly it'll pop up next, making route planning to avoid the protests somewhat problematic. Over the last several days, the protests have been nothing more than verbal demonstrations with no violence reported.

You're driving your pregnant wife and 10-year-old son to your son's nighttime little league game in a small crossover SUV. While on a two-lane city street lined with buildings, traffic in front of you suddenly comes to a standstill. Protestors are unexpectedly advancing toward vehicles on both sides of the street. You assume this will only be a slight delay, the crowd will keep marching past you, and no one will become physically aggressive.

The Complication

In a seemingly unprovoked manner, the protestors start antagonizing passing motorists going in either direction, spilling into the street to block cars. Some motorists slowly make their way through the converging crowd, honking and pushing ahead. As a sedan that's two cars in front of you makes a mad dash through the crowd, it appears that one of the protestors is injured by that driver's decision to make a break for it.

This angers the protestors, who quickly seek revenge by converging on the remaining cars. They attempt to open doors, throw objects to hit windows in an attempt to break through, and rock your car back and forth making you think they intend to flip it over. You're blocked on the driver side by opposing traffic, as well as cars in front of and behind you experiencing the same attack. You're essentially boxed in unless you try to drive up on the sidewalk. What steps can you take to help protect your family and alert authorities? Should you attempt verbal persuasion or look for an opportunity to flee your car and escape on foot? Are you justified in using your car as a weapon, possibly injuring other protestors or disabling your vehicle in the enraged crowd?

ATTORNEY JASON SQUIRES' APPROACH

Prep

I always have my SUV stocked with basic survival necessities. I break these into three categories: **1. People.** Items people need to survive such as water, clothing, and self-defense items; **2. Vehicle.** Goods to keep the vehicle functioning; **3. Mission-specific items.** For example: things needed for my son's baseball game.

While traveling with a pregnant wife, the matter is further complicated because of emergency issues related to the unborn child. I must have a bag specifically for the wife stocked with essentials like birth certificates, insurance information, cash and credit/debit cards, and preparation for a hospital stay.

People: While traveling anywhere you must have clothing to anticipate changes in temperature. Children have no concept of preparation, and extra care must be given to ensure each child has comfortable shoes and a warm jacket at a minimum. The wife, being pregnant, is susceptible to slight temperature variations. We always expect the cold to be the problem, but heat variations can be just as problematic. Each person has a durable water bottle, usually filled with water and ice. I also keep other large plastic water bottles to refill each individual bottle if needed. It's prudent to include sufficient snack foods for children, if for no other reason than to reduce stress when the children begin complaining. Remember, food can be quite comforting in a stress situation.

For self-defense items, as a lawyer, I'm always mindful of local, state, and federal laws related to firearms and weaponry. Generally, knife blades less than 5 inches are universally accepted in almost all jurisdictions. Just remember, you must be very close – too close – to an attacker to use a knife. Knife wounds are often more dangerous than bullet wounds. Items like flashlights, headlamps, and light sticks are essential. Where permitted, I carry a pistol and AR-15 with a reliable, long-lasting red dot optic. But, given this scenario is in Los Angeles, I'd have to leave my AR-15 at home in Arizona.

Vehicle: I always prefer SUVs. A crossover SUV offers extended mileage on a single tank of gas. I always reinforce the bumpers with a midrange, affordable bumper system that'd survive pushing the vehicle in front of me, if necessary. My SUV never goes below three-quarters full for any potential and unexpected long drives. Each vehicle has a seatbelt cutter in the sunglasses compartment. Since most SUVs ride higher than other vehicles, that allows me to see further ahead to anticipate trouble or traffic.

Flashlights, multitools, and a basic toolkit (metric and standard sockets, screwdrivers, tow rope, ratchet straps, etc.) are also kept in the vehicle. Additionally, any SUV should be outfitted with all-terrain tires and a full-size spare (not that ridiculous donut). Duct tape, lighters, 550 cord (200 feet), and cash are hidden in the vehicle. I also keep laminated copies of all federal firearms licenses and maps of the area showing alternate routes to areas of refuge outside the city.

I also keep meds for everyone, like EpiPens, NSAIDs, aspirin, and basic first-aid supplies. Remembering when to replace these items can be a chore. I replace all batteries on the longest day of the year (6/21) and the shortest day of the year (12/21). Also, I keep an inverter that plugs into the cigarette lighter as well as two battery packs that'll recharge cell phones five times each. Additionally, I carry a satellite phone, which I began doing when my wife became pregnant so I'd never have spotty cell coverage – yes there can be spotty satellite coverage, too (building obstructions).

Mission-Specific Items: I'm going to a baseball game and my wife is pregnant, so I keep those items for my person, vehicle, and what we need today (baseball equipment and emergency labor/hospital bag). When traveling outside the city, I also bring sleeping bags, more warm clothes, gloves, 5 extra gallons of water, 2 quarts of oil and transmission fluid, fix flat, etc.

On Site

I wouldn't knowingly take my pregnant wife and kid through an area known for trouble. I know that I'm literally a "sitting duck" if my vehicle is surrounded by angry protesters. I'd give a wide berth to any trouble or even potential trouble. I know, as a lawyer, that trouble usually means serious injury or handcuffs – this isn't an overstatement.

Remember, an angry mob has no collective intelligence. A mob is the sum of the individuals who'll say they were doing nothing wrong when you struck them with your vehicle. All assailants will claim they were "merely present," a legal term to suggest at the scene, but doing nothing wrong. Keep a watchful eye 10 to 20 car lengths ahead to scan for trouble; what constitutes trouble should be self-explanatory. Large groupings of angry people surrounding vehicles is trouble. Protestors are trouble. We might admire their First Amendment right, but we don't want to be victimized by it. I'd also keep at least three car lengths behind the vehicle in front of me. This distance allows me to quickly maneuver my vehicle and turn around at even the slightest suggestion of danger.

Let's assume I was doing everything reasonable. I was keeping a safe distance, scanning for threats, wearing seatbelts, had a cell phone charged and ready for use, and the mob suddenly appears seemingly out of nowhere. My friend is my accelerator. The vehicle is a target when stationary. Immediately, I'd utilize the distance I've kept between me and the vehicle ahead of me and conduct a three-point turn (learn this technique). I do this immediately. I move the vehicle quickly. I don't assume any angry grouping of people will remain peaceful.

I had this example recently where a group of teachers were protesting. I don't fear teachers; I love them. I know instinctively that troublemakers will embed themselves in large groups only to cause mayhem. So at first sign of trouble: I'm gone. If you're stuck in between cars (a person unexpectedly changes lanes into your lane seeing the protestors), I use the push bumper I had installed on the SUV. It's better to beg for forgiveness later than die. My insurance will pay damages to anyone's vehicle. But as a lawyer, I know this will mean future trouble – so I don't ram the vehicle in front of me when the Girl Scouts appear out of nowhere with cookies.

When I see the angry mob, I immediately call 911. I don't say on the recorded 911 call: "Well, ah, there are some people, and they're walking toward me." I know to articulate fear in a verbal manner. "911, What is your emergency?" "Help! There's an angry mob trying to hurt me, my pregnant wife, and 10-year-old son. I'm worried we're going to die."

In thousands of 911 calls I've heard and litigated, I've never thought a person expressing intense fear was lying. I've seen, many times, people appearing flat and unafraid. It's hard to claim I was afraid at the time when I don't sound afraid on the recorded call that will certainly be reviewed by someone else (insurance company and/or prosecutors). Protests are usually localized events. Whatever direction will take us away from trouble is the path I seek. I'd be doing this while on the phone asking for police assistance. While many people have differing views of law enforcement, I'll say these men and women are here to help. But make no mistake, if they're busy with other trouble, you're on your own. So I wouldn't pull over a block away and wait for the good guys.

I'm responsible for the safety of others. Let's say I've caused damage to the vehicle in front of me by utilizing the push bumper to safely get my wife and son away from danger. I call 911 and report what I did. There's such a thing as the necessity defense. It's legally grounded in the "Reasonable Person Standard," meaning: Would a reasonable person feel the need to push the vehicle in front of him to avoid any angry mob? It's not whether I feel the danger, subjectively, but rather, would another reasonable person do the same. Wide latitude is given to people who are acting in self-defense. Some people would cause damage, leave, and not want the potential legal headache. I'd run to the law and safely travel that distance to communicate with authorities the fear for my life and my pregnant wife and son, describing damage I created to avoid a potential criminal charge for hit and run.

If the mob gets me, my wife, and son, I know my fate is in their collective hands. I must do everything to avoid that possibility because, at that point, I'm lucky if I or my family isn't seriously injured or killed. I must utilize all available assets, but I must admit that I've done many things wrong if I find myself surrounded by this angry mob. I've failed to scan for threats far ahead of my vehicle. I've failed to keep a three-car distance from the vehicle ahead of me. I've failed to remove myself and family from the threat by using the accelerator. One of my last lines of defense is to plead for law enforcement to come get me. They'll respond by priority ... so maybe my pregnant wife speaks to the 911 operator and explains that while I try to maneuver the vehicle away from danger.

If I must drive on a sidewalk: Well, I say better to be judged by 12 rather than carried by six. I'll apply all force and fury to protect my family. Remember, legally speaking, a mob is comprised of individuals, and I will be held responsible for any injuries or damage to innocent people who are merely present. I can't drive blindly through the mob, running people over. You must maneuver away from danger, utilizing the bare minimum damage and injury to others. Let's say a child is with his mother who's a protestor. The law doesn't transmit mom's venom to her innocent child. So, think way ahead, be prepared for all reasonable contingencies, and flee at the first sign of trouble. Discretion is the better part of valor. The first line of defense is to live by that proverb.

SURVIVAL EXPERT TIM MACWELCH'S APPROACH

Prep

One of the most important things I can recommend before hitting the road is to study a street map long and hard. I don't care if you're looking at a map of your hometown, an area you work in, or a vacation destination. Get to know the connections and choke points of the streets, bypasses, and highways through the area. This helps you find alternate routes and avoid congested areas. Once the city streets are familiar, take time to study the map again periodically, and bring the paper map with you in the vehicle. I'm not suggesting that you ignore your phone's navigation apps or throw your Garmin out the window. On the contrary, use those tools as much as you like. But understand that nothing beats map study to really know the "lay of the land."

Once I know my routes and alternates, I'll think about the items that should be stocked our car. All the usual suspects make sense. Carrying food, water, tools, jumper cables, flashlights, first-aid kit, and the personal defenses we train with regularly will leave us prepared for most roadside emergencies. But preparing for a possible encounter with attackers on the road – this is a much more complicated matter. What if we had to defend ourselves against a crowd? If these were Mad Max times, things would be different, but depending on the circumstances, some jurors may frown on the use of your vehicle as a weapon, even if those shouting buffoons became physically aggressive.

Now there are some enhancements you can add to your car to thwart attacks and attempted break-ins. For the average Joe, turning your grocery getter into a fully armored vehicle is cost-prohibitive, and adding certain offensive capabilities may get you in trouble (think anti-carjacking flamethrowers seen in South Africa). Don't despair, there are a few things most of us can afford that would help to harden a vehicle. Buying puncture-resistant (run-flat) tires may allow you to keep rolling, even though you just got a flat tire in a scary neighborhood. After-market oversized gas tanks can keep you idling in traffic long after the other cars are out of gas. Consider a cell phone booster that could improve your communication options in case cell phone reception is spotty or you're separated from your family members. Finally, think about mounting a dashboard cam to record any incidents that happen so you have proof that can be shown in court.

We'd do our best to stay informed of protest activity, since information is one of our best defenses. It's important to know why the protest is happening, as well as the location of the event. Listening to the radio may provide some current local news, but who knows if that information is correct or current. Keep in mind that violence and crowd size are sometimes downplayed by the authorities and the media for various reasons. Check various forms of social media. These can sometimes provide local information; however, it may also be inaccurate. Whatever forms of news you find, use them to assess where the unrest is happening and why. Have a discussion with the family, preparing them for the possibility of running into some angry protesters and explain that your best defense is to get out of their way.

On Site

As a general safety precaution, vehicle doors stay locked and windows stay up when traveling in our car as a family or alone. Many of the newer cars on the road have automatic door locks that engage after driving for a minute or so, but why wait? Lock them as soon as you enter the vehicle. And even when it's hot, we like to keep the windows up and let the AC do its job. It'll cool off soon enough.

Once we're on the road, defensive driving is the name of the game. All drivers should watch the vehicle in front of them, but I go a step beyond and watch both the vehicle in front of me and the vehicle in front of them. This way, I have more time to react. But what about driving in tight streets with lots of company? Your driver's ed teacher would be proud if you could maintain the "two-car length" spacing between your grille and the rear bumper of the vehicle in front of you, but let's get real. In city driving, people will cut in front of you constantly when they see that much room. You won't be going anywhere fast with that much space in front. Keep enough room to give yourself space to make a quick exit if needed.

Once I spot the protestors coming down the street, I'd check the door locks again and get the phone handy in case we had to make an emergency call. Scanning the crowd, I'd try to absorb as much detail as possible to try and predict their behavior. With faces covered, they're not marching to save the whales. They're trying to prevent their faces from being photographed. This strongly suggests that they're planning (or at least hoping) to do plenty of things they shouldn't.

The Crisis

Look at the stats, and you'll find that most marches and protests are peaceful. But if they do turn violent, understand that riots are survivable events, assuming you know how to navigate the situation.

Pinned in place by gridlock, our vehicle isn't going to get us out of the area. Our exodus is will have to be on foot. I know my wife and son will be frightened to exit the imagined safety of the vehicle, but with car windows being smashed – it's well past the time to go. With multiple people on foot trying to break into or turn over our car, we'll make a break to the nearest store or business that'll let us in. It's not our job to police this crowd, but it is my job as a spouse and parent to protect my loved ones. We'll do that by getting away. Any provocation coming from my "group" could instigate an onslaught from the others. Just like bees, when one or more of those seen as threats are attacked – the rest may join in because they believe it's necessary to defend themselves.

Of course, the safest place to be during unrest is far away, but if we were caught in a mob and can't get to shelter – our best bet may be to blend in. Chant what they chant, and repeat the types of statements you're hearing the crowd say. Don't stick up for opposing views or groups. Pride won't help you. Tell them what they want to hear until you can get the hell out of there.

CONCLUSION

When a crowd becomes angered, tribal mentality often sets in. Bottles and rocks are thrown, nearby businesses are looted, cars are flipped, and fires are set. Whether it's after a sporting event with drunken fans pouring into the street or during a politically charged rally, sometimes it's impossible to predict when a group will suddenly turn into a rioting horde. When it happens, innocent bystanders often perceived as outsiders are treated as potential threats and pulled into the fray. That simple protest may escalate into a full-blown riot. Often the bigger the crowd and more attention they think they're getting, the lower their inhibitions and collective conscience becomes.

Individually, each protester has logic, beliefs, and reasoning, but as a group, their anger often leads to a criminal mindset. You can't reason with insanity; the best thing you can do is get out of its way until the tantrum is over, subdued by law enforcement, or just plain exhausted. Whether or not you know if you'll have to venture into the proximity of an unstable crowd, you should plan your vehicular belongings and alternate travel routes accordingly. The more options you have to escape, the better your chances of surviving the onslaught are. ⠶

17

YOU'RE IN A HOSTAGE SITUATION?

By Tim MacWelch
Illustrations by Cassandra Dale

So much had changed in just one minute. The look on my wife's face had turned from beautiful and bored to truly terrified and alert. A man lay dead on the floor, and the murmur of many people chatting had been replaced by the tumult of gunfire and screaming. A dozen questions struggled for the limited attention my mind could give them. Why had these men burst into our conference? Why were they restraining some people and killing others? What could I do to save my wife?

After being herded together like cattle, my mind began to go numb. The number of questions had settled down from so many to just two. "Why?" was the first thought, although knowing why this was happening didn't serve much purpose in the moment. The second question was the one that really mattered. "What am I going to do?" It was looping in my head, and I was running out of time to answer it. The men had almost reached us, binding nearby hostages with zip ties and duct tape. What should I do? I was out of time to decide.

In this RECOIL OFFGRID "What If?" column, we go out of the frying pan and into the fire of a violent hostage situation. To make matters worse, we're not on our home soil; we're in another country with a different way of handling this kind of crisis. For this "What If?" we'll explore some precautionary plans and actions we can take before traveling overseas. We'll also learn about a few "safety nets" for U.S. citizens abroad. Finally, we'll look at some strategies to stay alive in a hostage situation. So much can change in a short period of time. When it happens, will you be ready for it?

The Scenario

Situation type: Hostage situation
Your Crew: You and your wife
Location: Hotel, coastal city in the Balkans
Season: Summer
Weather: Warm; high 88 degrees F, low 62 degrees F

The Setup

You work for a renowned finance company with holdings and offices all over the world. Your travels often take you overseas to consult with wealthy clients. Recently, you were invited to a conference at a five-star hotel in Southeastern Europe, specifically the Balkan Peninsula, to discuss the economy and advise on international holdings. The event is taking place in a city that's a common tourist destination because of its picturesque beaches, so you decide to stay a little longer and make it a bit of a vacation. You bring your wife along as well, and plan for her to spend most days sunbathing at the beach and enjoying the local amenities while you're at the conference. Although you've visited the area before, you're not fluent in the native language, but are somewhat familiar with the instability and strife the region experienced after the fall of the Soviet Union.

As an experienced traveler, you do your due diligence to research any recent advisories on the State Department website, providing an itinerary to family members back home to make them aware of your travel schedule, flights, and overall agenda. You've also provided your contacts back home with a list of whom to call if trouble of any kind breaks out while you're away, instructing them what to do if they don't receive periodic status updates from you. The conference is expected to have over 250 visitors, many of whom are well-known within the investment industry as wealthy individuals, hedge fund managers, and financiers.

The Complication

The first day of the conference is a networking breakfast in the main ballroom on the ground floor where all the attendees get to mingle for a while before the keynote speaker takes the podium. You and your wife are socializing with some of the other attendees when you hear some commotion coming from the lobby immediately outside the conference room. You also notice two of the waiters look at each other and nod, before closing the double doors at either end of the room. While they both wait with their backs against the doors, you see one pull up his vest and remove a pistol from his waistband. He quickly hides it behind his back and glances around the room, a look of intense determination on his face.

As you're about to say something, the other individual dressed as a waiter fires a gun into the air. Several members of the crowd scream, but the only escape route is blocked. One of the waiters opens the door and lets in half a dozen masked men holding what appear to be AK-47s. You can hear more commotion outside, but you can't exactly discern what's going on. As the armed men burst into the room, the door is locked again, and several of them start ushering the crowd into the dining area while shouting commands in broken English.

Everyone is herded into the dining area and told to get down on their knees and to place their hands behind their backs. As other men take positions around the perimeter of the crowd, several start zip-tying people's hands and applying duct tape over their mouths and eyes. You hear one of the assailants ask a fellow attendee what his name is. The attendee responds with profanity and is promptly shot in the head. The crowd again screams while another assailant shouts, "Shut up and do as we say, or you'll end up like him!"

As you look in stunned silence at the lifeless body, you see the shooter pull out his wallet, look at the ID, confiscate his phone, and hand it to the man behind him, who puts it in a duffel bag. As they bind and blindfold the attendees and work their way toward you, you scan the perimeter of the room. There are no exits except the ones being blocked. Wallets, purses, briefcases, and phones are being confiscated and examined as each individual is approached. You recognize one man as a wealthy Swiss banker you've dealt with before as the kidnappers approach him. As they look at his ID, one of the kidnappers nods to another — then they drag the man out of the room. You aren't sure if this is a terrorist situation, a hostage ransom, or something else entirely. As the captors make their way toward you and your wife, you gingerly feel the outline of your small knife in your pocket, but you don't have any other defensive tools, what do you do?

TRAINED NEGOTIATOR KRIS SOUTHARDS' APPROACH

Preparation

It's been said that success is in the details. It's also been said that a plan is just a list of things that aren't going to happen. So you plan with high hopes but, in a situation like this, realize that you'll probably have to improvise. A lot.

Upon receiving the invitation to attend the financial conference on the Balkan Peninsula, I'd begin my pre-trip preparation. This includes reviewing not only the business aspect of the trip, but also the additional personal time I intend to take with my wife.

In this case, the venue is very nice and in close proximity to shops, restaurants, and the beach. So we decide to stay at the venue site, which would also facilitate opportunities to network after hours. However, if the town/province/village where the event lodging is located appears to be in a dodgy area, I might consider making my own lodging reservations. I'd try to research the venue itself as well as the immediate area to see if past travelers report anything untoward – shake-downs by the police, items missing from their rooms, and so forth.

This type of conference is ordinarily attended by a select group. Knowing who else will be there ahead of time is valuable intelligence. Equally important is who *isn't* going to be there. A collection of powerhouse personalities, or the conspicuous absence thereof, could impact how newsworthy the conference will be, which in turn affects how much outside interest it might provoke. This could be used to gauge the likelihood of intervention by the locals, whether through public protests or a bona fide threat to the event or its attendees. A review of foreign and domestic news sources in the days or weeks leading up to the conference could give an indication of possible disruption. If no alarm bells sound, or if they're at least muted, then it's on to the next phase.

Once I had a handle on the venue itself and the immediate area, I'd begin broader preparations. This would include checking the weather forecast for the region, as well as paying a visit to the State Department website to check for any advisories for the area and surrounding countries. The CIA also produces the World Factbook. While it won't have late-breaking information like the State Department's travel advisories, it contains useful information like the address of the embassy/consulate, primary languages, predominant religions, and small facts about local customs and courtesy. I might also run some Internet searches to figure out if there are well-developed criminal or terrorist organizations operating in the area.

Additionally, I'd check to see if there's a U.S. Consulate or other governmental presence in or near the venue – "near" meaning you could walk there in an hour or less. If not that close, I'd want to know how far I'd have to travel to reach U.S. soil and what my options are to get there. If I didn't have a rental car, I'd keep enough cash in reserve to take a taxi or bus to get me within walking (or running) distance of the embassy.

I'd make some predeparture lists for myself, including what clothes to pack; notes on exchanging currency; what personal security equipment, if any, could be taken and what electronic equipment to take. I'd also make copies of my conference itinerary, and my wife's intended day plans, and leave them with friends or family for safe keeping.

I'd establish a contact schedule that includes going over possible emergency code text messages with my wife, assistant, and best friend. The emergency codes would be simple three- or four-character text messages conveying the type of emergency, which dictates who should be contacted, i.e., the State Department, local authorities, boss, or family members. The presumption here is that I'd have little time, opportunity, or inclination to type a lengthy narrative via text.

When finalizing my reservations, if possible, I'd request a room no higher than the local fire engine ladder can reach. If not sure what that is, I'd request a ground or first-floor room.

On Site

I'd try to arrive at the venue in advance to allow some time to stroll the facility and surrounding grounds. I could use this time to make note of emergency exits, windows that can be opened, security cameras, fire suppression systems, security staff, and demeanor of hotel staff as well as others staying at the hotel. Ideally, I'd map at least two exit routes each from my room, the lobby, and the conference room. Also, if there appear to be hiding places to potentially escape a crisis, I'd at least give them a cursory inspection.

Beyond what's mentioned above, there's little more to do in terms of personal security because the likelihood of being able to carry a firearm or wear John Wick's bulletproof suit is about as good as the Titanic making it to New York. If local law permits a knife, I'd carry that. Barring that, there are any number of improvised tools to fill the void. Even in places where "weapons" are banned, getting your hands on a fruit knife or paring knife is probably pretty easy. Impact and stabbing weapons can be fashioned from all kinds of things. They're not pretty, and they'd provide little chance against armed and organized assailants, but having something on hand is better than nothing.

The company is paying a substantial sum for me to be there and is expecting a return on their investment. Absent a clearly defined threat, the two of us are committed to staying a few days at a five-star resort. However, I could still be on the lookout for anything suspicious. For example, you should take note if a group of military-aged males check in with six hard-sided golf bags when there's no golf course within 100 kilometers.

Crisis

Upon noticing the wait staff engaging in what I think may be suspicious activity, I'd work to position myself between my wife and the questionable characters. If I felt it necessary, I'd tap her right wrist, our agreed upon signal for her to stay close. As the situation developed, I'd take advantage of that initial chaos to get my phone out and send one of my preprogrammed emergency texts to those trusted contacts back home. I'd make sure to clear the screen and delete the message out of my recent conversations bar.

While conventional wisdom says to get out of there immediately, I also wouldn't have any idea what's going on outside the doors and if the hotel had been completely taken over. Regardless, with the exits sealed, fleeing would no longer be realistic. Now it's time to survive the next 15 minutes.

The commotion outside the door confirms that moving outside wouldn't have led to a better outcome. The presence of multiple attackers armed with automatic weapons eliminates any realistic thought of active physical resistance. But even if escape and physical resistance are no longer on the table, there are still things you can do.

During the initial confusion when the hostage-takers are asserting control is the time to move deeper into the crowd and get near a table. I'd be looking carefully at how the hostage-takers disperse around the room, take note of who's giving the orders and, if possible, who's the most agitated.

Once the first attendee is killed, it establishes a precedent by the hostage takers that violence is an acceptable first-line response. At that point, trying to be an alpha dog is a certain path to suicide. This is an important thing to understand about your captors, and to understand it quickly. However, if simply murdering everyone was their intent, as was the case in Mumbai and Paris, they would've come in shooting indiscriminately.

The taking of the one individual could indicate this is a criminal venture, but that doesn't necessarily change the circumstances for anyone else. While hostage response professionals prefer to deal with professional criminals, there's no guarantee of a peaceful ending.

While the bind team is making its way through the crowd, I'd continue to tell my spouse to stay as close as possible, physically touching her if it can be managed. I'd also try to tell those around me to throw themselves on the floor if shooting starts and stay there until told to get up. Not all hostage rescue teams are equal, but most don't shoot those laying still on the floor.

Once bound, attempting to break the zip ties is a nonstarter, unless I could do it without being noticed at any time or if I think things have gone so bad that physically fighting or running are the only choices left. Once bound, blindfolded, and gagged, the senses left are hearing, smell, and touch. I'd do my best to use them to try and track the movement of the hostage-takers and hear them speaking — even without understanding the local language, I could try to determine tone or urgency in their voices. I'd also try to sense changes in smell and vibrations through the floor. While the information gathered might have no practical use at the time, the better situational awareness I can maintain, the quicker I can respond when necessary.

In any hostage-taking scenario, once you're through the first 15 minutes, it's time to settle in and take a deep breath. The hostage-takers will have gotten through their initial adrenalin rush. At this point, it's better not to give them any reason to pump back up.

In the immediate sense, all of the steps I took prior to the doors being blocked came to nothing except perhaps the emergency message I was able to send out and that I'm appropriately dressed for the season. Even if I still had a weapon or escape tools on me to break restraint, being under the constant watch of heavily armed men and surrounded by panicking people who will behave erratically in the face of a sudden disturbance, the idea of making a break for it, or trying to overpower the captors, is a losing proposition. What I could hang some hope on is that my distress signal was received back home and that my loved ones are reacting appropriately — passing all relevant information to U.S. officials.

How the situation is finally resolved is outside of my control. My survival is mostly outside of my control, except for the little things I was able to do before full lock-down. At this point, I have to remain calm and accept that I've done everything I can for the time being to give my wife and me the best chance of survival.

SURVIVAL EXPERT TIM MACWELCH'S APPROACH

Preparation

During preplanning I'd definitely want to research any recent instances of crime, terrorism, kidnapping, or theft in the area I'd be visiting. A great place to start this research is the U.S. State Department website (www.state.gov). This site is packed with useful advice, current travel advisories, and general warnings about many countries. Most useful of all, the website can guide you to embassy and consulate websites that provide addresses and phone numbers for the nearest embassy or consulate in your destination country. You'll want to have these phone numbers and addresses on a durable card or sheet as you travel, since these outposts are your best means of help if you're an American citizen in a foreign land. Ask for American Citizen Services when contacting the Embassy or Consulate, and make sure you bring both the emergency phone numbers and non-emergency lines.

To limit risks while traveling, I'd prefer to stay at the hotel where the event was taking place. This would mean fewer trips around town and less movement. Before leaving, I'd also provide my travel details to my contacts at home. They should know my flight information, hotel address, and phone number, as well as information about any separate venues. This could all go to one person with whom I'd check in on a regular schedule, or my itinerary could go to several trusted people. We'd establish a "check-in" call or email schedule, and I'd leave instructions on what to do if I missed one or more "check in" calls. If I were concerned that my cell phone wouldn't work there, I'd also consider communication redundancy (like bringing a satellite phone in case my cell phone couldn't get through).

Since I can't exactly fly around with a personal arsenal, it'd certainly be a challenge to bring anything substantial for self-defense. A belt with a heavy buckle can be used as a whip, and a tactical pen can be used for stabbing. In our scenario here, I have a pocket knife, but belts, pens, and knives are poor substitutes for firearms.

When it comes to preparing for the conference, it would be a smart move to research the venue before attending. This could make me aware of issues that could throw up a red flag. Similarly, I might try to get a list of the attendees and have a private investigator attempt to vet any of them for shady backgrounds, questionable business dealings, or criminal association.

On Site

Once we landed in the Balkans, I'd check in back home and choose a respectable-looking ride to the hotel. The two main protocols we'd establish for keeping safe during our stay would be to stay alert together. We'd also want to work hard at blending in with the local population. This may not be possible when you bear no physical resemblance to your foreign hosts, as there's little you can do about being a head taller and a different complexion than the locals, but it's still worth the effort to minimize how much you stand out in a crowd. One simple trick is to avoid wearing a backpack. While people all around the world use backpacks, it seems to be a common part of the "American tourist" costume. Carry your things some other way. Once we arrived at the hotel, I'd also take a good look around at the property – inside and out. It's important to know where the exits are located and what your different options might be. Finally, I'd check out the venue where the conference would be held. I wouldn't expect to see any "deal-breakers" for our safety, but I'd reserve the final say on our attendance (and not leave it up to my employers, who aren't seeing the things I'm seeing). For example, a last-minute venue change and sketchy transport to the new location might cause me to skip the event.

Crisis

As soon as we've established that the crowd was being assailed and the situation was uncertain, I'd call the local U.S. embassy emergency line to communicate our distress. Even if I could only get in a few words in the time allotted saying that U.S. citizens were under attack at a specific hotel, it could start things in motion that would get the right professionals involved. I'd then leave the phone on and under the table so that they could continue to hear what was going on. At that point, compliance makes the most sense. One man had already been executed for mouthing off, and tensions are high on both sides of the situation.

Shortly after the initial conflict isn't the right time to try to negotiate, fight back, attempt to bribe any of the assailants, or to try separating ourselves from the group. I'd encourage my wife to keep her head down and not speak or try to resist (there would be better times for that later). Compliance equals survival in the initial stages of violent hostage situations. We should attempt to remain compliant yet aware during the ordeal. Count the number of men, note all identifying traits — essentially become a good witness. Of course, I'd attempt to stick with my wife, but I wouldn't expect it to go on that way indefinitely. Whether this event was a kidnapping for a ransom, or a politically motivated or terrorist attack, I'd bide my time before striking back — waiting until my captor's guard is down.

I may be able to break my zip-tie restraints by reaching up high and then slamming my wrists down against my belly, or I may be able to pick it like a lock by finding something thin and hard to act as a shim under the locking tab. I'd also want to stay alert to Stockholm syndrome (also known as capture-bonding), which occurs in nearly 10 percent of multiday hostage scenarios. Named after a 1973 robbery in Stockholm, this event involved bank employees who became so attached to their kidnappers that they defended their captors even after they were freed. Sure, it's possible that you could have mixed feelings toward your kidnapper when they provide food and drink or show their human side unexpectedly. But never forget that your captors are criminals who are denying your freedom. Keep your wits about you, pretend to be compliant, and maintain your watch for a set of circumstances that could allow attack and escape.

CONCLUSION

Despite our most meticulous trip planning, traveling abroad for business and pleasure can expose us to dangers we'd rarely face back home. That being said, our goal in this article isn't to scare you away from travel or cause you to never leave your home, but rather to make you better prepared than you were before picking up this magazine. This situation could just as easily happen domestically.

Going on a big trip can be one of the most memorable times in your life, and with the right precautions (and some good luck), it can be filled with good memories. As you immerse yourself in different cultures and get away from your day-to-day routine, make sure you stay alert to your surroundings. Even in resort areas, which are usually safer than the surrounding areas, nasty things can happen. Sometimes, you just can't escape your bad luck, but you can try to stay ahead of it. And whether you're at home or abroad, count the exits and keep an eye on the front door wherever you go. If you have a response that's a few seconds faster than everyone else, it might just give you the time to make a lifesaving decision. ⠿

18

YOUR FLIGHT IS HIJACKED?

By Tim MacWelch
Illustrations by Joe Oesterle

As a frequent flyer, you'd heard your fair share of commotions on airplanes. From fighting couples to drunken passengers – the cramped cabin of a crowded airplane was hardly a quiet place, even when most of your fellow travelers were being respectful. Yes, you'd been on noisy flights before, but this ruckus was different.

In the way that a parent can distinguish a child's cry of pain from a howl of frustration, these raised voices conveyed alarm to you. Turning to your spouse, you asked, "Honey, are you hearing this?" She looked up from her book and turned a bit to listen. A moment later, a woman's piercing scream tore through the low murmur of conversations in coach. It came from the front of the plane, behind the first-class curtain. You started to stand up in your seat, but your spouse pulled you back down. That was a good thing.

A loud and deep man's voice boomed just behind you. "Stay in seats! We take this plane now!" Craning your neck to see over the seatback, you saw two men in ski masks, holding a terrified flight attendant. The speaker shouted again, so all could hear "You stay in seats or we blow up plane!"

For this installment of RECOIL OFFGRID's "What If?" column, the editors have placed us in an airline hijacking scenario that pushes the boundaries of preparedness. And while this scenario is a painful reminder of the life-altering events of Sept. 11, it's also a valuable teaching opportunity. Here we'll share some potential strategies to fight back against fanatical hijackers, and we'll discuss some of the preparations and strategies that you might need to employ, should you find yourself in such a dire situation. Most of us will never forget Sept. 11, and we should never forget that this kind of crisis can still happen, despite all of the advancements in airline security. You never know when one person may make all the difference.

The Scenario

Situation type: Airliner hijacking
Your Crew: You and your spouse, airline crew, and approximately 200 other passengers
Location: During flight from Boston to Los Angeles aboard a Boeing 737
Season: Winter, late December
Weather: Clear; high 47 degrees F, low 31 degrees F

The Setup

You and your spouse are en route from Boston to Los Angeles to visit family for the holidays. Since two of the aircraft that were hijacked on Sept. 11 originated at Logan International Airport, security here is taken very seriously. As you prepare to board your flight, you feel confident that these protocols would prevent another such attack from happening at this airport. After the two of you take your seats, a well-dressed, middle-aged man sits down in your row's third seat and nods hello. The flight gets underway without incident.

The Complication

About halfway through your roughly six-hour flight, the mood is still and quiet. Suddenly there's yelling and commotion in the first-class section of the cabin. Initially, given all the cell phone videos posted on the internet of rowdy passengers, you think someone may just have had a little too much to drink. The commotion and arguing escalates, and you now hear screaming. People start to rise from their seats to see what's happening.

Suddenly, from the rear of the cabin, you hear a shout and two men start addressing the passengers in broken English to remain seated or they'll detonate a bomb on the plane. The two men are wearing ski masks, and one of them has a knife to a flight attendant's throat. The men start yelling at the passengers to stay seated or they'll be killed. The other man starts moving forward toward the cockpit with what appears to be a large, non-ferrous knife, while the first man remains in the rear holding the flight attendant as his hostage.

You're clearly in a hijacking situation. You also feel that the plane may be descending and deviating from its previous course. You're midair during this hijacking attempt, and according to the flight tracker on the back of the seat in front of you, you believe you're just east of Colorado.

You've no idea if they've managed to gain access to the cockpit. It's not yet possible to discern if they plan to divert the flight to an airport and hold everyone on board hostage, use it as a guided missile, or something else entirely. What are your options? Remain compliant? Is the bomb threat legit or a ploy to scare everyone? Can you attempt to call out using the jet's Wi-Fi or any other communication device you might have brought? Do you try to subdue one of the attackers and hope others will join in or that an air marshal is on board? If so, what can you use as a weapon?

FORMER FEDERAL OFFICER HANA BILODEAU'S APPROACH

We just reached the anniversary of one of the most devastating terrorist attacks on American soil. You often hear individuals preach "never forget," but I have to ask, are you living and preparing as if you'll "never forget?" We need only to remember back 17 years to find evidence that evil is present and terrorism exists.

As Americans it's our duty not only to never forget the lives lost but to also combat evil in the future. Preparation, and the wherewithal to survive, is a mental and physical exercise. Having worked previously in state and federal law enforcement, I understand all too clearly that crime can happen anywhere — even at 37,000 feet off the ground.

Being locked inside a flying metal tube with complete strangers doesn't provide me with a high level of comfort. Knowing whether there's a potential hijacker on the plane or not is inconsequential; there's always a potential risk. When I prep for travel, I ask myself, "What if my airliner was hijacked?"

Pre-Prepping

I'm a planner by nature; checking a calendar and making a to-do list is a daily ritual. So when planning travel I like to schedule accordingly and do so well in advance. During holiday travel, the airports tend to be a bit busier, security parameters are a bit tighter, and flights are usually sold out if not over-sold. Because of this somewhat unpredictable combination of elements, I purchase my tickets well in advance, and I always pay extra to board early (more on that later). I've learned by doing this that flights typically cost less, and I have the luxury of being able to pick where I'd like to sit. Like any individual suffering from a touch of OCD, travel during the holidays comes with a fair amount of anxiety, so prepping really matters.

To-Do

Carefully review the available flights and airlines for your destination. Typically the plane used to travel from Boston to Los Angeles is a Boeing 737 – this is important because you can easily learn the layout of the plane. On a Boeing 737, there are typically 33 rows, with exit rows at row number 17. There are galleys in the front and rear of the aircraft, two restrooms in the rear of the plane, and one additional restroom just outside the cockpit. I prefer to sit somewhere in row 15 to 20, giving me a good vantage point. I'm a curious person by nature, and this location provides me with the best overall visibility of the entire plane, without cornering me in one position. When traveling with my significant other, I always book a middle seat and an aisle seat, or two aisle seats next to each other. This allows for easy movement and visibility, as well as the flexibility to get up if needed and access to the front or rear of the plane.

To Pack

When traveling, my carry-on bag is always a backpack because it allows my hands to be free, with easy movement when I'm entering and exiting the plane, and while walking through a crowded airport. Inside my backpack, I utilize the laptop pouch to secure a Defender level IIIA plate that can be carried through security. This plate is designed for a backpack and weighs just 1.3 pounds. It can help protect you from fragmentation, edged weapons, and physical strikes. Easily accessible inside my backpack, I have an amenity kit containing a flashlight, batteries, large zip ties, duct tape, a couple sturdy ballpoint pens, tourniquet, hemostatic-combat gauze, pressure bandages, and socks – I always have socks in my bag so I never have to touch my bare feet on the airport floor when going through security, and they can also be used as a blunt striking agent when filled with change or batteries.

On Site

I like to arrive to the gate area of my departing plane early. This allows me to watch and evaluate the other passengers I'm going to be locked on a plane with for several hours. During this time, I look for other passengers who appear to be physically able to defend themselves if necessary. Personal attributes I note: 1) haircut: a high and tight suggests that the passenger may have been former military or law enforcement, 2) physical stature: a larger male or someone who appears to be physically fit and wears clothing advertising martial arts, CrossFit, military, or law enforcement entities could be a potential ally in a hijacking situation. Once located, I mentally document the passengers who might be able to assist me in a crisis if needed. This is precisely the reason I always pay the extra money to board a plane early — so I can find my seat, get situated, and watch the other passengers I've identified as they board, mentally noting where they sit, in case their assistance is needed.

In this scenario, I'm traveling with my spouse, so we also maintain our awareness as other passengers are boarding and watch their behaviors as they enter the aircraft. Once we locate our seats, I take the middle seat and he takes the aisle seat. I push the armrest to the rear and undo my seatbelt when safe, to prohibit obstruction of movement. I never put my carry-on in the overhead, keeping it with me and accessible at all times.

My spouse and I both worked in the defense world and train together in physical fitness, and hand-to-hand/edged-weapon defense. We communicate regularly on mission preparedness. Because of this, we're very good at non-verbal communication. From boarding to deplaning, we maintain awareness throughout the entire flight, which includes no noise-canceling headphones or ear buds, no sleeping, and no movies or entertainment that could divert our attention. We keep the lines of communication with each other open (for example: "I'm heading to the restroom in the front of the plane," or "I'm going to get a water from the flight attendant in the back galley," etc.)

Crisis

Midway through the flight, chaos erupts. It's clear that the plane is being hijacked, and at this point in time, as hard as it may be, it's essential to remain calm so you can assess, evaluate, and plan.

In the assessment stage I have three main concerns: 1) Is the pilot safe?, 2) Is there an explosive device on the plane?, and 3) How many hijackers are involved? Ever since Sept. 11, airline cockpits are locked, so if a hijacker has breached the lock it should be physically obvious. To identify the presence of an explosive device, visually inspect the hijacker's hands to see if they have something that could be used as a detonation device. And finally, scan the passengers to see if you can observe any additional potential threats.

Once my risk assessment is done, I'll evaluate the situation with my spouse and take note of our options. Can we rush the hijacker and end this situation? Are there other threats that need to be contained before taking on the hijacker? How do we create distractions? These are all questions to consider during the evaluation stage.

Now it's time to plan. I'll communicate with my spouse (verbally if possible, but non-verbal is always an option) and develop an actionable plan. In this situation, I'd suggest my spouse go to the rear of the aircraft due to his body size and immediate risk to the flight attendant's life. Next, I'll try to visually and physically communicate with the passengers whom I've identified to enlist their help to take down the hijackers. I'd also tell my seatmate about our plan (assuming I don't suspect he might be in on it).

Because of the positioning of our seats, I'd ask our seatmate to watch the plane and to verbally get our attention if any other risks arise. Before moving from our seats, I'd access and divide up the zip ties and ballpoint pens. The pens can be used as weapons, and the zip ties can be used to help restrain the attackers. I'd position my backpack so I can use it with my defender plate to protect my torso while charging the forward most hijacker. Finally, before separating with my spouse, I'd discuss with him how to exit our seats and the need for it to be fast and violent in hopes of taking the hijackers by surprise.

Once we're mobile, and our plan is in motion, I'd again make nonverbal cues to passengers I've identified as able to help, urging them to follow suit. Assuming we're successful and the hijackers are subdued and restrained, I'll scan the plane for additional potential risks, and have my spouse work with a flight attendant to gain communication to the cockpit. If the pilot or pilots are deemed safe, I'd relay pertinent information to him for communication to the ground for an emergency landing.

Nobody wants to fall victim to another Sept. 11 attack. If able, we'd all be willing to fight to ensure that doesn't happen again. In every instance the passengers will outnumber the hijackers, and if you're prepared, you have the ability to overpower them and take back control. In nearly every scenario, I'd make the conscious decision to violently fight back, because time is of the essence. It's common knowledge that the longer an incident lasts, the higher the likelihood a device will detonate and/or hijackers will gain access to the cockpit. I believe in being decisive and acting with speed, violence, and the element of surprise to overtake those seeking to inflict harm.

If you don't have the mental or physical wherewithal to survive, knowing whether or not a hijacker is on your plane is inconsequential. Taking accountability for ourselves and others is as important as acknowledging that harboring in place rarely has a positive result. At the end of the day, fighting for ourselves, fighting for others, and fighting for America is the only way to combat terrorism.

SURVIVAL EXPERT TIM MACWELCH'S APPROACH

Preparation

So how would one prepare for a flight where a hijacking might take place? It's not like the TSA would let you on the plane with all your tactical gear and a parachute. But thankfully, we can rely on more than mere luck for protection. Knowledge is one of our greatest assets, and while it might be unnerving, a great deal can be learned from studying the past few decades of airline bombing attempts and hijackings (particularly Sept. 11). While we're at it, I'd take some time to brush up on close-quarters hand-to-hand fighting, especially grappling and striking. I'd also read through the TSA-approved item lists at www.tsa.gov. Steel-toed boots are still allowed on planes, as well as leather belts with large metal buckles. Crippling kicks can be delivered with the boots. The belt can be used as a whip, or a restraint, as needed.

A tactical pen could be handy in a pinch, but why carry a little spike when you can still bring knitting needles in your carry on? The pen is cute, plus it writes on paper, but 14-inch hardwood or metal spikes can do a little more damage, most notably when shoved into a bad guy's ear canal. All you need is a ball of yarn with some half-knitted booties, and you have your excuse to carry them. Of course, the final decision rests with the TSA officer on whether an item is allowed through the checkpoint, but knitting needles and crochet hooks are on the "OK" list (for now).

To continue my preparation, I'd let the air crash statistics govern my selection of seating for me and any companions. This has little to do with terrorism, and more to do with the speed you could escape a downed aircraft. Generally speaking, the safest seats on an airplane are the exit row seats above each wing and the adjacent seating nearby. Choosing these seats will give you first crack at escape. Conversely, the worst seats (statistically) are the window seats furthest from the exits. You'd have to climb over seats, and possibly people, to get out. You'll also have to go further to get out of the plane. While we're on the topic of seat choice, the first few rows can be a gamble. Sure, you're close to the front exit, but these seats may be obliterated in a frontal crash. Whichever seat you choose (or get stuck with), make sure you know where the exits are located, even if you can't see them. In a smoke-filled cabin, you shouldn't be wondering which way to go.

One final prep would be communication. Your normal mobile phone won't be of much use at 30,000 feet, plus Airfones have pretty much become a thing of the past and are rarely found on airliners anymore. The altitude threshold for cell communication is roughly 10,000 feet in the air. And it's not just altitude that can limit your connection. Speed and "tower confusion" can also effect a cellular connection. Planes traveling more than 155 mph aren't likely places from which you can make a call. At great height and speed, your phone will try to link to many cell towers for signal, confusing both the phone and the network. While searching, the phone will emit a stronger signal, and the FAA says that this heightened signal can affect the aircraft's communications and navigational equipment.

Finally, when flying over rural areas, the towers will be fewer and farther between; and over the open ocean, there are no towers at all. So what's your viable option? Pick a flight and airline that has in-flight Wi-Fi, so you can still communicate using your mobile phones or devices, or bring a satellite phone. If you could get a message out with any device, there's no cut-and-dry answer for whom you should call. If the plane were low enough and slow enough to use your mobile phone and cell towers, you could certainly try 911. With a sat phone or working mobile, you could try the number for the airline you're flying. On Sept. 11, flight attendants Amy Sweeney and Betty Ong called the American Airlines office to relate that Flight 11 had been hijacked. You could also plan ahead by getting phone numbers for Homeland Security and the FBI.

On Site

Once we've boarded and gotten underway, we'd keep our seatbelts fastened. This isn't just to stay off the "naughty" list that the flight attendants are mentally compiling. Sometimes people die from injuries sustained during turbulence, and sadly, these broken necks and traumatic brain injuries could have been avoided by the simple use of a seatbelt. Roughly 60 people a year are injured from failing to wear their seatbelts on U.S. flights, and it's usually a patch of clear air turbulence that launches people from their seat. Yes, it's more comfortable to unshackle yourself, but do you take your seatbelt off in the car? No, you leave it on. And you should copy that behavior on a plane (except during in-flight bathroom breaks).

You've heard of the "wise old owl," right? The less he spoke, the more he heard. One simple safety protocol for my family is to limit our own talking in crowded places. Instead, we listen to what's going on around us. Of course, we'd look around a lot too, studying our surroundings as well as profiling the other passengers and even the crew. Our senses of smell can be valuable at certain times, too. As renowned tracker Freddy Osuna would say, "Weaponize your senses!" Plenty of people look nervous before flying, but unless potential hijackers have nerves of steel, they're likely to look extra nervous. Whether it's a copycat of Sept. 11, a hijacking for ransom, or some political statement, hijackers will have a lot going on internally, which may be visible externally.

Crisis

There has to be an evolutionary advantage to panic. Perhaps our remote ancestors survived unexpected attacks by bolting without hesitation and running in an unpredictable pattern. In our modern world of threats, panic isn't very valuable anymore. As soon as the hijackers are spotted, each and every passenger should remain calm, quiet, and compliant, no matter how badly you want to twist their heads off. In the initial moment, I would do my best to not fight or panic. Even if I or my spouse were grabbed or taken hostage, I'd endeavor to comply. With my eyes down and no talking, I'd listen intently and gather information. I'd also prepare myself mentally for the long haul.

If the hijacking were for ransom, the ordeal could carry on for days. So I'd find out everything I could about my adversaries and bide my time. By doing my best to not appear as a threat to them or a challenge to their plan, I can better determine what that plan actually is, then make the best choice. With the threat of a bomb onboard, a hasty action against suicidal terrorists could get everyone killed. If it's a hijacking for money, it's in the hijacker's best interest to keep everyone alive. If it's some other plan, we may be facing our final hours of life. In that grim setting, then we'll have to pick the right time and manner of attack. It might be worth the risk of communicating or coordinating with other passengers, if it could be done without alerting the attackers.

Since travel restrictions forbid firearms and knives on a plane, we'd have to get creative — improvising weapons, then attacking with surprise and savagery to retake control of the plane. Punch their throats, gouge their eyes, get them on the floor, and kick in their skull, or use a bootlace as a garrote. There are plenty of ways to fight without firearms or blades. If we managed to retake the cabin and the cockpit was never breached, the plane could make an emergency landing at the nearest airport. If the pilots are found dead, after retaking the plane, air traffic control may be able to walk someone through landing. There have been numerous successful landings by non-pilots, guided by air traffic controllers on the ground (many of whom have prior flight experience). And if you need to select a radio frequency for ATC, try 121.5 MHz (for civilian) or 243.0 MHz (for military use, also known as Military Air Distress), which air traffic control usually monitors.

CONCLUSION

There's nowhere to run and no place to hide on an airplane. You're caught up in the mix during any bad situation that happens in the air. Even if you sit still and don't make a sound, you're still an active participant in the events that are unfolding around you. That's right, choosing not to act is a choice, and making a choice is an action. You're still actively involved, and there are more actions to consider than just self-preservation that won't improve your chances.

When it comes to preparedness and survival, many of us start out prepping with a concern only for ourselves and our loved ones. But sometimes, as a person's survival knowledge grows, certain people realize that they need to help others survive as well. And this can be a crossroad in survival. Would you be able to sacrifice your own survival so that others might live? Some are willing to risk their life to save others, while some won't make that choice. We all want to believe that we're heroic, but you never really know for certain until you're in a situation that calls for that kind of sacrifice. We pray that none of us ever have to find out the hard way, whether we're craven or courageous underneath it all. ⁜

19

YOUR SUBWAY IS ATTACKED WITH CHEMICAL WEAPONS?

By Tim MacWelch
Illustrations by Joe Oesterle

The rhythmic vibrations of the subway car had almost lulled me back to sleep, even though the cabin was crowded with morning commuters. Strong scents wafted back and forth. The cologne and perfume of the passengers, as well as the countless cups of coffee, created a riot of scents assaulting my nose. I tried to ignore the odors in my groggy state, shutting my eyes and blocking everything out. It was working, until the passengers at the end of the subway car started screaming and a new smell caught my attention.

Nostrils stinging, I began to process the new information. My eyes opened as the stinging sensation traveled from my nose into the back of my throat. Scent can trigger memory, and as I fumbled for recognition, it hit me – bleach, it smelled like chlorine bleach! As frightened people began to rush past me, I wondered if this would be my last subway ride.

For this episode of RECOIL OFFGRID's "What If?" column, the editors gave us a nasty urban nightmare. We had to work our way through a terrorist attack in a crowded subway car. Continuing our new format, the editors asked us to explain what we would personally do in these emergency situations. This isn't some random character stumbling through a scenario, this is exactly what we'd do in a packed subway car full of panicked people and poisonous fumes. Try not to hold your breath while reading!

The Scenario

Situation type: Traveling to work
Your Crew: You
Location: New York City
Season: Spring
Weather: Rainy; high 47 degrees F, low 39 degrees F

The Setup

There's been recent news of intercepted communications that an unnamed terrorist group is threatening to attack a major New York City subway line with a chemical gas attack. It has been two months since the initial reports, but media coverage has subsided so you begin to assume the reports may have been exaggerated. While these current events are still unfolding, you're attending a daylong lecture at Columbia University.

Since you don't own a car and the subway is your usual method of travel, you board the subway near your home at the Bedford Park Station at around 7 a.m. on your way to the 116th Street station near the University. The train is full of the usual commuters and nothing seems out of place.

The Complication

After the train stops at the 155th Street station and then resumes its course, you notice a commotion in the car behind you. People start fleeing that car and entering yours, covering their mouths with their hands and clothing, acting like they're in pain and choking. At this moment, you notice a distinct acrid smell and yellow-green haze that, based on your research and knowledge, you believe to be chlorine gas.

You suspect your subway has been the victim of a chlorine gas attack/domestic terror incident. The conductor is obviously not aware of what's going on. What can you do? There may be multiple chemical gas attacks happening simultaneously in various cars; you're just not sure yet. What steps can you take to help protect yourself, save lives, and alert authorities?

SURVIVAL EXPERT TIM MACWELCH'S APPROACH

Prep

The sprawling public transportation system of New York City safely moves over 1-billion people a year, but with the threat of a terrorist attack in my mind I'd think long and hard whether to ride a subway car with that looming threat. Sure, more people die every year from automobile accidents than train wrecks and terrorist attacks combined — so much so that car accident fatalities rarely make the news. But that doesn't mean that I'd be eager to get into a crowded underground facility with limited exit strategies.

In my preparation, job one is to study the subway transit system. Learn its routes, its safety procedures, and escape routes, with particular attention to obvious bottlenecks or other points that would hinder evacuation.

My second specific piece of preparation for this type of threat would be to research previous terrorist attacks on subway cars and trains. In 2004 in Madrid, terrorists set off 10 backpack bombs on the commuter rail network, killing 191 people and wounding more than 1,800. One year later, a sarin gas attack occurred in a Tokyo subway. This attack was perpetrated by the Aum Shinrikyo (Supreme Truth) cult, a group of doomsday fanatics with thousands of followers all over Japan. Their insane leader, Shoko Asahara, gained access to the wealth of his followers and employed a chemist to create the sarin gas weapons that killed 12 people and injured more than 5,000. While the motives of these nut jobs are part of the research, their methods would be my primary area of focus.

My next job would be to research respiratory devices. Many of us include simple masks (like an N95 mask) in our everyday preps, but it's largely useless in a gas attack. Vapors, fumes, and gases go right through the mask — just like the air we breathe. And even though N95 masks will filter out anthrax and the cough droplets that transport the flu virus, you'll need something made for gases to remove them from the air you'll breathe.

One commonly available filter that can be found at most home improvement stores and attached to half masks or full face masks is the 3M Multi Gas/Vapor Cartridge (filter #60926). This affordable cartridge can attach to a variety of respirator masks and remove chlorine, hydrogen chloride, chlorine dioxide, plus a number of other nasty chemicals. Just remember that a mask is only as effective as the surface it seals against. Mustache, no problem. Soul patch, OK. But full beards keep the rubber mask from sealing against your skin.

As my final prep for close-quarters travel on a subway, I'd want a city-friendly EDC kit. This assortment of everyday carry gear would include a whistle, a flashlight, a first-aid kit, and a small pry bar. It wouldn't hurt to have an element that prepares you for a possible chemical attack too (besides the respirator). A product called Reactive Skin Decontamination Lotion is now available to civilians. RSDL is the only decontaminant cleared by the U.S. Food and Drug Administration to remove or neutralize chemical warfare agents such as tabun, sarin, soman, cyclohexyl sarin, VR, VX, mustard gas, and T-2 toxin. It's a simple little packet of lotion-like neutralizer. Each kit comes with instructions and a training product, so you can get a feel for it through realistic practice. It also comes with a packet of decontaminant for one person, which removes the chemical agent from the skin in a single step. It won't help with our chlorine gas scenario, but against other agents — it's better to have it and not need it ….

On Site

After deciding to take the subway, my first safety precaution would be to choose what I perceive to be the safest car on the train. But which car should I choose?

Conventional wisdom would lead us to believe that the front and rear cars of a subway train (or other type of train) are the most dangerous places in a crash. The front car would take the brunt of the damage in the event of a head-on collision, with the rear car taking damage if the train were rear-ended. But a terrorist attack is a very different event compared to a train wreck. In the event of a terrorist attack, the most crowded car would likely be the most tempting target.

Just one example of this sinister planning can be seen in the London subway bombings of July 7, 2005. In this attack, three suicide bombers detonated explosives onboard subway trains during the busy morning commute. While a number of people were also killed and injured that morning in a double-decker bus bombing perpetrated by a fourth group member, the subway portion of the attack killed 39 people and wounded hundreds more. Each of the three subway bombers sat or stood near the train doors, where the highest concentration of passengers would be located.

From my perspective, the least populated car is the least desirable target for someone intent on causing mass casualties. Once onboard the undesirable subway car, I'd take history's lesson to heart and stay away from the double doors in the car. Sure, this would typically result in more walking, but that's a small price to pay for a greater margin of safety. And whether I was in the subway in NYC or in a tube in any other part of the world, I'd find the emergency exits and alarms.

Once I've chosen my seat on the unpopular car (story of my life), I'd still remain vigilant for suspicious activity. In a less populated car, there would be fewer people to observe for any odd behavior or packages. This quieter area might be chosen as a setup or staging area, where a terrorist could potentially prepare to launch an attack.

The Crisis

In the midst of a chlorine gas attack on a subway, with the circumstances still unclear, the first thing I'd do is use the passenger alarm or passenger emergency intercoms to notify the train crew that something was seriously wrong. I'd have scouted out the location of these when boarding. Once the commotion started and I smelled a noxious gas, that's the time to hit the "panic button," though I'd want to avoid actual panic internally and avoid the frightened throngs of people that may be rushing my way. I could also try 911 on my phone, but there are no guarantees with mobile phone reception in a tunnel. It's also possible that the systems that support the phones would be flooded with calls during a crisis.

As for my position, I wouldn't want to be far from an emergency exit, but at the same time I wouldn't want to be in a spot where a crowd could crush me up against a wall or unopened door.

I definitely wouldn't try to get down low toward the floor. First, gaseous weapons wouldn't necessarily rise like smoke, and secondly, I don't want to be trampled.

Once I sounded the alarm, I wouldn't expect the train to stop between stations. If I had a multi-gas half-mask, I'd don the respirator and hide the mask by pulling up my shirt. I wouldn't want desperate people to rip the mask from my face. With the mask covered by clothing, I'd look like everyone else.

Without a multi-gas respirator, I'd have few choices for protection. I could use clothing as a filter and also attempt to limit my breathing. I could also try to move to an area with clearer air. If the agent gives any visual cues, such as dust, haze, or color — you could move the other way. Once the car stops (on route or at a station), I'd get out and seek medical attention. I may not immediately notice signs or symptoms of poisoning, so outside help is definitely warranted.

PHYSICIAN AND INSTRUCTOR LORENZO PALADINO'S APPROACH

Prep

Chlorine gas forms hydrochloric acid on contact when it's inhaled. Its victims suffocate to death from fluid accumulating in their damaged lungs, and escape is difficult when afflicted with burning, tearing eyes. There has been increased chatter of credible threats, and you know the subway has been targeted before. Preparing for your commute under these circumstances isn't being overly paranoid, it's the responsible thing to do.

Packing for the commute: Many discreet tactical bags, eschew an overtly military look, while still featuring plenty of rapid-access pouches, MOLLE, and Velcro in the interior to hold all your essential gear. While many are primarily designed to facilitate the quick draw of a firearm, in this situation having instant access to the key contents such as those below can be just as life saving.

⟩ Flashlight. In a confined space, a little bit of smoke or gas can severely limit your visibility. Also, yellow/amber lenses seem to reflect less (or appear to reflect less) than standard white light on particulates in the air (smoke and fog).

⟩ A cell phone. Remember, many phones have a flashlight feature. While not as effective as a tactical flashlight, it's another resource. Although your phone probably has a digital compass and GPS, the only directions you need to know are a route away from the source and up the stairs.

⟩ Backup power. A charger that's rugged, drop-proof, water-resistant, and has a built-in light can serve as an emergency backup to your primary light. Redundancy is always good. Aside from your phone, it can also power a rechargeable flashlight, should the situation get prolonged.

⟩ Knife or multitool. Assuming local laws permit carrying such an item, something sturdy that can pry and has a glass breaker is ideal. The glass on the trains is heavy duty and won't shatter as easily as a car windshield. They also have a plastic film that'll keep the glass in place to avoid injuring others when blown out. For these reasons, they'll require a forceful shove or kick after being shattered. You may have to kick through broken glass, and in the worst case, walk on the tracks.

⟩ Footwear. I'd wear a trail running shoe that's sturdy enough for climbing but comfortable to run fast in.

⟩ Gloves. Another carry item to consider is heavy work gloves. These will come in handy in case you have to hold onto a windowpane studded with broken glass and for climbing over debris once the train stops.

⟩ Bottled water mixed with baking soda (sodium bicarbonate). This mixture can be used to flush your face and wash out eyes if they're tearing and getting blurry.

⟩ Respiratory protection. A CBRN (Chemical Biological Radiological Nuclear) mask isn't as common or easy to carry as the above items, but there really is no safe solution that can be improvised. There are historic accounts of soldiers using urine-soaked socks to combat chlorine gas in WWI. This doesn't work well in actual practice (not enough ammonia) or logistically on a subway with only seconds of warning.

In a pinch, you could pour the water and bicarbonate solution over a thick cotton rag and attempt to breathe through it. You'd probably still get sick, but maybe not as sick as having nothing. Wool shouldn't be used as it's too difficult to breathe through when wet. Another problem is that holding the rag tightly to your nose and mouth would tie up your hands, impeding your escape.

⟩ Emergency escape hoods. These are a more practical alternative to carrying a bulky full gas mask on a commute all the time. More importantly, when an attack happens, you'll have little to no warning and will need to resort to something you can deploy and don quickly. Emergency escape hoods are one-time-use head coverings with built-in filters and an elastic neck seal. It's as fast and simple as opening the wrapper and pulling it over your head. They're packaged small enough to fit in your bag, briefcase, or in a pouch on your belt.

Emergency hoods provide chemical air filtration for 15 to 60 minutes, enough to escape a situation. They should deploy in one step, without straps to adjust. You should look for hoods that are CBRN-rated and "NIOSH-approved" (National Institute for Occupational Safety and Health). The Avon NH 15 and RSG CE 200 series are a few models that fit this need nicely.

Like all emergency equipment, you should train and familiarize yourself with their use before you use them in a real situation.

For even more portability, rapid deployment, and a quarter of the cost, Scott Safety has an alternative – the Emergency Escape Mouth Bit Respirator. It's like the mouthpiece of a snorkel with a filter attached, so it won't protect your eyes and face. You could put on swim or ski goggles if using this option.

It's important to point out that gas masks and hoods filter air but don't create oxygen. In a scenario of a confined space where a poison gas is displacing atmospheric gases, this deadly fact should be kept in mind. A solution to this and alternate option to an emergency hood is to carry a small portable air supply. The aviation industry uses the HEED (Helicopter Emergency Egress Device) and the diving industry uses a version called Spare Air. It's basically a small scuba tank the size of the water bottle you carry to the gym, so it'll fit in your commute bag. It supplies approximately 30 breaths or up to 3 minutes of air. Considering the average subway stops are two minutes apart, it should give you what you need to get out.

❭ Swim or ski goggles. These are useful if you don't opt for the escape hood, or as a backup to it. They can help to minimize burning to your eyes from the irritating gases, so you can preserve your vision while looking for an escape. Mucous membranes absorb faster than skin, so they may decrease the possible surface area for entry while protecting your eyes from burns and blinding. It's not what will kill you, but being blind in the subway might.

I wouldn't carry a chemical suit as it takes minutes to get into and tape up. Many aren't available commercially anyway without special certifications and substantial training to use properly. It's impractical to don in a subway car full of panicking people and will waste precious time. Suiting up can take several minutes, whereas escaping can take seconds.

Know your environment: The NYC subway system maintains two separate fleets with at least three different model cars. The dimensions of subway cars vary from 51 to 75 feet in length and 8 to 10 feet in width. Know how many steps this translates to for you. On average it'll be approximately 22 to 32 steps in length, depending on the car. I do a similar calculation in airplanes, counting steps from the entrance to my seat. I also count headrests with my hand.

In a dark or smoke-filled airplane, you may lose track of steps because you're taking longer strides or jumping over things, so the number of seats you can touch by extending your hand while running is a nice tactile backup. You can also make it a game during your morning commute to count how many stairs and steps from turnstile to platform edge. This will give you an idea of the average distance you'll need to cover to reach the relative safety of outdoors.

On Site

Sit at the front of the compartment by the door between the cars. This door is easy to open (even when the train is moving), doesn't require the train to be stopped, and doesn't have to be pried open to escape the compartment. In a panic, most people will stampede and crowd the exit doors to the platform; not many will think of escaping through the door in between cars if the train is stopped.

If the train is moving, people will quickly realize your door is their only escape, so be prepared for the rush toward you and possibly getting crushed. Being between cars while the train is moving is dangerous, but when the train comes to a stop you can jump to the platform from there. If you can, continue into the next car and keep moving further and further away from the attack, putting more distance between you and ground zero.

Why the front end of the compartment as opposed to the rear? It increases your likelihood of being upstream from an incident if it occurs. If gas is escaping a stricken car and spreading to other compartments, in a moving train it'll spread primarily backward, pushed by the wind currents, not forward and up wind in the direction of motion. You want to get upwind.

Crisis

When it comes to communicating for help and alerting authorities, the NYC subway system offers Wi-Fi and cellular service in all its stations. In a simple gas attack without structural damage from an explosion or collapse, the system will likely still be functional. Texts require less bandwidth than cellular calls. Oftentimes, a signal too weak for a successful phone call will still be sufficient to bounce around and eventually complete a text or post to social media.

If signal isn't good enough to call for help, you can alert authorities using these means. The NYPD and many large city law enforcement agencies have social media accounts such as Twitter and Facebook. The use of social media to alert and contact for help has been proven in disasters before. You should move toward the very front car of the train, placing the largest distance possible between you and the gas release and alerting the train operator to what is happening. They can radio the authorities.

If you're stuck in a compartment that is gassed and can't get out for whatever reason (doors jammed, crowd density, etc.), use your glass breaker on the windows and start ventilating to dilute the gas. This is where you'll be thankful that you always put your EDC gear in the same place in your bag every time and have rehearsed grabbing each item without looking. You need to find that glass breaker in low visibility, heavy smoke, or through tearing eyes. Instruct other passengers in the car to "ventilate" the train too.

Keep in mind you don't want to stick your body too far out of the broken window if the train is in motion, as you can get hit by a passing column. Stand on seats or climb up a pole if you can. The gas is heavier than air, so the higher you go, the less the concentration of the chemical agent.

This is the opposite of the crawl you're taught to avoid smoke when escaping from a fire. The reality is that this principle works best when we're dealing with greater heights, such as going up another floor or two, not so much the 2 feet you get by standing on a seat, but it may buy you a few seconds as you survey your escape route and break glass. If you were out of the train, getting to a higher level by stairs should definitely result in a noticeable change in concentration gradient of the gas.

Though getting away from the gas is the single most important key to survival, if stopped in a tunnel, leaving the train and heading out has its own hazards. There's also the danger of being hit by another train or coming into contact with the electrical supply and being electrocuted. Also, the tracks are the lowest point in the station and that's where the gas accumulates. Many of the tunnels are several blocks long. You'll have to weigh these dangers and decide if it's worth the risk.

Trains are frequent targets for terrorists. Escaping the epicenter of the attack to the outside is the key. Dilution is your friend – get to higher ground, as most chemical gases sink.

CONCLUSION

Terrorism does part of its job when people are harmed, but it also succeeds when people are afraid to go about their normal lives. Terror attacks instill people with fear, in addition to causing physical harm to people, systems, and places. This threat may cause some people to go about their business with a sense of unease. It may keep people from traveling to crowded places or visiting certain cities that may be considered a likely target. Or it may leave people paralyzed with paranoia.

So how do we find a balance between keeping ourselves and our families safe and walking boldly through life? Terrorists win when good people cower in fear, but this doesn't mean we should be foolhardy in our defiance and willingly place ourselves in harm's way to prove how brave we are. There's always a middle road we can travel, avoiding the greatest risks while exercising reasonable caution. And the key to staying on this middle road is situational awareness. During your daily routine, pay attention to people, places, situations, and your instincts. Be vigilant as you go about your day. Transform from a nation of sheep into a nation of sheepdogs, ever watching for the wolves that would try to harm the helpless. ⠿

20

YOUR CRUISE SHIP IS HIJACKED?

By Tim MacWelch
Illustrations by Lonny Chant

The ISIS flags. I had seen them many times on the news and in magazines. The black-and-white flags speak of God and his messenger, but the deeds done underneath them are never holy. Countless times, I'd seen pictures of this flag from the safety of my home, but this was the first time I had seen them with my own eyes. Fluttering from poles affixed to fast-moving skiffs, the black flags signaled these men were no ordinary pirates. They weren't just coming to rob us of our possessions or hijack the ship for ransom — they were coming to take our lives.

For this stomach-churning installment of RECOIL OFFGRID's *What If?*, the authors are continuing the new story style — explaining what they would do if they were personally caught up in the emergency situation. This oceanic survival story isn't some nautical nonsense about people with no survival background, muddling through an emergency. This is how we would personally plan for an international trip, and how we would react when things go horribly wrong. From our skills and survival tactics, to our plans and reactions, we hope you learn even more from this change in the format, and we hope you never need to deal with a situation like this.

The Scenario

Situation type: Ocean liner hijacking
Your Crew: You and your spouse, ship's crew, and approximately 150 other passengers
Location: Horn of Africa, Gulf of Aden
Season: Summer in the southern hemisphere (during our winter season)
Weather: Clear; high 100 degrees F, low 80 degrees F

The Setup

You've been saving for years to take a dream cruise with your spouse that lasts 44 days. It disembarks in Barcelona and makes stops in the Mediterranean before venturing through the Suez Canal into the Red Sea. It then proceeds to several more stops along the Arabian Sea and Bay of Bengal before reaching its final destination in Singapore. You plan to have an unforgettable summer vacation together to celebrate your anniversary and see parts of the world you've never been to before.

The Complication

Approximately 20 days into the cruise when you're nearing the Horn of Africa, your vessel succumbs to a coordinated hijacking by several skiffs. You're awakened around sunrise to an announcement. The captain comes on the loudspeaker, telling everyone that there are "unfriendly" vessels on the starboard and port sides and to stay in our rooms. The plink of bullets on the side was very noticeable.

You peer out of your stateroom window, and see a skiff flying the ISIS flag and a pirate with a rocket-propelled-grenade launcher. He takes aim in your direction and fires. You see the flash and dive to the other side as the rocket detonates in a stateroom two decks above your own. The pirates, four or five in each of the 25-foot boats, continue firing and try to board the ship. The captain then orders all passengers to assemble in an interior lounge for safety, and the ship accelerates in what appears to be an attempt to ram or outrun the assailants. While getting dressed and readying to leave your stateroom for the lounge with your spouse, the ship unexpectedly slows down.

You realize the ship has been boarded. Being that this is ISIS and not pirates, this is the worst possible scenario as the motivation is likely not ransom, but hostages and executions. There's no way to tell how many total hijackers there are, or if more are coming.

The New Plan

If you were home you'd call 911 and grab your gun. But you're in an ocean liner off the coast of countries that are poverty-stricken, generally unfriendly toward Americans, and your mobile phone has no reception. How do you deal with the hijacking? Do you hide? Attempt to communicate an SOS somehow? Do you take on the hijackers? Try to escape in a lifeboat?

FORMER FEDERAL OFFICER HANA BILODEAU'S APPROACH

Prep

Most vacations don't span over 44 days with multiple international destinations, but because of the uniqueness of this trip, I'd divide my pre-trip preparation into three categories: legal documents, intelligence on countries visited, and ship facts. Planning for a vacation in advance will hopefully help navigate any issues that may arise later.

Legal documentation: Before departing, I'd check with the cruise company to see what legal documentation they require to embark and disembark the ship. I'd then check our passports to ensure the issue date exceeds six months prior to the ship departure date and that expiration dates remain legal throughout the entire stay abroad. This is due to the six-month validity passport rule. Most countries won't permit a traveler to enter the country unless the passport is set to expire at least six months after the final leg of travel and was issued at least six months prior to arrival. Next is compiling a list of stopover destinations the ship will make throughout the trip. Using this list I also check the U.S. State Department website to see which countries require additional Visas or documentation to enter.

Once I have all the necessary government travel documentation, I make multiple paper copies of the documents in the event our passport is lost or stolen during the trip, so we will at least have some form of identification. I would be sure to carry one paper copy of my passport with me at all times and store each additional copy in different, secure locations while traveling.

I would also schedule a pre-trip doctor visit to obtain any necessary vaccinations and documentation thereof based on area of travel. Due to the fact that medical facilities will be limited at best, I would also purchase short-term international travel insurance that would cover any medical expenses outside the U.S. for a minimum of two days and a maximum of three years, and up to a million dollars in coverage. I'd keep copies of this coverage, vaccination documentation, and my U.S. insurance card along with our passports and other vital information.

Intelligence gathering: I'd first buy a paper map showing areas to be traveled and keep it in my luggage. I would also spend some time researching each country we'll visit and or travel through during our 44 days at sea. This would include checking the U.S. State Department's Consular Information Sheets for each country and current travel advisories for this part of the world, which is also on the State Department website. Next, I'd also familiarize myself with the culture, religions, and customs for each location to learn what formalities that, if not followed, could disrupt a peaceful visit.

Other contacts I'd want info on are the closest American resources for each international waterway that our ship passes through. Lastly, find contact information for the FBI and the U.S. Coast Guard for any of the U.S. ports as well as the U.S. embassy and local law enforcement contacts for all international ports of call. I would make a list of each and also make paper copies of each and store them accordingly.

Utilizing the cruise company's website I would gather facts on the ship to include:
> **Year Built:** 2011
> **Year Refurbished:** 2016
> **Gross Tonnage:** 66,084
> **Length:** 784.95 feet
> **Beam:** 105.646 feet
> **Maximum Draught:** 24 feet
> **Stabilizers:** Yes
> **Cruising Speed:** 20 knots
> **Guest Decks:** 11
> **Total Decks:** 16
> **Electric Power or Voltage:** 110, 220 AC
> **Guest Capacity:** 1,250 (Double Occupancy)
> **Staff Size:** 800
> **Guest to Staff Ratio:** 1.567 to 1
> **Nationality of Officers:** European
> **Nationality of Staff:** International
> **Country of Registry:** Marshall Islands

I'd also research the on-ship security and procedures, specifically noting if they have a security force and onboard holding facility. I would then identify and make a copy of the ship's evacuation plan. Next I'd check the cruise liner's prohibited items list. Then onto gathering info on the ship's infirmary to see what type of medical emergencies they're equipped to handle and their treatment protocol if a passenger needs higher medical attention.

Aside from the aforementioned documents, my emergency-preparedness packing list would include the following if allowed onboard:

> First-aid kit
> Flashlight
> Leatherman tool
> Knife with blade under 4 inches
> Battery-operated portable radios for ship communication if there's no cellular service
> Spare batteries for radios and phones
> Battery packs, cell phone charger (if international is not part of the cell plan, it's an additional cost, you can either use your phone on roaming or purchase an additional international plan).
> Electrical conversion and outlet adapter for each country
> Laptop, charger, and accessories
> Air card for internet and phone card (an air card is a cellular modem that attaches to the USB port of a computer and serves as a gateway to the internet antennas to improve cell reception)

On Site

Once onboard, first on the agenda would be checking into our stateroom, identifying where our stateroom is located in relation to the other important parts of the ship, and getting acclimated with its amenities. This includes unpacking and securing our personal documents. Next I'd develop an emergency plan for my spouse and I in case we're separated to include multiple meeting locations and modes of communication. We'd then want to familiarize ourselves with the ship's layout. Before doing so, stop by the information desk and grab a couple copies of the ship's map/layout.

With map in hand we'd head off to visit the most pertinent locations so we're better acquainted with where they are in relation to our cabin and the quickest ways to access them if needed during an emergency. These locations include:

> Customer service or information center
> Ship security office
> Infirmary
> Locations of fire extinguishers
> Locations of life vests and rafts
> Kitchen
> Captain's quarters
> Engine/electrical room

Crisis

And just like that, the captain makes an announcement that "unfriendly" vessels are on the port side of the ship and that passengers should assemble in the interior lounge for safety. Once confirmed that the ocean liner has actually been taken hostage, immediate action is imperative. Based on the history of ISIS, human life is of the utmost concern. Once the passengers have gathered in the interior lounge I'd spearhead organizing a mission plan.

First on the agenda is identifying any able-bodied passengers, preferably with military, law enforcement, or leadership experience. Establishing an operable militia of ship patrons to combat the hijackers is imperative. Organization and quick decisive action on behalf of the passengers is necessary to prevent the hijackers from becoming too embedded in the ship. Keeping the hijackers at bay and out of the interior lounge is essential.

Next, I'd ask all passengers to pool anything that could be used as weapons. Things that could be useful are kitchen utensils and knives, large blunt objects, fire hoses, extinguishers, rope, etc. Next is setting up a perimeter and using the ship's infrastructure as protection. One could do this by identifying things that could be used as cover/concealment and formulating a safe ground away form the threat.

Having a leader amongst the passengers is essential to maintain order, security, and communication. It's important that all passengers understand and agree to the plan of attack, convincing them that compromising that plan could disrupt the security of the group as a whole and cost the lives of everyone. The goal is to have all passengers in agreement. If that doesn't work through negotiations (strength in numbers), the passengers who refuse to conform will be separated from the majority to make sure there isn't internal hostility.

Once the militia has been established, it's all about dividing and conquering areas of concern. I'd take the most experienced passengers and send them to locate the ship's security forces to obtain any weapons kept onboard for such incidents. If possible, combine efforts with the security forces. Then it's on to locate and protect the captain, the engine room, and radio transmitting equipment.

If able to locate the captain, the goal is to immediately contact the U.S. Coast Guard, the closest embassy, and friendlies so an evacuation plan can be immediately implemented. The captain should be the person on board with the most working knowledge of the ship itself, so securing his or her safety is important. If there's firepower locked and stored on the ship, the captain is usually the only one with access. Make sure to provide as much pertinent information to the rescue efforts as possible, such as the number of passengers and location, estimated number of hijackers, and how and where the boat was compromised.

If possible, I'd send out another team out to identify the location and number of hijackers on board. Their secondary mission would be attempting to secure food and water. Being in the middle of the ocean, in the summer, and with extreme temperatures, hydration may quickly become an issue.

Success in this situation is reliant on remaining vigilant as a group, being prepared to fight, having a plan, keeping the hijackers at bay and maintaining strength in numbers until rescue efforts arrive.

SURVIVAL EXPERT TIM MACWELCH'S APPROACH

Prep

To get ready for a trip of this duration, here are four areas where I wouldn't skimp.

Hit the Books: Research is an important aspect of preparedness, and I'd take my time studying for our trip. From the areas we'd stop to the areas we'd be traveling through, I'd learn about the people and their customs. I'd also take a hard look at the cruise company and the ship itself. Learning about restricted items would be vital, as well as my communication options and the predicted weather for the season. And of course, I'd be worried about the troubled waters we'd be sailing through. I'd read up on the Somali pirates off the coast of Africa and the pirates on the Indian Ocean. Modern piracy is still big business, and some estimates put the worldwide loss at $16 billion per year.

Get a Satellite Phone: Communication can be critical in a survival situation, so buying or renting a satellite phone could be the most essential expense in the preparation for our trip. I'd do my homework on the models, features, and even the satellite networks. Just like your mobile phone, certain networks have better coverage in certain areas. A cheap sat phone may be found as low as $300, while a great one may cost $1,300. These higher-end units (like Iridium) have a greater number of satellites in the network. This offers the user global coverage, even in polar regions. In either case, it's a small price to pay for a greater margin of safety in the remote corners of the world.

Set Up a Contact: We'd definitely establish a regular contact at home. This is someone to check in with who'd have our itinerary and instructions on what to do if we became uncommunicative. Just as it wouldn't be smart to head out into the wilderness without telling anyone where you were going or when you'd be back, it's not too bright to travel without checking in with someone. A trusted family member or friend would be our contact. I'd also reach out to the U.S. State Department and create a contact there.

Pack for the Trip: For a month-and-a-half voyage through countries great and small, I'd bring the clothing and footwear you'd expect a tourist to wear. And everything we'd be legally allowed to bring. We'd also pack lighting such as headlamps and flashlights with spare batteries. A charger for the sat phone is a must as well. Cash in small bills would be a must, in U.S. dollars and other common currencies, though the foreign bills would be easier to pick up abroad than at home. Stateside currency exchanges aren't likely to have currency from every country. Tactical pens, belts with heavy buckles, and other simple travel-friendly tools for self-defense might be the best we'd be allowed to take. In some places, even pocketknives are forbidden. Double check local regulations on items such as these as well as the ship's list of any prohibited items.

On Site

After the long flight, and once we'd finally reached Barcelona, it'd be a great relief to finally board the cruise ship and settle into our room. Before we board the ship we'd get some bottled water and nonperishable food to stock our cabin. While this may seem strange to ship staff, you never know when there can be a hiccup in your food and water supply, even on a hedonistic cruise ship.

Then, after a bit of rest, we'd take a look around to get familiar with the vessel, looking for areas where we could potentially hide or fortify. Any weapons from the ship, conventional or improvised, would be on my mind as well, since we could bring very little for self-defense with us. I'd ask for a tour of the kitchen, if allowed, just to see where the big knives are kept. And once our voyage is underway, we'd see some sights with our group at each port of call, do a little shopping, and add a few more foods to our personal food pantry.

Crisis

Here's the part where we find out if there's such a thing as a "no win" scenario. With the ISIS flags flying, I'll expect no quarter to be given in the coming altercation. These mass murderers are typically religious zealots who cannot be swayed by logic or reason. And it would be likely that they should have no qualms about massacring every man, woman, and child onboard. I'd expect a distress call to have gone out as soon as the unfriendly craft approached the ship, but there's no guarantee that this occurred. This force may have an insider who could disable communications right before the attack. While it's likely that the cruise ship company has a standard operating procedure for pirates boarding the ship to get ransom money, the company probably doesn't have a game plan for religious nuts trying to kill every person on the ship.

I'd go along with the captain's orders to gather in a central spot as the ship tried to speed away from assailants who were firing on us from a small craft, but, with the small cruise ship lurching to a halt, I'd have to make a very dire decision. Would I join the group or avoid them? Rushing down the halls, bumping into uninformed people, I wouldn't know if the ship had stopped because it was under new command or it stopped because the captain had been instructed to stop and negotiate if pirates boarded. Whichever is true, these hijackers flew flags that showed they weren't the typical impoverished pirates looking for money. And the passengers gathered in one place would make a spectacularly easy shooting gallery.

With the sudden stopping of the ship, I wouldn't gather with the other passengers. I'd treat this like the active shooter scenario it is, and embrace the "run, hide, fight" mantra. If no distress call went out, it could be hours (or even days) before the maritime security forces in the area respond to the attack. And in just a few hours, dozens of motivated men could have every single one of our heads in a pile on the ship's deck.

So what's on a cruise ship that could act as a weapon? You're not going to go up against an AK-47-wielding attacker with a rolled-up magazine or a butter knife you stole from the captain's table. And with fire axes in short supply on the modern cruise ship, your choices are limited. So in this grim scenario, the best weapon at hand would be the weapon sitting in a drawer in our stateroom – the satellite phone.

We would barricade ourselves in the room and start calling our contacts. After notifying the State Department contacts we'd made before the trip, and making sure that the message would get to the multinational maritime task force for the region, we'd prepare to fight back if the door was breached. Perhaps some unruly passengers would buy some time for the anti-piracy task force of the region to organize, mobilize, and arrive on site. Using speed, surprise, and intense violence – we might be able to wrestle one rifle from an unskilled attacker. Or perhaps we could pick off a straggler who might be searching the ship alone. Then we'd finally have a proper way to fight back. Either way, I'm not dying on my knees.

CONCLUSION

In the past, piracy on the East African coast was much worse than it is today. Thanks to years of multinational naval operations, there's been a major reduction of piracy in the Indian Ocean. But the narrow sea passage in the Gulf of Aden has been favored by pirates for centuries, and in recent years, pirates have targeted scores of commercial vessels there (in 2008, more than 100 ships were attacked). This list of attacks includes several incidents involving cruise ships and private yachts.

Having done my homework before this trip, I would've known that in March of 2017, two-dozen pirates in two skiffs attacked and hijacked an oil tanker just off the northernmost town in Somalia. It was the first hijacking of a large commercial vessel since 2012. After boarding, the armed men turned off the ship's tracking system and demanded a ransom. A subsequent firefight with the local maritime police force and some tense negotiations ended the hijacking without ransom (largely because the pirates were afraid to get on the wrong side of the powerful Somali businessmen who had hired the ship).

So what's the takeaway here? Well, if you want to travel the world, you have to accept the fact that you'll be facing some serious risks and hazards. And while most trips end happily enough, some do not. Do plenty of research before you head out into the world. The U.S. State Department website is loaded with sound travel advice, and more importantly, travel advisories and warnings about dangerous areas. Criminal activity against travelers, terrorist activity, military conflicts, and many other hazards are explained and updated on their website: http://travel.state.gov. Give it a look. And although a cruise liner that goes slowly and close to shore off the coast of Somalia has certain risks, the potential for hijacking exists everywhere. ⁑

21

YOU'RE ON A TRAIN WITH A SUSPECTED SUICIDE BOMBER?

By Tim MacWelch

Illustrations by Sarah Watanabe-Rocco

It wasn't my call to make, and this wasn't some goofy action flick on TV. There were hundreds of lives at risk if the rat's nest of wires I glimpsed was actually a bomb. And if it was an explosive device, and if I sent a train attendant toward him, I knew that my sweet wife, everyone onboard, and I would likely find out if there was a God that morning.

My mind reeled with the weight of my predicament, and my stomach was close to losing its contents. I was absolutely sure I saw something to be worried about — and it was my job to say something. But if he really was a bomber and someone spooked him, we were all dead. For a second or two, I tried to figure out which end of the train would put us farthest away from the man, but I tossed aside the idea of escape. There was no escape on a high-speed train in a tight-fitting tunnel under the English Channel. So I rallied my courage, discussed the plan with my wife, and wasted no more time with indecision — since these might be the last few minutes of our lives.

In this gripping installment of *What If?*, we've been asked to face a disturbingly realistic scenario: What would you do if you and your spouse were on the same train as a suicide bomber?

To get different takes on this modern menace, RECOIL OFFGRID asked three survival writers to build a story from their own perspectives and experiences. For this installment, we have Erik Lund (a federal law enforcement agent with a bevy of tactical and survival experience) and Hakim Isler (a wilderness expert, martial arts instructor, and former psychological-operations sergeant with the U.S. Army). And for a third point of view, I've been a professional survival instructor for more than 20 years, and I've written multiple *New York Times*-bestselling survival manuals.

Scenarios like this make me wonder if there are such things as "no win" scenarios. Hope you're not reading this on a train.

The Scenario

Situation type: Potential suicide bombing
Your Crew: You and your wife, Sara
Location: The Channel Tunnel, from France to England
Season: Early summer
Weather: Partly sunny; mid-70 degrees F

The Setup

You're a fit male in your late 30s named Johnny, married to an equally fit wife named Sara. Living in North Carolina, you both own an online business selling protein bars marketed to outdoorsy types. You've run, hiked, and traversed almost every major trail in the eastern United States that doesn't require an ice ax and mountain-climbing rope. It's time to expand. You head to France, where you hope to see the sights, hit a few trails, and then take the underground Channel Tunnel (or Chunnel) to England for more adventures.

The Complication

At the Chunnel station in Calais, France, you and your wife enter the high-speed train looking for your assigned seats in standard class amongst the sea of tourists, Britons going home, and French headed for England. That's when you notice something: while everyone's wearing T-shirts and jeans or shorts, there's a man wearing a three-quarter-length brown jacket. Not exactly seasonal. Plus, he seems confused, or maybe anxious, as he looks for his seat.

Just as he finds his row, a rather large woman accidentally bumps him, briefly exposing what's underneath the jacket: a vest filled with an intricate web of wires and plastic bottles. Is this a prank? Or some kind of emergency drill, you think. *No, I have to treat this like what it looks like: a suicide bomber.* He quickly covers up his jacket, hoping no one noticed. No one does. Except for you.

The New Plan

As the train glides on the tracks roughly 150 feet under the seafloor, you have about 23 miles and 30 minutes to figure out a plan. Will this terrorist explode himself (and destroy this train) halfway through this engineering marvel called the Chunnel or wait until we've stopped at Folkestone on the English side? Or maybe he'll do it when we reach London to make a political statement in the heart of the United Kingdom? And how the hell did he get the vest on board? It doesn't matter. You whisper your plans to Sara and start steeling your resolve.

FEDERAL AGENT ERIK LUND'S APPROACH

I felt a small little punch on my arm and looked over at my wife, Sara. "Hellooo ... come back to Earth, spaceman Spiff," she said. I smiled back and apologized for being distracted, but my mind was still trying to make sense of what I'd just seen. It sure as hell looked like a bomb in some sort of suicide vest, but I couldn't be positive. My eyes tracked the man to his seat, while I tried not to look like I was watching him.

The man continued to stumble around, taking extra care to not let anyone incidentally touch him. The man finally found his seat, four rows up from mine on the other side of the aisle.

I whispered ever so quietly in Sara's ear: "I think the man in front of us is wearing a suicide bomber vest." Sara pulled back with a smile on her face until our eyes locked. We had been together long enough that she recognized the look in my eyes; this was no joke. She leaned back in and started to ask a question. I stopped her and motioned to our phones.

I texted her the man's description and seat location, followed by what I had seen. She looked freaked, but took a breath. "What do you want to do?" she texted me.

Over the next few texts I laid out my plan. I wanted to get a picture of the man, and then we would move forward on the train to the lounge car. When we found train officials, we'd notify them and give them the picture. Sara acknowledged the plan and nodded she was ready. I stood up and pulled down my pack, then slumped back down into my seat.

Reaching into the pack, I pulled out a 2-foot length of looped 550 paracord. On the outside of my pack was a large heavy-duty Masterlock keyed padlock. I unlocked it, attached it to the looped paracord, and stuffed it into my pants pocket. It would make a devastating impact device that could easily shatter a human skull if swung hard enough. I looked over at Sara as she was doing the same with hers.

"Just in case," I whispered, as a knowing smile slipped across my face. "I love you."

I stood up and let Sara get into the aisle, following her as we moved forward slightly. When I got next to the man I called to Sara, "Hey, come take a selfie with me." Smiling, she turned around and came back. As she did, I noticed the man shift his hand into his jacket. He clearly was on edge and possibly starting to panic at the thought he might be discovered. This wasn't going to work, and I needed to change my plan – fast – before he decided now was as good a time as any to detonate the explosive. I threw out my hand and pushed Sara back.

"Let's do it up there, the light is better," I said, pushing Sara up a few rows. She didn't know why I changed our plan, but played along.

A few rows up, an older man stood up from his seat and held out his hand, blocking Sara in the aisle. *Aww ... f*ck me. This guy is on to us!* I shoved my hand into my pocket, grabbing for the paracord on my improvised medieval mace.

The man blocking our path started saying something in French. I had no idea what he was saying, but the determination in his voice was clear. As I went for my improvised weapon, Sara spun around and grabbed my hand, still in the pocket. "Hey honey," she said," he wants to take our picture for us." Sara's intelligence and fluency just saved my illiterate ass from striking this dude. I said, "Tell him thank you, but we'll do it ourselves." Sara nodded and translated the message.

When we got a few more rows up, we turned around, hugged each other with big smiles. I held out my phone like I was taking a selfie of us, but intentionally didn't switch the phone camera to face us. I snapped a quick picture of all the people in his section of the train with nobody the wiser. To complete the charade, I showed the picture to Sara. She smiled and kissed me, then we turned around and moved into the next train car.

I stopped briefly to look at the picture. It was near perfect; I was able to zoom in on the man as he sat in his seat. All of his facial features were crystal clear, and the police should have no problem identifying him. I even noticed that he'd taken his hand back out of his coat.

Arriving in the bar buffet compartment, Sara and I found an empty spot and waited for a waitress. After a few moments, she came over to take our order. I pulled her close and whispered what I had seen. The waitress tensed up, then collected herself. Stepping back, she smiled and said she would check to see if the train had that wine available and quickly left the compartment. In a flash, a man who identified himself as a manager arrived, asking us if we could come with him to view the limited selection of wines the train had for special occasions. Sara and I nodded, following him out of the compartment.

The manager led us through a door marked "employees only," and we soon found ourselves in an operations room near the power car. There I explained to the security chief what I had seen and showed them the picture. He asked a few questions about the details of the bomb and thanked us for our quick action in reporting the incident. The security chief left the room, and the manager guided us back to a premier cabin. He advised us to stay in the cabin until someone came for us and that we'd reach our first stop in about another 10 minutes.

We sat in silence in the cushy seats. Picking at a loose thread, Sara finally said, "What do you think they're going to do?" I didn't know, but figured that if the man wanted to blow up the train in the tunnel, he'd have done it already. It seemed that we'd be OK at least until the first stop.

We sat in silence for the next nine minutes until the train made its first stop. As people started to disembark, a train attendant led us off the train and guided us through the station to a security area, where we met a police officer. He asked us to provide a detailed statement and description of what happened.

After a few hours, Sara and I were allowed to leave. I asked the one of the officers what happened. He reported that several undercover agents boarded the train as passengers, taking up several seats around the man. Without warning, the agents converged on the man and were able to subdue him. The suicide vest he was wearing was a real vest, but it had no explosive compounds. Sara and I gave the officer a look that betrayed our lack of understanding. Seeing our confusion, the officer added that terrorists often like to perform test runs to see if they can get a simulated vest through security screenings.

Laughing, he said that the terrorists don't like to waste suicide bombers, so they do test runs to see if they can effectively breach security before the actual attempt. Who would have thought terrorists are concerned for the safety of their suicide bombers?

FORMER U.S. ARMY PSY-OP SERGEANT HAKIM ISLER'S APPROACH

Without a doubt, I saw a bomb strapped to that man. Before I said anything to my wife, Sara, I wanted to get more details. After the train pulled away, I tapped the video camera app on my phone and hit record. I covered the screen with a hand towel while I walked to the bathroom. On my way there, I surveyed the exits and the passengers.

Once in the restroom, I checked my footage. It had a decent view of the man, but mostly from behind. I decided to record again on my way back. Once back in my seat, I reviewed the video again. It was crooked, but I got some really good frontal video of him.

As I began taking screen shots from the video, Sara asked, "What are you doing?" Even whispering felt too risky, so I opened the notepad app and wrote a message. I typed that she shouldn't get alarmed, then summarized my observations. Sara immediately went pale. I showed her the photos and the location of the man. Without hesitation she typed, "We should try to stop him!"

We had to come up with a plan. Because of our lack of professional security know-how, I felt it would be best to get a train attendant involved.

Sara and I crafted a note on my phone detailing my observations, a photo of the bomber, his seat number, and what seat we were in. We used her phone to find Eurostar's website. There was a contact form, but no direct email address, so I couldn't figure out how to attach the photo. I started to curse under my breath, but my tech-savvy wife grabbed my phone. Mumbling something about Google Photos, she managed to come up with a link for the photo and pasted everything into the contact form. At least if the bomb went off in the next second, they'd have all the details. Then I emailed it to my dad for good measure and rang the button for the attendant.

When he arrived, I said, "Someone dropped their phone, and it seems to have their name on the home screen. Do you know who this is?"

I handed him the phone with the note on the screen: "This is not a prank! Do not look suspicious. The guy four seats up with the coat on has a bomb. I saw it under his jacket when we got on. Please alert your supervisors. Walk away with my phone and please email my wife with any instructions." The rest of my message included Sara's address and a summary of what we'd already done.

The attendant went pale, frightening me as I thought he was about to break down. Suddenly, he straightened up and smiled: "Thank you sir, I'll see if I can find the owner." Then he walked away.

A few minutes later, Sara received an email: "Thank you for informing us about the situation. We are aware and taking measures for everyone's safety. Please do not make contact with anyone else, as we do not want to start a panic. Stay seated until otherwise notified."

Sara and I looked at each other in terror. We held each other's hand and sat back.

For the next 10 minutes, we waited to see what would come next, but the anxiety became too much to bear. This guy could detonate his bomb at any time, and I would rather go down fighting. I wrote Sara a message – she agreed. She had a small 8-by-6-inch mirror in her bag; I wrapped it in my towel, wedging it at an angle between the seats. Carefully breaking it while I coughed to mask the sound, I was left with a sharp point. I wrapped the other end in the towel and gave it to Sara.

We formulated a plan. I would walk toward the bathroom then pretend to feel ill and dizzy, apologize to the others, and sit down in front of the bomber. Appearing motion sick would be much less threatening than behaving like a loud American, trying to spark a conversation with no good excuse to sit down near him. Sara would sit in the seat behind him with her improvised shank in her purse. I was stronger, so if either of us might be able to restrain his hands, it would be me. From our positions, we'd wait for the authorities to act. However, if the man made a move before then, we'd be close enough to do something.

This was a Hail Mary play at best, but it was a better backup plan than sitting back, waiting to die. Sara and I looked into one another's eyes. We kissed each other for what might be our last time.

I took a deep breath then I was off. I started to stumble toward the bomber's seat. "I gotta sit here," I said, trying to sound weak. "I'm feeling dizzy." I plopped down, apologizing to the people around me, and leaned my head back. The bomber didn't say anything. I felt a small bit of relief. I raised my head slightly to see Sara just reaching the seat behind the bomber. Instead of a subtle cough, I nervously exploded with a mucus-laden bellow. The guy glared at me. "Sorry," I said, as Sara quietly took the seat behind him. At this point, it occurred to me that perhaps I shouldn't have given my phone away, as I could no longer communicate with her.

After a few minutes, two attendants we'd never seen before entered from the front. The bomber took notice. Then two large men dressed in regular clothes entered from the rear. This agitated the bomber, as his head swiveled back and forth. The attendants tried to play it cool, but it was clear to me the four men were headed toward us. Clear to the bomber, too.

In my periphery, I could see the bomber's hands reaching. He wasn't waiting to see what would happen next; he was going to detonate the bomb. I screamed, "Bomb!" as I sprung out of my seat and grabbed his hands. I barely got a hold of them when one of the attendants joined the fray, but fell on me and broke my grip. He also obstructed the other attendants' path.

The bomber shifted away from the aisle, toward the window. I had smashed the detonator out of his hand in the struggle, but now he was reaching for it as I grabbed his legs. Suddenly, the side of a closed fist suddenly hit him in the neck.

Blood began to squirt from between his fingers as he frantically clutched his neck.

Everything felt like it was moving in slow motion; I followed the hand back and saw it was Sara's. Without hesitation, she stabbed four more times.

"His hands!" I yelled. The attendant on top of me leaped forward and grabbed the bomber's wrists, joined by one of the plainclothes men who dove over the seats and onto the bad guy. The three of us held his limbs down until his resistance melted away. The other attendant kept watch of the passengers in case of an accomplice, while the other plainclothes man took out plastic zip ties and cuffed the bomber's feet together and his hands above his bloody head.

Hours later, in the safety of the Folkestone station, we learned from a police official that the two attendants and two plainclothes men turned out to be undercover security agents. The official admonished us for intervening, forcing the agents to act earlier than they had planned and saying we were lucky to be alive ... but reluctantly thanked us for our bravery. The blank look on Sara's face told me we'd be dealing with the aftermath of her heroism for many years to come.

SURVIVAL EXPERT TIM MACWELCH'S APPROACH

"Sara? Did you see that guy?" I whispered to my wife. "What guy?" she replied. A surge of emotion welled up inside me. It felt defensive, a blend of being afraid for my wife's safety and anger over the fact that she might be at risk. Sara had always been able to read me like a kid's book. Big letters, simple words. The color drained from her face as she picked up on my fear. "What's going on?" she asked in hushed tones.

I quickly but quietly explained what I had just seen – the man with the long coat, the wires, and bottles. She rose in her seat a bit, pretending to adjust how she was sitting, to sneak a glance in the direction of the man. She whispered back to me that she just saw the back of his head, nothing more.

My wife stared at me for a few moments, while I stared at the man who might have been planning to kill us all. She broke my concentration when she quietly said, "Whatever you're planning, I'm in."

Her words echoed in my head. I loved my wife more at that moment than ever before. Not only because I was afraid I might lose her, but also because I'd never been more proud of whom she was. My mind raced as I considered the possibilities. Finally, I concluded, "We have to immobilize him. If he has a bomb, he'll have a trigger. Keeping him from getting to it is the only way that we can all get off this train alive." Her eyes locked with mine, and I could see her thinking it through. She nodded, signaling that she understood.

"How are we going to grab him?" she asked. "You pull him out of his seat by his left arm, and I'll come in from behind and grab his right." Sara nodded again, and asked, "armbar?" I nodded and gave a halfhearted smile, even though this was hardly the time for smiling. Still, she was ferocious at jiu-jitsu and, for a second, I felt something close to hope.

She grabbed my hand and squeezed like she was trying to make diamonds. I pulled her hand up to my lips and kissed it softly. After a bit, we both stood up. Sara took the lead down the train aisle, stopping in front of the man. I was nearly behind him when the unimaginable happened.

A man stood up suddenly, right in my face. He spoke French, and it seemed like he was asking my pardon for something. He blocked my view of my wife, which set me on edge. And apparently she wasn't the only one who could read my emotions like a book. The man's jovial tone switched gears quickly to a tone of loud annoyance, and people were starting to stare at us. As a torrent of French words fell on my uncomprehending ears, I thought I picked out the word "American," then some bad words, and thank God, I picked out the French word for "bathroom." Then I understood and backed into a vacant seat, allowing him to pass.

With a snort of derision, he walked away and I finally saw Sara again. When she saw me start toward her, she knew it was showtime. I slid into the space behind the man, ignoring what the people sitting there might think. My muscles were tight, ready to tear from their tendons or spring forward. As the bomber looked up at my wife, Sara hit him with her most dazzling smile – the one she used to get my attention for the first time so many years ago.

"I love your coat!" she exclaimed, "You must tell me what brand it is and where I can get one." I stared down at the back of the man's head, his dark hair wet with sweat. Sara grabbed the man's coat sleeve, feigning to look at the fabric. As the man rose from his seat to protest, he was halfway under Sara's control, and I grabbed his right arm to lift him out of his seat.

He cried out in surprise and anger, as I tightened my grip and tried to thread him between the seats toward the floor. Slender and sinewy, Sara had already applied an armbar to the man's left arm as soon as his back hit the floor. And I did my best to pin his right arm. During the scuffle, his coat opened up.

It wasn't long before an Irish woman saw the wires and screamed, "Bomb! He has a bomb!"

Then all hell broke loose. The roar of screams and exclamations was almost deafening in the tight quarters. One man started to kick the bomber in the head, but lost his balance and nearly fell on my wife. But most people just scrambled away from us. That's when I noticed the bomber's feet. He was kicking his left foot at the heel of his right shoe, as if trying to remove the shoe. My wife and I were locked onto his arms and torso, but neither of us could reach his feet without letting go.

As his shoe finally came off, I saw a red wire attached to the shoe and running up the man's pant leg. "The trigger is his shoe!" I yelled. There was only one person left in our vicinity, the hefty blonde woman who had bumped into the bomber earlier. She had been sitting there in her seat, right next to the empty seat of the bomber. Her mouth had been agape in surprise, until I called her attention to the shoe and the wire. She frowned and slid down from her seat, not gracefully, until her knees and calves covered the man's ankles and feet. He cried out in pain, and she looked directly at me.

In a thick British accent, she said, "Don't worry, love, I've got this. I'm from Manchester, and where I'm from, we get things handled."

My muscles began to tire as I held the man like a tourniquet, but in a few moments, several train attendants and a uniformed police officer came to our aid. As they handcuffed the man to seat legs, keeping him in a spread-eagle position, I grabbed my wife and held her as tight as my waning strength would allow. I could tell she was spent too, and it was then that I finally noticed that the train had stopped moving.

As she and I moved away from the bomber and the growing pool of authorities and train personnel, a strange pulse rocked the train, as if some giant hammer had just struck it from above. Sara looked at me and tears began to pour from her eyes. "He wasn't the only one," she said.

And then the lights went out.

CONCLUSION

In every edition of *What If?*, we encourage our readers to ask themselves some key questions. Did the characters do the right thing? Could this situation happen in real life? And if this happened to you, what would you have done differently?

In this tale, my character saw something and didn't say anything to the authorities. This is a piece of fiction portraying a very specific scenario. It shouldn't necessarily stand as an example of your behavior in a similar or different situation.

In this day and age, everyone should say something if they see something amiss. It's our duty to our fellow humans — to be the extended eyes and ears of the law enforcement professionals who strive to keep us all safe, every single day. And unless we have the training, resources, and backup that law enforcement would have, we typically should leave the confrontation to the professionals. That said, every life-or-death situation is unique. It's up to you to practice your situational awareness every time you're out in a public place, and to trust your instincts. You never know when these two assets will save lives. And we'll say it again — if you see something, say something! ⠭

22

YOU'RE TRAPPED IN A MASS SHOOTING?

By Tim MacWelch
Illustrations by Joe Oesterle

It wasn't the popping gunshots that shocked your senses the most in that crowded mall. You've fired enough rounds in your life to be familiar with the sound of gunfire. It was the screaming child who made you stop in your tracks. The sound you heard wasn't the commonplace tantrum of a spoiled child screaming for a new toy. No, this was a shriek of pain and absolute fear from a young one.

It was a piercing wail, and the instincts of a parent took hold. You had to find the child. As you ran hunched over, zigzagging toward a stone planter, the screaming grew louder. You were almost there! Then the ground rose up to meet you. You didn't remember losing your footing and falling, you simply realized you were suddenly on the ground. Just feet away from the crying of the child — just feet away from the decorative stone structure that would afford you solid cover — you were down and if you didn't move fast, you could die right there.

Whether the attackers are foreign-born terrorists or homegrown bad guys, their goal is the same — to kill as many easy targets as they can. In this edition of *What If?*, we pose the question: What if you're in a crowded shopping mall when a mass shooter starts a killing spree? To get different takes on this deeply troubling threat, RECOIL OFFGRID asked three different survival writers for their knee-jerk reaction.

So, we have Candice Horner, a U.S. Marine Corps veteran, registered nurse, and competitive shooter. Next, we have Erik Lund, a longtime contributor who's also a federal law enforcement agent with a bevy of tactical and survival experience. And to round things out, ROG asked me what I would do, as well. I've been teaching people how to survive almost everything for the past 20 years, and I've written multiple *New York Times*-bestselling survival manuals from my experience.

It's an honor to continue writing for RECOIL OFFGRID, though it's far from comfortable to wade through this all-too-real-feeling *What If?* story.

The Scenario

Situation type: Mass shooting
Your Crew: You
Location: Chicago, Illinois
Season: Winter (late January)
Weather: Cloudy and windy, 15 to 30 degrees F

The Setup

You're visiting the Windy City and decide to have your last lunch in Illinois at Water Tower Place, the eight-level mall located inside a 74-story skyscraper. You figure you can hang out there for a few hours, buy some souvenirs, and still have plenty of time to catch an Uber to O'Hare International Airport. More importantly, you'll be out of the bitter cold!

The Complication

You're about to enter the Oakley store when a loud noise echoes throughout the mall. Everyone flinches, then freezes. Suddenly, several more bangs ring out. It's gunfire! Immediately, people scream and sprint in every direction. You instinctively duck behind cover and carefully scan for the safest way out — instead of seeing an exit you spot a gunman fire randomly into a crowd of people then head in your direction. He didn't see you, but he's about 35 yards away and approaching. What do you do?

The New Plan

With this bad guy shooting at people indiscriminately, you'll have to formulate a plan (and fast) for what to do. You need to deal with the environment (the store and mall), the gear you happen to be carrying, and the reaction (if any) of other shoppers, security guards, or police.

U.S. MARINE VETERAN CANDICE HORNER'S APPROACH

As usual, I procrastinated. This time, I waited until the last minute to buy my husband a birthday present. But, an extra day in Chicago, after my friend's wedding, provided me with just enough time to get him a new pair of Oakleys. Thanks to a wannabe badass, I didn't even step foot in the Oakley store.

Just as I was about to enter the store, shots rang out with a systematic, thundering cadence. Just from the tone, I knew it was a shotgun. The herd of people in front of me froze, until someone yelled, "Gun!" Then the frozen crowd dispersed into unorganized chaos, flaring out in every direction with unguided purpose. I quickly scanned for the shooter and spotted him about 35 yards away, reloading his shotgun while coming up the escalator. I made haste to the largest store next to Oakley.

The Oakley store was too wide open; I needed a better place to hide, so I ran to American Eagle Outfitters. I hurried toward the back of the store, where other people were also running. I didn't want to get caught up in their large, flock-sized target. So, I hid inside of a circular clearance rack — the type that's always over-stuffed and never organized.

As I crouched down in the circle of clothes, I damned myself for not staying in the hotel and shopping with Amazon Prime. This wasn't like me; I don't like shopping malls. Being in large groups of people is outside my comfort zone. What the hell was I thinking by coming here?! I felt I was getting what I deserved for coming to a city with terrible gun laws, a place I couldn't legally defend myself. Damn it. Thank goodness I have an insatiable affinity for knives and carry several in my purse. I was armed, but to use a knife during a gunfight would take a little bit more than courage. I had to use his firearm of choice against him, capitalize on the weak points of a pump-action shotgun.

Shotguns are like good beer — they're always empty. Knowing this was my advantage, as the sounds of his shots got closer, I counted each round. One, two, three, four … *and five.* After the fifth shot, there was about an eight-second delay – he was reloading.

By the intensity of the screams, I could tell the shooter was within the walls of my makeshift safe haven. The clearance rack provided enough concealment to hide me, while still allowing me to view the masked shooter's location. He followed the sounds of screams coming from the back of the store.

I held my breath as his one-track mind guided him inches past me and to the screams coming from the dressing rooms and storage area. With a tormented sound of joy in his voice he yelled at the door, "This will be your tomb!" He discharged another five rounds until running the gun dry. Eight seconds of pure terror passed until the next five rounds of buckshot penetrated the door. The souls barricaded on the other side didn't have a chance; he was determined to reach them. I had to do something.

After sizing him up, I knew my tiny frame wasn't much of a match for his strong, tall build. I had to get him closer to the ground for a fair chance. Thank God for tunnel vision because as I slid out from behind the discounted skinny jeans, the gunman was laser focused on loading one shotshell at a time. With a knife in my strong hand, I kicked him with all my might to the back of his lead knee, which supported most of his weight. He stumbled toward the ground, his finger still on the trigger, accidentally discharging the shotgun toward the roof.

Since it was a pump-action, he couldn't fire another round without racking the fore-end. In that instant, he was closer to my level, and I wrapped my left arm around his neck while simultaneously slicing through his trachea and right carotid with my Medford Micro Praetorian Knife. I kicked the shotgun out of reach, standing over him as his artery spurted blood all over the sand-colored tile. I stared at his lifeless body for what seemed to be an eternity.

I must have been in shock, because I was numb to my surroundings and seemed to be out of my own body as my eyes were locked on the carnage beneath my feet. But it wasn't over, and I snapped back to reality.

The ringing in my ears from all the shotgun blasts was overpowered by the cries for help on the other side of the buckshot-riddled door. I pleaded with the survivors to open the door, explaining I'm a nurse and want to help. They hesitantly did. There were 12 of them behind that door. I scanned the group for serious injuries; no one was dead. There was a young boy, gray in the face with blue lips and bleeding profusely from his elbow. I grabbed a new belt off the storage shelf and tightened it around his upper arm until the bright red bleeding slowed.

By now, more people had joined us in the storage room. Several of them had hidden near me and saw me take down the gunman. A couple of them looked at me like I was dangerous. I didn't care. At that point, anyone who had enough life in them to judge me was lucky they didn't get shot by that crazy man. Their discontent was somehow comforting to me because it meant they made it through this ordeal.

About 10 minutes later, police and EMS arrived. The injured were taken away, and I was taken into custody. I didn't have time to process the emotions that would come once the adrenaline eventually settled.

My adrenaline quickly turned to anger when I was told that I had to be held in custody and questioned by police. And, as expected, they took my knife. They charged me with carrying an illegal weapon, because Chicago law states a concealed knife can only have a 2.5-inch blade; mine had a 2.8-inch blade.

The charges were dropped after the story made the news, heralding me as a hero. Once released, the cops offered me protection while traveling back home. I gladly accepted because the motives and connections of the gunman weren't yet known. I was, essentially, a walking target until they figured out why the shooter attacked. I didn't regret my actions though. Some people just don't belong on this Earth, and I categorized him as such.

What I learned from all of this was to trust my gut and not go into a city that doesn't support the Second Amendment. Had I been able to have my everyday CCW, I would have been able to react sooner rather than waiting for him to reload. I also learned that sometimes due diligence isn't enough. When I looked up the laws in Illinois, I read that knives with a 3-inch blade were legal – but Chicago has a stricter knife law than the state.

So, the next time I'm invited to a wedding in a state with such highly restrictive gun laws, I'll just send my love and congratulations by mail.

FEDERAL AGENT ERIK LUND'S APPROACH

It didn't take long for me to spot the shooter. The rolling booms echoed throughout the mall, but my eye instantly spotted a man cycling the action on a pump shotgun. The full-face ski mask confirmed this was indeed the shooter and not a mall security guard. The shooter touched off another round and then turned, walking in my direction while reloading more shells. Seeing the opening, I instinctively started my drawstroke by lifting my cover garment to access my pistol, only to stop and realize that I had no pistol.

Chicago is one of the most gun-restrictive cities in the entire country. Only the elites can obtain a concealed carry permit in Chicago, and I most certainly didn't qualify as an elite member of society.

I quickly stepped behind a large square pillar right at the Oakley storefront entrance. Time for plan B. I'd never make it if I tried to run for it. I could try to find a back way out of the store; a work exit or maybe a fire exit. But being unfamiliar with the store, there was no guarantee of success. Even if I were successful, could I live with myself for not trying to do something to stop this rampage? I had the training and the skills to make a difference.

No, I will not run, I will fight back. If not me, then who? I needed a plan, and fast, but only one option seemed viable at the moment. *If he comes into the store, I'll have to try and ambush him from around this pillar and go hand to hand with him.*

I pulled my SOG Kiku folder out of my pocket and deployed the blade. While I was pretty sure it was illegal to be carrying this knife, it was more important to survive this incident than worry about what kind of legal trouble awaited me. Win the fight first, then worry about lawyers. A quick scan of the interior of the store revealed complete chaos. People were running all around, some were starting to hide behind counters and displays, while others were trying to find another way out.

Good, all of this commotion and movement will keep him distracted and give me the opening I need. Two more booms echoed over the screams in the mall, only much louder this time. *He's getting closer.*

I slowly shifted my head just enough to let one eye see past the pillar. The shooter was 15 yards from the entrance and still headed toward the store. He briefly stopped and raised the shotgun. I quickly pulled my head back as another boom rang throughout the mall. A scream drew my attention back into the store. A woman was running from behind an overcrowded display to another less crowded place to hide when buckshot impacted her hip. Screaming as she fell, she slid several feet along the floor until coming to a stop almost in the middle of the display floor.

The sound of the pump action cycling was followed immediately with another blast directed at the woman. Fortunately, it went a little high and the shotgun pellets passed over her body by a couple of inches. The shooter cycled the pump action again and by the proximity of the noise, I knew the shooter was extremely close. My heart was jackhammering in my chest as final thoughts popped into my head. *Time to sack up. Drive him into the ground. Be fast. Be brutal.* Every muscle in my body was twitching, ready to explode and attack with all the speed I could muster. Everything I could bring to the fight was set on a visual tripwire, ready to launch. Then I heard the loudest sound you'll ever hear in a gunfight ... *click.*

It wasn't the visual stimulus I anticipated. No shotgun barrel or human body walking past the pillar where I lay in wait to ambush the shooter. No visual cue whatsoever; just an extremely loud click. My brain instantly processed the sound and sent the launch command. *Go, go, go! He's empty!* Every muscle fiber released, and I accelerated around the pillar. The shooter had paused for a second after he heard the click of the empty shotgun. He was in mid-cycle when his eyes caught a flash of movement and he looked up at this figure that had appeared from nowhere, rapidly bearing down on him.

He was only three steps away from me, but the distance between us felt like a mile. It didn't matter; I was committed, and the only thing I could do was continue to accelerate and close the distance. My plan was to hit him like an all-pro linebacker until I could get him off his feet or get him pinned up against a wall. Taking him to the ground or pinning him against a wall would make it virtually impossible in the tight confines of a hand-to-hand fight to use the long shotgun against me, but it still would allow me to use the knife in my right hand against him.

A step away from making contact, our eyes locked. I could see the shock and fear in his eyes. I had caught him totally off-guard, and I thought, *You better brace* *for impact, mother f*cker.*

My shoulder slammed into his midsection. (Later, my old high school football coach would track me down and send me an email after seeing the store surveillance video of the incident, congratulating me on the best hit he ever saw me make.) I made contact with enough force to lift the shooter off his feet and into the air. We crashed down onto the store floor in a tangled mess of limbs. I heard a loud groan as the air in his lungs escaped his body, sandwiched between me and the floor. Before he could recover, I quickly scrambled on top of the shooter, who was flat on his back.

Still holding my knife, I instantly reared back and rained a right-handed punch straight at his face. He was dazed but still putting up a fight, instinctively raising his left arm to block my strike. That's exactly what I wanted him to do, and at the last moment, I changed my punch to a push, driving his arm across his neck as I collapsed my body down onto his. At the same time, I slipped my left arm around the back of his neck into a half headlock. As I pushed his arm across his throat, I ducked my head down behind his left elbow and used my head to pin his arm across his throat. I then curled my left arm toward my head and tightened my grip, pinning his arm and head in one position.

Using my head to pin his arm freed up my knife hand to strike and prevented him from protecting his left side. I made several rapid-fire strikes just under his left armpit into the upper lung. The strikes had the desired effect – he screamed and did everything he could to free his trapped arm and protect his left side. Now was my opportunity to finish this fight.

Releasing pressure on his pinned arm allowed him to move his arm down to protect his body. This also opened my next target area, the side of his neck. I reared back to begin a series of strikes into the side of the neck and throat when another body jumped onto us, followed by several more in quick succession. Several people from inside the store had jumped in to help me and in short order had the shooter completely overpowered and pinned to the floor.

In a matter of minutes, the local police had secured the area. The shooter acted alone; it was over.

He was transported to the hospital for emergency surgery to repair his damaged and collapsed lung – he survived to stand trial.

Several days after being interviewed and giving my statement, store surveillance video indeed showed that I made a perfect tackle, driving the shooter into the ground. It also showed that upon impact with the ground, the shotgun fell out of the shooter's hands and skidded several feet away, out of his reach. Upon reviewing the footage, the local district attorney stated that because the shooter no longer had access to the shotgun, my use of the knife upon him was excessive and that I should have just held him down.

Apparently in Chicago, no good deed goes unpunished, and he charged me with carrying a concealed weapon and assault. My lawyer said that no jury would ever convict me and not to worry. I sure hope he's right.

SURVIVAL EXPERT TIM MACWELCH'S APPROACH

Snapping out of my shock from falling to the ground, I scurried behind the stone planter just in time to see a panicked mother dragging her screaming child from the sturdy cover into a nearby clothing store. Thank God there was no blood on either one of them. It was one small victory in the sickening ordeal. But that might not last. I remember thinking, Racks of clothes may hide you, but they won't stop bullets. At least the little family wasn't in the open, and they did have some concealment. I popped up for a brief second to survey the scene, and then sunk my head back behind the stonework.

There was one man walking my way with a black down-filled jacket and a black ski mask. I wasn't sure from my one-second glance, but from the profile it looked like he was carrying a shotgun.

My mind raced with questions. Was he acting alone? Did he have training? Where were the police and mall security guards? Why choose a shotgun for this?

But the questions stopped flowing when I heard the distinctive sounds of a shotgun being racked and another shot being fired. Since I had been traveling, I had no firearm and precious little in the way of everyday-carry (EDC) gear — just my phone, which I decided to use by dialing 911. I waited until the operator answered, whispered "Shooter in the Water Tower mall," and set the phone in the greenery, still connected.

Since the shooting began, the mantra of "run, hide, fight" had been playing in my head, almost like some kind of religious chant. I could simply run away. I could keep hiding behind the planter. Or I could run up and try to seize the weapon. Or I could go with plan D, which was "none of the above." Even if this murderous assailant had no training, his shotgun blasts could still be effective at killing and maiming people. I had to make a decision. Since I could be easily engaged with a close-range shotgun blast if I popped up from my cover and ran, I decided to stay behind the planter for the moment.

There was too much screaming in the mall to hear the shooter's footfalls, and I couldn't predict which way he would go to pass the planter. If I went around it to the right or left and made the wrong choice — I could crawl right up to the muzzle of the shotgun.

But then I heard another round rack and another blast, very close and to my left, so I began crawling to the right of the circular stone structure. I looked over the rim quickly, with the plants giving me some concealment. The culprit was just 10 feet from me, but walking away. He was heading toward the clothing store where the mother and child had fled. I thought about staying behind the stones, safe from the shooter.

But could I live with myself if he walked over and shot that woman and child? Then the little one started screaming again. I knew what I had to do.

I couldn't see the woman or her child in the cramped and overloaded clothing shop. But I could hear the child's wail coming from the back. The store's space was filled with long racks and circular stands packed tight with clothing on hangers. The mass shooter stood in the doorway of the store, looking inside as I padded up behind him as quietly as I could. It was the dumbest moment of my life, very likely the bravest as well, and possibly the last moment too, if I screwed up. My goal was to grab the gun, but as he swung around toward me, everything changed.

His head turned toward me first, and as our eyes locked, I felt a very real sense of time slowing down. I felt as though I had all the time in the world. I could see that he had the shotgun firmly gripped in both hands. It would be no easy task to pull it from his grasp, so I grabbed his mask and spun it on this head as I shoved him hard. The thick black ski mask blinded my would-be killer, and he roared with anger as he stumbled back and I ran past him to the back of the store. There I saw the mother and child huddled on the floor in front of the cash register, as well as a young woman who was frozen in fear behind the counter.

I grabbed the mother by the arm without a word, raising her up as she clung tightly to her offspring. I also grabbed the petrified clerk as I passed and pulled them into the store office. I shut the door and locked it, then pushed them all to the floor. I had no idea what kind of shells the shooter was firing, but the door and wall looked rather flimsy. As the women lay on the floor in shock, a shotgun blast flew through the feeble door. The big holes told me he was using buckshot.

Thank God I had the presence of mind to get away from the door and lie down. I knew that average doors and walls won't stop a 9mm round, so they're not true cover, just concealment. As I heard the doorknob jerk, I pushed a file cabinet against the door with my legs, then several boxes, all while continuing to lie on the floor. He shot the doorknob next, the mangled assembly of metal falling onto one of the cardboard boxes I had pushed over. Without saying a word, the shooter began kicking the door.

The terrified clerk just lay there on the ground with her face covered. The young mother started screaming alongside her little girl. On the floor, we were out of the line of fire, but we were hardly out of harm's way. The shooter seemed hell-bent on getting into the small office. He fired two more rounds into the door, each in the area of the hinges. He kicked a few more times, then stopped. I looked toward the mother and put my finger to my lips as if to say, "Shhh." She quieted a bit and covered her child's mouth, though they still whimpered a little and continued to breathe loudly. The clerk seemed to have gone catatonic or fainted.

Scanning the office, I found no phone or anything particularly useful. There was a fire extinguisher, which could be used as a blunt object or to spray flame-retardant dust in an attacker's face. I picked up the extinguisher, broke the plastic safety line, and pulled the pin.

Did the shooter move on? I wondered. How would I know for sure? I didn't dare peek through any of the holes in the door; he might see the movement and fire. Were we done? Was this over?

We had barricaded ourselves and fortified the door with office goods. He couldn't get in, but I still didn't feel safe. I put my ear to the wall and listened intently. There was shouting that seemed remote, at least from outside the store. The shouts seemed short, like commands. I thought I heard something like

"Put your weapon down!" Finally, the police had arrived, but we weren't out of harm's way. One of the Chicago SWAT teams had the shooter cornered, in the store. I told the girls to stay down; the police didn't know we were back there, and we could easily be hit by friendly fire.

In desperation, the shooter began kicking the door again – likely thinking that it was an exit. After another blast to the upper door hinge, he flung his full weight into the cheap door, buckling it inward. He scrambled to climb over the door and the blockade piled behind it. His hood righted again, those eyes stared at me through the mask holes full of recognition and hate. With one hand on the door and the other on his shotgun, he tried to slither over the caved-in door and take aim at me. I launched the fire extinguisher chemicals into his face, and my ears rang again as he pressed the trigger again.

By the grace of God, the buckshot went into the wall behind me and not into my body. That shot was all the police could take, and they stormed into the shop. Clearing each aisle of clothing, they found the coughing suspect standing there near the broken door. When he leveled his shotgun at the point man, several team members opened fire. Startlingly white puffs of feathers spewed from his down jacket as each round tore through his flesh. The shooter fell, and the team rushed forward, not sure if there were more shooters.

They found us in the hazy dust-filled room, coughing, and sputtering – but alive.

CONCLUSION

It should be with great humility that we admit the flaws of our age. Despite social media's claim that the world is more connected than ever, we see people who have gone the opposite way. Some make national headlines by acting out against a world where they feel no connection, whether due to mental illness or other factors. And terrorist groups continue to add to their ranks, spreading their twisted ideologies and recruiting foot soldiers to carry out their evil deeds.

Mindset, preparedness, and situational awareness have always been important, but they're especially so these days. The police can't be everywhere at once, and the FBI can't read minds. No one knows exactly when or where the bad guys will strike. But there's one thing that we do know. At the end of the day, it's up to us to be invested in our own self-defense and family security. It's up to us to learn what to do, how to do it, and when to act. ⠿

23

A DIRTY BOMB GOES OFF IN YOUR CITY?

By Tim MacWelch
Illustrations by Jordan Lance

Five seconds. Only five seconds had passed. But it felt like five hours as your mind slowly processed what had happened. The booming sound outside of your home, the rattling of the old single-pane windows, the screaming you heard on the street – all of it let you know that something horrible had struck.

You were just a kid when the Sept. 11 attacks happened, but it had a major impact on your childhood. Maybe today it was happening again.

Terrorism is the new Cold War. Many of us today worry when the next big ISIS or ISIS-inspired attack will occur and in what form it will take. Some of us are so concerned that we've taken measures to be prepared for it. But what happens when it's time to leap from theoretical plans to a state of action? In this edition of *What If?*, we pose the question: What if a dirty bomb explodes in your hometown?

This would invariably create a cascade of unpredictable events. To explore as many possible outcomes and viewpoints, RECOIL OFFGRID asked three different survival writers whether they would hunker down or hit the road. For this installment, we have Candice Horner, a U.S. Marine Corps veteran, registered nurse, and competitive shooter with experience in federal law enforcement. Next is Mike Seeklander, a former law enforcement officer who's also a Marine Corps combat veteran, firearms instructor, and a martial artist.

And for contestant number three, our editor asked me to craft a story as well. I've been teaching people how to survive almost everything for the past 20 years, and I've written *New York Times*-bestselling survival manuals.

And now it's time to find out just how prepared we really are.

The Scenario

Situation type: Terrorist attack
Your Crew: You (mid 20s) and your 3-month-old baby
Location: Baltimore, Maryland
Season: Autumn (October)
Weather: Cloudy, 63 degrees F, with slight wind

The Setup

You're an electrician in your mid 20s. Recently separated from her deadbeat mom, you now have sole custody of your infant, Ashley. With your babysitter (your mom) on vacation, you also take a two-week vacation to spend some quality time with Ashley in your townhouse in the Federal Hill neighborhood. In the shadow of our nation's capital, Baltimore can be a rough city – you consider the government dysfunctional, the infrastructure in disrepair, and the crime rate impressively high; but it's home.

Just as you introduce Ashley to the glory of televised Ravens football, you hear a distant boom followed by some rumbling. Then the texts, tweets, and posts start flooding your smartphone. Something about a building collapse. Next, the commentators stop their pregame show to report there was some sort of explosion at Johns Hopkins University. A big one. Eventually, the network's breaking news alert interrupts the game: A massive explosion has vaporized the campus' entire School of Education building on Charles Street and destroyed much of the surrounding residential and business buildings. Terrorist attack? Unless it's the biggest gas leak accident ever, most likely.

The Complication

As news reports grow scarier by the minute, you realize you can't go numb. After putting Ashley down to sleep, you start gathering your supplies and gear. That's when you see the TV and online updates: ISIS has claimed responsibility for the explosion, saying it was a truck bomb laced with radioactive material. They say they struck at "the heart of a blasphemous education system that teaches Americans how to hate Islam." The phrase "dirty bomb" echoes in your head, stopped only by another ISIS threat: "There will be more."

The New Plan

You don't know if there'll be another attack that's closer, but you know that the university is only 5 miles away. And if that attack really was a dirty bomb, exposure to radioactive debris could spell bad news – and you're not willing to do nothing with Ashley in your care. So, do you use your preps, supplies, and survival skills to shelter in place and fortify your townhouse? Or do you grab your baby, climb into your work truck, and hope to get as much distance between you and any possible fallout or follow-up attack?

FORMER U.S. MARINE CANDICE HORNER'S APPROACH

In an instant, the city went into a synchronized panic. Screams of terror seemed to come from all directions. Word had quickly spread that ISIS was responsible for the bombing. I didn't need to look outside to know the city was in chaos.

I love Baltimore, but unfortunately I've seen firsthand how quickly a crowd can turn into a violent mob. Because the news reporters were providing conflicting statements, I had to believe no one actually knew the full story. With limited information, but enough to know it was dangerous outside, I decided we were staying put.

I quickly scanned the Internet to get a Cliff's Notes version of how to survive a dirty bomb attack. Most of what I found advised staying inside if we were already sheltered in a safe place at the time of the attack. I wasn't sure if we were upwind or not, but I figured I could look into that once I had a clear plan for our "staycation."

I double-checked to make sure we had enough food, water, baby formula, diapers, and wipes to tide us over for a few days. After scooping up Ashley and her Pack 'n' Play, we headed down to the basement, which doubles as my man cave.

My man cave has many comforts, but a bathroom is not one of them. A 5-gallon bucket with a lid became my makeshift throne. The small windows in the basement were old and could potentially leave and allow the infiltration of radiologic dust, so I sealed them with duct tape. My paranoia took me a step further by cutting my shower curtain liner slightly larger than each window and completely covering the frame and again sealing it with duct tape. Even though the heat wasn't running, I shut off the air system and taped the air vents in the basement. If there was dirty bomb dust outside, it was going to have one hell of a time getting into my safe haven.

Ashley was sound asleep by the time I finished taping the air vents. The sight of her peaceful slumber had a calming effect on me. I sat down, closed my eyes, and focused on the feeling of clean air rushing into my nose and then slowly exhaling out of my mouth. In that moment, all I thought about was the blessing of those breaths.

Then, déjà vu erupted, but from a different direction. ISIS meant what they said, and initial news reports said they annihilated Fort McHenry with another dirty bomb. Not only were we now sandwiched between two dirty bombs, but these bastards also destroyed the birthplace of our national anthem. Fearing things were getting worse by the second, I ran upstairs to get my shotgun and extra OO buck just in case local punks took advantage of the situation to loot homes and businesses.

On the way back down, I grabbed the air purifier so the basement wouldn't get stuffy while we waited out this nightmare. The most terrifying aspect of the whole situation was not knowing what to do, or how long we would be in danger. I had the news on TV, the radio on, and the Baltimore Police Department scanner broadcasting via my laptop. Although I loathe social media, Twitter provided the most up-to-date information from eyewitnesses. The hashtag #baltimorebomb was in full effect.

I needed to learn more, but part of me didn't want to delve deeper only to find my man cave could quickly turn into our coffin. I had to mentally compartmentalize the turn of events so that I could be productive and, if nothing else, attempt to prepare for our doom. I looked up the current wind direction report online. The wind was drifting slowly northeast. This meant the dust from the first bomb wouldn't come near us, but the fallout from Fort McHenry could hit us.

Because the windows of my house were drafty, I was concerned they'd let radiologic dust in and possibly slip into the basement via the door. I taped up and covered the basement door in the same fashion as the windows. My mother sent me a frantic email that she'd been trying to call. Everyone must have been calling their loved ones in Baltimore, because I couldn't call her back. Thankfully, the Internet was working, and I was able to give email and Facebook updates to everyone who wanted to make sure sweet Ashley and I hadn't perished. Being connected while bugging in was reassuring and it ever-so-slightly softened the hard edge of doom surrounding us.

It had only been three hours since the first bomb, and the future possibilities were slowly setting into my mind. I'd do anything to go back to yesterday, as mediocre as it was. The day prior to the bombings was normal; I came home from work and had the usual discontent toward my job, but loved the life I could live thanks to it. The sounds of cars driving down my street and kids laughing on the stoop next door were now replaced with rumbles of a city in distress.

Hopelessness set in, my heart sank, and I closed my eyes. I guess stress had gotten to me so much that I passed out from mental exhaustion. I was startled awake by high-pitched screams coming from the street.

I peeled back the shower liner from the window and saw my elderly neighbor, Ms. Thompson, kneeling on the sidewalk cursing the sky. She looked angered, but equally terrified. I knew she lived alone. I assessed the situation for what seemed like an eternity. I felt like I should help her, but I didn't want to put Ashley or myself at risk.

Ashley started crying. Luckily she wasn't old enough to comprehend what was going on – she was just hungry. But I had to go help Ms. Thompson; she was going to scare herself to death. Peeling back the barrier on the door upstairs felt like a knife to my gut. I got over myself and pushed forward with my rescue mission. As soon as Ms. Thompson saw me, the look on her face affirmed my decision to help. She was relieved. Once we got inside, I instructed her to take a shower in the extra bathroom to wash off any possible radioactive material, and to put her clothes in a plastic bag. I gave her a set of Ravens sweats and told her I'd meet her in the basement. Since I had gone outside, I followed my own directions and took a shower in the master bath, albeit without a shower curtain, before returning to the basement.

By nightfall, Ms. Thompson was very sick. She had continuous bouts of vomiting; she was drenched in sweat and became lethargic. The next morning I was able to get a call through to 911, and they said someone would be there as soon as possible. As soon as possible is a relative term, and they were able to take her to the hospital the following night. Once she was in capable hands, I was able to make the most out of my basement retreat with Ashley.

Disaster relief workers took us to a safe area five days later. But, we still weren't out of the weeds since the effects of the fallout could take weeks to show. Baltimore would never be the same.

FORMER LAW ENFORCEMENT OFFICER MIKE SEEKLANDER'S APPROACH

I remembered my parents' reaction when the Twin Towers fell in New York City, the horror on their faces. As a 10-year-old at the time, I had no idea the emotions they felt – until today. Now father of a beautiful girl, I truly understood what it meant to have kin possibly face harm or even death. My gut told me that the explosion was only the beginning, and, if ISIS repeated the pattern that Osama Bin Laden planned 15 years ago, there were certainly other targets.

"Move!" I heard my father's voice in my head. A former U.S. Marine (there are "no ex-Marines, just Marines"), he would always say action trumps intent every single time. I had to act, and speed was of the essence.

Baltimore was both beautiful and sinister, and I knew from experience that when things went bad, the bad people came out. My lovely city had one of the highest crime rates around, and if food, water, and power started to dry up, all hell would break loose. Not to mention there was a dangerous cloud of potentially radioactive dust headed in who knows what direction. And there was no hope in waiting for the government to step in. I figured they would be suffering from HUA (head up ass) disease for at least several days before reacting properly. Nope. Time to bug out.

And thanks to being raised by a Marine, I knew what to do. When I was a kid, we'd often head out with minimal gear and tell my mother that we'd be back the next morning. While these outings were only a mile or so into the wooded area behind our house, each excursion taught me something new. The one constant? Always make a packing list. I know, it didn't really sound like such a cool survival lesson. But the way it worked with my old man was that if you forgot something, you lived a night without it. Forgot your bug spray? Live with ticks. Forgot your fire-building kit? Sleep cold.

A packing list was a great tool for gathering the right items quickly, but also something you could tweak depending on your trip. Because I would be jumping into my work truck – a 2011 Toyota Tundra Rock Warrior 4x4 outfitted with the tools of my trade – I had plenty of room to pack the essentials.

My goal wasn't to grab my baby and live off the land for an extended period of time, but rather get clear of the crime-ridden areas with the potential to succeed in any environment that I ended up in. My destination was one that I lucked upon several years ago while on a project. A longtime customer, a rich dentist named Richard, hired me to do a complete wire job of his family's old cabin that he inherited. It was on secluded acreage near Chambersburg, Pennsylvania. If I helped keep the place up and do any electrical work he needed, I had a key and free access.

The cabin was about 100 miles northwest of Baltimore – well outside of any potential radioactive dust cloud and far north of other potential targets, such as Annapolis and Washington, D.C., but not so far that I couldn't reach it by truck with my spare fuel cans.

I opted for my full camping kit plus a few creature comforts for Ashley. This included a small tent, air mattress, sleeping bag, fire-starting kit, solar charger, and my drop box of small supplies – ranging from silverware to a coffee pot. While I had plenty of comfort items at the lodge, I had many miles to cover to get there and had no idea what I might encounter.

Next, I stowed my Smith & Wesson M&P 9C and two spare magazines into a Vertx sling bag then placed my Marlin 336BL lever-action rifle and a .30-30 Winchester with an 18-inch barrel in a secured compartment in the truck bed. After double-checking my list, I headed out. Total packing time: about 25 minutes, getting me out ahead of the mass of panicked fans leaving the football stadium.

Luckily, my job required a lot of driving, so I knew how to navigate through my Federal Hill neighborhood without hitting the major thoroughfares. My goal was to avoid Interstate 95 and 83 altogether and instead use surface streets to eventually get to Maryland Route 26, which would take me northwest to my destination.

All was going well until the 26 neared the Interstate 695. I could see the line of traffic ahead of me. I wasn't sure if the jam was caused by panicked drivers or it might actually be a roadblock set up by law enforcement.

Based on the radio reports, there were at least two more explosions, and now at least two cells of terrorists were playing hide and seek with local and state police. Several gun battles had erupted, and the city was placing all residents on a lockdown, warning them to stay inside their homes. And while I appreciated what the police were trying to do, there was no way I was getting trapped inside the Baltimore metro area covered with a cloud of potentially radioactive material and relying on the government to save me.

As traffic inched forward, I was able to switch lanes and get out from behind a semi-truck. I could see police lights in the distance; no doubt a road block. Sitting like a frog stuck in mud was not an option. I decided to do something about it.

One thing I had learned from years of camping and off-roading was that there was almost always a way around an obstacle, especially on the East Coast with hundreds of years of old trails and small winding roads. I drove up onto the curb, cutting into the parking lot of a restaurant to double back. I found a set of residential streets that paralleled the roadblock and knew that if I could navigate another half mile west I could probably jump back on a main road and be good to go. A few backtracks later I finally found a decent route and made it back to the 26.

After an intense first hour trying to bug out from the Baltimore area and a smooth 90 minutes after that, we finally rolled up to the Chambersburg property. Exhausted, I took Ashley out of her car seat and put her in a baby carrier on my chest. As I was about to grab the baby bug-out bag I had packed, a silhouette stepped out from behind a bush. Instinctively, I grabbed the M&P handgun from my sling bag and kept it in the low ready position as I turned.

I breathed a huge sigh of relief to find it was Richard, the dentist and cabin owner.

"Thank God you made it," he said, stepping forward like he just saw a ghost. He was at the cabin with his family for a weekend trip and had heard the news about the attacks. I discreetly put the gun away, opened the truck door, and gave him an embrace. I had never been so happy to see a dentist before.

SURVIVAL EXPERT TIM MACWELCH'S APPROACH

Leave or stay? The debate raged in my mind. Every instinct urged me to flee, but I knew how bad traffic was in Baltimore at rush hour. And a panicked exodus out of the city would be worse than any rush hour imaginable. The friendly flat screen TV that was about to show my favorite football team was spewing forth information that I just didn't want to hear. ISIS was threatening more attacks in my area, and the emergency broadcast system was instructing people to "shelter in place."

I didn't want my little girl to breathe radioactive dust. I just wanted to get out of town. But I knew the traffic could turn into gridlock in a heartbeat and just one automobile accident could leave thousands of people trapped in their cars – with no shelter from the tainted air. Despite the fact that every fiber of my body wanted to put my sleeping baby in my work truck and drive away, I knew I had to stay put. It was the only logical choice, and after several minutes, I finally came to grips with it.

But how could I make sure the air in our poorly insulated townhouse was safe to breathe? I didn't have duct tape and tarps to keep the dust from creeping in, and I wasn't even sure which way the wind was blowing that day. Did I have time to seal off all the windows in one room, or would the wind blow all of the dust out over the water and away from our home? I just didn't know.

I had to find out if we were in harm's way. Pulling out my phone and searching for weather maps with wind direction and speed, I found a weather webpage from a local news station. *Thank God*, I thought – the wind wasn't blowing from the university toward my house. But it was blowing between my home and the school.

Then the situation finally hit me. The bombing site was a busy university. All those people, dead or dying. I felt as if I'd throw up, but I knew I had to control my emotions.

The wind wasn't blowing the dust in my direction at that time, but that could change with a moment's notice. I had to seal up my daughter's room, but I didn't have the duct tape and plastic sheeting recommended for shelter-in-place situations. I did have plenty of electrical tape in my work truck. I quickly ran out to the vehicle, astonished by all the people in the street. They were watching the smoke cloud rise into the sky and drift to the south. "You should all stay inside!" I yelled to a few of my neighbors. They looked at me questioningly, as if they didn't understand what I said. But I didn't have time to stop and explain the situation.

I unlocked the truck, grabbed a cardboard box of black electrical tape, and headed back inside. I had 15 tape rolls, and I wasn't afraid to use them. I locked the front door and taped the door cracks behind me. Then, I headed to Ashley's room and taped the cracks around the window sashes. I taped the electrical outlets and light switch, as well as the HVAC duct in the floor.

After doing all that, I went over everything again with more tape, making wider seals. I hurried to the kitchen, and filling up a grocery bag with clean bottles, nipples, and pacifiers. Then, grabbing a can of formula and a jug of distilled water, I stashed all these things in my baby's room. Finally, I grabbed my get-out-of-Dodge bag and all the drinks from the fridge and headed to the baby's room. I looked at the weather on my phone again, hoping that the wind hadn't shifted my way – thankfully it hadn't. I cracked open a beer as quietly as I could to avoid waking Ashley and took a long swig of the cold brew. But just as I started to feel like I had everything under control, all hell broke loose.

A second explosion rocked the city of Baltimore, much closer to my home this time. The old windows in the baby's room rattled and one of the panes cracked.

Ashley awoke from her nap, screaming. This was the ISIS threat made real. And much closer to home. I rushed to tape the crack in the window pane and check all of the tape strips for a good seal.

Through the one window of my child's room, I saw a hazy smoke begin to pass by the window. The dread built as I realized that I was smelling smoke. This meant that the outside air was still getting in. I'd worked in these houses for years as an electrician, and I knew just how shoddy the construction was, but now these half-assed homes were a real threat. I checked all the tape again with my right hand, holding and bouncing the baby in the crook of my left arm to calm her. I could still smell the smoke and dust, but all the tape was tight. How was I going to keep the dirty air out? I stressed. If only I had a way to pressurize the room.

Then it hit me – my uncle's carpentry tools! When the housing bubble burst on the East Coast, a lot of small construction companies went out of business. My uncle was among them, and he asked me to store a few of his power tools, including an air compressor. I pulled open the bedroom door, breaking the tape seal, and ran to the basement. The air seemed musty, but much cleaner down there, and I plugged in the compressor unit. The loud motor kicked on and soon the large tank was full of air.

Rushing back upstairs, I re-taped the door and put a small nick in the hose with the tip of my pocketknife. The air hissed out very slowly, and as I held my daughter, I aimed the leaking air toward our faces. After a few minutes of this, the smoke smell didn't seem so noticeable. "This might be working, baby" I said to my little one. Maybe the air pressure in the room was higher than that outside the room, and it would keep the dust and smoke at bay.

The air had cleared outside of the window, and it seemed that an autumn breeze had picked up. *Maybe we might just make it,* I thought. *Maybe.*

CONCLUSION

There's nothing that isn't alarming about a dirty bomb, but it isn't quite as dangerous as it sounds. Of course, anyone in the blast radius of any bomb is at great risk for traumatic injury or death, but what terrorists would be banking on with a dirty bomb is a greater panic due to the inclusion of a scary substance, namely something radioactive.

Sure, radiation is bad and enough of it can kill you, but a dirty bomb is hardly a nuclear warhead. Avoid the dust, stay indoors, let the prevailing winds disperse the dust and smoke, and – above all – don't panic. It's likely that you'd get more radiation in a dentist's office than in a city that's been dirty bombed, and when we panic, the bad guys get the exact reaction that they want. (For more, see "Dirty Bombs" in issue 16 of RECOIL OFFGRID.) ⠿

24

A HACKER BRINGS DOWN THE GRID?

By Tim MacWelch
Illustrations by Sarah Watanabe-Rocco

Was it betrayal? Was that the sickening feeling that grew in my stomach as the skulls on my monitor began to pinwheel? They spun and they laughed. It felt like they were laughing at me. Computers were my life, and my livelihood. How could they turn against me like this?

My intern, Mimi, stood behind me, peering over my shoulder at the demonic images unfolding, unwelcomed on the computer screen. I knew exactly what this was. This was the work of some high-level hacker, or a group of them. How big was this event, I wondered. If they hacked Google, what other systems did they get into? No sooner than I completed that thought, I discovered another place they had entered. The lights, the monitor, the AC, and all of the other powered devices in the office suddenly shut down, all at once. Mimi quietly gasped as the office went dark. She gripped my shoulder.

"What's going on?" she asked, trying not to sound scared.

"It's not good, Mimi." I said as the weight of the situation settled on me. "I think the electrical grid has been hacked."

This edition of "What If?" poses the question many of us have asked since the rise of the Digital Age: What if a computer hacker brings down the grid? To find different approaches to this technological disaster, your favorite urban survival magazine asked three different writers to tell you a tale about surviving this scenario. In this installment, we introduce you to first-time "What If?" contributor, but long-time writer, Jim Cobb. Not only has he published numerous survival books, he's also a well-respected disaster preparedness consultant. Returning to the fold is Erik Lund, a federal law enforcement agent with a vast array of tactical and survival expertise. And then there's me. I have been a professional survival instructor for the past 19 years and am the author of a new book on survival and emergency preparedness, *How To Survive Anything*.

Here's what happens when we wave goodbye to computers, electricity, law, order, and civility.

The Scenario

Situation type: Computer hack leads to a grid-down scenario
Your Crew: You and a college intern, Mimi
Location: Houston, Texas
Season: Autumn
Weather: Normally in the 70s F, but unusually hot in the 80s with high humidity

The Setup

You're a female graphic designer in your early 30s and have a small but successful creative agency doing artwork, marketing, and website design for various small businesses and non-profit organizations. Your boutique is located in the trendy Washington Avenue Arts District. It's 7 p.m., and the sun's starting to set after a hot and humid day full of sunshine.

The Complication

You go to Google to confirm how your client's website looks via a search engine, but rather than the usual white page with the Google logo, you find instead a black page with morbid skulls and an ominous threat: "You are all pawns. Wake up or sleep forever. You've been warned." Both you and Mimi get the same menacing webpage on your smartphones. Then, it appears on all the websites and apps you visit. You turn on your office's TV to find that all the news stations are reporting about this online phenomenon. As time passes, the broadcasters report breaking news of blackouts in downtown Houston and other parts of town. After some time, they start showing footage of some skirmishes between looters and police. Then, the power in your shop goes out. You realize the whole arts district has fallen prey to the same situation that's happening on the news. How far does this online attack go?

DISASTER-PREP EXPERT JIM COBB'S APPROACH

I knew as soon as the lights went out that we'd waited too long. Mimi and I should have beat feet as soon as the first news reports about the hack began to surface. Instead, we just sort of assumed things would return to normal quickly, just like always. I mean, we'd had power outages before, but they'd never lasted more than a few hours at the most. This, though...this was different.

The good news was that the temperature outside had dropped considerably. It was still pretty darn hot, but at least it wasn't sweltering. The bad news was that, like in any city, the freaks came out at night. And that was during "normal" times. There was nothing normal about what was happening. The news reports had mentioned several incidents of looting and rioting. And, unfortunately, several of the spots they'd indicated were between us and Mimi's apartment complex.

Even so, I figured her apartment was a more realistic goal, at least for now, than trying to get to my house 7 miles away. Mimi could usually bike from my studio to her apartment in about 10 minutes. Walking, it was about triple that, give or take – so we hoped, at least.

There was still enough ambient light to see our way around the studio a bit as we gathered supplies. Mimi said that she didn't have much food in her apartment, so we wanted to bring with us as much as we could with us. Which really was sort of laughable, given the meager stocks on hand. I mean, c'mon, this was a marketing business, not a supermarket. If this would've happened a couple of months ago, though, we'd have been set. One of our clients, a small but growing publisher, previously had us handle a book release party for them. While it was a great success, we had leftover cheese, hors d'oeurves, and other finger food in the fridge for what seemed like weeks. All of those goodies were long gone.

While I scanned the shelves in my break-room's kitchenette, I asked Mimi to pull all of the batteries from our digital cameras. I had a couple of small flashlights that took the same size batteries. Thankfully, our cameras used AA batteries rather than battery packs. For once, my avoidance of buying the latest and greatest photography gear worked in my favor.

Mimi had her ever-present messenger bag, and I had my small backpack that served as a purse as well as briefcase. We emptied our bags of all non-essential stuff to make as much room as possible. I hated the thought of leaving my laptop, as I'd already convinced myself the studio would be gutted by looters. But, as a business asset it was insured against theft, so I had that going for me, at least. We filled each bag with water bottles, sleeves of crackers, and apples.

I knew the basic route to Mimi's building, having driven her home a couple of times, but didn't know the neighborhood that well. Being that we'd have to take a roundabout way to get there, hopefully avoiding the looting and such, I figured we'd better take the time to make a plan and check a map of the city. I was embarrassed to admit the first thing I did at that point was pull out my phone to go to Google Maps. Old habits die hard, I guess. As I was racking my brain, trying to remember if the gas station down the block had maps – assuming they were even still open during the power outage – Mimi suddenly jumped up and ran over to the reception desk. I swear, I could almost literally see a light bulb burning over her head as she rummaged through the desk drawers.

I heard her exclaim, "Yes!" and she came back and sat down, setting on the table the Yellow Pages. My puzzled look was answer enough so she opened it up and rifled through the first few pages. Street maps! I'd forgotten that phone books often had maps in the front or back. Now we were in business. We plotted a route that would take us around the areas we already knew were bad news, keeping our fingers crossed that we'd avoid the looters and rioters. Even so, safety was still a concern.

Neither Mimi nor I carried a handgun, though I'd grown up around guns and could shoot fairly well. She at least had a small canister of pepper spray. She said her boyfriend had insisted she carry it when she began riding her bike back and forth to the studio. I thought for a moment then walked back to the kitchenette. From a drawer there, I pulled a large bread knife. The blade was about 8 inches long and serrated. It was pretty thin, but I knew it was sharp. I had no idea if I'd be able to actually use it to harm someone, but I felt better knowing I was armed. Since I had little interest in sliding a sharp blade down the back of my pants, I grabbed the empty cardboard box from the crackers we'd put in our bags. Folding the cardboard over the blade a couple of times, then cutting it to size and covering it with duct tape, I made a fairly decent sheath. I slipped it into my belt at the small of my back. Not the greatest solution, but it would have to work for now.

The basic plan was to get over to Mimi's apartment and spend the night there. Mimi's roommate, Victoria, was out of town visiting family and had left her bicycle behind. If the trains weren't running in the morning, I could borrow the bike to get back to my house. While Mimi's apartment building wasn't really on my way home, it was still closer to it than my studio, in a roundabout sort of way.

I tried calling my neighbor to see if she could run over and check on Vinny, my Maine Coon cat, but neither Mimi nor I could get a call to go through on our

cells. The phones would just search for a signal for a few minutes, then disconnect. There was no dial tone on the landline, either.

We headed out the back door, after making sure all of the blinds and curtains
were completely closed at the front of the studio. I figured there was a slim
chance looters might pass it by if they couldn't see anything worth grabbing.
Mimi unlocked her bike and began pushing it. Our initial plan had been to sling
our bags onto the handlebars, but once we were actually outside, we were both
very reluctant to do so. If we suddenly had to bolt, the bike would probably be
left behind. I toyed with the idea of just leaving the bike locked up, but figured
it wasn't much extra effort for one of us to push it and we might end up needing
it at some point.

The city was surreal. I'd never seen it so dark. No streetlights, no neon lights
over the restaurants and taverns — it was downright spooky. I could see candles or oil lamps in a few windows as we walked by apartment buildings. The
occasional passing car shone like a beacon, as there was nothing else competing with the light from the headlamps. Mimi and I talked in whispered tones,
instinctively wanting to match the darkness with quiet.

We stuck to the side streets as much as possible. Despite the late hour, there
were a lot of people walking around. Most of them were just hanging out,
talking to their neighbors, presumably about the blackout and related matters.
There were a few small groups here and there that caused us some concern,
but we managed to avoid being accosted. Thanks to the maps we'd torn from
the phone book, we got lost only once.

After just shy of an hour of walking, we made it to Mimi's building. Rather
than leave the bike locked on the rack outside, we took it into the apartment
with us. Then, just to be safe, we went back downstairs and grabbed Victoria's
bike, too. I turned on one of the flashlights and balanced it on its butt on a table,
lighting up much of the room. Mimi quickly pulled down the shades and closed
the curtains in the living room. A bit of searching through drawers found a few
candles and some matches. The food in the fridge was still somewhat cool so
we grabbed milk, lunchmeat, and some odds and ends for dinner. I told Mimi
that whatever we didn't eat soon would end up just going to waste unless the
power came back on overnight. She had some ice in the freezer, but didn't have
any coolers, unfortunately. We each took quick, lukewarm showers. Obviously
the building had electric water heaters rather than gas. But the fact that we had
running water was a blessing.

Cleaned up and with full stomachs, we settled in for the night. We each said
a prayer that things would be back to normal by morning.

FEDERAL AGENT ERIK LUND'S APPROACH

The darkness only lasted for a few seconds before the boutique's emergency
lights activated. I could feel Mimi's grip on my arm starting to relax. The emergency lights created an eerie mix of light and shadow that almost resembled
some private party room in the basement of a nightclub.

"What do we do now?" Mimi asked.

"There's nothing more we can do," I replied. "Let's get everything locked up and try to find a way home."

After shutting down the computers and securing some important documents and computer hard drives in the studio's safe, it was time to find a way home.

I wiped away the sweat from my forehead. The power had only been out about 15 minutes, but it was already getting warm inside the boutique. The stagnant air was thick and humid with no options for relief. The idea of opening the windows and front door for circulation was out of the question. Even if it was cooler out-side, doing so would risk inviting in the wrong people – the kind who were look-ing to take advantage of the situation and possibly loot the place. No, the doors and windows would have to be locked, but that also meant that we would have to leave. It wouldn't take long before the temperature inside the store would climb into the 80s. Trying to sleep in this virtual oven would be nearly impossible, and staying up all night in a sweatbox wasn't an attractive option, either.

Getting home was my only real option, and it wasn't going to be easy. My house was only a quick 7-mile train ride away, but trekking that distance in heels was simply not going to happen. I made a mental note to myself: "Leave a set of running shoes at the office from now on." If I ever had to walk home again, I would be better prepared next time.

I decided my first option was to phone a friend for a ride. I wiped away the sweat and started scrolling through my phone, looking for someone close to hit up for a ride home. Ahh, Joshua will do it. A quick second later and his phone started ringing. Then my heart sank a little – his phone went to voice-mail. "Damn!" I yelled out of frustration and a bit of panic. Mimi handed me a cold bottle of water and a cup of yogurt she had snagged from the break-room's refrigerator. "Here take these while they're still cold," Mimi said. "We never did stop for dinner." I looked at her and smiled and remembered why I had select-ed her from all of the intern applications. Despite her fear of the dark, she had a strong work ethic and always offered good options for getting the job done. "Thanks," I said. "That sounds perfect right now."

I sat down and sent a quick text to Joshua explaining my situation and then started to eat my yogurt. Mimi asked, "So what's the plan?" Thinking through my options for a second, I said, "I can't walk home in these heels, so it looks like I'm just gonna wait for Joshua to get back to me. I can always call a cab to take me home, but don't worry about me. You've got your bike – you should go home. I'll be OK." Mimi cast a very disapproving motherly look at me. "Uh, no, I'm not leaving you alone," she said. "I'm staying with you. We'll get home to-gether." I smiled and gave her a look of thank you. I didn't want to be alone, but I couldn't ask her to stay with me, so I was very glad to hear her say that. "OK, let's figure out how to get us home," I said.

After trying for almost a half hour, all of the cab companies were booked. Apparently, a lot of people in the Arts District work late and needed rides home too. I was on a callback list for when a cab became available, but the waitlist was long and it might be several more hours before my turn came up. We started calling ridesharing services, but that's when the phone lines stopped working. The network was probably overwhelmed or affected by the black out, too. The heat in the store was almost unbearable, and my shirt was now almost completely soaked. I said to Mimi, "I need to get some air; I'm going to go outside." Mimi nodded, and went with me to unlock the front door. Stepping outside provided some relief. A gentle breeze made all the difference. It was still hot, but it felt cooler outside than it did in the store. Looking around the area, everything was still dark except for a few buildings that clearly had emergency generators, as their lights were still working. Still, it was as quiet as a cemetery.

"Let's just go to my apartment," Mimi said.

"Thanks, but there's no way I can walk 2 miles in heels," I responded.

Mimi smiled and said, "You won't have to."

I shoved several bottles of water into Mimi's backpack along with my heels. I grabbed a knife from the break room and taped it to the shoulder strap of the backpack. It was just enough tape to hold the knife in place, but it would break free if I needed to grab it. It wasn't much for defense, but it was better than nothing. I pushed the bike outside and locked the front door. I looked over at Mimi.

"Are you ready?" I asked. Mimi stood up from her stretch and with a smile said, "Yep, try to keep up."

While I knew a lot about Mimi's professional skills, I knew next to nothing about her personal life. Turns out she was an amateur triathlete, which is one of the reasons that she rode her bike to work every day. It was a way to get in some bike training. She also ran cross-country in high school, but started competing in triathlons when she got into college. She said the 2-mile run home would be just a little warmup for her. I would ride her bike barefoot and carry the pack with our supplies should we need to detour and head away from trouble.

I laughed at her and said, "I don't think it'll be a problem."

"Challenge accepted," Mimi said, and took off running.

I started peddling and did my best to keep up. About a mile into the journey we crossed out of the blackout zone. The oppressive heat had brought some people out into the streets looking for relief, but being that the Arts District was a business area, there were very few homes or apartments located in the blackout zone. A short 15 minutes after we started, we arrived at Mimi's apartment complex.

"Home at last," she said. "Good job keeping up."

I laughed off the remark, but was ashamed to admit that it about killed me to do so. Note to self: get my fat ass back in the gym and buy a bike, a backpack, and some supplies to keep at the office in case this crap happens again. As I got off the bike and pushed it over to Mimi, she said, "I think it's time for a big glass of wine."

"Ya know," I said, "that's the best idea you've had all day."

SURVIVAL EXPERT TIM MACWELCH'S APPROACH

I had two questions that I could not answer: How widespread was this hack, and how long would the electricity be down? If the power would be back soon,

Mimi and I could just stay at the office. But if not, we might want to get out of Dodge while the getting was good.

But where to go?

I tried several times to call my mom, who lived an hour's drive west of Houston, but the only sound the phone made was a beeping pulse. Mimi got the same noise, desperately trying to call her friends and boyfriend. All of the phone calls of a frightened city must have swamped the system. It sank in slowly that we might be on our own for a while.

Mimi looked like she was ready to bolt, but I lied to her and said that everything would be OK. I knew it wouldn't, but it was what she needed to hear. I asked Mimi what she had at her apartment in the way of food and supplies, and her response was none – Keurig coffee, plastic utensils, and maybe a package of instant ramen or two. She was a college student after all.

Mimi's place was about 3 miles south of the shop, while I lived more than 7 miles away. But at my home I had food, a propane grill to cook the food, and several water cooler jugs of water, among other supplies that I had purchased after the last hurricane. We talked over our options of leaving or staying at the office, even talked about staying at a hotel or trying to hail a cab. Neither of us had much cash though, and we knew that the plastic cards we lived off of would be little help to us with the power out. "Looks like it would be our best choice to go to my house," I said, and Mimi reluctantly agreed. We talked about taking turns on Mimi's bike, one walking and one riding. But I was afraid that the nice new bike would be a tempting target for theft. I had been robbed for my bike when I first moved to town, and I still had a tiny scar under my chin where my face hit the asphalt during the attack. Again, I urged Mimi to side with my plan – we stick together and we just walk.

We had worked through dinner, before things took their bad turn, and we were both in need of food and drink. We pooled our cash, locked the door, and went a few doors down to the sandwich shop. As we walked, we saw that the street was packed with cars, most of them abandoned. This seemed odd, but we didn't give it much thought at the time.

The doors were open at the eatery and some flashlights had been set about for lighting. The shop owner and his son were the only ones working and the place was packed. It turned out that they were just giving away the food. "It won't keep in this heat," they said. I had gotten to know the owner and his family since opening my business around the corner. I felt bad asking, but as he handed me and Mimi a brown paper bag of sandwiches, I asked him if they had a car and could give us a ride out of town. He said a car wouldn't do any of us any good. He went on to explain that before the power went out, all of the stoplights went green. The hacker's doing, no doubt. Every intersection had wrecks, and many people had been killed. The ambulances couldn't even get to most of the accidents. Things were far worse than I initially guessed.

I hated to ask him, but I did: "We've going to have to walk several miles in the dark tonight. Can we borrow one of your flashlights?" He looked hesitant at first, but glanced over at the dwindling stack of meats and cheeses. "Sure," he replied. "At this rate we'll have to close up shop in a few minutes anyway." I asked where they were headed, hoping they were headed the same way as us, but was crushed when he said they were walking east. My place was to the west.

I took a flashlight, thanking the man and his son profusely. Mimi and I walked quickly back to our office. No more than 10 steps from the sandwich shop, I noticed two men peering into various cars, and thought they were up to no good. Our movement caught their eyes and they began staring at us. The larger man, a fat and sweaty looking oaf, called out, "Hey honey, what's in the bag? What's the matter? Cat got your tongue? You got a place to go for tonight? We've got a place. You can go with us."

They were about 10 steps behind us as I unlocked the front door, pushed Mimi inside, and locked it behind us. Without a word, we both started drawing the blinds shut. Mimi and I both jumped when one of the men started banging on the door. "We know where you are," the voice jeered.

Retreating to the back of the office, I tried to dial 911 on my mobile phone, but only heard the beeping again that indicated the lines were jammed. We agreed that any thoughts of staying overnight were out of the question now that we had stalkers.

By the light of the flashlight and the decorative candle from the bathroom, we scavenged the office for everything that could be remotely useful. We found some chocolates at the bottom of a desk drawer and an old bottle of salad dressing from the small fridge in the break-room. There were several bottles of water in there, too, and some odd bits of clothing and a broom in the closet. As I looked at the mismatched items, an idea started to form.

"Mimi, who would you walk right past on the street? Who would you not even look twice at?" I asked her. "A salesman, or one of those guys with fliers," she responded. She gave several other answers, until she hit the one I was looking for: "A homeless person!"

"Yes," I said with a growing smile, "a homeless person is ignored by almost everyone." Every day America allows people to suffer on the streets with very little in place to help them. But today, it was the thing that just might make us invisible.

We still had running water, and in the bathroom we washed off every hint of makeup from our faces. Then, I took a piece of the chocolate and melted it in my hand. I wiped it randomly on Mimi's face and hands, and mine as well. We looked like we hadn't had a bath in a year, but we still smelled of perfume and now chocolate. As I mentioned that hole in our plan, Mimi grabbed the oil and vinegar salad dressing and said, "This is expired — let's try it." She wiped a handful through her normally pretty hair and soon looked like a greasy drowned rat, a rat that stank of rotting food. I beamed with pride at my crafty protégé. "Me next," I said.

Then I put on an ugly, oversized shirt left at the office by an ex-boyfriend, and Mimi donned a sketchy looking trench coat that a former intern had left behind. A little more chocolate wiped on the clothing made the garments look like they came out of a trash heap. I took up the trash bag from the larger office can, with trash and all. In it I placed our water bottles, brown bag of sandwiches, the chocolates, and our purses. I slung it over my shoulder and handed Mimi the broom. "You carry this – it's the closest thing to a weapon we have," I said. Just as we were ready to make our exodus into the parking lot behind the shop, there was a banging at the front door like before.

"Hey, girlies!" the man called. "If you open up the door, we'll share some drinks with you!"

I unlocked the back door and we fled, leaving a lit candle on the desk so the men would think we were still inside the office. We ran for the first few blocks, attracting some very strange looks as we went. To the average passerby, it must have looked like one bag lady stole a bag of trash from another bag lady, who was chasing her with a broom.

After a few more blocks, we slowed to a walk and caught our breath. People still looked at us, but quickly averted their eyes and looked at anything else as we passed them by. It was as if they could catch homelessness by looking at us too long. Due to our run through the neighborhood, we reached the freeway sooner than I anticipated. It was gridlocked, with vacant vehicles everywhere. Plenty of people were milling about in the failing light, but our path was relatively clear. We walked side by side on the road, and anyone who glanced our way quickly turned and looked somewhere else.

We paused for a moment, draining two water bottles and sharing a sandwich, but we didn't dare delay too long. As we hid behind a vacant box truck on the freeway, we saw fires spring up on either side of the freeway. Random vehicles, businesses, and homes were burning. This night would never be forgotten by anyone who can survive it.

We walked on and saved our flashlight until the twilight had completely faded and we really needed it. About a mile from my home, people started to approach us in the dark, drawn like moths to the light. Most were asking about the flashlight. But as soon as they drew near, I lifted the light beam to shine upon our faces, as if telling some campfire ghost story. Our appearance and our smell were more than enough to inspire people to say "Sorry, don't worry about it," and "Never mind, thanks anyway." One kind older man even offered us some bottles of water, saying that we looked like we could use them. Mimi smiled and said "No, thank you. We're fine now." Walking down my neighborhood's exit ramp from the highway, I finally felt like we would be fine.

The lie I had told Mimi earlier had turned out to be true. We were going to be OK, but this night could have easily gone another way. And as I saw my house numbers in the dying glow of the flashlight, I knew we were going to be safe – for a little while, anyway.

CONCLUSION

I hope it was worth it. I hope you're happy with your high-tech world of push-button ease and the inevitable vulnerability that comes along with it.

Computer hacking is an everyday part of the modern world, and a looming threat to the modern American way of life.

When a few disenfranchised weirdos living in their mom's basements or a few well-schooled hackers from an opposing ideology are able to steal information, drain bank accounts, shut down utilities, and bring our world to its knees – at the end of the day, we really only have ourselves to blame. We handed them the keys to it all. So what do we do to keep this work of fiction from becoming fact? Should everybody go Amish overnight? No, that's not possible, nor is it the right approach. As individuals, the best we can do is become more self-reliant and more independent from modern technology. This gives us a cushion to fall back on, in any type of crisis. And those of you who are part of big business or are bureaucrats, you need to take hackers as the serious threat they really are. Spend a little of your money to fight them, or lose it all when they shut you down.

Finally, our culture needs to understand that newer, faster, fancier, and more interconnected technologies aren't always a good thing. The more parts there are in a system, the more parts that can fail – or in the case of this story, be used against us. Take this edition of "What If?" very seriously, folks. Don't let your precious computers and high-tech gizmos become the Trojan Horse that gets all of our cities sacked. ⠶

25

YOU'RE STRANDED ON A REMOTE BACKROAD?

By RECOIL OFFGRID Staff
Illustrations by Joe Oesterle

Every year, we hear stories of stranded motorists who, for one reason or another, end up in a situation that culminates in a fatality. Although we'd like to think we'd never end up in a similarly grim position, the people who actually found themselves in those circumstances probably assumed the same thing. Our overreliance on the GPS systems found on our phones or in our vehicles, as well as the belief that we can "just call someone" whenever we need to, has made us a little too complacent in our preparatory measures. If those luxuries proved to be out of service or just plain useless and your vehicle broke down in a remote location, what – besides luck, hope, and instinct – do you have to rely on to help mitigate a bad situation?

The Scenario

Situation type: Stranded on a remote dirt road
Your Crew: You and your adolescent son
Location: Rural New Mexico
Season: Winter
Weather: Cold; high 60 degrees F, low 24 degrees F

The Setup

You've decided to take your 12-year-old son on his first hunting trip in rural New Mexico. The ranch you're headed to doesn't publicize its whereabouts. Only a select few people know of this location since it's invite-only, but you were able to make the arrangements through a friend who hunts there regularly. He provided the GPS coordinates and contact info for the owners who don't live onsite. There's no one else staying at the ranch, but you do have access to their facilities, food, and have key codes to enter and exit. This trek is several hours from your home in Texas, but you figure the road trip will give you some bonding time with your son and provide a chance to enjoy the scenery. The closest major city is about four hours away and the closest major highway is about a two-hour drive from the location where you'll be staying. There's a long, unmarked, unpaved road that leads from the main highway to the ranch. You're all packed up with your firearms, clothing, and some snacks and drinks for the drive. Your assumption is that if you get lost, you'll be able to call the property owners for directions or clarification.

The Complication

As you approach the ranch down the long, winding road and the sun begins to set, your cell phone's map app tells you're about an hour from the location. Then, the unthinkable happens. Your truck's engine suddenly loses power, clunks loudly, and then shuts off. You step out of the cab to find a long trail of oil and metal chunks on the road – there's no way this engine will be taking you any further. You still have about a half tank of gas and the truck's battery is good.

Since you're a considerable distance from the ranch or the highway, you're not sure if you should risk walking either direction in the dark. Also, your cell phone has no reception, and you have no other means of communication. Although the outside temperature is currently in the mid 50s, temperatures at night can drop below freezing. Since your son is asthmatic, he'd have to stay behind if you walk to get help. Cold air can trigger asthma symptoms and flare-ups, especially if it's dry out. All you have is what you brought with you to make do until you find some assistance.

What do you do? Walk to find help or until your cell phone has signal again? Wait it out on a remote road that gets little to no traffic? You have a big bag of potato chips and some beef jerky, four 500ml bottles of water, changes of clothing, hunting rifles, ammo, binos, and your cell phone. How can you survive being stranded for hours or even days? We asked protective specialist Mel Ward and disaster management specialist Nila Rhoades for their takes on how to handle this situation.

DISASTER MANAGEMENT SPECIALIST NILA RHOADES' APPROACH

Preparation:

Planning a hunting trip like this would take a lot of foresight. The potential for things to go sideways are many. When planning any kind of trip, whether it's to a theme park, an overnight getaway, or a hunting excursion, one must plan for the worst-case scenario and pack supplies accordingly. As the old saying goes, "A failure to plan is a plan to fail."

To prepare my child mentally for this trip, I'd have long discussions with them on the pillars of survival: fire, water, food, shelter, and medical. We'd then pack items for each of those pillars before we left for our trip. My child would have a good understanding of the rule of 3s as well. One can go 3 minutes without air, 3 hours without shelter, 3 days without water, and 3 weeks without food.

If my son and I found ourselves in a situation like this one, our first priority is finding shelter, since air is a given. The truck's cab will shield us from the elements, but at some point, we'd have to find help or a way to communicate with emergency services. We wouldn't move from the vehicle for at least 72 hours. It takes approximately 24 hours to be able to file a missing person's report, so I'd give a little extra time for search parties to attempt to locate our vehicle. One primary rule of getting lost or stranded is to stay in the current location so emergency services have a better chance of finding you based on your route. If a communications plan wasn't put in place, we'd stay in the vehicle until help arrived or until we felt we had waited enough time to embark to a secondary location. Having a paper map and compass is critical here as well as having an outlined route that's followed alongside the GPS on the cell phone. After my 48-hour mark, I'd start doing some map route recon and asking questions like:
> How far am I from the ranch?
> Where is the nearest service station?
> Where is the nearest town?

> Which is the closest walking distance?

> How long is walking to the nearest aid going to take?

> How much time should I add on that pace to account for my asthmatic son?

> What supplies have to come with me, and which can stay in the vehicle?

An important aspect of planning trips where communication is intermittent, is establishing a GOTWA plan prior to embarking on the trip; also known as a contingency communication plan.

G- Where I'm Going.

O- Others I'm taking.

T- Time of my return.

W- What to do if I don't return.

A- Actions to take if I'm hit or actions to take if you're hit. (Meaning, actions to take if I miss my communications window in this scenario.)

Prior to such a trip I'd have my vehicle properly inspected so an engine malfunction would be a literal act of God. Many auto shops offer pre-trip inspections and would hopefully have found any major issues prior to such a trip. Bringing a hunting rifle is essentially a no-brainer as is it a hunting trip, but I'd also take my EDC Glock 19 as well because the trip between the ranch and my home is a fair distance

Researching the local area is always a must. Not only weather, but also terrain, indigenous wildlife, local flora, and fauna, as well as nearest towns and service stations. As far as supplies go, a satellite phone is going to be my biggest asset on a trip like this. It is my lifeline in case of emergency. Being a mother, I always pack a few extra days of supplies wherever I go. Whether it's to a local water park for the weekend, or a two-week-long cross-country road trip. I always bring more than I anticipate using. A camping /hunting trip like this would be no different. Therefore, I'd have extra food and supplies like a Sawyer filter that could be used to filter water we found in the area. The foods I brought would most likely consist of calorie dense granola bars, protein bars, Slim Jims, and probably a few MREs. A little bit of that food can go a very long way, especially for a child and especially when we aren't physically exerting ourselves yet.

On Site:

The one practice I'd absolutely avoid is leaving the vehicle for at least 72 hours. That's our shelter and our safety from animals and the elements, so we'd stay put with our supplies until help arrived. Being in the middle of nowhere, there's still always a propensity for evil to thrive. My main concerns wouldn't be human in nature, but rather animals like coyotes, mountain lions, snakes, etc. Again, staying inside our vehicle will prevent any unwanted and dangerous visitors. The weather is nearly perfect during the day, but the night could prove to be chilly. Layering the clothing that we brought for our trip would provide warmth during the evenings if the temperature got unbearably cold.

If a GOTWA or contingency communications plan wasn't set up prior to departure, I'd still stay put for at least 72 hours. I'd assess my car for items to signal with. My side mirrors would work for a signaling device to get the attention of aircraft.

I'd also take my spare tire and be prepared to burn it to signal those nearby. Black smoke from the rubber would hopefully catch the eye of passersby.

Being stuck anywhere can be scary. Therefore, keeping calm and maintaining a level head is critical. Children feed off their parents' emotions and reactions so keeping calm for your children is important and necessary. Especially with an asthmatic child, I wouldn't want them to get worked up or in a panic. Upon first realizing that my son and I were stranded I'd assess our supplies and attempt to ascertain our location via our map. Having already established a GOTWA plan, when I don't check in at the ranch my family back home should start initiating the emergency plan that we laid out prior to departure.

Another aspect of my supplies would be a SPOT device. It's essentially an emergency beacon (Emergency Locating Transmitter). As soon as the vehicle died and I realized that it was approximately 60 miles away from the ranch, it could be time to turn on the emergency beacon. Depending on my GOTWA plan, if I didn't have help by sunup, I'd initiate the SPOT device, per my GOTWA plan.

Crisis:

My main concern would be the medical items needed for my son's asthma. I'm a big believer in the phrase, "a pair and a spare." Therefore, I always carry an extra dose, bottle, inhaler with me at all times; on top of what my child carries on them for emergencies. Because he's got a medical condition and because he's my child, I won't leave him under any circumstances. I cannot guarantee his safety if I'm not in his immediate vicinity.

Due to the lack of physical exertion because we're essentially waiting in our vehicle for help to arrive, we could stretch our food and water supplies over the course of many hours, if not many days. Our biggest concern would be water intake and staying hydrated during the warm days.

Having prepared for this trip to the point where I have multiple contingency plans, I wouldn't anticipate being on my vehicle for more than 24 hours. However, being a parent, a lot of my supplies would be able to last for many more days. My SPOT device would work as a signaling beacon. Being the parent that I am, I also always carry a mini SERE kit in my purse, that also has a signal mirror and a few methods of starting fire to keep warm along with water filtration.

PROTECTIVE SPECIALIST MEL WARD'S APPROACH

The Mindset of Mitigation

I treat every outing like I'm leaving the wire. My home is my Forward Operating Base (FOB). Everything else outside that perimeter is unknown. Whether I'm going to the store or heading into the New Mexico desert, I bring things that let me shoot, move, talk, and heal. These are like my four basic food groups.

How much of this stuff I bring depends on where I go, with whom, and for how long, but I always bring the same things. I like to have things that make mild to wild inconveniences much simpler to contend with. That's my personal strategy. I can't easily prepare for everything, but I can prepare to make everything a little easier.

Our society has made us victims of our own success. As a recovering survivor of stable power, hot and cold running water, and the mostly peaceful transfer of power, I carry with me things that take the place of that which I've seen fail us.

Pandemics can empty store shelves. Supply chain shortages delay products and services. Freak winter storms wreak havoc in states that aren't prepared for extreme weather. Hackers half a world away can make gas expensive and hard to come by all because they ransomed a pipeline company's computer network.

Regardless of what I'm doing, I want to plan like it's the 19th century rather than the 21st. This is especially the case when I travel. I'm preparing like I'm going back in time. I'm not going to rely on smartphones, power grids, and minutes-away Emergency Medical Services. I'm going to account for these modern conveniences, but I'm going to plan like they won't be there when I need them.

Reconnaissance

The first thing I like to do if I'm going somewhere I haven't been before is a map reconnaissance. I not only want to review the route and have an alternate in mind, but for something like hunting or hiking, I'd like an idea of the area of operations I'll be working in. You can use Google Maps if you want, but I like to stay away from that stuff and go with apps like OsmAnd or Maps.me. Both of these work offline.

Speaking of offline, I'm a paper map guy. I keep a road atlas in all my vehicles. Gas station maps of your region are also great to have as atlases tend to be more compact. It's nice to have something you can spread out on the hood of your vehicle and do some figuring on. You can also get laminated versions of these from bookstores and use map markers to highlight routes, gas stations, hazards, etc.

Concerning the route, I like to know where hospitals are along the way as well as the closest advanced care to where I'll be operating. I might identify a few with trauma capabilities as well as some walk-in clinics for bumps and bruises if we incur something minor. Since my near-teenaged son will accompany me, I want to include him in the route planning and points-of-interest along the way so he's participating rather than just observing. While doing this, I'm going to give his mother, or someone reliable not coming with us, a five-point contingency plan.

I'll tell her where I'm going, who I'm taking with me, how long I'll be gone, what to do if I don't come back on time, and what I will do in response to an emergency. Some of you might recognize this from your time in the military. I think it's just as useful for civilian activities like hunts and hiking and keeps us in the right mindset. It's easy to do and much better than the usual, "I'll call ya when I get there." What if I don't get there? What if I can't call?

Since we're exploring an isolated region on this trip, I'm going to use either mytopo.com or USGS.gov for some topographical awareness. Both of these resources offer cheap ways to print detailed maps of your chosen AO. I might like to identify some high ground, key terrain features, and water sources in the area. If I give myself a top-down preview, the land is likely to make more sense to me when I see it for the first time.

I'm also going to check the weather forecast for the areas I'll be passing through as well as my ultimate destination. Farmersalmanac.com has lots of info on weather, phases of the moon, and long-range forecasts for trips I might be planning down the road.

Now would also be a good time to talk to people who've been where I'm going. What are the temperatures like there? What kind of wildlife is in the area? What gear do they recommend I bring? What should I watch out for? For me, this is like an intelligence briefing. I like to treat the trip like a mission. I'll enjoy it when it goes well, but I'm prepared for when it doesn't.

Now that we have an idea of where we're going, how to get there, and maybe what to expect; let's get the truck ready.

Vehicle Readiness

I'm going to inspect my truck like I've never seen it before. I like to check the usual things we take for granted: tires, fluids, belts, and hoses. I'm going to make sure the spare tire is present and ready to go as well as ensuring I have the proper tools to change it. I can also reference a site like AAA.com for vehicle inspection tips if I feel like I'm missing something. I'm also not above scheduling an inspection with the local dealership or auto repair shop. Some dealerships even offer free inspections on the items above and can point out areas that need to be addressed.

Once I'm satisfied the truck is mechanically sound, I'm going to inspect all the gear I'm taking with me. As mentioned earlier, I have all this with me all the time. I may add or subtract amounts given the situation I'm heading into.

Most of what I keep in the truck is recovery and road-side repair related. In rugged terrain I might bring two full-size spare tires. I have a hi-lift jack and shovel as well as a heavy-duty bottle jack (not the one that came with the truck). I carry a full toolkit with sockets and wrenches sized for my truck. I have chains, at least one kinetic recovery rope, winch supplies like tree-savers and snatch blocks as well as two sets each of soft and hard shackles.

In the toolbox I keep a spare serpentine belt for my motor and extra vehicle fluids. I have 5 gallons of water, 5 gallons of gas, 1 gallon of anti-freeze, 2 quarts of my engine oil, power steering fluid, sealed brake fluid, and transmission fluid. I also bring along a lithium-ion jump starter kit that can start multiple dead vehicles or charge my phone. I have a high-output portable air compressor, tire repair kits, tire spoon, and extra valve stems to round out fixing all but the worst tire issues.

Provisions and Gear

For the New Mexico trip, I'm bringing what my son and I need to be there three times as long as my planned stay. I'm setting up our kit and vehicle in a way that serves us if we don't reach the ranch, lodge, or campsite. It's just me, him, and the truck and I want to keep thinking and planning like that's all there will be.

I'll have with me my rifle and pistol with spare mags and ammo. I always bring along my ragged copy of the SAS Survival Handbook for its many useful survival tips the success of our society has demanded we forget. Water purification is top of my list since taking enough water with me for even a week-long trip can start to strain a single-vehicle outing. I like Guzzle H2O's portable Stream system. As long as I have a water source, I can quickly and easily refill my water tanks. I also like to take a two-person tent along with me regardless of if I'm staying in a lodge-like setting or not. Sleeping bags are relatively lightweight insurance against cold nights even if I don't plan on using them.

I obviously have my cell phone for primary comms, but also like to have a satellite phone for remote outings. I also carry a backup pre-paid cellphone. While working in the AO, I have several General Mobile Radio Service (GMRS) radios. I like these because they're relatively inexpensive for intra-group communication and are repeater-capable for situations like the one we're about to get into. For repeaters in your area, you can check mygmrs.com.

I always have several GPS-capable devices with me regardless of what I'm doing. My wife got me the Garmin Tactix Charlie one year for Christmas which is a nice tool to have on your wrist. I still run my old, but trusty 60CSx as well. Of course, I have my phone's GPS, which I use the most, but trust the least. For some extra peace-of-mind I'm looking at the Garmin InReach Mini personal locator. To aid with reception issues, I've been researching the weBoost Drive Reach OTR. This is basically a 5G/4G signal amplifier that drastically increases your coverage in more remote areas.

For emergency medical I bring plenty of tourniquets staged in, on, or around each vehicle door. I like to use North American Rescue products like their Combat Casualty Response Kit. This lets me deal with various traumas and provides enough resources to deal with multiple patients. I also have individual bleeder kits I keep in response bags that contain light, ammo, and medical. Further, I have normal non-trauma first-aid kits, so I don't have to use my good medical supplies on routine scrapes and cuts. Rounding this out I have a pole-less litter just in case.

If anyone is dependent on medication, like my son is, I make sure to bring extra along with me. I'll store it in several places in the vehicle and among my gear in case I lose a pack so I'm not losing everything I have.

Now that I've done nearly everything I can to make sure nothing goes wrong, it's time to break down on the side of a dirt road.

Are We There Yet?

So, the truck is mechanically down hard, we're not yet at our destination, and we're pretty far from where we last had cellular reception. Before I get into what I might do from here, I'd like to go back to my paper maps and suggest something. One thing I like to do is make note of when my cell signal starts becoming spotty. I'll mark my paper map with a last-known spot of solid signal as I wind my way into the badlands. This gives me a sort of rally point I can navigate to if all else fails so I can make an emergency call. I want to go through all my various modes of communication before I start thinking about hoofing it or wearing animal hides and crafting spears.

Without a good cell signal, I'd first try OnStar, or similar service, if I have it. OnStar still uses the same cellular network as your telephone, but the system might have more range than your handheld due to it pushing more watts. It's worth a try. If I had the aforementioned weBoost antenna, now would be a good time to power that thing up.

If cellular isn't going to happen, I can try a couple things. First, I'd send some texts and emails to the person I gave my five-point plan to describing the situation, where I am, and what I'm planning to do. Sometimes when signal is faint, a text might make it through whereas voice cannot. I'd next see what I could get on my GMRS radios. I have both a high-power unit in the truck as well as handhelds. Since I took the time to visit mygmrs.com, I've already programmed in any available repeaters in my area that can extend my range. If I absolutely have no comms working, it's time to start figuring out exactly where I am on the map and where the closest help might be whether I try to signal to it or walk there.

Remember those offline navigation apps? Now I'm glad I had those installed on my phone as well the pertinent regions downloaded so I know exactly where I am and can communicate that position via latitude and longitude, Military Grid Reference System, or even key terrain. Now would also be a good time to disconnect the negative battery terminal on my truck to preserve it since it's not going to be running anytime soon.

Now I know where I am and what my options are looking like. Since no one is supposed to be headed out this way for some time, staying in place and waiting for someone to come along may not be my best option. It looks like I'm facing an hour (by vehicle, much longer on foot) either to the ranch or the highway. I'm not sure if the ranch has a landline or any other form of communications equipment since I've never been there. I do know, however, that I marked on my map the last known location for cell reception back towards the highway.

Given that I'm not currently under any additional duress like injury or lacking food and water, walking back toward the highway is looking like the most direct route to getting some help. Alternatively, I could walk in the rest of the way to the ranch and continue the trip, but at some point I'm going to need my vehicle recovered, so I should probably get that ball rolling and then see about salvaging the rest of the trip.

So, what I'd probably do is set up the tent for the night at the truck and walk back to my known reception point in the morning. I'll keep a signal fire going throughout the night just in case. I'll ration my supplies, even though I brought extra, in case what looks like a simple plan to do some walking becomes more complicated. If I did have something with me like the Garmin InReach, I'd probably save that for a medical emergency or last resort.

Before bedding down I'd also ensure there's no possibility of a fire hazard with the truck. I'd probably cover that oil spill with dirt under and around the truck and make sure to keep my fire well away from it. I want a signal fire, not a signal explosion. The entire time I'm talking to my son and including him in the decision-making. If he's worried at all, it may help him to be a part of the process of how to fix the situation and give him some comfort that we're taking steps to mitigate hazards. We might make what was going to be a fun hunting trip into even more of an adventure.

When morning comes, I pack up the guns, water, radios, first-aid, food, don some hunter orange, and prepare to hike back to that last known point on my map. I'll open the hood on the truck as a signal as well as use rocks or a shallow dirt trench to create an arrow on the ground indicating my direction of travel. I'd also tape a note to the inside of the window describing our plan and how to contact us should anyone come along and find the truck.

I would also compose some updated texts and emails and send them even if it tells me they're not going through. As we walk, I might catch just enough signal for them to be sent as well as possibly receive word back. As we step off, I make sure to mark the truck's location on my GPS as well as my physical map making note of key terrain in the area I can spot from a distance.

Even though my son has a medical condition, I don't recommend splitting up and leaving him with the truck. Too many unknowns. I take what I need to care for him with me and walk to a known point together. I can use my map or GPS tools to roughly measure the distance we'll be covering. I'd bring the tent and camping gear just in case we have to overnight while waiting for help.

Once we reach an area with enough reception to send and receive messages, we can initiate our five-point plan. Our emergency contact person can pass on our location, status, and requests and act as a relay for us if needed. We can set up a temporary camp and wait for help depending on the time of day and estimation of how long it will take aid to arrive. If there's time left in the day, we can return to the vehicle and wait there until help arrives.

CONCLUSION

To sum it all up, preparation and planning can go a long way, even when things go sideways during a road trip. The key to success is planning for the unexpected — for the worst-case scenario like we see here. We should always be prepared for medical issues, vehicle issues, food supply issues, water contamination issues, and getting lost. The most crucial aspect is remaining calm and having an emergency contact plan in place, so if a communication window is missed, then friends and/or family have a protocol to follow to send emergency response aid to your general vicinity.

Assume your conventional means of communication and GPS may not work when you need it most, so having redundancies may mean the difference between life and death. Review multiple routes to and from your location and pinpoint whatever key facilities are closest: police substations, hospitals, etc. Jot down and keep direct contact info for these facilities. Leave an itinerary with predetermined contact times/dates for those back home so they know there's something wrong if they don't hear from you. A little effort on things like this beforehand will save you a lot of headache if you find yourself in the proverbial middle of nowhere. ⠿

26

YOU'RE STUCK IN A COUNTRY CONSUMED BY POLITICAL TURMOIL?

By RECOIL OFFGRID Staff
Illustrations by Cassandra Dale

It's 2021 and many travel restrictions have lifted, offering people the opportunity to finally vacation internationally or visit other countries for business. Although it may have seemed like COVID was the only big concern when considering foreign travel, political turmoil can be just as contagious, unpredictable, and deadly as a conventional disease. Whether it's the 8888 Uprising in Burma, 2016 attempted coup in Turkey, or recent presidential assassination in Haiti, situations can often unfold with little to no ability to estimate how it'll impact national stability or treatment of foreigners.

Despite whatever planning you may have thought was adequate and thorough, your overseas travel may put you in the wrong place at the wrong time with only local resources to assist you in seeking safe haven. If you were stuck in a country that was suddenly reduced to chaos and the political rhetoric on the ground shifted blame to people of your nationality, how would you deal with potentially being labeled as a threat to the local government? Risking capture could result in interrogation, imprisonment, or even death.

The Scenario

Situation type: Traveling abroad
Your Crew: Yourself
Location: Southeast Asia
Season: Autumn
Weather: Humid; high 88 degrees F; low 63 degrees F

The Setup

You take a trip to Southeast Asia, a region you've traveled to many times in the past, to visit a plant that manufactures goods for your company. You plan to spend a few days visiting with your associates there, but you only have a marginal understanding of the local language, culture, laws, and key facilities, such as the American embassy. Protests have been frequent in the area during the last few weeks, and most have culminated in a few arrests before crowds were dispersed by police. This time feels different. Over the next few days, you begin to worry as police presence and the size of the protests seem to be escalating. The national news is continually blaming Western influence for the corruption and continued civil unrest. As if the guilt by association couldn't get much worse, you're also informed that all foreign diplomats are in the process of being expelled, embassies are being forced to close, and all foreigners – particularly Americans – are being explicitly named as subversives by the government.

The Complication

You wake up a couple days before your flight home to the sound of gunshots outside your hotel. Peeking out your window, you can see a column of military vehicles moving down the street, with uniformed troops marching alongside. Citizens are fleeing in fear. You turn on the TV, and the American news channel in your hotel room is saying that protests have morphed into an attempted coup that was crushed by the government. In response, the government is now detaining and questioning any foreigners.

After speaking with a few other Americans in your hotel, you learn that the government is intermittently shutting down internet access, similar to what went on during the Arab Spring and more recently in Myanmar. You're also informed that secret police are beginning to monitor hotels for foreigners, and that access to the airport has been compromised by a military blockade. As an American, you fear your passport may put you in jeopardy. The prison conditions are terrible, and you're aware that many people have been incarcerated in this country indefinitely without even having a trial.

What do you do? Who can you call? Do you have any rights whatsoever? The language barrier proves an even greater obstacle to navigate. What steps can you take to explain the situation believably and receive assistance from family, the State Department, or anyone else who can help you out? We've asked security expert Danny Pritbor as well as international media correspondent Miles Vining for their recommendations on how to deal with the situation.

SECURITY EXPERT DANNY PRITBOR'S APPROACH

Years ago, a mentor and longtime friend shared a quote that stuck with me throughout my years of service: "Movement without observation equals death." At the time, the context was in reference to a low-light firearms course, where he was explaining the constant need for situational awareness. To be effective in the tactical environment, you need to process and prioritize data rapidly — in other words, stay "switched on." As my career progressed, and the areas of operations shifted from domestic to international, I realized the saying couldn't be truer. But based on my experiences, I'm going to add to the quote, "Movement without observation *and preparation* equals death." I, along with countless others serving in operational roles, often in hostile environments, have learned some hard lessons, usually after the action takes place, and many times after lives are lost.

Preparation

Prior to an overseas trip, I conduct a risk assessment. Using open-source satellite imagery, I get an overview of the area. First, I locate my hotel, the airport, and worksite. Secondly, I start to identify where my friendly locations are, like the U.S. Embassy or allied embassies. Other key locations are hospitals, alternate airports, or maritime ports.

I identify my primary routes and secondary routes to frequently traveled locations. I research information on activities such as crime, terrorist actions, and government/civil unrest. My focus is initially on the city or town I'll be traveling to, then working outward to the provinces and country. I pay close attention to the entire region as well; neighboring countries may have turmoil that can bleed over and affect the area of travel. By taking these steps, I establish where and when these significant acts are taking place and pinpoint the highest risk. Then, I can take steps to mitigate the risk.

For example, I advised a group of college-aged individuals who would be traveling through parts of North Africa. They wanted to take the train, which was the common mode of transportation. There was a low to moderate threat of terrorist activity in the region. After the group attended our travel security course, they quickly understood that the train would make them vulnerable to "time and place predictability" as well as place them in a crowded environment where women are often sexually assaulted. Because they understood the risk, they developed an alternate plan which allowed for greater flexibility in how and when they traveled.

Now that there's an understanding of the risks and situational awareness of the environment, I develop what's called a "base monitored movement plan." It's pretty simple: I have someone back home who is my base monitor. I share my communications and travel plans with them. For example, I'll check in every 24 hours at 6 p.m. local time on primary communications, which I'll have listed as a text from my cell phone (alternate is an email; contingency is satellite text via Garmin inReach Explorer+).

For any missed check-ins, I establish a shorter window. If I miss my 6 p.m. check-in, I attempt again as soon as possible; but if it's midnight with no contact, my base monitor will need to consider calling the listed emergency contacts of the area I have listed in the plan. When civil unrest takes place, airports are the first to shut down. Haiti is the prime example of this and Egypt during the Arab Spring. I build options for alternate means of departures from the country. Along with my alternate communications plan, I take into consideration establishing evacuation plans which include air, land, and sea (or other body of water) options.

What I typically do is have a pro word — a shorthand procedure word representing a predetermined meaning — designated for each city and/or evacuation plan. Should I need to affect a specific plan, I'll send the pro word to my base monitor, and they know which plan is in effect. That way I keep my travel plans off communications.

As a traveler, I carry two lines of gear. In principle, each line consists of the following categories: medical, communications, and personal defense. I add to these, but don't omit any of the three. This system has served me and others well by ensuring an overlap of these critical items. If I were considered a resident or living abroad, I'd expand my lines of gear to a third (vehicle) and even a fourth (residence) line. Important note: the lines shouldn't appear military/tactical, so leave the MOLLE and Velcro-covered bags at home.

The first line is carried on my body. For medical, I carry a pressure bandage, usually a 4-inch Israeli bandage, stripped out of the package. I remove it from the primary marked packaging to give it a sterile look (no government markings) to avoid any questioning should my bags get searched. The bandage is packaged in a second, clear unmarked wrapper to keep it clean. I also carry a CAT Tourniquet in a non-tactical color (i.e. orange). Both these items are carried in an ankle med kit and/or cargo pockets.

My primary form of communication is my cell phone. On it, I have my navigation and various communication applications. These apps require cell signal or Wi-Fi. Many of the navigation apps can be used offline, without cellular signal. (We could go down a rabbit hole with digital security, so that'll be left for another time.)

Carrying weapons abroad is always tricky. Personal defense gear will have to be a personal decision; choose items that can be explained and have a plan to do so. I try to stay within the law of the land, making every attempt to avoid scrutiny when crossing the border. I carry a SureFire Tactician flashlight and often opt to travel without my name-brand fixed blades. Once on the ground, I've been known to head over to a night market or hardware store for items such as a screwdriver or paring knife. I make a sheath out of cardboard, duct tape, and string (for a lanyard). These items can be disposed of in a hurry, or if questioned, I can provide a reasonable explanation as to why I have the items. The bottom line is I have a plan for personal defense.

It's important to note, I discreetly stash my passport in my first line. This is just in case I get separated from my second line/go-bag. During stressful situations people have been known to leave go-bags behind. I usually bring emergency cash ($2K to $5K) and/or items that can be used to barter with. Credit cards will not be useful during lawlessness and disorder. These items are hidden away in my first line.

My second line is a medium-sized backpack or messenger. I carry additional medical, communications, and items for personal defense. For medical, a full-sized individual first aid kit (IFAK) along with a booboo kit (Band-Aids and over-the-counter meds). Communications consists of Garmin inReach Explorer+ (satellite texting unit), spare batteries, charging cables, and 20,000 mAh (minimum) external battery pack. Additionally, I have a couple of headlamps, a spare flashlight, batteries, snacks, baby wipes, gloves, water purification tablets, copies of my passport/documents, compass, and rain gear.

An often-overlooked aspect of foreign travel is "denying evidence." Understand that your social media footprint provides a great deal of information about who you are, what you do for a living, and where you stand politically and religiously. If you're detained by the local authorities, and questioned about why you're there and who you work for, what will they find on your social media feed? Many cultures operate on what is called a "shame and honor" system. Will your feed depict you as an honorable person? I want my social media to support my reasons for being there.

If questioned about who I am and what I'm doing there, I should be able to provide a short, legitimate statement (SLS). For example, "I work in the textile industry, and I am visiting companies A, B, C, regarding our manufacturing needs." If I'm in the textile business, then my feed should reflect that. No political statements, pictures of the wild night of partying, provocative behavior, and statements that would be considered disrespectful to the local religion. I'm mindful that I'm in their country and U.S. civil rights no longer apply. In other words, I have a solid "backstop" and show that I'm honorable.

On Site

If my business requires multiple trips to a location, I work toward improving my initial plans. Once on the ground, I hone in on the patterns of life: what government officials dress like, what the checkpoints look like, where the checkpoints are located, traffic patterns, interactions between locals, just the day-to-day routines. The purpose is to determine what "right" looks like, so I know what "wrong" looks like. I build my network of strategic relationships, determining which locals can be of assistance, especially should I need to implement an evacuation plan or need a safe house.

Perhaps my contacts in shipping at the textile factory can assist with a water evacuation via the port if necessary or a trusted official can help me lay low for bit. I work to make sure the evacuation plans developed back home are a reality on the ground. This will require familiarization of routes and scouting key areas. As my network of strategic relationships expand, I work to develop additional emergency communications plans and possibly implement a mesh network such as GoTenna Pro or similar.

If I'm located near an embassy, I arrange a meeting with the Regional Security Officer to introduce myself and explain my travel and/or company's purpose. Just as with the local relationships I mentioned, I work on building relationships with the embassy staff to get invited to functions and stay informed.

Don't ignore the danger signs! There's usually a buildup to civil unrest and critical incidents. If you have your head on right and paying attention, you should be able to make your exit prior to any major shutdowns or disruptions. If you find yourself pinned down in your hotel room or somewhere in the "open," you need to determine the best option based on the information on the ground. Remember, movement without observation and preparation equals death.

In the tactical community, there's a great deal of emphasis on the hard skills, like various shooting and combative programs. There's nothing wrong with having these skillsets, but keep in mind hard skills will be used after the "bang" takes place. For today's world traveler, there should be an equal amount of time dedicated to honing soft skills, which focuses on mitigating risk and avoidance. A few of the topics to study are: Situational Awareness, Medical/TCCC, Surveillance Detection, Active Shooter Response, Security Driving, Actions on Contact, Digital Security, Building Risk Assessments, and Base Monitored Movement plans. Learn more about how to train for these in my author bio at the end of the article.

INTERNATIONAL MEDIA CORRESPONDENT MILES VINING'S APPROACH

Preparation

If knowledge is the lightest piece of gear one could put in their travel bag, then interpersonal communication skills has to be the second lightest. The most important point I'd like to stress is that the crisis prompt is essentially a man-made problem that requires human solutions. If you can't build tangible relationships and connect with other people on a personal level, no amount of survival gadgets are going to get you out of a bind of this magnitude in a foreign country.

One thing we shouldn't fool ourselves with is being some sort of Jason Bourne or James Bond figure who sneaks through the shadows of a foreign locale. Looking to historical precedent, it needs to be pointed out that for many of the great "Western" explorers who have conquered Everest (Edmond Hillary), crossed the Empty Quarter of the Arabian Peninsula (Wilfred Thesiger), or ran humanitarian missions into war-torn Burma and Syria (David Eubank), there has always been an equally competent or even more ambitious local counterpart/guide who has helped to navigate the human and terrain environment. This is why every successful news crew in the world has behind-the-scenes "fixers" whenever they go into foreign countries.

So, when it comes time to deal with a crisis, don't think for one second that you won't need the assistance of the local populace. In fact, to not take local cooperation into account is to doom yourself to failure. Whether it's an actual guide, a driver getting you across the city, a shopkeeper to provide you with food and water, or a friendly translator, you're going to have to negotiate, barter, explain, and even beg with people who don't share your language, nationality, religion, or values. How successful you are at this process could mean the difference between going to a foreign jail or going home.

Gear

For communications, I usually want to have several types of data and cellular service. Ideally, I have a local SIM card, an international SIM card, and preferably two cell phones. One phone I like to call my "dirty" phone, where I download and interface with all the host countries' applications and registrations. The other one, my "clean" one, I try to keep separate with my personal information, my more confidential calls, etc. Beyond cellular phones, some very good devices that exist are satellite pagers where I can get GPS coordinates, send SMS messages via satellite, and even push preset emergency messages to designated recipients. Spot X is one such company that has very economical packages. For a full communications capability, I no longer need to lug around a bulky Pelican case with the ubiquitous folding antenna sat phones that barely work half the time. SatSleeve from Thuraya is a very compact clip-on device that simply connects to my iPhone or Android device via Bluetooth. But with these two types of devices, I need to take into account the fact that, if I'm held in a foreign country already suspicious of my intentions, finding unregistered satellite communications technology in my luggage is a solid indication that I'm some sort of spy.

In regards to more gear, I like to be as efficient and self-sufficient as possible. My electronics need to be compatible with the host country's outlets and voltage; if I can power them myself via solar chargers that's a plus. I like to bring a repair kit consisting of Shoe-Goo, gaffer's tape, and a sewing kit to fix small tears and issues that might come up. But much more important than gear, I need to realize what I have, and be able to replace these capabilities in-country with local amenities. I should be browsing local stores to see what might work better or is equal in comparison to the kit I'm bringing in. Amazon isn't going to be there for me when I need it the most. I don't want to be a hostage to my equipment, and I need to adapt when items fail.

With communications, I have to assume that everything I'm transmitting is being bugged, censored, or recorded some way or another. Applications such as Signal are great, but it doesn't make a difference if the host country is able to covertly download software to your phone that monitors your keystrokes. Pre-arranged brevity codes are good to develop with family members and friends, but they have to be kept simple and dummy proof. For example, one brevity code I've used with my spouse is in referencing the third floor of our apartment if I were to get into a bind, but still have communications. Of course, our apartment doesn't have a third floor, it only has two, but that's the point. I can call her and say, "Would you mind looking through my hockey sticks in the third-floor storage room," in response she could make up the flow of the conversation, but instantly realize that something is very wrong in my part of the world.

On Site

Whenever I'm in a new location overseas, I need to try and seek out whatever environment I'm in, both the physical and the human terrain map. For the human terrain, I want to know who is in the area every day. The security folks, restaurant employees, gym employees, and receptionists. Can I establish a rapport, even a friendship that might be able to help me? Knowing my physical environment is critical as well. What roads, pathways, buildings, and structures show up on maps that don't exist anymore, and vice versa. Offline mapping applications such as Maps.Me, or OsmAnd are fantastic when the network is down, but a thorough scouting should still be in order. On one occasion when I was climbing a hill in China, I came cross a patchwork of small-gauge power lines anchored on steel poles only knee-high. Sure, I could low crawl underneath them, but that wouldn't have been an efficient route if I needed to get over that hill in a hurry with gear. Satellite images of the hill showed a bare surface.

When I'm staying in an unfamiliar sleeping location, I want to consolidate my belongings in a way that still allows me to efficiently get to them and use them, but also so that I can easily work from them. I can't live in a state of hyper-preparedness, but I also don't want to get caught with all my overseas worldly belongings littered across a hotel room. What I try to do is minimize the number of places where I keep my belongings. I pick three or four locations in a room and stick to them — the closet, the bathroom, my bedside table, and maybe a desk. I use my existing bags as organizers and wardrobes for my belongings.

Having a designated go-bag is definitely nice, but let's keep things in perspective here. I'm in a foreign country, I need all my belongings. I don't want to just survive; I want to thrive with all my equipment. Maybe I bounce out of that hotel room with my sweet go-bag and end up having to hunker down somewhere in-country for weeks at a time because the borders are closed due to the volatile political situation. If I have the liberty of 20 to 30 minutes in my room, wouldn't I have wanted to at least attempt to gather the rest of my belongings, which should've only been in several locations to begin with?

That being said, I need to come up with a realistic evasion logistical plan. If I'm starting with no time at all, I can only leave with what I have on my person. That should be my passport (and a small laminated copy thereof in another location on my body), shoes, what I'm wearing, an ability to see at night, whether that's a headlamp or a handheld light (which also works nicely as a blunt force weapon), my mobile device and a way to charge it, and a jacket (which can double as a blanket). This sounds simple, but let us imagine a scenario where you're in your hotel or around the corner from it, and you cannot access your room due to a hostile takeover, a police barricade, or an angry mob rampaging and looking for foreigners (CWO Bryan Ellis was killed in this manner during the 1979 U.S. embassy riots in Islamabad).

Our second time slot is going to be that several-minute window where we can get our go-bag, throw a couple extra necessities in, and scram out the door. Now, we have a more nuanced approach to how we can live out of that bag for a limited period of time.

Our third time slot will be half an hour to perhaps an hour. You know a crisis is ongoing and you have to leave. If we can leave with all our belongings, let's try for that. If we're limited to our go-bag and maybe a secondary small bag, that works too. Now we can prioritize what we can jettison or keep when it comes to space. This would also be a good time to organize bags on priority, starting with what's on your person first. If you have to jettison all your bags, what do you need to ensure stays with you? If you have to jettison one or two, which ones are they going to be, based on priority? We probably don't want to chuck our laptop, power banks, and hard drives, but that suitcase with souvenirs, extra clothes, or items we can probably get locally anyway could probably go.

Crisis

When I'm in a foreign country that might be third-world, totalitarian governed, and even at peace, I'm working with the notion that everyone I meet already assumes I'm a spy, an agent, or some kind of intelligence officer for the United States. I'll actually never be able to rid myself of this assumption. But I do have the ability to either lessen the spy bias or increase it. By owning or carrying tactical items – even something as innocent as a C-A-T tourniquet, for example – the assumption of being an agent has been heightened. If I try not to lie and try to be honest with authorities, the spy assumption might be relaxed. How I present myself through my physical belongings, demeanor, attitude, and actions will bear a tremendous amount of weight in the minds of those whose authority will determine whether I can get on a plane back home or rot in an overcrowded jail. Now isn't the time to be coming up with a cover identity or a supposed origin story.

When I'm questioned, I want to stick to the facts. I don't need to be opining about which side I support in the country, what I think about the deteriorating situation, or the United States' role in the mix. What's my business, what I am doing, what items I'm carrying, where I want to go, and how I want to leave.

Bribes are an incredibly tough subject overseas. They're just as likely to get me in trouble as they're able to get me out of trouble. Especially with bribing official authorities, because that adds more fuel to my case of being a no-good foreigner in someone else's country. If I were to attempt a bribe, I'd try to relegate it to small, tangible actions that can be completed soon and in my vicinity — bribing a guard to open a gate, a ticket manager to change a ticket. I'm in no position to make open-ended, complicated, behind-the-scenes negotiated agreements that'll lead to my release. This isn't my turf, and I don't know the human terrain with the right relationships in positions of power. What kind of language I use is especially key as well. Many authorities who take in bribes regularly don't like to refer to it in such crass terms. Instead of saying, "Can I pay you to open this gate," maybe try, "I would like to give you a bonus for your hard work," or "If you can help me with something, I can monetarily return the favor." An outright bribe of "I'll pay you a certain amount to do this for me" might end up insulting someone severely. Put on your best thinking shoes and work some diplomacy.

When looking at international organizations for help or escaping to neighboring countries, I'll have to tap into pre-existing networks somehow. There are numerous emergency travel insurance companies out there that work in ways that can be very beneficial. This doesn't mean they'll be fast-roping into your compound with an armed extraction team, but it does mean they might be able to arrange plane tickets with travel agencies they're friendly with, or have folks in those countries come and provide places to stay or advice. Global Rescue and Ripcord are two such companies, but there are several out there.

CONCLUSION

The key to any of these situations is going to be your intuition and people skills. Work through some of these scenarios with an assumption of being stripped of everything you know apart from your clothes, then revisit how you would handle that situation. The gear is great, but your interpersonal skills need to be one step ahead. Stay cool, calm, and collected, build up your sources, verify your news, act with confidence, and go with your intuition.

Pay attention to escalating problems in any area you plan to visit. A population's confusion and overall disposition about a situation can be easily exacerbated by mass media and sudden turmoil. Check the U.S. State Department website for travel advisories prior to venturing abroad. Having redundant forms of communication to relay information to anyone back home, multiple escape routes, and friendly local contacts are just a few necessities that could mean the difference between survival and incarceration.

No one needs to know anything about you other than what you look like to form inaccurate and dangerous assessments that could put your life in danger. Although the reality may be that regional unrest has nothing to do with you personally, the perception on the ground may be that it does. Don't assume this situation is only specific to other countries. You may have to apply these lessons to a domestic situation if civil stability continues to decline. �֍

27

YOU'RE LOCKED
UP ABROAD?

By Tim MacWelch
Illustrations by Robert Bruner

The air in the jail was hot, humid, and foul beyond words. You were separated from your friends and shoved in a cramped concrete holding cell. There were no beds or chairs. The space just had three rough walls, a low ceiling, a filthy floor, and a row of rusty bars bearing a locked door in the middle. There wasn't even a toilet in the cell, just a hole in the floor near the back corner of the room. You thought this was likely to be the source of the stench that filled your nostrils, nearly making you retch; but this wasn't the most worrisome thing in the room.

Three local men were also in the cell with you. The expressions on their faces were varied. One man looked at you with a vacant expression and another stared at you with utter contempt. The third man, however, was the most unsettling. He looked at you hungrily, as if his jailors had just provided him with a treat. He muttered something to the contemptuous-looking man in a language you didn't understand. There was some nodding, as if an agreement had been made, and then they both started to move slowly toward you.

For this installment of RECOIL OFFGRID's "What If?" column, we are taken out of our normal surroundings and thrust into a situation that's beyond our control. It's a place where almost everything is stacked against us, and it's an unfamiliar landscape where our normal rights, protections, and freedoms do not apply. We'll look at some of the precautionary measures you should take before you travel overseas. We'll also look at some of the resources that are available to U.S. citizens abroad, and things to do at the first sign of trouble. Finally, we'll talk about some ways to preserve your sanity in a situation that looks hopeless. You're going to need a good lawyer … if you ever make it to a courtroom at all.

The Scenario

Situation type: Traveling for vacation
Your Crew: You and a few friends
Location: Southeast Asia
Season: Fall
Weather: Humid; high 90 degrees F, low 63 degrees F

The Setup

You and a few friends take a trip to a Southeast-Asian country for some rest and relaxation. You plan to spend your days relaxing on the beach, enjoying the local bars and cuisine, fishing, and spending a few carefree days with your pals. There are a total of four of you, but you have only a marginal understanding of the local language, culture, laws, and key facilities such as the American embassy. Although this country is generally considered friendly toward Americans, you also know there's a significant local criminal element that dabbles in everything from kidnapping to petty theft, as well as known terrorist groups who have a history of operating in the area. If something goes sideways, the ability to get help is questionable.

The Complication

You head out one night to a bar in the tourist-friendly downtown so you can hopefully comingle with some fellow Americans and English-speakers. You sit down at a table to have a few drinks with your friends. As a friend of yours is bringing drinks over to your table, he inadvertently bumps into one of the patrons and spills a drink on him. He appears to be local and is offended, because he's dressed better than most who are at this bar. After some hard looks from this individual and a few curt words in another language, your friend does his best to apologize profusely and offer him a drink as a peace offering. The individual scoffs and returns to his table occupied by three other well-dressed locals. Your friend returns to your table and seems to brush off the incident as a misunderstanding and you all continue with the night under the assumption that the worst is over.

You occasionally look over at the table of other individuals who continue to stare at your table with looks of contempt on their faces. Although you only know some of the local language, you can definitely make out that they're talking about you as you overhear them using common slurs that you know refer to foreigners. After about 30 minutes, your friend returns to the bar for another round. In a seemingly unprovoked manner, another man from the table of locals gets up, walks up behind your friend standing at the bar, and slams a beer bottle into the back of his head. It doesn't take long for everyone else at the bar to take notice. Now the sh*t's hit the fan. Your other friends get up to quell the situation, which provokes the rest of the table full of individuals who were staring at you to rush the bar and begin shoving and swinging at your friends. Your friends struggle to defend themselves as customers flee the bar. In a few short minutes, the local police have entered the bar and are blowing whistles to calm the situation.

Your friends are immediately handcuffed, and so are the locals who started the fight. You can't understand what the locals are saying to the police, but as you sit at the table dumbfounded that this is going on, an officer grabs you and immediately puts you in handcuffs. Here, you're in a foreign country with probably little to no "rights" as you know them. It's your word against the locals – assuming you can manage to communicate with the officers. You know your friends didn't provoke this fight. You're all brought outside and put into the backs of police cars, where you're whisked off to the local jail – you already know it's the stuff nightmares are made of. The conditions are terrible, and you're aware that many people have been incarcerated in this country indefinitely without even having a trial. What do you do? Who can you call? Do you have any rights whatsoever? The language barrier proves an even greater obstacle to navigate. What steps can you take to explain the situation believably and receive assistance from family, the State Department, or anyone else who can help you get free?

INTERNATIONAL MEDIA CORRESPONDENT MILES VINING'S APPROACH

Getting arrested or detained in a foreign country will ruin anyone's day. As responsible world travelers, we need to understand the extent of the situations we'll be putting ourselves into.

Preparation

Having a background of the threat environment we're entering is critical, and something we shouldn't let our guard down on, even on vacation. Find out what local problems are common in the area you're visiting. What are some of the more frequent crimes against foreigners in your vacation destination? What kinds of valuables do local thieves like to target? What scams are being employed? You can find answers to these in forums, social media groups, and news articles, but more importantly, try to get a feel for these when you're on the ground — talk to locals and other foreigners. Many locals will claim their part of the country is crime-free, as they don't want to discourage guests in their country. But if you can establish a rapport with them, they should tell you more about what the crimes, threats, and scams are in the area.

An important part of traveling is to bring our passports, but we can't always rely on having them in our possession. Maybe they'll be stolen and sold on the black market. Maybe we'll give them to a law enforcement official and end up conveniently "lost" behind a desk. Either way, we cannot depend on this material object.

We need to make copies, preferably in color, and keep them waterproofed. Printing a high-definition image of your passport on paper and laminating it so you can keep it folded in your pocket would work well, but just having a paper copy in a small sealable plastic baggie works fine too. This copy shouldn't be kept with your actual passport or your wallet. Remember, we're operating on the assumption that both your wallet and your passport are gone. Having a digital copy on your phone is a good move too, but accessing it in a jail cell might be tough. If it's hosted online, then you could access it through an internet connection given the opportunity to jump on a borrowed cell phone.

Establishing your identity is important when being held in detention, because you'll have to prove a need to contact the U.S. embassy or nearby consulate. U.S. embassies and consulates will have a 24/7 duty officer which is usually one of the employees that rotates into that position. Before you travel, find the local emergency contact number for this role. This isn't the general embassy contact number that'll usually come up on the specific U.S. Embassy's website, but is usually listed under an emergency contact page online. If you cannot find it, give the embassy a call beforehand and ask for the phone number directly. Another good set of numbers to have are options for English speakers in the country's law enforcement. For example, Thailand and Vietnam have designated tourist police divisions designed to work with foreigners and have English-speaking officers on staff.

Having these phone numbers on hand, listed in your phone, and/or printed along with your passport copy is essential. If you're only allowed one limited phone call from a prison, a U.S. State Department official or an English-speaking law enforcement officer in that country is the person you want to talk to. The State Department can notify your family in the United States, possibly pay you a visit, maybe even recommend local lawyers that you might be able to work with. An English-speaking law enforcement officer might be able to smooth things out with the police that are holding you.

Any time you travel, it's always a good tactic to routinely check in with family or friends back home every day, even if it's just a casual greeting and update on current events. Don't give in to the temptation to post this publicly on social media along with some amazing beach photos. This could open up the possibility of thieves (or "friends" of yours with unsavory accomplices) targeting your residence in the States for a break-in because you aren't home. Another point to consider is to develop a low-key alert plan with someone you trust. For example, something you can say or do if you're in detention or maybe even kidnapped, without raising the attention of your abductors. This method has to be simple but effective and easy to remember. Maybe your family has never owned cats, but you send a message asking how your new kittens are getting along with each other. Just something to quietly let them know that not all is well and instruct them to get in touch with the U.S. embassy in that country.

There are a number of items that would be great to bring with you overseas in terms of a personal EDC kit. In regards to being detained, we have to remind ourselves that we might be separated from everything in our pockets, or even our clothes themselves, as they could be switched out for prison uniforms.

That being said, a few items certainly cannot hurt. In terms of self-defense, I always have a short, durable flashlight with me. I can use this to possibly blind an attacker, establish my presence without escalating a situation, or as a blunt-force striking tool. The beauty of a small metal flashlight is that I can have a self-defense weapon of opportunity almost anywhere, inside a plane, in a cinema, etc. A physical notebook and pen are useful for writing down important information if my phone goes dead.

It's always a good idea to purchase an international cell phone service plan in the United States before traveling. It's an even better idea to buy a local SIM card in the countries you visit. Not only is it going to be cheaper than overseas service, but it'll most likely be more efficient for the local environment. Realize that the Third World depends much more on data than calling or text; this is why WhatsApp is so popular. But before you do this, check the countries' networks to see if they are CDMA or GSM, and whether or not your own phone is unlocked for international use. Many times, I travel with two cell phones, an iPhone as my primary and an Android model as my secondary. If charging cables don't fit or are unavailable, or maybe my phone gets stolen or broken in a scuffle, I still have a backup means of communication.

On Site

We generally have this impression of indigenous Southeast Asian peoples being very conservative, kind, and maybe even shy in the eyes of Western social norms. But like anywhere in the West, locations of social interaction such as nightclubs, bars, and popular restaurants will have their fair share of trouble-makers and scammers. Look up videos of "Walking Street Pattaya" for examples of these scenes. We need to be vigilant as to the social environment around us and what could possibly escalate into a situation beyond our control. If we're going to be drinking, we must be watching our consumption and understand that while intoxicated, we're raising the possibility of a confrontation.

Different cultures bring all sorts of intricacies that can take many years of local immersion to comprehend. You don't have the time, education, or experience to begin to understand these. Instead, what I've found is that if you genuinely feel something is off or probably wouldn't fly in the States, then it probably is the same elsewhere, within a few degrees of magnitude. Listen to your instincts and watch what the locals do in response to a crisis happening. Don't be the drunk tourist trying to mediate a situation or even escalate it. Play things conservatively and swallow your pride.

Think about what you're wearing and what's in your EDC kit in terms of how it could be perceived locally, either by a civilian who might confront you about it, or by a law enforcement officer who's on the fence when looking at your case. Wearing a Grunt Style T-shirt with an oversized American flag printed on the right shoulder might not be the best attire in a country where hundreds of thousands of people were killed in a period of heavy U.S. intervention. Likewise, having some odd EDC survival gadget might also be looked upon with scrutiny by a law enforcement official searching your personal belongings. If they suspect you of being a spy or a criminal, this could serve as confirmation in their eyes.

Crisis

Let's come to terms with one very important reality. You're not James Bond, and you aren't going to clandestinely sneak yourself out of a jail, slit some guard's throat with your fold-out credit card knife, and make it to the extraction submarine waiting in the harbor. You're an American citizen on holiday in Southeast Asia, now being detained by local police forces on suspicion of whatever it is they want to charge you with.

Our first priority should be proving our identity to the arresting officials and getting in touch with our diplomatic representatives in the local country. Our embassy isn't an instant "get out of jail" card, nor can diplomats from the State Department even represent us in a court of law. But it can get information back to our families in the United States and at the same time might allow for some facetime with a State Department official who can explain some of the laws and various options we might have. Hopefully, we either still have our passport, our waterproofed color copy, or at least a digital version. Then, we should be able to call that emergency duty officer at the embassy obligated to answer at all times of the day and night.

Throughout your ordeal, your biggest asset is going to be your attitude and your code of conduct in dealing with law enforcement. Realize you're in a situation beyond your control. What little there is you can control (asking for a phone call, requesting to speak to higher leadership, improving prison conditions) might completely depend on how you act and appear to the officials in charge. If you play the role as an arrogant, loud, insulting foreigner who couldn't care less about local rules, then you'll get treated as such. More importantly, in many of the respect-driven, conservative, and hierarchal societies that make up Southeast Asia, people tend to shut down when it comes to emotional temper tantrums. If you're patient, respectful, and ask politely, officials will almost certainly respond in kind.

Unfortunately, in much of Southeast Asia, living with corruption is a part of daily life for the indigenous population. Understanding this, it's dangerous territory to recommend that foreigners should simply bribe their way out of a sticky situation, as this is compounding one crime on top of another. Potentially offering a bribe to local law enforcement personnel is a personal choice that an individual has to make based on their own conscience. If the decision to offer a bribe is made, then it must be done so very tactfully. Southeast Asian police officers often don't see bribes as themselves breaking the law so much as them being able to provide more for their families from their meager salaries. Of course, if you're already in detention, officers could simply take your money and not do anything to help.

Law enforcement always wants to probe for information. As a foreigner, the scrutiny can be greatly amplified. Local cops have seen their fair share of foreign drug smugglers, scam artists, pedophiles on the run, and mafia types (Pattaya in Thailand is practically owned by the Russian mob), so another foreigner in trouble could be one or all of the above. Some might even suspect you to be a spy. To counter all of this, you need to be completely honest about everything. Don't try to hide some fact because it's embarrassing or makes you squeamish. If they suspect you of some foul play, then a single lie could be their smoking gun find. This advice goes with any interaction with law enforcement, but only state what you know happened during the incident. Do not be conjecturing, fishing for clues, or otherwise filling in gaps.

Facts and Figures

As a snapshot of foreigner-related or targeted crime, here are some stats by the Thai Tourist Police in January 2019: https://www.tatnews.org/2019/01/thai-tourist-police-release-statistics-highlighting-crackdown-on-illegal-activities/.

State Department Assistance During an Arrest

Using Thailand as an example, here's what U.S. representatives are legally obligated to do in the event of an arrest: https://th.usembassy.gov/u-s-citizen-services/arrest-of-a-u-s-citizen/.

SURVIVAL EXPERT TIM MACWELCH'S APPROACH

Preparation

It's a dangerous mistake to skip the steps in preparing for a trip to a foreign country with a known criminal element and a different language. Any prospective vacation of mine would involve a lot of preparation.

Starting with my supplies, there are a few items I always like to carry on my person while traveling. The simplest everyday carry items include my mobile phone, some cash for emergencies, and practical clothing. These would be clothing and footwear selections that offer good movement, some protection and some defensive/offensive capability. For example, sturdy boots aren't very breathable or comfortable for a hot and humid climate, but certain footwear works better for kicking bad guys than those goofy sandals and flip-flops the other tourists are wearing. I'd also want to carry a light source, like a small inconspicuous flashlight. And since traditional defensive tools like firearms, knives, and pepper spray are forbidden in so many places, a leather belt with a heavy buckle and a discreet tactical pen may be the best I can do while in transit. The belt buckle can act as a flail and the pen can add an extra jolt when striking.

Another facet to my preparation is research. A travel guidebook is an excellent resource to study, even before I make the decision to book a trip to another country. These books can give us some remarkable details about the destination, as well as dos and don'ts to observe. I'd also want to know about the crime in the area, particularly against travelers. Is it a high kidnapping area? Is it risky to use cabs for transport? Where are the "no-go" areas? It's also smart to learn a few basic words and phrases in the local languages. "Yes," "no," "please," "thank you," "hello," and "goodbye" can go a long way in a strange land. Simple phrases like "stop that," "where's the bathroom?," "I'm sorry," "how much does this cost?," and "what's your name?" are even more valuable.

Learning a little bit of the local language is a step few travelers bother to do, but it's not only useful – it can create a much warmer reaction from local people. Prior research of the country's customs and general laws can start paying off for me. For example, I'd want to know about major local holidays, as these will certainly affect my ease of travel. I'd also need to know the things considered rude or offensive, that an American might never recognize. Finally, I'd need to know the most common things that would be legal at home, but illegal when I'm abroad. For example, insulting the royal family of Thailand is punishable by 3 to 15 years in prison per incident. In 2011, an American named Joe Gordon spent nearly a year in prison after being arrested for a blog article he had posted prior to visiting Thailand.

And let's not forget about communicating with our friends and family back home. I'd choose a person who I'd check in with on a regular schedule. They should have my itinerary, the hotel phone number and address, and some kind of instructions on what to do if I missed one or more check-in calls. Check the U.S. State Department website (www.state.gov) as part of your research it's loaded with helpful advice, travel advisories, and warnings about the country you intend to visit. It can also direct you to embassy and consulate websites, which provide addresses and phone numbers for these vital resources.

Take down the information, especially the separate emergency and non-emergency phone numbers for the embassy and consulate in the area. These American outposts are ready to help in the event of a death, serious illness, violent crime against, or the arrest of an American citizen. Ask for American Citizen Services when contacting the embassy or consulate. ACS is the office that'd assist us in our jailhouse scenario.

On Site

Once checked into the hotel, I'd call home and then call the local U.S. embassy or consulate to inform them of our group's arrival in the county, how long we're planning to stay, where we're staying, and how we can be reached. This information puts our names on their desks, which is helpful in the event that we have legal issues. It's also important in an emergency situation where Americans would need to be evacuated from the country.

I'd also set up our hotel room for emergencies. Stocking some food and water (in tamper-evident containers) is a great start, and I'd learn the layout of the hotel. Whether we head to the hotel bar or out on the town, we'd make a plan to stick together. I always strive to sit against a wall, toward the back of any eating or drinking establishment. This allows me to watch the door for better situational awareness. I'd also encourage a bathroom buddy plan, where no one heads off to the bathroom alone (this is a good place to get jumped). I'd keep an eye on the crowd, and most of us don't need a translator to understand the universal language of dirty looks.

If I began to suspect any problems with the locals (particularly a problem that could escalate), we'd simply leave the bar and go somewhere else. In some parts of the world, it's easier to use the "gray man" tactic, attempting to blend into the background and avoid calling attention to yourself. This may not be possible when I'm a head taller than most of the local people and bearing the wrong complexion, but it's still important to avoid bringing unwanted attention onto myself. For that reason, I wouldn't bring valuables such as jewelry and watches on the trip.

Crisis

Despite our best efforts to avoid trouble, sometimes trouble has a way of finding us. In the event that some local inhabitants decide to give me and my friends a pummeling, it's unlikely I'll be able to talk my way out if it with a limited vocabulary. I'd attempt to circle up our group and stave them off until the authorities arrive. Despite our instincts to beat these attackers to death with our beer mugs, it really looks bad if we're "winning" when the cops finally bust in. Some of the non-combatants may explain to the LEOs we didn't start the fight and were just trying to defend ourselves. Ideally, we'd have a few bumps and bruises and be told to go back to our hotel by the officers. But let's say that didn't work. I certainly wouldn't want to have anything that could be construed as a weapon or drugs on my person at the time of my arrest. Once placed in custody, I'd keep saying

I'm an American citizen, and they're required to inform the local embassy if they detain me (which is usually true). We wouldn't resist arrest. I wouldn't expect my "one phone call" like you'd get here in the U.S., but my communication plan with my contact back home would have them calling the hospital and police station if I missed my check-in by 12 hours (or some other preset time period).

After the arrest, it may be made clear that those who are holding me are operating by the book, or they may have a looser interpretation of the rules. I'd have to cautiously broach the subject of paying my "fine" to be released. All the while, I'd have to determine whether a bribe would solve my problems or add to them. However, without access to a translator, the chance to buy my way out from the authorities may never happen, and if the local PD that took us are crooked — we probably wouldn't have our wallets anymore to offer a cash bribe in the first place.

As a final thought for our article, I'd like to address the one thing that you may be able to control in a situation that is completely beyond your control — your thoughts. It's really hard to control other people, the things they do, and the situations that occur, but with the proper mindset and control, you may be able to stay in charge of your own thoughts. This could be a sanity-saver and lifesaver in both short-term and long-term survival settings. Your thoughts control your attitude, which in turn affects your emotions and experience. So, if I was stuck in a squalid foreign prison and had no idea when I might be released, I'd do everything possible to keep my thoughts positive and be there for my friends.

CONCLUSION

Despite our tumultuous history in the region, Southeast Asia is one of the safest places for American tourists to spend time on vacation. Hundreds of thousands of tourists from all over the world spend weeks and even months in Thailand, Cambodia, Laos, Vietnam, and more recently, Burma as it has opened up to the public. These countries truly are a fantastic combination of awesome people, breathtaking sights, delicious food, and unforgettable experiences. Don't let the tales of a few taint a possible visit to the region. But on the same token, be smart and prepared about the possibilities of being the victim of criminal activity or ending up in a jail cell, no matter where your travels take you. Understand the situations you're in and the consequences of acting rashly or making poor decisions. Ultimately, realize your biggest asset in a complex and chaotic dilemma is going to be a clear mind and a successful attitude.

The laws and customs of other countries can be completely different than those back home, and unfortunately, ignorance of a law or custom is rarely a valid excuse for breaking those rules. To further compound our problems, the local authorities may take an above-average interest in the activities and missteps of outsiders. These law keepers may range from being suspicious of travelers to being downright hostile to foreign citizens. Before you buy that plane ticket, take the time to do your research to determine if your destination might be a high-risk area or a place notorious for incarcerating foreigners. The ass you save may be your own. ⠿

28

YOU'RE LOST
AT SEA?

By Tim MacWelch
Illustrations by Robert Bruner

The smooth Pacific water had been full of biting fish that morning. You were overwhelmed with the feeling that life just couldn't get any better. Floating on your friend's boat in the warm glass-like ocean had seemed like a dream in the early morning hours. The sunrise over land had been impressive. The two of you had laughed, reminisced, and pulled fish after fish out of the productive waters. Then everything changed.

Just a few hours after the fishing was over, your good friend who captained the boat the two of you were on now lay dead on the deck beneath the ignoble shroud of a black plastic trash bag. As the sun beat down burning your skin, your pleasant dream had shifted into a dark and disturbing nightmare. Only one of you knew how to pilot the boat and navigate through the shallows and sandbars to get back to land – and that person lay dead at your feet. You were alone, far from shore, with limited food and water. Was there any course of action that would keep you from joining your friend in an untimely demise, or would all paths lead to the same dark end?

For this episode of RECOIL OFFGRID's "What If?" column, the editors have asked us what we'd do if stranded on the ocean in a rather grim scenario. There'll be no scavenging the neighborhood or the backcountry for emergency supplies in this situation. If we didn't bring it on the boat, we don't get to use it! To complicate things, we don't have nautical skills, the emergency takes place in foreign waters, and we don't even speak the local lingo.

The deck is stacked against us, and that's when we need our preparations the most. During this installment of "*What If?*" we'll look at some survival strategies on the water and the preparations to consider before heading out onto the ocean. A boat can be different things to different people. Sometimes it's a toy to be played with, other times it's a mode of transport. But in rare situations, that vessel can become a floating prison, or worse, a sinking tomb if you don't make the right choices.

The Scenario

Situation type: Stranded on a friend's motorboat
Your Crew: You and your friend George
Location: Pacific Ocean, off the coast of Baja California
Season: Summer
Weather: Hot; high 98 degrees F, low 63 degrees F

The Setup

It's a Saturday morning and you've ventured to beautiful San Quintín in Baja California to fish for yellowtail. You've traveled down to stay at your friend George's summer home. As an avid fisherman, you're looking forward to this outing and its promising fishing reports. George owns a Boston Whaler 315 Conquest, which is a 31-foot, twin-outboard-engine motorboat that the two of you will be using. He tells you about a spot where he's had good luck lately, and says that not many of the other charter boats know about it, so there's a good chance there won't be anyone else around. You're only mildly familiar with deep-sea fishing, this is your first time to the area, you don't speak Spanish, and you have only a little bit of knowledge about maritime rules, boating, and basic navigation. You're relying primarily on George's knowledge to get you where you need to this newly discovered fishing honey hole and back to shore safely.

After loading up the fishing gear and a cooler with some sandwiches, beer, and water bottles, you shove off. You make a quick stop about 10 minutes from where you launched to catch some bait fish for the day. Then George says the spot you'll be fishing at will take about another hour to get to. He tells you on the way out that it's a tricky run, explaining that the path to get there and back is very narrow and shallow in places, and inexperienced boaters have run aground in the area before. He also tells you that after nightfall San Quintín is reportedly a delivery spot for offshore drug trafficking and that boats operating in the later hours are often connected to cartel activities. After you arrive, it's approximately 7 a.m. and there's no one else around. You begin fishing, but also notice that land is no longer visible.

The Complication

You and George have had a successful morning, but after about two hours of fishing, George tells you he's feeling a little sick and says he's going to the bathroom. After about 15 minutes, you go to check and George and he has fallen in the bathroom and is unconscious. You suspect a heart attack, check vitals, and immediately begin CPR. You're unsuccessful in your effort to revive him and fear your friend has died. Here you are, stuck somewhere in the Pacific Ocean with minimal boating experience and no idea how to get home safely.

You begin to look around and find what you can. A flare gun, a few life jackets, extra fishing equipment, inflatable life raft with a small paddle, some spare clothing, tools, a fire extinguisher, some charts and registration paperwork, mooring rope, but no extra fuel. What steps should you take? How would you weigh risk versus reward on staying put and hoping help would come to you versus attempting to pilot the boat back to land or find other fishermen? Should you toss the anchor over and wait things out? Attempt to use the radio to communicate with anyone nearby, hope they understand English, and possibly risk being overheard by drug runners who would exploit your situation? Would you attempt to pilot the boat yourself in search of help without fully understanding how to recognize the areas that are shallow and could rupture the hull? For this installment, our situation is fraught with potential complications.

MARITIME EXPERT DAVID MARTIN'S APPROACH

Preparation

With practice, even last-minute travel invitations can be met with a logical order of thought to boost your own safety and success. Remain mindful of seasonal swings in weather, elevation, and temperature differences from your home conditions. Research your destination and host expectations. Do not rely entirely on one person in your group to figure out the details so that you can "just show up."

Even though you may travel on short notice as a guest of a trusted host, find time to get hands on with a chart, map, any source of computer-based orientation to get the lay of the land, or in this case, an ocean involving a border crossing into Mexico. Working in reverse order from my destination, I'd create my itinerary to share back home with those tracking my travels. Next, I'd assemble a compact carry in a Watershed bag of essential documents, licenses, passport, insurance cards, and required forms of ID to ensure safe passage along the water or overland route, including cash.

Moving to communications and navigation, think worst-case scenario — separating from the mother ship. Pack a second sea gear ditch bag with a few key lightweight essentials, from electronics right down to a survival mirror. Topping the list, I'd bring a Garmin Inreach Mini, which is a two-way communication device, complete with the essential water bundle subscription service to enable messaging to friends, family, or satellite-relayed emergency calls, including key GPS coordinate mapping/tracking capabilities for loved ones at home.

Also along for the trip I'd have a handheld Garmin GPS, a waterproof camera, a non-flashy digital watch, and a compact, portable handheld Horizon VHF radio capable of tracking weather, communicating with other vessels, and relaying lat/lon coordinates through a distress signal. A submersible, portable locator beacon and accompanying emergency strobe light are so affordable, including the registration and lessons, that there's no excuse not to stop at your marine supply store to inquire about them. Your cell phone will be of limited usage beyond many costal waters. I would explore renting a satellite phone for extended, remote coastal trips.

Illumination tools I'd take with me would include water-resistant headlamps, plus a small SureFire Invictus flashlight, which comes with SOS settings capable of running for hours. Grab chem' break lights and kayak strobes for each life vest or raft.

I'd pack clothing such as sun-protective, quick-drying long-sleeve shirts and pants from Simms, gator face mask, hat, gloves, ankle-high boat booties, and two-piece rain gear and fleece vests to ward off overnight temperature drops. If the motors went down and help is days away I don't want to risk exposure, dehydration, sunburn, or chills during an overnight or extended float. In extreme heat, a towel, dunked in the cooler ice water and draped around the neck, will help reduce the risk of heatstroke.

Items like lighters, a water distiller or desalinator, duct tape, tourniquet, a med kit containing hook removal line, pliers, and bug juice would all make sense, especially if you must abandon ship into a survival raft. Flying without a blade? Make a mental note to pick up a small filet knife in the first marina you see.

Ponchos offer protection from the sun and can double as a decent cistern for catching rainwater aboard a life raft in the event you lack another source of potable water. Ponchos with grommets or small tarps and rain jackets can be rigged with cordage and broken oars to serve as sails for rafts, conserving energy in strong currents. I'd triple check that my Wiley X shades with polarized lenses were in my bag.

After covering contingencies for our fishing trip, I turn my attention to our brief overland journey from California south by first reviewing the U.S. State Department site, my first stop for any trip south of the border. On the revised 1 to 4 scale, with levels 3 and 4 including "Reconsider Travel" to "Do Not Travel" I see nightmare scenarios of violence bullet pointed to serve as examples of random to organized targeting of tourists. Baja largely falls into the Level 1 to 2 range of "Exercising Caution" to "Exercising Increased Caution." I'm troubled by the advisories that disclose that tourist resorts are no longer exempt from brushes with seemingly random or even targeted violence, especially after dark on remote roads.

Last, I'd make a quick call to Global Rescue to verify my coverage was up to date. In a recent sporting trade show, one of their brochures stuck with me, reading, "The best fishing spots are the worst places to have an emergency." This membership organization provides integrated medical, security, travel risk, and crisis response services. These services include on-demand medical advisory, field rescue, security extraction and evacuation services with affiliations with leading sports conservation organizations. Global Rescue's mobile app connects clients with medical and security sources throughout the world.

On Site

Local knowledge is golden in any angling community, but that can be a somewhat guarded set of hard-won facts. I was completely dependent upon George for local knowledge. Pay particular attention to maritime hazards from rocky shallow reefs outside the surf line, simple sand bars, tidal swings and water clarity, prevailing ocean currents, forecast winds, and the boat's capabilities. Due to my limited Spanish, I was particularly interested in offshore jurisdictions and emergency protocol, including laws, limits, and any local customs for communication protocol with local authorities.

George shared with me a detailed route, including a couple of key points that I relayed to the family back home complete with plan to return no later than sunset. With this info the family would be able to track our progress and exchange text messages during the journey, including the ability to receive any emergency or distress declaration. He did not file a float plan with the marina, but they knew to look for him before dark, he said.

Dockside, I'd want George to provide a brief rundown on operating the basic controls and electronics, plus the boat's layout to separate creature comforts from operational necessities, especially GPS mapping, waypoint books, and sonar. Before casting off, I'd take the tour from bow to stern. The Whaler's foam-filled hull has a reputation for being unsinkable.

Openly discuss your floating emergency response plan with your captain or group leader. Use the five-step "range safety emergency" for worse case scenarios: First, take control of the situation; contact authorities and medical responders if needed with your location details; render care to the extent of your medical training while continuing communications and guiding responding rescuers to your location. Last, once the emergency is resolved, prepare to fully record or document your actions for your own protection, especially your chronology of decisions. In the aftermath expect scrutiny. Anticipate your actions will be not only questioned, but also second-guessed. Events recorded in a Rite in the Rain notebook, portable camera, or on video may prevent your loss of freedom, reputation, or avoid liability during the investigation that follows any life or death incident.

Openly discuss the availability of any onboard firearms and the requirements for returning to port or being inspected. Florida anglers are well aware of strict accountability for every last bullet awaiting them upon entering Bahamian waters, for example. George is not a gun guy, tells me our vessel is without weapons, and explains that Mexico has strict gun laws, especially for non-residents. He wants to avoid trouble with authorities and so do I. Do not board someone's boat with a firearm without permission or knowledge of laws.

Crisis

If you suddenly find yourself without a captain, try to determine where you are. Pay attention to your horizon, conditions onboard, and navigational hazards to determine whether self-rescue opportunities will suffice or whether emergency assistance is required. Communicate your situation and location early on to responders via VHF, even if your distress call is not a call for a rescue, yet. Know in advance which channels are monitored by the U.S. Coast Guard or national authorities. In foreign waters consider activating your emergency signaling devices and two-way satellite communicators, including distress signalization. Hailing any vessel on multiple channels may bring about people with maligned intentions.

In one common event running aground on sandbars may simply require awaiting a tidal cycle to resume safe operating. In the extreme, severe structural or hull damage may result from collisions with submerged reefs, other vessels, unlit channel markers, or floating debris. In the event you're taking on water in a volume that exceeds your ability to plug, pump, or salvage the vessel, get the life jackets, communicate your situation, and start gathering emergency supplies, especially if you have a backup vessel like a dinghy or inflatable emergency raft.

Your visibility and survival chances increase greatly by staying with the vessel. Only in the most extreme example of an uncontrollable boat fire would I consider abandoning the Whaler. Stay with the boat until it begins to submerge.

Larger commercial craft with life rafts will secure these in above-deck storage containers. These are usually inflated via a compressed air tank connected to the raft, pre-equipped with rescue supplies, including insulated floors and tent-like covers to prevent exposure and increase visibility. Supplies may include a V-shaped forward sail, oars, or a sea anchor to remain near the disaster site and avoid drifting away.

Smaller private pleasure craft with inflatable life rafts usually stow the rafts in dedicated gear lockers or in cabins to prevent theft. These smaller rafts are usually not equipped with survival gear so prepare to grab at least two separate ditch bags, one with survival gear and one with emergency comms, including visual distress signals. Don't attempt to paddle home unless a destination is in sight. Paddling is exhausting and dehydrating.

If I had to abandon ship I would attempt to carry all portable water and nonperishable energy foods. A Katadyn Survivor 35 Desalinator is capable of producing 1 ounce of water every two minutes. Stored in a separate waterproof container I would want the combined emergency distress and locator signaling devices in both electronic and flare forms. Consider SOLAS class magnum flares, including parachute flares capable of attaining heights visible for miles. During daylight hours handheld or floating orange smoke signals are capable of guiding in aircraft or rescue helicopters.

I owe it to my old friend to return him safely to loved ones. I don't want to be intercepted transporting a deceased man. If possible, I'd text my family and one trusted friend of the situation, advising my plan. I repeat this message to USCG authorities via text, advising my approximate route and arrival time. I reviewed readings at the helm to gauge fuel levels and approximate burn time.

SURVIVAL EXPERT TIM MACWELCH'S APPROACH

Preparation

Not being a seaman, I would definitely want to do my homework before chugging out onto the ocean. Finding a polite way to ask, I'd question George about his plans to get fresh water (since saltwater isn't safe to drink); and I'd inquire about his safety equipment and communications equipment. Since there aren't many cell phone towers bobbing around in the ocean, I'd consider bringing my own satellite phone for an outing like this. These can be rented, if funds are limited. I'd also need local emergency numbers like the nearest USCG station. And whether you rent or buy a phone, shop around for a more rugged model (something that a splash of saltwater won't destroy).

While on the topic of communication, I'd ask George what kind of radio his boat has, how it works, how to send distress signals, and anything else that seems handy to know. Before the trip, I'd also pester George about desalination equipment (just to make sure he had something onboard). There are hand pumps (like water filters) that remove salt from the water. Fluid Technology Solutions makes a Mariner F2O bag that will pull the salt from seawater. The pump is expensive and takes a lot of physical effort to operate. The osmosis bags are much cheaper and easier to use — just fill and wait for the salt to be separated from the water. But these desalination bags can only be used once.

As far as research goes, it would be wise for me to study previous "lost at sea" situations. Even though they may not instill me with confidence to leave my beloved terra firma, reading real-life ocean survival stories could show me how other people survived in open water circumstances and provide insight into the psychology of nautical survival. As you should do for any trip, I'd have a "what if" discussion with someone at home about my travel details and create a "check in" plan with them.

For example, I might plan to call home every day at 5 p.m., just to check in, remind them of my plans for the following day, and of course, let them know if any plans have changed. I wouldn't be shy about asking George for the specific latitude/longitude of the area we'd be fishing, even if he protests about his secret fishing spot. Someone else needs to know where I am, and it's not a bad idea to determine how much time should pass before they take action if I didn't make the call in within a certain number of hours or if I went missing. Sure, it sucks a little fun and freedom away from a trip to have these daily check in's, but their worth far outweighs the hassle.

Before we leave the dock, I'd ask George to walk me through his boat for the grand tour. With unbridled curiosity, I'd let the questions fly. Show me how to read a map. How do I use the radio? What are the local ocean current patterns? What do these instruments do? How do you file a plan with the harbormaster to go boating off the coast of a foreign country? I'd be like a hyper-curious 5-year-old with the questions. What's this? What's that? How's it work? Hopefully, George will interpret this enthusiasm as a shared interest, or at least understand that it's from a desire to be prepared.

On Site

George is gone to his final rest, and after I said a prayer for my lost friend, the first thing I'd do is get on the radio or hit the button on the emergency beacon. I wouldn't have let George leave the harbor without showing me how to use the communication equipment in an emergency, and this situation definitely qualifies. The size of the vessel will have an impact on the type of communication and emergency signaling equipment required by law. On a vessel like George's, the radio might be a very high-frequency (VHF) or single-sideband (SSB) radio. Vessels in distress can radio for help on VHF channel 16, if they don't have a beacon. With the radio on the correct channel, press the button and say "Mayday, Mayday, Mayday, Coast Guard this is (your vessel name)." Await their reply and they will ask for your location and type of distress.

Once you've established communication, the local authorities may direct you to another channel (to discuss your situation off the main channel). If the vessel has an emergency position-indicating radio beacon (EPIRB), it will notify rescuers via a global satellite system. All you have to do is push a button.

Again, the size of the vessel will dictate whether an EPIRB is required or not. Luckily for this scenario, the U.S. Coast Guard is very active in western California/Mexican waters. There are several small boat stations down the coast of California, as well as several large cutters that patrol those waters.

Once the beacon was activated or the radio call was successfully made, I'd sit tight. Even if the boat did have enough fuel to get back to the harbor and then some, I'm no captain and would not attempt to drive the boat with limited experience. It takes a lot of training to read charts, navigate shallow waters, and drive a boat safely. If I didn't have that knowledge, the best thing would be to stay put. Furthermore, having relayed my position to local authorities, the last thing I'd want to do is move. Unless the boat is engulfed in fire or sinking quick, I'm staying on the boat to keep vigil over my departed friend and the boat is staying anchored. But this wouldn't be a good "what if" unless we compounded our problems. So let's say a rogue wave slammed the boat into a reef and the vessel started bringing on water.

Crisis

Since the boat is my shelter in an unforgiving environment, I'd do my best to patch the leak, if it were accessible, once I realized that we were taking on water. If there was no risk of being crushed between the hull and the reef that ruptured it, I could get in the water and try to improvise a patch on the outside of the hull. If it is merely fractured due to impact (there isn't a big chunk missing), I could place a large thick piece of plastic sheeting across the leak on the outside of the hull. Secured in place with ropes, the pressure of the water will help hold the plastic in place and slow the leak (if I had nothing better to use). Tape that can be used underwater (like Flex Tape) would be even better.

If the vessel caught fire and couldn't be extinguished or is taking on water faster than any onboard pumps can bail it out, it's time to start thinking about abandoning ship in favor of the life raft. After inflating the raft and tying it off to the sinking vessel, I'd start loading the supplies. I'd bring the fresh water, any desalination equipment that was on the boat, and my sat phone. I'd also grab all the food, some fishing tackle, the mooring line, the flare gun, and some spare clothing. If time allowed, I'd salvage as much as possible and tie my friend's remains to the boat. This would prevent him from being lost in the water and allow his loved ones a proper burial after his remains are recovered. Rather than trying to paddle the raft toward shore, I'd stay anchored by the sunken boat. By running the mooring line around a boat rail, the sunken and anchored boat becomes the anchor for my raft. This keeps me from drifting away in the current. Even If the boat sank completely in the shallow waters, I'm still in the right place and able to signal when other craft approach (with flares, smoke, mirror, air horn, etc.).

Now, let's say the whole day has passed and no rescue came. Then at dusk, I signal a passing vessel with my flare gun. The other boaters approach and seem to be offering help, but I don't speak their language. Would I board their vessel? What if they're drug runners or human traffickers? If the "bad guys" heard my call for help over the radio, they wouldn't be likely to come investigate or hang around the area. They'd be concerned about getting caught by USCG patrols. I'd have to trust my gut, but I'd probably go with the help that is offered rather than wait for a more legitimate-looking rescue vessel.

CONCLUSION

I'd like to conclude this article by thanking all Navy servicemen and women, U.S. Coast Guard members, and other maritime emergency responders for their service worldwide — in times of conflict and peace. Your service and sacrifices have not gone unnoticed. I'd also like to remind you that as long as a ship, boat, or rubber raft isn't on fire or sinking, it's important to understand that the watercraft is your "shelter" in the world's largest wilderness — the ocean. Without that shelter, you can only stay afloat for so long before you drown or exposure kills you. Even if you've lost your anchor and you're adrift, your craft is still the most lifesaving asset you have. Without it, you're at the mercy of the sea — a survival setting where no quarter is given. So when the water rations are low and you think you know which way to swim to shore, think again! Making the choice to abandon ship is often the last choice made by those who are claimed by the ocean. ⁑

29

YOUR CHILD DISAPPEARS WHILE TRAVELING?

By Tim MacWelch
Illustrations by Jordan Lance

One minute, she was there — holding my hand, just like she always did. And the next minute she was gone. The sickening panic began to rise within me, like a surge of nausea — but far worse. I whirled in circles looking for her, but in the press of people, there was no trace. As soon as my wife saw the look of fear on my face and realized our child wasn't standing with us, she began to shout our daughter's name. But over the din of the busy public square, no response could be heard. Our child was gone.

In this installment of RECOIL OFFGRID's *What If?*, the editors asked us to explain our own approach to one of the most horrifying scenarios that a parent can face — a potential abduction. Continuing our new format, the authors explain what we'd personally do, should we find ourselves in this type of emergency situation. As a parent, this has been one of the most unsettling *What If's* that RECOIL OFFGRID has formulated.

The Scenario

Situation type: Traveling in a foreign country on vacation
Your Crew: You, your spouse, and your 6-year-old child
Location: Paris, France
Season: Winter
Weather: Rainy; high 47 degrees F, low 39 degrees F

The Setup

You've finally made good on your promise to take your spouse to Europe, and as it happens, you're taking your young child along too. You've planned an unforgettable vacation together, and you're looking forward to giving your spouse an unforgettable anniversary.

The Complication

While visiting Paris during a walking tour you prearranged, you're venturing down the Champs-Élysées with your group when you stop to listen to the guide's spiel on the Arc de Triomphe. Your 6-year-old lets go of your hand for a moment, and you think nothing of it. Only a minute goes by while you're watching the tour guide. You look down to discover your child is no longer next to you.

As you search through the group and the immediate vicinity, you cannot find your child. What do you do? Did they just get distracted by something and are aimlessly wandering somewhere you can't see them? Were they abducted by assailants stalking the tour group? What's your response plan? There's no way to determine for sure what happened, and you're losing precious time.

If you were home you'd call 911 or ask people in the vicinity. But you're in a foreign country where residents may be unfriendly toward Americans, your child doesn't have their own phone, you don't know any French, and people in the area might speak limited English. How do you deal with this? Contact the police? Attempt to communicate with the rest of your tour group and mobilize them? Do you search with only your spouse? Try to call the child's name?

JOURNALIST AND MOTHER JACKI BILLINGS' APPROACH

Prep

As any parent knows, a simple trip to the grocery store with a child in tow can quickly turn into a nightmare without some foresight; so a trip overseas definitely entails some heavy preplanning. To avoid any hiccups, I'd focus on four areas:

Research and more research: Months before we even set foot on an Air France flight, I'd begin to meticulously gather data about our French destination. Aside from the usual hotel and restaurant recommendations, I'd seek out specific data on the tourist locations we intend to visit. I'd want to know when the busiest times are, if there are any sketchy neighborhoods nearby, if there are travel advisories for the area, and the location of important establishments like police stations, hospitals, and the U.S. Embassy.

I'd pick up a physical map of the areas and mark all these locations on my physical copy, then also store the information in my smartphone. Since I always carry a notepad, I'd also jot down relevant numbers like police, hotel, etc,. to keep on my person should I need to dial a number from another phone. To round out my research, I'd familiarize myself with local customs and etiquette so my family could better assimilate into the local culture.

Bring on the tech: During the research phase I'd also tackle technology. My first step would be to call my particular cell phone carrier and verify whether they offer international service and ensure I was placed on that plan. I'd also inquire as to whether my cell phone would work overseas. If not, I'd purchase an unlocked phone that would allow me to make and receive calls and texts while in France. While I'm tracking down tech-related information, I'd also take the time to research GPS devices for my child. Though we heavily emphasize sticking together, the reality is that sometimes kids wander off. To ensure we keep tabs on our 6-year-old, I'd purchase a good GPS locator that we can use while in France to track his location should we become separated.

Learn the language: Communication and the ability to understand basic concepts and words is vital when traveling overseas. While I don't expect my family to become native speakers overnight, I'd insist that we start learning French months before the actual trip. I'd most likely sign us up for actual classes, but if cost or scheduling proved too difficult, we'd, at the very least, use software or online tutorials. Setting time aside each day to study, I'd make it a priority for us to know how to communicate on a basic level. In addition to actually studying, I'd invest in a pocket phrase book/dictionary equipped with basic and commonly used phrases for us to keep on our person while in France. This would prove useful if we need something specific and are conversing with a French speaker who knows little English.

Prepping my child: One of the most critical steps in the preplan process would be prepping my child. Though visiting France would be an exciting and fun-filled adventure for him, it does mean lifting him out of his normal schedule and routine. Doing so might cause some unpredictable behavior that I'd want to mitigate before stepping on French soil. We'd start by including him in the French lessons, teaching him basic words and phrases to help him communicate. Knowing how to tell someone who he is, who his parents are, and key phrases like "Help me" or "I'm lost" would be vital should he become separated or one of us become hurt or injured while overseas.

We'd also make a point to continue reviewing our policy on "bad guys" and how to defend one's self — information we've already covered with our child but that we want to continually refresh. Since he's just 6 years old, wielding a gun or knife isn't really practical, so I'd focus on encouraging him to use basic self-defense skills to ward off potential kidnappers. Criminals rarely want attention drawn to themselves so if my child creates enough of a distraction, he might prove too difficult for a kidnapper to move to another location — an act that likely leads to death.

To prep him for what he might face in the real world, we'd role play to allow him to practice yelling our names, screaming, biting, scratching/gouging, kicking, and hitting. Though we regularly reinforce what to do if he becomes lost, we'd certainly amp up those conversations. We'd review that it's best to stay put and yell for mom or dad, using our real names, until we locate him. If we're nowhere in sight, we'd reinforce that he should look for police officers or security guards to ask for help. Lastly, I'd purchase a whistle for my child to wear while in France. Since it can be heard more clearly over street noise, we'd practice using it if someone tries to grab him and run.

On Site

After a long flight trying to entertain a 6-year-old, I'd be ready to kick back at the hotel for a bit. Before slipping into a jet-lagged coma, I'd take a little time to attend to some details. First, I'd confirm that our cell phones do, in fact, work in France. If they consistently show no signal, we'd purchase burner phones to use while in country.

Once we got some rest and before we headed out on our Champs-Élysées adventure, I'd snap a picture of my child on my phone. This picture could prove useful if he became separated, with the most up-to-date information on what he looks like and what he's wearing. Speaking of clothes, I'd also outfit him in bright colors or patterns, such as oranges and lime greens, so he'd better stick out in a crowd and thus be easier to spot.

We'd review safety information with our child, including what to do if he became lost (look for police officers in the area) and what to do if someone tried to take him (fight and draw attention). I'd also whip out the whistle for him to wear around his neck as well as the GPS locator watch I bought to track him. Before we left the hotel, I'd verify the GPS system is working properly with my phone to make tracking my child easier and efficient.

Finally before heading out, I'd equip my son with a sliver of paper from my handy notepad with his name and age in addition to our information on it. This paper would serve as an important tool should he become too nervous to recall his French and unable to communicate who he is and who his parents are.

Once we arrived at the Champs, my husband and I would, once again, reiterate that our child should always have "hands on" mommy or daddy and that, at no time, should he wander off or let go of us. We'd also, again, review what to do if he became lost or someone attempted to take him somewhere else.

While we gather with our tour group, I'd take special note of the area. I'd look for any individuals that seem out of place or as if they're paying special attention to my family in particular. If anything seems off, I'd alert my husband so we could keep an eye on them and a tighter grasp on our child. This awareness would continue throughout the tour.

As we prepare to embark on our tour, we'd want to also take some time to familiarize ourselves with our tour group and guide. We'd look for anyone within the group who speaks English and suss out any potential dual French-English speakers. Introducing ourselves would be the easiest way to ascertain that information and become friendly with those we'll be spending the next few hours with. We'd need to take some time to introduce ourselves to the tour guide. While I'd have selected a tour with a dual French-English–speaking tour guide, we'd need to check out just how much English he/she knows so that if we need anything we know the level at which we'll have to communicate.

Crisis

A parent's worst nightmare — what started out as the trip of a lifetime has quickly devolved into panic as our child has gone missing. Despite the fact that we've discussed at length that he should never let go of mommy or daddy's hand, he's no longer beside us. We're left wondering whether he simply became distracted and walked off or if more sinister forces are at play.

After calling his name and quickly searching our nearby vicinity, we'd make the decision to alert the tour guide and group. Putting those French classes and our dictionaries to use, my husband would communicate to the tour leader and group that our child is missing. While he was informing our tour guide, I'd grab my cell phone to call the police. Let's say it had no signal in the area — I'd want to locate a working cell phone as soon as possible.

When we arrived on site, I found the English speakers in my tour group. I'd immediately ask them to help me locate a phone and start sweeping the area for signs of my child. Even if my phone has no signal, it does carry a vital piece of information — the picture I took earlier. I'd pass the picture around the group while I continued to call out for my child and track down a phone.

Once we got a working phone, we'd use the notepad I carry with emergency numbers to dial local police. We'd want to report our child missing as soon as possible. If our child turns up nearby, a simple case of wandering off, we can simply apologize for his misbehavior with just mild embarrassment. On the other hand, if he has been taken, quick police response and a perimeter might save my child's life.

While my husband is working with the tour group and members begin spreading out in search of our child, I'd look at my device to see if I can track our child via the GPS watch I had slipped on his little wrist earlier. Best-case scenario, it'd alert me to his location nearby; however, if we couldn't establish his proximity, we'd relay the GPS information to police as we followed the tracker. During this time, we'd keep eyes and ears peeled for any signs of struggle in the crowd. Knowing that we taught our child to fight back, create a scene, and cause as much noise and disruption as possible, I'd be listening for my name or the whistle and watching for gawking crowds or signs of distress.

Assuming he hasn't turned up by the time police arrive on scene, I'd produce the picture of my child I snapped that morning. With police now on hand, my husband would call the embassy and notify them of the situation, hoping to be granted additional resources to locate our child.

Conclusion

A missing child is a terrifying ordeal for all parties involved, but preplanning to eliminate certain variables as well as staying aware and responding quickly to his disappearance would maximize our chances to bring him back safe and sound.

SURVIVAL EXPERT TIM MACWELCH'S APPROACH

Prep

Do My Homework: Planning and research are a vital part of all forms of preparedness. So the planning for a trip so far from home would be much more extensive than the planning for a local getaway. I'd endeavor to find out as much information about higher crime areas in Paris, then pick a hotel and plan activities in a "safer" part of town.

We'd also take the time to learn a little bit of the language. Yes, English is a common language in Europe, but it'd be foolish to expect everyone to speak a little English. To increase our chances of successful communication despite the language barrier, I'd pick up an English to French dictionary. Any traveler should know more than just "Where's the bathroom?" in the local language.

Wherever you travel, it's smart to learn the words for "yes," "no," "please," "thank you," "excuse me," "hello," "goodbye," "I don't understand," "I'm lost," "Do you speak English?", and of course, "Where's the bathroom?" And make the effort to pronounce your new words correctly — it really helps.

Set Up My Phone For Travel: The ordinary mobile phone may not work "as is" if taken to another country, but that can usually be remedied. Before the trip, I'd visit my local phone carrier store and ask for help. A great deal of confusion can be avoided by working face-to-face with a professional. There are several issues that can prevent a phone from working abroad, and a knowledgeable customer service rep should be able to handle them all. They can tell me whether the phone is locked or unlocked, if the carrier has a partner in the city and region I'll be traveling to, and so many other tech issues.

I'd also look into the possibility of purchasing a local SIM card when I arrive in Paris, France. This may be much cheaper than buying an international phone plan or paying the high price for roaming. And speaking of phones, we'd need some phone numbers to call if we ran into trouble. I'd write down the local emergency numbers in Paris, and, just as important, I'd get the number for the U.S. Embassy there.

School My Child: The lessons of "stranger danger" tend to take away some of a child's innocence, but these are necessary lessons in today's messed-up world. Child abductions are a painful reality that must be faced by today's parents. The best way to face this issue is to give our kids the tools they need to recognize and react to a dangerous situation. And while we don't want to make children paranoid, they really should be prepared for dangerous situations.

Teach your little ones (and even your teens) that they should never go with a stranger, regardless of what the person says. They should never get into a vehicle, go into a room, or enter a building with a stranger. Finally, children should be taught to listen to their instincts. If any adult (even family friends and acquaintances) asks them to keep secrets, go with them unexpectedly, or do anything that makes them uncomfortable, the child should shout "No" loudly and go for help.

Going a bit further, children don't always need conventional weapons to defend themselves. They can be taught self-defense tactics (screaming, biting, gouging eyes) that can be used during an attempted abduction. And when the emergency isn't an abduction, just a simple matter of getting lost, we teach our children to stay put.

A simple set of instructions (like stand still and start counting) will give them something to focus upon (besides fear), and standing still makes them easier to find. Finally, if your child realizes they're in trouble, instruct them to go to a uniformed police officer or similar law keeper. You can even specify that they go to a female law enforcement professional, who may be naturally less intimidating to a little child than a male officer.

On Site

Once we reached Paris, my family made our way to the hotel to relax. Our phones were working, thanks to our efforts to ready them for international usage. Due to the flight time and the short winter days, we arrived late in the evening, so we decided to get a good night's sleep before we began our exploration of the city. While the girls were getting ready for bad, I slipped out to the hotel's little gift shop, where I bought an overpriced local map.

Since I had no familiarity with the area, this map would be a key part of navigating through the city. Bringing it back to the room, along with some interesting-looking French snacks, I then studied the street layout carefully. This map would go in our daypack as a reference, but we'd try to avoid walking around with it. Standing there with a map would be a dead giveaway we were tourists, and that could draw attention that we didn't want. After tossing and turning on the hard small bed (and suspecting that bedbugs were biting me), we ate a cold and wildly overpriced room service breakfast.

During the meal, we went over the hotel name and address with our child, as well as mom's phone number just in case we became separated. Every child should know at least one parent's phone number by heart, starting at the youngest age possible. We also made sure she was carrying a card in her pocket with the hotel name and phone number, and her name and our phone numbers. As we left the hotel, I grabbed one of the hotel brochures for our daughter to carry. It had a picture of the building on the front, as well as the address and phone number. I folded it in half for her and she slid the brochure into her pocket.

Crisis

From the first moment we lost track of our child, my wife and I tried our hardest to swallow the panic that'd be threatening to overwhelm us. With our child missing, and since we didn't know if it was a kidnapping or just a lost child, we informed the tour group leader and approached the nearest authorities patrolling the area. And we continued to follow any parent's instinct – calling for our child – but we knew that a law enforcement BOLO (be-on-the-look-out) would be even more helpful than our frantic searching.

With the English-to-French dictionary in hand, I communicated "lost" and "child" to the first police officers we found in the square. Since our child had the hotel information, my wife decided to go back to the hotel, and I stayed in the park with a few officers and the tour group leader. After a very tense 15 minutes, my mobile phone began to ring. I was in shock from the whole ordeal, so the phone rang a few times before I was responsive enough to answer it. The call came from my wife. She was at the hotel with a very nice young female police officer – and our daughter – who had left my side to look at pigeons and gotten disoriented. It turned out that when the officer saw a lone child crying and looking around in a panic – she intervened.

Our upset child didn't remember the info card in her pocket, just the brochure from the hotel, but that was all that the officer needed to see. Overwhelmed with relief and gratitude, I told the officers and the tour group leader, and I ran back to the hotel. My wife, my daughter, and I held each other for several minutes – so relieved that this had only been a "lost child" situation and nothing more sinister. And after another chat with the police, we headed back to our room to regain our composure and rethink our plans to visit crowded places in Paris.

CONCLUSION

When the worst has happened – your loved one is missing – what can you do to help? The first and most important thing you can do to help your loved one is to maintain your calm as best you can in the terrifying situation and contact the authorities. If the incident has happened in your home country, of course you'd contact the local authorities (and federal law enforcement, if abduction was suspected). But if the issue has occurred abroad, try to reach your embassy or consulate to seek help. In France and most other countries, you can reach out to the U.S. Embassy and ask for American Citizen Services. They can coordinate with local law enforcement and any American FBI offices in the area.

If (for some strange reason) you can't get help from your own countrymen, then you'll have to rely on the local authorities or local government office. Whoever ends up assisting you, be patient with those who are helping you and don't expect a quick resolution to this personal crisis. Even though the odds of your child being kidnapped by a stranger are very low in the U.S., France, and most countries, it'd be very nerve-racking to wonder "what if" for even a short time while your child is lost.

For more information on protecting your family, visit the website of the National Center for Missing and Exploited Children at www.missingkids.com. ⠿

30

YOU'RE STRANDED IN THE DESERT?

By Tim MacWelch

Illustrations by Cassandra Dale

Y ou woke up slowly, grudgingly, and in a state of confusion. It was so cold, shockingly cold. As you lay there, curled up and shivering on the bench seat of the old pickup truck, with only your jacket for warmth, you couldn't quite reconcile the facts. It wasn't too long ago that you very nearly had a heat stroke. And just 10 hours later, you felt as though you were going to freeze to death.

"How can all of that heat be gone?" you asked yourself, zipping your work jacket up to your chin and laying out spare clothing in your lap like a blanket. If only the truck would start, you lamented, wishing you could drive to safety (or at least run the heater for warmth). But the truck was beyond your skill to repair, and you were slowly starting to realize that the situation may have been beyond your skill to survive.

The desert is a harsh backdrop for any kind of survival scenario, and the life that does exist there is highly adapted to the climate. If we don't play by the rules of this dry environment, our chances for outlasting the situation are slim.

So, in this edition of our *What If?* column, we pose the question: What if your vehicle breaks down, leaving you stranded in the desert?

To explore different approaches to survival in an arid landscape, RECOIL OFFGRID asked different survival writers to create a fictional story that contains real survival tips and tricks. Joining me for this installment is Jared Wihongi, a SWAT officer, firearms instructor, and defensive tactics teacher who holds a master rank in the Filipino combat art of Pekiti-Tirsia Kali. He has real-world experience thriving in sweltering conditions, having traveled the globe to instruct everyone from elite police units in Asia to special-operations forces in his home (and arid) state of Utah.

As for me, I've been teaching people how to survive almost everything for more than 20 years, and I've written multiple *New York Times*-bestselling survival manuals from my experience. As always, it's an honor for me to be a contributor to the *What If?* feature. Now, let's see if our character can hack it in the dry lands.

The Scenario

Situation type: Stranded
Your Crew: Just you
Location: New Mexico
Season: Late summer
Weather: Sunny; high 100 degrees F, low 55 degrees F

The Setup

You're a portly sales executive in your early fifties named Mark, about to depart on a long road trip back home to Wichita, Kansas. You dropped off your daughter, Laura, at her new home for the next four years: New Mexico State University. Despite the tears and laughs, the trip was a success, thanks to your trusted '90 Ford F-150. Time to head home.

The Complication

The trip to the Las Cruces campus was fairly straightforward, as you just needed to make it there in time for freshmen orientation. But on the way back you decide to take a much-deserved detour: visiting Roswell. As a sci-fi buff, you've always been fascinated by the city's love affair with UFOs. But after passing Alamogordo, you must have taken a wrong turn. Are you on U.S. Route 70, U.S. Route 82, or some unnamed county road? Every two-lane road is starting to look the same.

The Google Maps printout isn't helping, and even though your iPhone has a GPS fix, you're not getting any data. So, your location on the screen is just a lonely dot, floating unattached to reality, in the middle of virtual New Mexico. Immediately, you regret not buying a *Thomas Guide*. To make matters worse, your truck's temp gauges jump, and lights start blinking. You pull over. With nary a shoulder, you roll off the pavement onto the rocky dirt and slink to a stop. Steam billows from the hood. You think it's the thermostat — but no way of knowing without checking for leaks and pulling everything apart. As the morning gives way to the afternoon sun, the temperature climbs. You haven't seen another soul, rest area, or gas station in the last 70 miles. You're officially stranded and lost in the desert.

The New Plan

Realizing that simply sitting in the hot sun with a broken-down truck won't help your situation, you reevaluate your situation and your supplies. You don't have your usual toolbox or spare parts. But you have the following:

> '90 Ford F-150 and its parts
> Wallet, keys, CCW license, concealed carry Kimber Master Carry Ultra, TOPS MIL-SPIE 3.5 folding knife
> Fleece-lined, heavy-cotton Carhartt work jacket
> Luggage containing street clothes and travel-size toiletries
> Windshield sunshade
> Paper printout of Google Maps directions
> Small YETI cooler with a 16.9-ounce bottled water, two sandwiches, and a chocolate bar
> Jumper cables
> Spare tire and jack
> One 12-ounce can of dog food (found under the seat)

CQC EXPERT JARED WIHONGI'S APPROACH

You have to be freaking kidding me! Seriously?" I muttered to myself. I was familiar enough with my truck to know that this was a serious issue and wouldn't be a quick fix. Oh well, it was what it was, and whining wasn't going to change anything. I needed to focus my energy on the situation at hand ... so what was my next step? It was 100 degrees outside and climbing. I needed to stay calm and figure this out, but time was of the essence.

I did a quick survey of my surroundings and the horizon. I was fully aware I was lost even before my vehicle broke down. So, outside of dumb luck, there wasn't a good chance I would find my way out on foot, especially considering I hadn't seen civilization for at least the last 70 miles. In the distance, I saw some mountains with greenery and the prospect of water, potential food sources, and high ground to get a phone signal. All of which I'd need if I were to survive any length of time.

I estimated it must be about a 10- to 15-mile hike. *Not exactly the same as my walk to the mailbox*, I thought as I looked down at my beer belly, *but not out of the realm of possibility.* After all, I used to play college football, and cardio wasn't foreign to me.

I took a quick inventory of what I had in my truck and put together a hasty survival kit in my travel backpack. The sandwiches and chocolate bar I brought for the trip would come in handy — I could stretch those over a day or two. Whenever my friends made jokes about all the weight I gained over the past 35 years, I told them I was saving up for the zombie apocalypse. Now those jokes seemed poised to become reality, sans the living dead. Luckily, much of this weight gained came from snacking while laying on my sofa watching episodes of Bear Grylls' *Man vs. Wild*, so I figured I had a few ideas of what I needed to do. If there's one thing I knew, it's that my body would survive off its abundance of fat stores — but dehydration was going to be my biggest enemy. I'd have to stretch my one bottle of water out; take a sip every few hours or so.

As I finished assembling my survival kit, it hit me. I was already sweating profusely, and the day just seemed to be getting hotter. I came to the stark realization that I'd probably never reach those mountains. I needed to conserve my energy and hydration if I hoped to last more than just one day. What on earth was I thinking? I wasn't the physical specimen I was 35 years ago, and with this plan of action I'd probably end up one of those people whose abandoned vehicle is found months, if not years, before my skeletal remains were discovered.

Change of plans: back to Boy Scouts 101, stay put and wait to be found. If I were to be rescued, I needed to stay hydrated and make myself visible.

First things first, I had to get my body temperature down. In this desert, every movement seemed to make me sweat more. The inside of my pickup was like an oven, and the pavement around my vehicle seemed to be radiating heat. About 50 yards off the road I could see a small rocky outcrop. I could use my windshield sunshade combined with some natural shade to get out of the heat.

Before I made the much shorter hike there, I used the spare clothes from my luggage to cover my arms and legs to protect my skin from the sun. I also grabbed a shirt to cover my head, as well as my mouth to help prevent moisture loss from breathing. I recalled a memorable episode of Bear Grylls peeing on his shirt and wrapping it around his head to further control the body's temperature. Rather than get that drastic, I took my chances with some windshield washer fluid from my truck — though I didn't want to get it in my eyes or ingest it, as it has some toxic content. Either way, it seemed the least disgusting of my two choices.

Next, I opened the hood of my truck and arranged some rocks to fashion a crude SOS sign on the road, with an arrow pointing toward the rocky outcrop I spotted. I also wrote a note on the back of an old maintenance receipt from my truck's file cabinet (also known as a glovebox) and left it on the dashboard, detailing the date, time, and where I was headed. The last thing I wanted was to miss a potential rescue by a passing motorist or helicopter.

I quickly made it to the rocky outcrop – 50 yards was definitely smarter than 15 miles – and found a good spot to prop my windshield shade. As I started to cool down in the shade, I took a bite of my chocolate bar and started thinking through my next options.

I'd need to make myself visible from as far as possible if I were to stand a chance of being rescued. I needed to make a fire! Smoke by day and light by night; that seemed my best chance. I anticipated that it would start getting cold at night, so a fire would also help me stay warm. At sundown, with the temperatures more bearable, I'd try my hand at getting my truck back up and running. I'd also take a short walk to the highest ground within reasonable distance to see if I could get a cell signal or some data for my GPS.

As the day dragged on and broad daylight started to give way to dusk, I knew I only had a short period to work in the cooler hours before nightfall and darkness. I began to gather as much combustible material as possible, mostly dried brush and tumbleweed. I included some green brush to create as much smoke as possible in the daytime.

Next, I grabbed a couple of worn socks from my luggage to soak up oil and gasoline from my truck to help start the fire.

Then I got to work trying to figure out what was going on with my engine, now that it and the weather had cooled down. As I twisted and pulled on parts trying to diagnose the problem, it became more apparent that I'd never figure things out without my tools. Temper and stupidity got the best of me, as I slammed my hood shut out of frustration. Big mistake. My smartphone was on the engine bay; it fell to the road, breaking the screen and putting the phone out of commission entirely. Any hope of finding a signal was gone.

"Can things get any worse?" I thought to myself as I walked to some nearby bushes to pee. Just at that moment I heard the frightening noise I'd heard all too many times on TV... rattlesnake!

I glanced around and quickly caught sight of the serpent a few feet off to my side, well within the animal's coiled striking distance. Thanks to what I used to think were unhealthy TV watching habits, I knew these are vibration-driven animals – so I remained still. The snake's rattle stopped briefly and intermittently, but never completely, for what seemed like an eternity. The rattle told me it remained in alert and potential attack mode. I slowly drew the Kimber I'd kept in my waistband all day, took a steady aim at its head, and *blam* – direct hit.

Not knowing how long I would be stuck out there, I used my knife to remove the snake's guts and whatever was left of its head, being careful not to touch any fangs or venom. "I'm sure it'll taste like chicken, right?" I asked aloud, knowing full well snake meat wouldn't and acknowledging that I was now talking to myself. I wrapped the body in a large Ziploc bag from my luggage and placed it in my cooler.

I piled the dried twigs and vegetation, slipping the gasoline-drenched sock beneath them. Connecting my jumper cables to the truck's battery, I ignited the gasoline and got my fire going.

Looking at the bloodstain that was once the rattler reminded me that there were dangerous critters out there, so I opted to layer up with my extra clothing and Carhartt jacket and sleep in the cab of my truck. Not super comfortable, but a little warmer and safer than being out in the elements. During the night I got up occasionally to re-stoke the fire. It was ironic how cold the desert was when the sun was gone.

As morning arrived, I began adding green shrubs and an oiled sock on the fire to create more smoke. I kept the fire going as much as I could to signal my location.

Two days into this ordeal and it quickly became apparent that although my efforts at thermal regulation were prolonging my life, my food sources were certainly going to outlast my water sources. I had conserved my food knowing that eating would just make me thirstier, but my water was completely gone and I was starting to feel faint and have hallucinations. I tried to make peace with the fact that I wouldn't last much longer out there, but my imagination started running wild with worry for my daughter. Just as I started to feel hope was lost, all the steps I had taken to survive began to pay off.

A BLM ranger saw the smoke from my fire and came to investigate. Following my SOS sign, he located me in the shade of what I thought would be my deathbed. I barely had the strength to thank him, rejoicing silently in the fact that I would live to see my daughter graduate from college. Although, next time, I'll fork out the cash for a flight.

SURVIVAL EXPERT TIM MACWELCH'S APPROACH

Since I had no idea how long I would have to wait for another vehicle to appear, I decided to pass the time by sifting through my stash of supplies. There were so many things that I owned … that weren't with me on this trip. But those possessions wouldn't help me while they were sitting at home, so I decided to stop worrying about them. I focused on the supplies that would help right then.

In the blinding sun, I made a mental list of the goods, and then put on my sunglasses to scan the horizon in every direction. No buildings, no towers, no sign of human existence were to be seen, other than myself, the road, and the broken-down truck. There was no point in trying to walk anywhere. That much was clear. I didn't have enough water to make it anywhere on foot, so I decided to stay with the truck. It's big and easy for people to spot, I rationalized. I could even turn on the flashers while the battery lasted. And it was the only source of shade in a landscape devoid of trees.

Two hours had passed since my truck rolled to a halt on the side of the god-forsaken road. Over and over, I tried to call and text virtually everyone in my phone's contact list – to no avail. There was no signal.

I opened both truck doors, but there was no breeze to help with the growing heat in the cabin of the truck. I placed the shiny silver windshield cover in position to block some of the sun, but it didn't help much. Sweat poured down my face and back as I sat there, constantly shifting my gaze from the side window to the rearview mirror. I looked at the road ahead of me, and the road behind, desperately hoping to see some kind of vehicle headed my way. But as the heat built up, there was still no one in sight. I decided that open doors weren't enough of a signal of distress, and I wanted to save the battery to run the hazard flashers after dark, so I left the scorching truck cab and lifted the hood. It was hard to tell which heat was worse – the direct sunlight or the baking sensation inside the cab.

Opting for the cab again, since it at least offered a seat, I climbed back inside. I couldn't shake the feeling that I was in some sick fairy tale; I felt the like the boy crawling into the oven of some gingerbread house witch.

After another hour, I finally had enough. The oppressive heat of the truck cab felt dangerous, and I was so hot and thirsty that I had stopped sweating. My pulse pounded and my head felt light as I climbed down out of the cab and walked around the truck looking for relief. There's wasn't any significant shade cast by the vehicle, and I began to contemplate whether I should crawl under the truck to get out of the sun. I dropped the tailgate to give myself a seat where I could do some further thinking, immediately realizing that the tailgate itself cast a small patch of shade. Crawling underneath, the hot ground began to cool and soon the temperature was a little more tolerable.

I tried again to call for help on my iPhone, deciding to power down when the battery reached 10 percent. Through sheer boredom and lethargy, I remembered my food. Realizing the sandwiches wouldn't keep in the heat, I ate them both – only to find myself even thirstier. A little too late, I remembered something I had heard ages ago, in Boy Scouts or some other place. If you don't have water, don't eat. Whoever said it, they were right. My thirst had built from mere discomfort to a parched dry-mouth sensation. Down went the water bottle, still reasonably cool from the YETI.

My thoughts cleared a bit, sitting in the shade and feeling the water's effect on my body. I went over the plan. If I still didn't get any help, I'd run the flashers after dark and build a fire to catch people's attention after the battery runs low, though I didn't remember seeing any matches or a lighter when I inventoried my gear. The thought quickly passed from my mind, since the heat left me with no interest in making a hot fire right then. I watched the sun grow closer to the horizon – and I watched the empty road.

Eight hours had passed since the truck broke down, and the sun sank low. Finally, I had to answer nature's call. It had been 12 hours or more since I had last urinated. I walked to a nearby bush and made a pathetic stream of strong smelling piss. I was done quickly, and glad of it. But sheltering in the sparse shade of the scrub bush was a rattlesnake.

It hadn't made a sound as I released my urine, but as I backed away, it decided to give me a warning rattle. The tail shook, reminding me yet again that I was out of my depth and not welcomed in that place.

That was all I needed to incentivize me to try the engine again. My energy had returned a little as the air reached a more habitable temperature (and I began to think about sharing the terrain with rattlers), but the engine still wouldn't turn over. I thought I might have 30 minutes of sunlight left, so I stood on the front bumper and peered at the engine's parts and systems, looking for the weak link in the chain. As the shadows grew longer, I turned my phone back on to use the flashlight feature. Reaching down into the engine compartment, holding my phone for its light, my bad luck continued. The phone slipped from my clumsy fingers, and fell on the rocks below. Not only did the case come off, but the screen shattered. Tiny glass shards skittered across the stones and disappeared like insects into the cracks.

Climbing down from my perch, and reaching under the truck, I retrieved my phone — now broken and even more useless. As I knelt on the stony ground, holding the broken bits of my phone, reality started to gnaw at me. I had no way to reach out for help, I had no water left, and there were rattlesnakes around the area.

My thoughts of scavenging for firewood in the cool dark evening seemed more like a death wish and less like a survival strategy. Absent all day, the breeze began to move as the last rays of sunlight disappeared behind distant hills. At first, the cooler air was very welcomed. It felt like an air-conditioned room after a hot day, though it wasn't long before a chill ran though me. I climbed into the truck, glad to be away from the wind (and the snakes). The remaining warmth of the vehicle's metal was a mild comfort, and my head began to nod.

Lying down on the bench seat, I closed my eyes, thinking I would take only a moment's rest. When I opened my eyes again, full darkness was upon me, along with a noticeable chill. I cursed my sloth, not knowing how many cars passed by me while I slept. I hit the button for the hazard flashers and opened the driver-side door. For several hours, I sat there. Finally, when the flashers grew noticeably dim, I closed the door and shut them off. Using my jacket as a blanket, I managed a few fitful hours of sleep. Dreams of a rattlesnake in my truck, and my shivering, finally woke me. I laid there feeling utterly defeated, taking stock of all my failures. All the "should haves" and "could haves" haunted me like desert ghosts, and I wondered what it would be like if I became a ghost myself.

As my thoughts turned their darkest, I noticed a faint light in the rear window of the truck. Dawn must finally be here, I thought. As I began to think about writing a will when I had enough light to see, new colors joined the light pouring into my truck cab. White light and blue, pulsed across the cab ceiling as I sat up. The sheriff's deputy approached the driver-side door, and my uniformed savior asked if I needed help.

CONCLUSION

In the world's toughest deserts, you might as well be on the moon. There's almost nothing there to help you in that inhospitable set of surroundings, and if you didn't bring the things you need to survive, you won't find them out there.

For those who live in, work near, play in, or travel through desert terrain, you'll want to load up your vehicle like you're getting ready to colonize another planet. Bring more water than you think you'll ever need, more food and first aid gear than you expect to use, more tools and spare parts than you know how to use, and everything else that you have in your bag of tricks. The desert doesn't coddle the incompetent or forgive the foolhardy. She's a brutal adversary, with a host of weapons at her disposal.

As my mom tried to explain to me about girls when I was a pimply adolescent — and what I'm trying to explain to you now about the desert — pretty is as pretty does. And to me, there's nothing prettier than turning your vehicle into a rolling warehouse of survival supplies, especially before driving into remote areas. ⁑

31

YOU'RE TRAPPED IN A COUNTRY UNDER SIEGE?

By Tim MacWelch

Illustrations by Sarah Watanabe-Rocco

There it was on the huge HD television at the bar. I could see it happening as clearly as if I were there myself. The news footage showed the beautiful statue, just down the street, being pushed over by a huge mob of angry people. The blood drained from my wife's face as she watched, and she gripped my arm. I quietly said to her, "This isn't good" – the understatement of the century.

As we looked at each other, I realized that the lack of color in my wife's complexion made her stand out even more from the tan, bronze, and copper-skinned locals all around us – some of whom were shooting dirty looks in our direction. "I want to go home," my wife said plaintively, her voice cracking with emotion. "Me too," I said. But I had to be honest at that moment, I wasn't sure that we still could.

What happens when political frustration reaches a breaking point? The correct answer is, almost anything!

This edition of *What If?* poses the question: What if you're on vacation overseas when a coup breaks out? And to embrace the almost limitless directions that an event like this can take, we asked three different survival writers to fight their way back to friendly soil – or die trying.

For this installment, we have Ryan Lee Price, a freelance journalist and outdoors enthusiast who has contributed to the *SHTF* column in our sister publication, *RECOIL*. Next we have Rudy Reyes, a martial arts instructor, former member of the U.S. Marine Corp's 1st Reconnaissance Battalion, and actor. And for lucky number three, *OG* asked me to tell a fictional, but realistic tale as well. I've been teaching people how to survive for over 20 years, and have been blessed with the opportunity to share stories in many *What If?* features and write multiple bestselling survival manuals.

Much like Issue 12's *What If?*, there will be no fictional characters. *OG* asked us each of us what we'd do personally if placed in the aforementioned precarious position. Here are our takes.

The Scenario

Situation type: Coup D'état
Your Crew: You and your loved one
Location: Rio de Janeiro, Brazil
Season: Southern Hemisphere's Winter (late June)
Weather: Sunny, 75 degrees F

The Setup

It may be winter in the Southern Hemisphere, but you can't tell. It's mild T-shirt weather here in Rio. You're here for work – a large U.S. corporation connected to the Summer Olympics has hired you as a consultant to come to Brazil to teach a course as part of its annual company retreat for executives. It's a chance for upper management to build leadership skills through outside-the-box activities. You make it a working vacation by buying a ticket for your lady and having her room with you.

The Complication

You've wrapped up a successful course and had planned to spend the next few days sightseeing with your wife. You know things have been tense since hearing from your client that police just killed four protestors, including a 10-year-old boy, in a nearby favela during a protest against the U.S.-backed government. But on this morning, while at an outdoor cafe, you notice an unusual level of street activity. Cars pass by carrying men with shirts tied over their faces. You decide it's time to change your flight, but the Internet is down and your cell phone doesn't want to work.

You go inside to find the staff glued to the TV. News reports show widespread chaos. Rioters burning U.S. and Brazilian flags, storefronts smashed, and armed confrontations. The manager tells you the news says the president, many of his cabinet, and the police have disappeared after protestors, backed by members of the armed opposition, stormed the capitol grounds this morning. Now government paramilitary forces are fighting their way to the capitol. The battle is only a few blocks north and coming this way.

The New Plan

You realize that you have to move before you're caught in the crossfire. What do you do? Head to the airport? The U.S. embassy? And how do you do it when there's fighting in the streets and you can't even speak the language?

AVERAGE JOE RYAN LEE PRICE'S APPROACH

The beaches and landscapes of the Marvelous City are the best on the planet. The soulful music, nightlife, and people are all part of a woven tapestry of a rich and beautiful culture. Two weeks to celebrate our 18th anniversary couldn't have come sooner, and Rio just before the Olympics was a city of constant movement.

For the first few days of our vacation, it was funny not to be able to speak Portuguese. My wife Kara and I made a game of trying, but the waiters and cab drivers would just laugh or offer some grammar advice. *Posso tomar uma cerveja? Leve-nos para o mercado.* My Google translation app worked wonders (but I never carried my phone outside the hotel), and nobody seemed to mind too much; we came across as clueless American tourists with too much money to spend. And we were welcomed for that, it seemed.

By the fifth evening, however, not being able to speak the language became terrifying. Hushed rumors, small groups of hotel staff gathered in sober huddles, whispering. The sudden emptiness of the city was deafening. The Copacabana beach, desolate. Taxi cabs, gone. El Glaetoo Bar, the Amir, the Bacara do Lido around the corner, all deserted. When Kara and I went down to the lobby, Francesca Lins, the Porto Bay's guest relations manager, was wringing her hands, obviously fraught with despair.

She was little help in telling us what was happening, except to explain through strained English that something – she wasn't clear about what though – had suddenly changed. President Rousseff was facing impeachment, and the manager advised us to get out of the country, that America was again to blame for tampering in Brazil's government. Again? There were flag burnings, effigies of our president hanging from the lampposts, houses and hotels being searched, people rounded up. Most of the Americans staying at the Porto Bay, she said, had made their way to the airport.

On the Atlântica, outside the lobby doors, several pickup trucks raced by filled with men bristling with rifles. They were shouting "golpe!" as they sped past.

Up in our room, I tried to use my phone to change our flights, but the Internet was down. My phone was a brick. We decided to head there and take the next flight out, regardless of the cost.

The news on TV was not too helpful, since we didn't understand any of it. Some in the Brazilian Democratic Movement Party and many politicians were being indicted in a multibillion-dollar kickback scheme with the state-run oil company, Petrobras. It showed clips of military units rolling down major streets in Fortaleza and Natal in the north and Sao Paulo to the south. Chaos, bloodshed, violence.

I heard the word, "coup." It was time to leave.

Forget the luggage. Forget the clothes. Forget the souvenirs. We put on some jeans and tennis shoes, a worn hat, and drab shirts. We felt we might have to blend in; at least my wife's Argentinian heritage gave her darker features, but I was European white. We took off our wedding rings and tied them to the laces of our shoes, and we stuffed our driver's licenses and credit cards in our socks, so we would walk on them in our shoes. Cash was stashed in the other sock, and I tucked our passports into the waistband of my underwear.

We gathered some things together in a small bag — toiletries, water from the mini bar, a hand towel, tissue, anything we might need. I created a "dummy" wallet with $40 U.S., some colorful bills of Brazil's *real*, my library card, and our room keys to act as a decoy if we were mugged or stopped. We did the same thing with Kara's purse. Nothing of value could be taken from us without a detailed search. We put our phones and other jewelry in our luggage and left it in the room with my business card on top, hoping that the hotel might ship it to us if we got home.

Down in the lobby, there were a dozen other tourists waiting in a panic by the front doors. I grabbed a paper map from the front desk. A small bus pulled up, and we were herded on by Lins; Kara and I headed to the very back by the emergency exit. Out of the window by the side of the hotel were three bodies and a burning car. Sirens, gunfire, and explosions crackled through the air, and everything smelled like cordite and flames.

The bus made a quick left from Duvivier onto Atlântica and sped east on the wrong side of the road. Burning cars, barricades, and mobs of militant young men with faces covered spilled from the side streets. They shouted *"Golpe! Golpe! Golpe!"* and fired weapons in the air. The bus turned onto Princesa Isabel, dodging cars and still on the wrong side of the road, headed toward the Túnel Engenheiro Coelho Cintra that led underneath the mountains toward the airport. This seemed like a very bad idea.

Before we even got 100 feet into the pitch blackness of the tunnel, we were stopped by a pile of cars, stacked up to block the tunnel entrance. Men with guns stood tall in the bus' headlights, hands outstretched for us to stop, weapons at the ready. The bus's doors were pried open and several men came up the steps. One of them shouted something at the driver, but all I could make out was *"Americanos."* Seconds later, a shot rang out, and the driver slumped over the steering wheel. The bus erupted in a panic. More shots were fired.

I threw open the emergency door, and Kara and I jumped out the back along with two other men sitting near us. We headed toward the fading light at the end of the tunnel and ducked down an alley next to the Real Residence Hotel.

The alley ended with a small fence, and beyond that was the confusion of a favela, the scattered shanties, the winding streets snaking into the mountains. People were strewn about in all manner of escape. Cars were being packed, bicycles loaded up. We turned left on Dona Alexandrina and headed up over the hill. At the crest, a Volkswagen bus stood idling, its driver staring at us as we approached. *"Americanos?"* he called out, motioning us to come closer. We had no idea what he was saying, but I heard *"entre"* and that sounded like "enter." He slid open the VW's door.

This could either be a good Samaritan or a fatal trap. My wife and I looked at each other, trying to decide what to do. But the sound of approaching gunfire decided for us. We jumped in, and he circled the bus around and down the hill. The cargo area of the bus was filled with various things; obviously he was leaving town.

"Aeroporto," I said, one of the few words I had picked up while in Rio. "Can you take us to the *aeroporto*?" He shook his head and barked something in Portuguese. He lurched and jerked his VW through the bumpy twisting roads of the favela. It was dark by the time we got down the hill and out on the main roads. Fires lit the night, and chanting mobs shooting guns and rioting spilled all manner of debris into the streets.

We followed Praia do Flamengo past the University, farther into the Guanabara Bay, and north toward the airport, when suddenly, the driver stopped in the middle of the street. He turned quickly to us with a pistol in his hand and growled at us in Portuguese as he motioned to my pockets. I didn't understand what he said, but I knew what he wanted. I handed him my dummy wallet stuffed with loose cash that he didn't immediately count, and he jerked the gun toward the VW's door.

Seconds later, we were standing on the streets of Rio in the confusion of a governmental coup, pilgrims in an unholy hand.

Our best bet for survival now was the U.S. consulate, which, according to the map from the front desk of the hotel, was only a couple of kilometers away. Up ahead was the World War II tomb of the unknown soldier, where an extremely large crowd had gathered. They were shouting *"Golpe! Golpe! Golpe!"* It was going to be a long couple of kilometers.

FORMER U.S. FORCE RECON MARINE RUDY REYES' APPROACH

I had just completed a weeklong consulting project for a U.S. corporation in Rio, helping their security team ramp up for the Olympic Games, and finally had a few days of R&R with my girlfriend, Alicia. The tensions in the city and nation escalated dramatically since police killed several protestors including a young boy. It hadn't been too safe for sightseeing alone, so Alicia was poolside all week and getting a little stir-crazy, yet she was almost unrecognizable due to a savagely dark tan.

After a day of exploring, we decided to relax and enjoy some late afternoon caipirinhas at a little café not too far from the hotel. The sweet lime drinks hit the spot, but our tranquility was interrupted by gunfire.

I stood up to look down the street to get an idea of where it was coming from when several cars raced by; the passengers were all masked with AKs and MAC-10s sticking out the windows. I ran back to the table, chugged a pitcher of water to dilute the alcohol, and walked into the bar where a crowd was gathering around the TV. The bartenders were translating the news reports to the crowd of foreigners, and the reports weren't good. There was a full-fledged coup underway and the Brazilian elite, along with Americans, were the targets of the mass rage. I noticed the staff at the café started slipping out the back door. It was time to go.

I grabbed Alicia and told her we needed to run to the hotel, grab some of our things, including my Iridium phone, and get to safety. She asked where safety was, and I told her that I was working on that. As a Recon Marine, I knew it was time to incorporate my SERE training: survive, evade, resist, escape.

As we left the bar, the air was filled with layers of noise, screams, cheers, sirens, and automatic weapons. After a couple of blocks, I noticed the shops were desolate, and we needed to peer around every corner to see if the street was safe. I caught my reflection in a store window and knew the button-down shirt and Recon cap reeked of tourist. I poked my head into an abandoned shop and grabbed a Brazilian flag T-shirt and matching cap. In a situation like this, blending in was key to survival.

We had a few blocks left to reach panema Beach hotel when a nearby car screeched to a halt. We quickly took cover behind the wheels of a van. I carefully peered around the van and saw two rebels get out to chase a bunch of fleeing tourists. Near my foot was a glass Coke bottle — I grabbed it and whispered to my girl to stay put and cover her ears.

The driver was smoking a cigarette and looking in the other direction. I threw the bottle over his car, and it smashed against the sidewalk. As the driver got out to look, I took advantage of the 21-foot principle and bolted toward him. He was barely able to move his rifle in my direction when I crushed him against the side of his car. His AK hit the ground as I drove his head into the side of the car several times. He was out of the fight. I picked up the weapon, racked a round, and disengaged the safety. The two other gunmen were firing on the scattering tourists. Using cover along the way, I moved toward the other two rebels. With a couple of tight bursts from the AK, the threats were neutralized. I called to Alicia as I returned to the car and told her to get in.

Moments later we pulled up to the hotel; the lobby was filled with anxious guests, and the staff was gone. We took the stairs up to our room. I grabbed my satellite phone, knife, some clothing, and a few bottles of water. I told her to only grab a few items of clothing and grab all the water from the mini fridge. I went out on the balcony and saw smoke rising across the city.

Within minutes we were running down the stairs back to the main floor, when gunfire and screams filled the lobby. We waited for a few minutes in the stairwell. I heard movement coming toward me when the door swung open. Three armed men came rushing in, and one after the other fell as my AK barked several more times. I grabbed a magazine from the chest rig of one of the rebels, reloaded, and then filled my pockets with five additional mags. I popped my head out to look around. There were bodies everywhere, but the other gunmen fanned out throughout the hotel. I told Alicia to grab my belt and run with me.

As we exited the hotel, I took out two men standing out front who were firing at people on the street. We made a move toward the car, but more gunfire told me the rebels were too close, and we would never make it. We needed to hide.

We went back into the hotel and quietly made our way to the basement. It was clear that the workers and rebels were looting rooms and killing guests. I found a dark area near the laundry room and was about to tuck in when we were spotted by two hotel employees, a male and a female, who turned the corner about 10 feet away. I held my hands out as a gesture of good will when the man began to run and yell – "Americanos!" I easily caught him and tackled him, not wanting to smoke the poor guy. A USMC choke applies pressure to the carotid artery, resulting in loss of consciousness in less than 10 seconds. He was out in five. As I stood up and turned around, the woman with him began to scream so my girl hit her with broomstick. To cover our tracks, we dragged them into a closet, sliced several towels, and bound and gagged them.

Once the threats were hidden away, we found a secure nook in the basement and tucked in for a while. I told her to get some rest. We were going to wait until 0300 to venture out. "Where are we going to go?" she asked. "The U.S. consulate?"

I told her that any U.S. embassy or consulate would be a target, and we wouldn't be safe there or near there. I figured we had two options. We could move inland and try to make our way to Paraguay, or get to the marina only three clicks away and steal a boat. The latter was the better choice. I tried my sat phone, but the basement was too fortified for a signal.

At 0300, I woke Alicia and we made our way out of the hotel through a side entrance. The city was in flames, the power was out, and the sounds of gunfire still echoed through the streets. We ran, hugging the foliage near the beach, and moved quickly to the marina. As we approached, I spotted a few rebels standing guard at the entrance. I moved to an area where I could recon the area and saw the boat I wanted to take. It was a modern 50-foot sailboat with an engine. I could easily man her myself, and I knew she would have radar and comms.

We made our way back to the gate area and secured cover behind a Jersey barrier. I moved the selector switch to semi-automatic fire and picked off the two guards standing outside the gate. The third guard had a bead on my position and returned fire, but sprayed rounds wildly. After he emptied two mags, he came out to look around since I didn't return fire. The second he cleared the gate, I released a round, hitting him center mass, followed by a single shot that struck him in the side of the head.

We now had a clear path to our escape. I directed Alicia to run to the boat at slip 25, as I entered the harbor gatehouse and saw keys on the wall with corresponding numbers.

I ran to the slip, finished untying the boat, and started her up. A long two minutes later, we were moving. Once we cleared the mouth of the harbor, I called one of my Department of Defense contacts on the Iridium sat phone. He told me that the U.S. Navy was en route, and called back with coordinates to sail to for a rendezvous.

Well, at least we would have a couple days on the water as a vacation.

SURVIVAL EXPERT TIM MACWELCH'S APPROACH

I threw a few Brazilian *real* (dollars) on our table as we hurried out of the café. We had to get back to the hotel, but we didn't have much to work with. I had my wallet with some U.S. dollars and some *real*. My wife had a small purse with a mix of cash and credit cards as well. We each had a phone and our passport. Our route to the hotel was only a few blocks long, but it crossed the reported path of the rioters.

"If we're lucky, we'll get to the intersection ahead of them," I mentioned to my wife, as we walked briskly hand in hand. We both had every interest in running the distance, but I convinced her that walking would draw less attention.

As we strode, I tried my mobile phone again, desperately hoping to reach my contact. Before leaving the USA, I had a long talk with my friend, Paul, who works for the State Department. He had given me many travel tips and had a contact in the U.S. Consulate General Rio de Janeiro. He had given me her name and number, just in case, neither of us knowing what would later erupt.

While walking, and continuing to try the number, it finally rang. We stopped and stepped into a doorway. My feelings of hope were dashed when my contact's voicemail kicked on. "Hello, you've reached Stacy Wells with the United States Consulate General Rio de Janeiro. I'm sorry I can't take your call ..." I left her a brief message, including my mobile number, my wife's number, the hotel information, and I begged her to call us back. We continued our trek, heads down and trying to stay off the radar. People rushed in every direction, and each time they ran toward us, I stiffened, unsure if I would have to defend the both of us. Thankfully, they were running past us to join the fray.

There was one more intersection to cross, and we'd be at the hotel. But things took a dark turn. As we reached the street corner, a mob of people dressed in black clothing with black cloth over their faces marched toward the crossing from a side street. With guns in hand and wearing mismatched pseudo-uniforms, these thugs must have been the militia force. As the front lines reached the open intersection, a teen rushed out and began yelling at them. We'll never know what he said in Portuguese, or why he confronted the armed group, but we would never forget the sight we beheld. Several of the militia's frontrunners opened fire on the teen, riddling his young frame with bullet wounds and blowing a large hole in the back of his skull. It only took a second, but the young man slumped into a grotesque folded position – face down in the middle of the intersection.

It took a few seconds to snap out of the paralysis I was in. I'd never seen anyone murdered before, and it was only a few yards away. "Change of plan," I said aloud. Grabbing my wife, who was still in a mild form of shock, we started trotting in the opposite direction from the militia. My stomach sank as I realized that our path away from the militia was also leading us away from the hotel.

The next block down, traffic was moving slowly. My wife spotted a cab that was available, and we made our way toward it. I had planned to get to the hotel, use the landline phone to call our family back home, the U.S. embassy, and half a dozen other places. But right now, I just wanted to get us on a plane. I told her that we weren't going back for our luggage, and she looked strangely glad to hear it. My wife and I both felt a strong wave of relief after getting inside the cab. Our breathing became slower and deeper, and I told the driver "*aeroporto*," one of the few words of Portuguese I had picked up during our trip. We saw the back of his balding head nodding and he said, "OK, sir" in English.

The traffic was stop and go, with many cars shooting forward quickly – only to jerk to an unwelcomed halt. It was during one of these halts that three men stepped in front of the cab with handguns raised. Clearly rioters, their faces were covered and the thin façade of our safety was ripped away. They shouted something at us or at the driver. We didn't speak Portuguese, but we could understand the tone. Words full of hate and accusation were spouted in our direction. The driver didn't lower the window, even though the man tapped the muzzle of his handgun on the grimy glass. The gunman nearest to the driver spat a few words that ended in "*inglês.*"

I knew enough Spanish to know that he said something about English. The gunman aimed the sidearm at the driver's head. Then my senses were bombarded by three things at once: the air pressure inside the cab jumped sharply, my ears hurt from the deafening boom, and my face was pelted with sharp cubes of glass and something wet, which turned out to be some of the driver's blood and brains. I pushed on the door handle on the opposite side of the shooter, but the driver had locked the doors from his controls. We couldn't escape. My wife started to cry, and I was sure this was the end. But as our hearing returned, I could make out the sound of a whistle blowing repeatedly.

The shooter locked eyes with me for a second, with a look of pure and malevolent animosity, then he ran to catch up with his retreating companions.

In seconds, the police had surrounded our car. All traffic had been stopped. Two of them tried to open our locked doors, and one officer reached through the shot-out window to hit the door-lock release. They half helped and half pulled us out of the cab, saying things we couldn't understand and motioning for us to sit on the curb. When I said "thank you," the nearest officer said, "American?" When I nodded yes, he raised his weapon to my head. It was in that moment of shock that I looked past the threatening officer and saw the cab driver's door. There was a little hand-painted phrase near the top of the door: "I speak English."

He'd been killed just because he spoke my language. As I sat on the dirty curb, I pondered whether these would be my last few seconds of life, and I silently cursed myself that I'd ever come here – or talked my wife into coming. Do I attack the officer? As I was processing the thought, I was startled by the phone ringing in my shirt pocket.

With the officer's handgun still aimed my way, I slowly pulled the phone from my pocket and swiped the icon to answer. It was Stacy from the consulate. The officer was speaking to us in slow and hateful tones, but the only words I really heard were Stacy's. She asked what was happening, and I told her that a police officer was about to shoot us. After that, she began screaming over the phone in Portuguese. I switched it to speaker mode. The officer hesitated, lowered the weapon a bit, and looked at the phone. I *very* slowly handed it to him, and he listened to the ranting woman for a moment. He said a few words to Stacy, and she screamed at him some more. He then lowered the sidearm completely and handed me the phone. "Stacy?" I asked. "Thank God!" she replied. "He thought you had killed someone."

She went on to explain that she told the officer that we were important diplomats and he would be personally responsible for an international incident if he didn't release you to the consulate right away. She asked where we were, and told us to stay put for one of the State Department guys to come get us. Stacy said it wouldn't be long; he wasn't far away.

My wife held me tightly as we sat on the curb until a tall man with a soldier's bearing approached us. "Mr. and Mrs. MacWelch?" he asked. "I'm here to help you get home."

CONCLUSION

There are two basic reactions that people have always had toward "foreigners." The first is positive. We're curious about them and make friendly contact. Our ears seem to enjoy hearing new accents, and we want to find out about their world. This reaction has allowed trade and the exchange of information for centuries.

The other reaction that people have is not so gracious. The "you're not from around here" mentality keeps strangers at arm's length. Suspicion and mistrust lead to hostility and hate.

"Stranger danger" is certainly not a new reaction. And it's certainly not a nice reaction when you're the stranger receiving this negative attention. This is why it's so important to take some precautions when you're traveling to a place where you could be viewed as an outsider. Do your research. A lot of it. Learn as much of the language as you can, especially the phrases that can help you travel and negotiate. Learn the lay of the land, and discreetly carry a map of the city or town you are visiting. Adopt the local dress as well. The last thing you want to do is wear out-of-place clothing and stand on a street corner peering at a big map. This is a dead giveaway that you aren't a local, and it opens the door for trouble.

And if trouble starts of its own accord, your best bet is to discreetly tuck tail and get out of Dodge. Travel with several forms of ID and a high-spending-limit credit card (or two) because last-minute plane tickets cost a fortune. ⠶

SOLD OUT until Next Year

2

32

CRITICAL SUPPLY LINES ARE INDEFINITELY INTERRUPTED?

By RECOIL OFFGRID Staff
Illustrations by Sarah Rocco

It's impossible to predict the flashpoint that could reduce a city to chaos in a matter of hours. One thing is for sure: There will always be some among us who are looking for an excuse to see the world burn. We've watched certain U.S. cities silently condone violent civil unrest in 2020, blithely lumping it into the same category as peaceful protests. What will that flagrant disregard for safety and stability culminate in this year? Rather than throw caution to the wind and assume "everything will be alright," we decided to look into a situation that could potentially have a devastating impact on commerce. What if your hometown was so consumed with rioting that the services and supplies you take for granted suddenly became unavailable?

The Scenario

Situation type: Long-term supply shortage
Your Crew: You, your spouse, and your children
Location: Calumet Heights, IL
Season: Summer
Weather: Hot; high 90 degrees F, low 70 degrees F

The Setup

You live in a major city that has been under siege with nonstop civil unrest. The weeks of ongoing riots have not only forced many city centers and local businesses to close but have also interrupted commerce for the average citizen. Everything from supermarkets to hardware stores have stopped receiving deliveries. Roadblocks, because of protests as well as trucks being looted, have not only made it difficult to conduct business, but some companies are flat-out refusing to send their drivers into areas where their lives are in danger. Curfews and limited public movement have only exacerbated your inability to replenish supplies you used to take for granted. Store shelves are empty, fighting over what's available is a regular occurrence, and you have no clue when things will subside enough for life to resume as normal.

The Complication

Since you're not able to just pick up and leave your home that easily, and the suburbs have experienced a run on their supplies, you're forced to improvise with what you have and stretch supplies as far as you can to make them last. Of course, traveling through areas that are fraught with unrest comes with its own risks, not to mention the fact that there are long lines at gas stations due to a diminishing fuel supply. It's summertime, and the heat only makes a bad situation worse — the scarcity and chaos are weighing heavily on the mental state of an already agitated local population.

Although mail has continued to be delivered, you fear that the USPS may be the next link in the chain to break. Services like UPS, DHL, and FedEx have stopped delivering goods in order to protect their staff, making it somewhat difficult to purchase supplies via e-commerce. For this "What If," we've asked survival instructor Kevin Estela and agriculture and natural resources educator Phillip Meeks how they'd adapt their lifestyle to these conditions. Each writer was asked to consider things like food storage/cultivation, making or improvising needed household items, finding alternatives for medication and first-aid supplies, and self-defense resources like ammo without consistent availability of commercial goods and services.

SURVIVAL INSTRUCTOR KEVIN ESTELA'S APPROACH

The daily morning news has given me no hope of this current civil unrest stopping. The government has failed the people and has let the lunatics run the asylum. My normal supermarket has been trashed, my favorite local family owned deli and convenience store was burned for allegedly aligning with the politics of the mob's apparent oppressor, and desperation around the city is at an all-time high. Cellular service is still consistent and access to the internet has given me a chance to collect valuable intelligence from my environment. I'm going to let the looters fight over scraps as I direct my attention elsewhere.

For most people, running out of food is a death sentence. Many of my neighbors have left town for the suburbs, but I'm holding ground. I've heard reports of those who left late being met by ad-hoc militia-type groups with skewed politics and maniacal leaders. I've seen photos of the evacuees' trashed cars, but haven't seen any of the evacuees themselves. We can only speculate. Those who remained have told me they are in the same boat as I am, and we've talked about our homes as our castles that we'd be willing to defend. We are trying to stay low-profile, and we've even adopted the clothing color scheme of the "protestors" to blend in. If only they could see how much I loathe their reckless actions behind this stupid disguise I'm choosing to wear.

Most of the leftover families have backgrounds in self-reliance much like my own, and many are weekend sportsmen with a modest home armory of at least a .22 rifle, 12-gauge shotgun, and .30-06 bolt gun. In many large cities like this one, politicians have limited our ability to own most pistols and modern sporting rifles. My sister and my nieces have come to my house, so this fight for survival isn't mine alone. If I only had to worry about myself, I'd suck it up and sacrifice comfort voluntarily. With kids around, this isn't going to be easy. We have a stocked cupboard, but that food won't last long. Canned food doesn't require reconstitution, but the trade-off is weight and space. We're part Asian, so we were fortunate to have a healthy supply of rice on hand already. I need to think of ways to extend those meals. I need to find fillers out there to get us through this winter.

We stocked up a modest medicine cabinet with more vitamins, dietary supplements, and bandages for boo-boos. Since we don't plan on moving about much, we've moved the bug-out kits from our vehicles to our house. Car windows are just fragile doors that haven't been smashed open yet, so we don't want to leave anything of value out on the street.

Appearances vs. Reality

Knowing we'd need to get across town from time to time, I secured the rattiest- looking shopping carts I could find. The "protestors" loot and steal from stores, shops, and wealthy individuals. It's a gamble, but I doubt being seen as a bum would attract too much attention, especially at hours of the day when most are preprogrammed to sleep and definitely when the cold of winter keeps most "protestors" indoors on their computers and phones.

We all know the actions of this mob don't constitute lawful protest. I watched it play out time and time again and was quick to stock up on freeze-dried foods at the local Walmart. I also grabbed plenty of canned goods at the supermarket as soon as I suspected something like this was happening in my backyard. I let the idiots fight over toilet paper while I grabbed another large sack of rice, plenty of cooking oil, and tuna packets.

The way I look at it, with just these three ingredients, I have carbs, fat, and protein. I grabbed some spices and seasoning packets before I left, knowing I could provide some variety to my unexpected guests who experience food boredom easily. One last thing I picked up on my way out of the store were oversized clothes for my nieces and sister. I want them to look like they have been without food and unable to fill out their normal clothes. Perhaps that'll help to keep prying eyes from looking too closely at us in our well-prepared state.

Coordination

It pays to have friends. Thankfully, the bonds built around campfires and in hunting camps are hard to break. Outdoor pursuits like these tend to attract similar mindsets. Before all this nonsense popped off, my hunting buddies and I discussed using our phones as a primary means of communication along with two-way radios as an alternate means of communication. Some of us don't have our license to transmit over civilian amateur bands, but we're pretty sure law enforcement has bigger fish to fry than some guys chatting on open lines the mob likely isn't monitoring. Using past cases of civil unrest, we're fairly confident phone and internet service won't be interrupted, as people were tweeting and calling from inside occupied zones in the Pacific Northwest.

Should the local government services or utility providers shut down, they'll only temper the resolve of the mob to stay on mission. My hunting buddies and I decided to use a simple code along with GPS hunting software (OnX Hunt) on our cell phones to keep track of mob positions that we could share with one another. We could also pool our resources if times really got tough. We decided to pop common critters found in most cities as survival food, and save them with the tools found in most of our kitchens like Kitchen-Aid meat grinders, vacuum packers, and food dehydrators.

As a community, we feel the strongest resource we have is one another. Even though we don't have a medical doctor in our immediate group, we've identified who will be our "doc" with the highest medical training. We've used text message chains to inventory our medicine cabinets by sharing the photos of what we have. Who knows, maybe someone has a leftover prescription or remedy someone else may need. Without a regular doctor to visit, this will have to do. The rest of us will work in support roles, and we'll fall back on print resources like the book *Where There Is No Doctor*. We know this isn't perfect, but we can work with what we have and address what we face.

Redefining "Food"

If I've learned one thing about eating in the wilderness, it's that hunger is great sauce. I know what it's like to fast, but how do you convince kids to eat conservatively? My sister is a good mother, and like most moms, she'll sacrifice her comfort for her kids. Some of the kids' picky eating habits will make this scenario more difficult. I'll have to field dress and butcher out in the field, and return with cuts of meat that resemble what could've been bought in the grocery store. Doing this in the field will make me more vulnerable, but the trade-off is having to carry less weight over distance.

Drop cakes and fry bread are easy to make with just basic ingredients. Additional nutritional ingredients can be added and snuck into the girls' food like a dog mama sticking a pill in some peanut butter for her pooch. We've got a meat grinder attachment. I know I can mix random scraps of meat, fat, cheese, and spices to make what should remind the girls of meat snacks.

Discreet Food and Water Collection

Even though I live in a city, I know there's a major body of water directly east of me, Lake Michigan on the outskirts of Calumet Heights. Should I run out of food or if the water gets shut off, I'll take my shopping cart, don a disguise — most likely a utility worker outfit with a hard hat, vest, and clipboard — and head there. I won't chip through the ice with my hatchet until long after dark. The good thing about ice fishing is that I can set multiple homemade tip-ups and bail multiple hooks on a single line. It's a form of passive fishing that'll let me seek out resources while the baited hooks do the work. If I resort to active fishing, I'll be a sitting duck and an easy target.

My friends and I decided we wouldn't take from other families in the same scenario we're in. If we ran out of food, we would fall back on taking food from government buildings and, in particular, schools. Schools serve hundreds if not thousands of meals each day. The supplies found in the cafeteria, the athletic trainer's office, school nurse's office, and various family and consumer science classrooms would give us plenty to sort through. We know the looters and protestors are more interested in high-value real estate like department stores and political buildings.

We can work efficiently and without disruption by going where the agitators won't be. The frustrating lack of action by the federal government to harden schools, despite numerous calls for basic physical security measures to protect against school shootings, means easy access for us. We asked officials to block off ground-floor windows and create security corridors to prevent unauthorized access, but since they took no action, we know there'll be multiple easy entry points.

The Enemy of My Enemy is My Friend

I've already mentioned how most residents of Illinois don't have the firearm resources of less restrictive states. Standing toe-to-toe with the rioters is foolish and strategically irresponsible. While I know my hunting partners are capable marksmen and the value of a single well-placed round can't be measured, there are better options that draw on strategy than force. From watching the news, we know there are multiple domestic terrorist groups "protesting," but without any real direction. We know mob mentality is often reactive and driven by emotion, which is how we'll divide the mob and direct their attention at one another instead of the populace. All it takes to incite a mob is a perceived threat. A few bricks with gang colors or inflammatory notes thrown through some rival windows will send a strong manufactured message. Enough bricks can build a house or break down the perceived structure of an organization when equally disorganized groups turn on one another.

We know this civil unrest can't last forever. In all the cases in our recent history, the government has eventually stepped in. This isn't a matter of surviving indefinitely; it's simply a matter of holding out. While some of society has crumbled around us, the backbone of this nation is still holding strong and working together through a secret network. Compared to a mob looking for attention and likes on their social media hashtags, we value community and cooperation. We're going to outlast and see this through.

NATURAL RESOURCES EDUCATOR PHILLIP MEEKS' APPROACH

Both peaceful demonstrations and riots increased significantly around the globe from 2011 to 2018, according to data published by the Cross-National Time Series. Last year alone saw some of the most costly civil unrest in U.S. history, with one set of protests extending to 140 U.S. cities and leading to personal and corporate insurance losses in excess of $1 billion, says the Insurance Information Institute.

It seems that unrest capable of impacting local businesses and grinding day-to-day life to a halt is a greater possibility than it's ever been, especially in cities. And these events won't necessarily come and go within a few days.

Indoor Preparations

When I was a kid, I learned a lot about preparedness from a space my parents referred to simply as their "utility room." They'd converted their carport into a new kitchen, leaving the old refrigerator and cabinets behind. Over time, my folks filled this space with razors, shampoo, toothpaste, adhesive bandages, Ibuprofen, salt, and practically any other worthwhile item they caught on sale. In the same way, the old refrigerator got packed with condiments, ground beef, soft drinks, and frozen pizzas. This continuous and long-term larder-loading is what I've tried to adapt as an adult. It can be an affordable way to build enough supplies to carry a family through a long-term event ... but only if you start now.

You may use a lot of disposable items in your normal, day-to-day life – things like paper plates, paper cups, paper towels, and wet wipes. It's good to have a few weeks' worth of these things in stock, but for the long-term, there'll come a point where it'll be more sustainable to switch to real dinnerware and towels to be laundered. For an emergency that stretches on for months, plenty of laundry detergent and dish soap are good investments. Some ultralight backpackers forego the need for a lot of toilet paper by using a squeeze bottle as a makeshift bidet. The thought makes some squeamish, but the fact is it's an acceptable way to keep oneself clean when paper products run out.

Another angle regarding the replacement of disposable with reusable items is this: if trash disposal is disrupted for weeks or months, what will the accumulation of garbage in your home mean to your family's health and morale?

Buy drinking water in reusable 5-gallon containers to cut down on waste. Hygiene and household cleaning can be accomplished with pool water or a rain barrel. It's possible the rainwater can be made potable in a pinch, too, depending on the surfaces it touches.

Plan to cook during an extended crisis, and give the entire family a role in the process. (A selection of easy-to-prepare instant meals will be fine for when time and energy run low.) Canned meats, vegetables, and fruits have a long shelf-life, as do pastas, flour, and cornmeal. Powdered milk is great to have on your shelf, but liquid milk can be frozen for several months, too. Have family members select recipes now that use a minimal number of ingredients, and concentrate on putting those items in your pantry.

If you haven't stockpiled first-aid supplies and medications such as over-the-counter painkillers and allergy relief for both children and adults, begin doing so immediately, always being mindful of expiration dates. Keep appropriate amounts of ammo for hunting or defense stashed away. In fact, double what you think is a reasonable amount. Dry pet food will store for a long time, so be sure to have some extra, as well as common pet medications.

Pick a room in the house such as the master bedroom, and equip it with solid locks and extra shelves. Store communications equipment, first-aid supplies, extra food, and defensive tools in there. This can be where you lock up your supplies should you have to leave for a few hours, or it can serve double duty as the spot to which your family retreats in an emergency.

Have some cash in small denominations set aside, as well as items that can be used for bartering with your neighbors: hard candy, instant coffee, sample bottles of whisky, cigarettes and cigars, travel-sized toiletries, and so on.

Outdoor Preparations

Most vegetable seeds will keep for years in the freezer, so stock up when those go on clearance. Snap peas and beets are versatile in that their leaves can be eaten, too. Radishes are ready for harvest in under a month. Vegetables with many fruits per plant do well in containers on a balcony, and a nice crop of potatoes can be harvested from buckets, mulch piles, or even cardboard boxes. To work edible components into the landscape, blackberries, raspberries, currants, serviceberries, and strawberries can all be used in attractive ways.

Embrace the concept of "succession planting." Once you harvest onions, for example, fill that spot with snow peas or kale. Understand which vegetables are best direct-seeded into the soil and which need to be grown first as transplants, and invest in a few trays and a bag of starter mix for cabbage, broccoli, and tomato transplants. Cool-season crops that you'd normally grow in early spring can typically be planted again in late summer for a fall harvest.

A roll of "floating row cover" will extend the fall growing season by at least a couple of weeks, providing fresh produce until Thanksgiving or beyond.

On Site

Family and friends outside the area may still be able to access supplies normally. Take advantage of that silver lining as long as USPS delivery is still happening to fill in gaps with medications, toiletries, or other supplies.

Parks and greenways can prove to be a source of wild edibles, especially in the summer, and the fact that maintenance of public green spaces may cease will mean a proliferation of blackberries, greenbrier, wild carrot, pokeweed, and other food-worthy plants. Be wary of collecting edibles from previously well-maintained lawns and golf courses, though, as these could still cling to some pesticide residues. Don't overlook the many species of weedy mints that could be used for teas. Most home lawns (once maintenance subsides) will host good yields of dandelion, chickweed, oxalis, violets, and other edibles.

While fish and crayfish can be easily harvested from nearby water bodies, water quality is likely a concern in the city, and the harvest of squirrels or groundhogs from a city park may draw undue attention. However, those protein sources are there if desperately needed, as are winged options such as starlings and pigeons.

Entomophagy (the practice of eating bugs) is ranked as a last resort by most, but with a little cooking and lots of barbecue sauce, it's possible to convert grasshoppers and cicadas that emerge in the summer into novelty dishes to stretch the food supply.

Fuel, herbicide, fertilizer, and pharmaceutical runoff can all make urban streams and ponds questionable, so be cautious when seeking an emergency water source. Focus instead on rainwater catchment, if possible, and treat drinking water by boiling or using a backcountry filter system.

Crisis

An individual or household can easily navigate through many short-term disasters, but the longer the emergency, the more you need community. That can be your physical neighbors, members of a faith-based organization to which you belong, or a group of buddies who all live within walking distance of each other. Studies have looked at the value of community in disaster resilience, and the bottom line is that those neighborhoods and broader communities able to invest in their own recovery from the bottom up — as opposed to waiting for authorities to fix everything — stand a much better chance of emerging from a serious disaster. There are two ways to view your neighbors: as competitors for limited supplies or as potential allies whose knowledge and skills can complement your own.

A coordinated neighborhood gardening effort can minimize idle hands and involve men, women, and children in preparing for their own nutritional needs. A few folks with shovels, mattocks, and wheelbarrows can easily convert turf to garden in a few hours. Within days, every yard and vacant lot on a given street can be prepped for vegetable production.

Children can be given the task of overseeing small plantings at their own homes, monitoring the patio tomatoes for hornworms, for instance, or picking slugs off the cabbages.

Another community effort directly related to gardening — and an important one given that urban soil is often less than ideal for growing — is the development and maintenance of compost. A team can be responsible for collecting all compostable materials from the neighbors (newspapers, coffee grounds, fruit and vegetable scraps, grass clippings) and keeping it aerated. The more a compost pile is turned, the quicker it becomes something useful.

Beyond gardening, a coalition among just a few neighbors could help address other needs, such as those that relate to clothing, repairs, or medical emergencies. "Maria has some new sheets she'll donate if we agree to replace them after all this is over, and Stan is handy with a sewing machine."

It can be surprising what tools and skills you may uncover on the block. Mark has a tractor with a bucket and a rototiller attachment; Lisa spent two semesters studying veterinary medicine; Richard is a retired tailor. A neighborhood swap meet can be a good way to exchange any surplus you may have for items the family next door can part with: shoes, tools, disinfectants, seasonings. The social aspect of these kinds of activities can help keep everybody sane at the same time.

A good, progressive approach to preparedness that's been presented to me is to first think about a 72-hour event. After that, make it a goal to have all you need for two weeks, and so on. It's good to maximize all available storage space over time with your family's nutrition, hygiene, health, and safety in mind. In thinking of disasters that could potentially go on for months, it's also wise to consider what neighbors might bring to the table.

CONCLUSION

Lots of situations can interrupt the flow of commerce. COVID, snowstorms, the Suez Canal blockage, and the Colonial Pipeline cyberattack all recently contributed to an interruption in goods reaching their destination. Civil unrest is just another piece in the puzzle that can also indefinitely affect our ability to procure the goods or services we take for granted. Many in the ammunition industry believe that the demand has exceeded the supply so dramatically that it may take at least two years to catch up. Ask yourself what would happen if that type of demand impacted food, medical supplies, and other items you absolutely need to live.

Do your part to not only use these techniques to maximize your self-sustainability during an emergency, but also consider forming neighborhood groups with like-minded individuals who share your concern. Determine what everyone's willingness to participate is, what their strengths and weaknesses are, and what role they can fulfill when everyone needs to pool their resources to survive a supply shortage. A little extra planning now will pay dividends when another unforeseen event threatens to force the average citizen to do without the conveniences they've grown accustomed to. ⁑

33

WE ARE HIT BY ANOTHER PANDEMIC?

By RECOIL OFFGRID Staff

Illustrations by Joe Oesterle

In Issue 28 of RECOIL OFFGRID, we wrote a feature on Operation: Dark Winter (ODW) – a senior-level government exercise from June 2001 that simulated a bioterrorism attack in the United States using smallpox as its agent of choice. Its findings were discouraging to say the least.

The results of the ODW study revealed a gut-wrenching reality that many Americans weren't aware of until COVID-19 found its way here – we as a nation are drastically ill-prepared for pandemics. Problems range from a lack of sufficient training, delays in developing vaccines or drugs to treat a new illness, and the collateral damage it causes to our infrastructure and commerce.

Fast-forward to 2020, and the world has seen firsthand how devastating the effects of a highly communicable disease can be on every aspect of human life. The question now remains, how can we prepare for the next wave or another outbreak with a contagion that's even deadlier?

The Scenario

Situation type: Another pandemic
Your Crew: You
Location: Your hometown
Season: Autumn
Weather: Clear; high 68 degrees F, low 45 degrees F

The Setup

In a matter of months, the COVID-19 pandemic wreaked havoc on the United States. Businesses and schools closed. Workers were furloughed and laid off. Students and parents had to adapt to online learning. There was a run on groceries; some items sold out immediately with very little replenishment. Firearms and ammunition sales spiked, and first-time gun owners realized how difficult it was to purchase a firearm, not only due to legal formalities, but also because many retailers were left with nothing but empty display cases.

Hospitals were not only overwhelmed with new admissions, but the staff was often limited and, in some cases, quit for fear of exposure. Medical supplies were also depleted quickly due to a shortage in the national stockpile and the fact that many were made overseas. Our economy took a huge hit, and the unemployment rate is still high. With rumors of certain jobs not being reinstated, there's a lingering fear that another recession is on the horizon.

The Complication

If another pandemic happened, how would you prepare for it, drawing on your experiences and what you witnessed with the COVID-19 pandemic? What if a new pandemic involved a disease with an even higher mortality rate? What would you stock up on, and how many weeks' worth of supplies would you keep on hand? How can you better prepare financially for another period of indefinite employment? Who would you rely on for accurate information regarding the status of the pandemic? How would you protect your health during necessary ventures into public places? What can you do to bolster your medical knowledge and preparedness if you're forced to stay at home and medical help and supplies are limited?

FIRST RESPONDER JOEY NICKISCHER'S APPROACH

Having just gone through an "easy" pandemic, namely COVID-19, and having tested my preparations on multiple fronts, I have to say that I'm happy to have had a "warm-up round" before the next wave hits us. Not only will you and I be better prepared, but the government and private sector will be better prepared, too.

If *and* when another pandemic hits and we return to full lockdown, remember that stores will probably remain open, even if with limited hours. You'll eventually be able to get food, toilet paper, and other basic necessities. The difference is that during the pandemic, things may not be available at will, which is what we're used to. We have become a society that thrives on "just in time" inventory, which means that most stores have just enough inventory to get them through a few days' worth of their average sales volume. Beyond that, products usually have to be ordered from the manufacturer. Understanding this business principle will help avoid the panic buying and a repeat of the dreaded toilet paper hoarding incident of 2020.

Use the lessons learned about shortages to stock up on some of your personal staple items. If you have a preferred brand of toilet paper, buy double your usual amount. There's plenty of toilet paper in the United States, but if people begin hoarding again, you might not be able to get your preferred brand for a few weeks. Additionally, have enough face masks and sanitizing supplies to last a few weeks. And remember, the less you venture out into public, the less you'll need those masks and sanitizer.

Personally, the only things I'm really stocking up on are food staples — particularly meats, both canned and frozen. The 2020 pandemic hit the meat industry pretty hard, and I was informed that some of the meat processing facilities had employee infection rates around 50 percent. That's huge, and it did cause some shortages. Again, it didn't mean that there was no meat to be found, only that my preferred cuts or quantities weren't always available when I wanted them.

My other staples include rice, beans, flour, yeast, sugar, and baking powder. With a generous supply of these items, combined with various meats and vegetables, I'll never be without something to eat. I'll continue to shop as needed, about once every two weeks, and consume the fresh stuff first. If there's something in short supply at the store, I can easily pull from my stockpile and simply replace that item when it becomes available. In general, I keep about a 60-day supply of my personal food staples at home.

The other plus about having extra supplies in your personal stockpile is that you can make less trips to the store during a pandemic. Less trips to the store equal less exposure.

It's good to have other items on hand, too. I keep a few standard medications, such as acetaminophen, aspirin, decongestants, and naproxen, also with a 30-plus day supply at maximum dosage, per person in my home. My house is on a private well, but there's also 20 gallons of potable water handy in jugs for emergencies, plus a few cases of bottled water. I keep 40-plus disposable lithium AA batteries in my cache, plus half a dozen adapters to convert AA batteries to C and D size. My batteries are primarily for flashlights and my emergency AM/FM/weather radios. I don't currently have a backup generator for my house, but I have a vehicle that has a 2,000-watt inverter on board. In an emergency, I can plug in my freezer and re-frigerator to keep things cold. Our dog food is also kept at the 60-day supply level.

All items in soft packaging, such as paper or plastic bags, are kept in clear plastic bins in the basement with lids securely attached. This is primarily to ensure that no errant mouse chews through the package, but also helps to keep the packages dry if there's a water leak. The clear bin makes it faster and easier to find what I'm looking for. Canned or jarred foods are kept in the kitchen cupboard, in the back of the hall closet and on dedicated shelves in the basement. I found that if metal cans were stored on my concrete floor, they would rust much, much faster than if stored on a shelf. A dehumidifier also helps keep the basement, and supplies, dry.

We also take safety precautions with all store-bought supplies that come into the house. If it's something that can sit outside in the sun for a while, we start with that so the UV can help kill any germs that might be on the package. Then, the item comes inside and sits in a "quarantine area" of the basement for seven days, being careful not to cross-contaminate other items. Items that must come straight into the house are cleaned with a mild bleach solution, by submersion or wiping. While these steps might not be 100-percent effective, every step we take helps lessen our risk of exposure.

I'm not particularly worried about communications problems during a pandemic, but I maintain several communications options, just in case. First, there's the cell phone with multiple chargers plus a few small rechargeable battery packs. I also keep in mind that the phone can be charged in my vehicle with the standard power port. I've also exported my cell phone contact list onto my computer, have a hard copy printed for emergencies, and leave a copy in an envelope at mom's house. I'll never forget mom's number, so I can call her and get whatever important contact info I need from that list.

Other emergency communications abilities I have include two-way commercial radios, both mobile and portable, plus a HAM radio. They're preprogrammed with all my local frequencies, plus the common FRS, GMRS, and commercial frequencies. I also have a hard copy list of the frequencies and PL tones I might use in an emergency.

One of the most important things to have available during any emergency is an excellent support network close to home. Besides maintaining a great relationship with my neighbors, I'm the chief of my local volunteer fire department. Belonging to a fire department is like having a second family — everybody pitches in to help each other during hard times. We have members who are making shopping runs for other members and some are even preparing meals for those who are self-quarantining. We're also sharing information about what stores have shortages or surplus of critical supplies, such as sanitizing wipes.

I also have a responsibility to help keep the public safe, and that starts by making sure that my firefighters and EMTs have all the safety equipment and training that they need. Our preparations for the pandemic began in January 2020, mostly with becoming educated on what COVID-19 was, what its symptoms were, how to avoid becoming infected, and how to avoid transmission to/from others. I can say that N95 respirators were already in short supply, nationwide, in January 2020, as government and well-informed private sector groups geared up for what was coming.

In the process of equipping my fire department for emergency response to COVID-19 infected residences, we needed to issue each firefighter protective N95 masks and hand sanitizer. Just as important as having proper PPE is knowing how to use it. We see far too many people wearing quality masks inappropriately, thereby negating the positive attributes of having the higher-quality N95 mask. Whatever level of protective equipment you have access to, make sure you seek out knowledge about how to properly use it.

As the reports of the next pandemic are released, my family will increase our social distancing and remind others to do the same. We'll also take note of whether our neighbors are following recommended guidelines, and if they are not, we'll minimize in-person contact with them. We'll stay out of public contact to the largest degree possible, including preparing all of our own meals and ensuring that as many precautions are taken as possible.

DISASTER MANAGEMENT SPECIALIST NILA RHOADES' APPROACH

This most recent COVID-19 pandemic has shown many avid preppers and survivalists where the holes in our supplies are. This is both a blessing and a curse. While my area wasn't hit as hard as others, walking the grocery store aisles with my children and seeing the empty shelves definitely gave me a surprising level of anxiety even though I have a well-prepared stash of items tucked away. Knowing what I know now, there are things that my family would do differently prior to a future pandemic.

Knowledge: To set the stage, having a stash of essential items is critical. Items like basic toiletries, food items, water, medical supplies, and yes, even toilet paper. However, one frequently overlooked resource to add to your supply cache is books. Having a well-rounded library of medical, survival and preparedness, fishing/hunting, and target-hardening literature can be extremely beneficial. Make sure your library is relevant to your needs – in urban environments, learning how to fish, hunt, or build an improvised shelter from fallen logs isn't as practical as it would be in the wilderness. Having hard copies of resources can be lifesaving. We found a great library of survival resources on www.superessestraps.com and Amazon. Military manuals like the *Ranger Handbook*, *Winter Survival Manual*, and *The SERE Handbook* are also crucial additions.

Toiletries: The most surprising aspect of the COVID-19 pandemic was which items flew off the shelf and how quickly the online vendors ran out of personal hygiene products. Panic buying hit the American people early, and it hit hard. There have been many videos posted on social media of parents searching stores for diapers and wipes for their children, only to leave empty handed. This was one area that I hadn't adequately prepared for, and it was the first thing to change in preparation for the future. We purchased a case of the current size, and one size larger to be safe, along with a large case of wipes.

Food: Our food supply techniques won't change much other than gathering more on a regular basis. More is always better. Barring any major food allergies, you can never go wrong with MREs, followed by copious amounts of fiber supplements. They're compact and can last for an awfully long time when stored properly. Other long-term emergency foods like Mountain House, Wise Company, Augason Farms, Northwest Fork, and Survival Tabs are also great products to keep on hand. We ensure that each person in our family has approximately 2,000 calories per day. We don't differentiate between child and adult. It's our built-in surplus.

Water: Water can be a tough one. Water bottles expire (not the water itself, but the plastic as it starts to degrade) and take up a lot of space. Knowing what we know now, I wouldn't worry so much about water as nothing drastic happened with water supplies in the United States that wasn't already an issue prior. However, having a few cases of Blue Can Water can never hurt. They aren't cheap, but they have a 50-year shelf life.

Our rule of thumb is to keep at least three months' worth of food, water, and supplies on hand and rotate through or add to them as needed. We figure that each person needs 1 gallon of water per day. Again, we don't differentiate between child and adult. That helps us come out ahead.

Vitamins And Personal Protective Equipment (PPE): I keep a small stock of vitamins, but finding COVID-19 appropriate vitamins was a challenge. It took me weeks to find things like multi-vitamins, colloidal silver, vitamin C, and elderberry supplements. While these aren't specifically prescribed to help with COVID-19, we believe they help the immune system for those times when we had to leave our home to restock.

Obviously, as many of us found out earlier this year, finding masks, gloves, bleach, and hand sanitizer took the strategy and planning of a war-time sand table. Stocking up on PPE is suddenly at the top of our list. MOPP 4 gear wasn't necessarily appropriate to wear to our local grocery store – although we considered it going to Walmart a few times – but simple PPE was adequate and even mandatory in some businesses. From now on, we'll always ensure that we have a case of hand sanitizer, masks, latex gloves, and cleaning agents at the ready.

Finances: Financially planning for another pandemic takes patience and sacrifice. Many of us already feel this in our finances even without being insecure about our jobs or ability to put food on the table. My family follows a modified version of Dave Ramsey and The Budget Mom techniques for financial preparation. Essentially both schools of thought want you to have a $1,000 to

$5,000 emergency fund, then pay off all consumer debts, then have three to six months of expenses (not income) in a savings account or money market. It won't always be easy to reach this point, but it can aid in having cushion if your hours are cut, if you don't know when unemployment benefits will kick in, or if you want to stock up on items in the early days of a disaster. I strongly recommend following both individuals on social media and getting Dave Ramsey's book, *The Total Money Makeover.* At the very least, it'll give you guidelines to start building what will work best for your family and your unique situation. While researching what financial preparedness method works for you, also research unemployment options should you ever have to file and keep up to date on new unemployment benefits (like the ones during the COVID-19 pandemic) to know to what to expect.

Information: During the height of the COVID-19 outbreak it seemed like everyone on social media was now suddenly an infectious disease expert. It made finding relevant and accurate data incredibly difficult. It seems like there's a scientific publication to back up anyone's opinion on COVID-19. New data may fluctuate, but common sense and a little bit of science goes a long way. The presidential addresses are a good place to start for an overview of the latest medical information.

Because of all the ever-changing data, it's increasingly difficult to abide by any stringent rules. Stick to the most consistent information rather than focusing on sensational headlines and outliers. Speaking with medical professionals in your area is always a good course of action as well.

Community: The stay-at-home order was the worst part of the COVID-19 pandemic. As a work-at-home parent being able to go to the library, the park, a MOPS group, or a friend's house was a godsend. With all our outlets taken away, it made occupying and entertaining my kiddos a challenge. My advice is to connect with friends via Zoom, Facebook Messenger, Facetime, or Skype often. Getting together in person is a calculated risk that must be assessed by each party; but seriously, nothing virtual can replace a hug from a close friend. Also, be sure to let the kids talk to their friends – they need their tribe also.

Building a sense of community is paramount should another pandemic hit the country. Text or call your neighbors, friends, and family often. In my community, someone started a public Facebook group called, "Oops, I ran out of..." This group was created to help community members find the items that they were searching for without having to drive to a dozen different stores. This enables grocery shopping to be a group mission rather than a free-for-all. It also presents opportunities to barter and trade to gather supplies that you may be missing. Neighbors can also help you lock down your street if riots and looting are happening in your area. Emotional and mental aspects are important, but they don't matter much if you don't have safety or food to eat.

Safety: Having a home that's alarmed is just smart these days. When the alarm is tripped, it calls dispatch for you, which allows you to manage the threat until law enforcement arrives. Installing a Ring or Nest video doorbell is a great option as well. While alarms aren't always a criminal deterrent, they can buy you precious seconds to respond to danger.

Most criminals don't want to be seen, so investing in exterior motion-activated lighting that can be secured to the exterior of the property can also mitigate a specific level of criminal.

During an uncertain time, awareness of what's normal and abnormal in one's surrounding environment is critical. We should never be afraid to say that something is abnormal or to respond accordingly. If something feels off, don't let normalcy bias persuade you to rationalize it. Investigate further and be ready for the most dangerous outcome.

Communication: Communicating with others wasn't a huge challenge during the COVID-19 pandemic. Sure, Zoom calls were overloaded or slow at times, but communications were fairly uninterrupted. That being the case, having a secondary or tertiary method of communication is always wise. Satellite phones, ham radios, walkie-talkie systems, and CB radios are always a great choice, if you have a method of charging and/or replacing the batteries.

SEARCH-AND-RESCUE SPECIALIST ANDREW SCHRADER'S APPROACH

Preparation: I remember being at Home Depot back in 2017 when the forecasted track of Hurricane Irma was shifting toward my home in Tampa Bay. My town suddenly and collectively realized that we were all about to have a bad time. Shoppers pushing their carts looked around bug-eyed, watching for signals of a stampede from the rest of the herd. Tense conversations and cart-bumping spilled into every aisle of the store, as everything even remotely related to survival and comfort got picked off. No more generators or gasoline containers, no more solar lights. When the plywood sold out, folks started buying decorative siding and trim — anything to help Band-Aid their homes against the storm. It made me realize what many of our readers probably already knew: The panicked animal inside all of us isn't very far underneath the surface.

Personally, I consider having two weeks to a month of supplies to be appropriate. Non-perishable food and water are a given. I have many cans of Chef Boyardee and Campbell's soups, as well as Mountain House freeze-dried meals and a little Jetboil stove. Besides food and water, the other thing I have to constantly remind myself of is to make sure I have a month's supply of whatever prescription medicines the family needs.

Helping to ensure mere survival is good, but I try to go beyond that to determine what will make my life much more comfortable if things get shut down. Many of us are used to 48-hour deliveries from Amazon. However, we all saw how quickly the supply chain can get shut down, or simply redirected to other priorities that are considered more essential. To figure out what I should plan on stockpiling, I take a good look around my home and see what we're actually using on a daily basis. When I do this, I find many things that go beyond what I'd really consider "survival" items, such as those that make me feel better and keep my spirits up. This includes items like shampoo, dental floss, and coffee. The more little "nonessential" goodies you already have in your house, the less you'll be tempted to leave your house and expose yourself to potential infection. Also, you'll have a better means to trade with your neighbors.

After waiting eight days for my power to be restored after Hurricane Irma, I paid for a natural gas line to be run to my house from the neighboring street. Now, I have both electric and natural gas availability at my house. The main point of the natural gas was to run a 22-kilowatt Generex generator. Simply installing propane tanks would've been less expensive, but I didn't want to worry about getting refilled when a disaster hits, and I also figured the below-ground installation was less prone to damage or vandalism. Although my house is mainly powered by electricity, my water heater is powered by gas, as are my firepit and outdoor lamps. If the power goes out, I could boil water and cook food over the firepit. Also, I purchased 10 or so inexpensive solar security lights from Amazon and stuck them all over the perimeter of my house. It's nice to be able to see where I'm going at night, and if we lost power, we'd be able to charge them during the day and use them for at least part of the night.

In case our cell phones go out, I use a Garmin inReach Explorer+, which allows me to message anyone from anywhere, and also provides navigation capability.

On Site: When a disease reaches pandemic levels, I do my best to take no unnecessary risks. I try to reduce trips to the store, avoid enclosed spaces with crowds, and generally follow Center for Disease Control (CDC) recommendations. I also avoid nonessential activities that might inadvertently send me to the hospital. For example, I'm not getting up on the roof just to blow leaves off. I'm not doing heavy lifting yard work and risking throwing out my back. The nonessential "honey-do" list can wait until the pandemic is over.

To stay informed, I source my information globally from outlets such as the BBC and Al Jazeera to get more than just an American perspective. If there's a story that sounds like it might be politically motivated, I simply Google it and try to look at it from several websites to get a broader picture. I use social media to keep up with friends and hobbies, not as a news source.

During a disaster or any national crisis, I pay special attention to watch for scammers and those who try to exploit the vulnerable. There will always be someone trying to make money off of disaster victims or play off of people's fears. Mr. Rogers told us that to feel better we should always look for the helpers. I believe that, but I also know we need to keep one eye out for the scoundrels who are never far behind.

Crisis: When facing an unprecedented situation like this, we give ourselves the best chance of success if we practice preparedness as a mindset. I used to keep my bug-out supplies in the garage, trying to save space for something that (hopefully) wouldn't be used very often.

What I eventually realized, though, is that when it's in the garage I just forget about it. I never bother to check on the items or think about if I should add something to it. And worst of all, I don't notice if things are deteriorating. Obviously, anything you may be entrusting your life to should be stored in the best conditions possible.

I currently store my bug-out supplies inside of my air-conditioned house, and not inside of a closet, either. I like to have them out where I can see them. I think it helps me keep a preparedness mindset if I have to walk by the gear every day. In a way, it's almost helpful if you store gear in an inconvenient place. Like a blister on my toe or a thorn in my thumb, to me it's a daily reminder of the next unknown threat that could be quietly coming down the pipe any day.

I store my especially valuable gear in a gun safe and scatter a few low-dollar items which appear high-dollar – such as a broken laptop computer and a fake Rolex – out in easy sight in the hopes that a would-be thief would take the bait and leave the rest of my valuables alone. I also use an inexpensive Wyze Cam system to keep an eye on the house and have scattered an area of functioning and non-functioning webcams around the outside to give the appearance of a seamless security system. For me, it's not really about stopping the thief who is truly prepared and determined to rob me. Instead, it's more about trying to look like a better-defended house than the one down the street.

For income, I've done my best to diversify my revenue streams and not just rely on my day job. I've earned additional certifications, and I've learned a side hustle or two just like so many others have in this gig economy. If I thought I was in for a truly disastrous dry spell, I'd maintain my checking account by putting everything I needed on credit cards until they got shut off. The long-term bankruptcy issue could be handled once I no longer had to worry about the short-term survival of my family.

A safety net is about more than what you can do on your own, though. It's invaluable to maintain the best possible relationships with your neighbors and strengthen a local support network. Bring them booze at Christmas, mow their lawn once in a while, and actively search for how you can contribute to their well-being. Having a blood-relative 50 miles away isn't nearly as valuable as having a good neighbor one mile away. So, think in terms of maintaining resources (like good neighbors) within walking distance. Because when your city gets locked down, walking distance may well be the furthest you can go.

This "What If?" column hits close to home for me, and I'm writing this as much to myself as to our readers. I've no doubt that another pandemic will visit us again – it's just a matter of time. And, to my shame, enduring a globe-crossing infection of this size was something I never really thought would occur. I suppose that if this were 1920 and I had just seen the ravages of the 1918 influenza pandemic, I might've been better prepared. But time washes away all of our collective memories, and it's tough to keep threats in mind that seem more like stories and legends. It's made me appreciate this magazine more and be glad I held onto my back issues.

Working as a structural engineer and Urban Search and Rescue specialist deployed primarily to hurricane events, I naturally compare any disaster to a hurricane. And in the case of COVID-19, the effects on my world have been similar. I've watched this thing shutter my local businesses and put a damper on my own livelihood in the construction industry. Neighbors get sick and go to the hospital — some come back. Even my wife contracted the virus; watching her struggle to breathe gave me a feeling of helplessness I hope to never feel again.

CONCLUSION

Those who choose to procrastinate their survival planning will be the first to experience the world's indifference to their situation if they're caught with their proverbial pants down. Socking money away, stocking up on supplies, checking multiple sources for information on an outbreak, and above all, remaining level-headed will pay dividends for you when the unprepared masses start running around like headless chickens.

Preparing for a future pandemic doesn't have to be a scary process, but it does have to have a level of precision and forethought. If you're new to survival and preparedness, always start with the basic pillars of survival: food, water, fire, shelter, and medical. Having a good supply in each of these categories will help build a foundation that can handle just about anything. Also, remember that survival isn't just about what you have; it's about what you know and the skills you've developed. Seek training in key areas such as first aid and self-defense and practice these perishable skills frequently.

The good news is, there are actions we can take for next time. Although we can't control the outcome of the game, we can make sure that we give ourselves the best possible odds going into it. ❖

34

YOUR UTILITIES ARE INDEFINITELY DISRUPTED?

By Tim MacWelch

Illustrations by Cassandra Dale

The baby was sleeping quietly and your spouse was catching a much-needed nap on the couch. Your daughter was trying hard to stifle her giggles as she watched her favorite cartoon on television. If Norman Rockwell were still alive to paint scenes of modern domestic tranquility, your household could be the model.

As you settled down into your favorite chair and the dog curled up at your feet, the mood of the day was contentment. Without realizing it, your eyes had closed for a moment. Sleep was starting to take hold of you, until something caused you to stir. It felt like the rumbling of a truck, until you realized that it wasn't a vehicle. The shaking intensified. The baby started crying, and the dog began to whimper. The flat-screen TV fell off the wall and crashed onto the floor. Your daughter screamed, and you were barely able to stand as the earth shook violently.

Remembering the "triangle of life," you scooped up your children and pushed your family into the corner of the room. The ceiling drywall began to crack and virtually every object that could fall over ended up on the floor. The children wailed in fear, and just as suddenly as it began – everything stopped, including the illumination from your light fixtures.

For this installment of RECOIL OFFGRID's "What If?" column, the editors have asked for our preparations and reactions to a severe earthquake that knocks out all your utilities. In this scenario, we're not tucked away in the countryside at some self-sufficient cabin – no, that would be too easy. We're smack in the middle of a large city (just like many of you) and are now without power, gas, phone lines, and water. You have no idea how long this cavalcade of outages will last.

How do you provide for your family's basic needs after suddenly being thrust back into the dark ages? How do you keep your family warm with winter approaching? What's your strategy to deal with looters and marauders? Pay close attention, there's nothing that any of us can do to prevent Mother Earth from shaking like a wet dog, but there's a lot we can do to be ready for the utility outages that follow.

The Scenario

Situation type: At home
Your Crew: You, your wife, and two young children.
Location: Tulsa, Oklahoma
Season: Late Autumn
Weather: Rainy; high 58 degrees F, low 38 degrees

The Setup

You're at home with your spouse, your 2-month-old baby son, and your 9-year-old daughter, and pet German Shepherd, enjoying a leisurely Saturday when there's a 7.3 earthquake 67 miles northwest of your location. Structural damage has been moderate to severe in the areas closest to the epicenter. Although your home has only had minimal damage, a byproduct of the earthquake is that utilities have been knocked out within a 150-mile radius of your location.

The power grid is disabled indefinitely, local cell towers are inoperable, and landline phones are also down. Natural gas and water pressure have dropped to zero. Winter is approaching, and it'll begin snowing soon. A situation like this can not only cause fatalities for those who suffer from cold, dehydration, food shortages, overwhelmed hospitals, and other collateral effects of the outage, but desperation in the form of looting may quickly take hold.

The Complication

Since you have no electricity and conventional communication has been wiped out, your ability to get media updates on the restoration of utilities is limited. Without water, your ability to remain hydrated, bathe, have proper sanitation, and cook is extremely limited. The possibility of looting is high, and you're in a major city. Winter is coming and without gas and electricity, the cold may wreak havoc. What steps can you take to endure this long-term utility outage, feed and protect your family, and endure without modern conveniences? Realizing that these outages may extend to an indefinite radius and road blockages may be everywhere, rather than attempt to leave the area in search of another place to hole up, you decide to bug in and rely on the supplies you've stockpiled. The grid is down and, just like hurricane-ravaged Puerto Rico, may not be up again for months.

FORMER U.S. ARMY PSY-OP SERGEANT HAKIM ISLER'S APPROACH

Prep

Because I live by the "not if it will happen, but when" motto, my family and I have been preparing for long-term disasters for many years. When my wife and I decided to put money toward stocking up on supplies, we knew that purchasing a large quantity in one fell swoop is cost prohibitive. On average, we go shopping every two weeks, so we started purchasing small essentials during our shopping trips to gradually increase our emergency supply cache.

Over the last two years we've set aside $125 per month plus half of any remaining discretionary funds to help pay for items that we'd need for a disaster. Every two months we buy a bucket of freeze-dried food. Our biweekly shopping trips also lead to the acquisition of bottled water, protein bars, hygiene products like antibacterial soap, medical supplies, and vitamins.

Some of the larger items that would be useful in an event like this are a gas generator with four months' worth of fuel to power it, a small solar generator, 20 small propane tanks, eight months' worth of drinking water, 16 months' worth of freeze-dried food, and four months' worth of pet food. A CB radio and hand-crank radio would also enable us to have another way of receiving information if power is out. Having paid attention to how much firewood we consumed during an average winter, I'd also make sure we had at least a winter's worth of fuel for the fireplace. In an emergency situation where gas and electricity are off, it'd make sense to have even more than that amount as we'd be using it to do more than just keep warm.

Speaking of power and light, how many batteries do you consume in a month? Television remotes, game console controllers, flashlights, electric turkey carving knives ... whatever. Have you ever added it all up to see what your monthly battery budget is? Knowing this could help you keep some critical capabilities up and running during a time like this. Having candles and lighters would also be something to keep enough of in case the battery supply began to diminish. We store most of our supplies along with our food and water in our basement since the temperature stays cool and dry all year, even without artificial temperature control. Some freeze-dried food can last up to 25 years, but unfortunately we can't say the same for our 2-month-old son's baby food.

To account for little ones, consider stocking up on a year's worth of powdered milk and baby food. Since breastfeeding would be our baby's initial food source, it'd be important to keep my wife (and thus the baby) well-hydrated and -nourished in a situation like this. My wife could exclusively breast feed him for 6 to 8 months, then start providing him with a combination of breast milk and baby food. The shelf life of baby food is about 24 months as long as it's unopened and stored appropriately.

An additional preparation is harvesting rainwater for tasks like showering and sanitation, instead of using our stored bottled water. The bottled water may be used as a last resort for bathing if sanitary water, especially for bathing our baby, was in short supply. We could potentially reuse bottled water numerous times for cooking. Another item worth storing is several gallons of Clorox bleach. This should be rotated regularly since it has a shelf life of one year before it starts to break down. Mixing 1 tablespoon of bleach with 1 gallon of rainwater can be used as a cleaning solution. Having four people and a dog living in a home during a disaster can get pretty messy and unsanitary. Being able to clean surfaces is especially important to help reduce the potential for illness, especially for children with weaker immune systems.

We collect our rainwater in barrels connected to our gutter down spouts on the side of our house. We can also use the rainwater to irrigate any food we're growing. An above-ground kiddie pool could be emptied, filtered, and consumed if the situation were desperate, but it could also serve as a receptacle for snow and rainwater. Using empty water bottles to collect rainwater could also be practical so we'd hang onto as many as we could make room for. Our rainwater barrels have a screen filter over them, however, when we collect the water we'd still run it through a LifeStraw pump system for increased filtration.

With the understanding that good people can become desperate in bad situations, my wife and I have spent years training with firearms and taking self-defense classes with our daughter. We have a shotgun and two pistols ready at all times. We keep a minimum of 1,000 rounds of ammo in stock for the pistols and 50 rounds for the shotgun. We routinely run drills to practice how to respond if someone tries to break into the house. This type of training became even more important to us after the birth of our son, who is too small to escape or defend himself.

As an additional security measure, we put our German Shepherd through Schutzhund training so he's able to carry out protection commands against any assailants. It's been a long-standing rule in our house that during a power outage we all move to the living room close to the fireplace and stay there to know each other's whereabouts. This also helps us easily identify any intruders, and keeps us close to what may ultimately be the only source of heat in the house.

Even with all these preps, safety comes in numbers and we created an emergency survival group with our neighbors. To ensure easy contact among our neighbors we use GoTenna – a device that allows us to create our own wireless network in the absence of an established cellular grid. We all have small solar chargers for our phones to ensure they stay working if cell service is restored. Running training drills together every so often will make sure survival skills remain fresh and organized so there's no confusion about responsibilities during adrenaline-filled emergencies.

On Site

After the disaster happened, we'd immediately turn on our radio to see the extent of the damage, paying particular attention to anything related to infrastructure conditions (municipal buildings, hospitals, surrounding homes, and nearby road damage). Simultaneously, we'd use the GoTenna to ensure the neighbors are all OK and find out where they're located. This could help lift some of the fog of chaos. We'd set a time to meet at my house that night to go over what to do and see if anyone needed any immediate help. With the loss of infrastructure there may be no waste management and no immediate medical or law enforcement support. A neighborhood or family group would need to discuss how to implement an interim plan to deal with the lack of resources.

To avoid unsanitary conditions developing inside the house, I'd suggest converting any sheds into outhouses and improvised bathing units with passive solar water heating systems for the hotter months (during the colder months, we could heat the water over a fire). I'd also build a compost site behind my house that we can use for food and human waste, and we can build additional ones if necessary to handle the waste generated by our neighborhood.

For collective defense, if you're able to organize to that degree, consider blocking off the street with a couple cars to make it harder for potential looters to access the neighborhood. I'd also suggest making a nighttime security rotation – one family would watch over the street each night for a four-hour shift to communicate anything suspicious. Lastly, we'd put each house on rotation for daily cleanup duty for the outhouses – it's nasty, but with no municipal refuse system or sewage everyone would have to pitch in so it doesn't become a health hazard.

Crisis

With all our combined preparations, and with the support system of our neighbors, I estimate being in good shape for at least a year without help and supplies. When grid-down situations switch from short term to long term, though, food supplies will eventually run out. The unprepared who've already run out of food will be searching for it. When enough people join together in desperation, there's a chance of being overwhelmed by a force you can't withstand.

In the event that hordes of desperate looters start heading your way, I'd suggest also preparing a separate bug-out location well in advance. Several years ago, my wife and I bought 60 acres of land. The land has a water source and is very secluded. We built a small shelter there with hidden supplies and have solar power on the property. The ability to hunt deer, turkey, rabbits, plant crops, and harvest wood for fires and other makeshift construction purposes makes it a good long-term location to hold up. The impracticality of bringing other people with us poses a challenge. To discreetly keep movement away from our neighborhood, we chose three routes to the property that are in wooded areas away from the city and any commonly-used roads.

It's important to remember the old saying, "accept the things you can't change and change the things you can." The most primitive things every human needs to survive are heat, water, food, security, and adaptability. Prepping for these things by gradually acquiring supplies and training betters your odds. Know what natural disasters may occur in your area and get to know the people around you to build a strong support system in advance of any calamities.

SURVIVAL EXPERT TIM MACWELCH'S APPROACH

Prep

This scenario is a great example of the concept of "prepare for one disaster very well, and you're well prepared for most disasters." As far as our family is concerned, an earthquake taking down our utilities isn't much different from several other crisis situations knocking out those things. Sure, there's probably more damage with a quake and it will take longer to repair than a cyber attack, for example, but we prepare for long-term utility outages (that may result in civil unrest) just like most other disasters.

Immediate Priorities: There are plenty of supplies that you could buy in advance that'd help in this situation. In the city, I'd want to have a utility shutoff tool, available at most hardware stores. This can shut off municipal water and gas, both of which should be shut off right after a quake for many good reasons. A top-shelf first-aid kit is high on my list too, since injury is likely in disasters. Water is my next priority. We bought a large-capacity home water heater for extra storage, which can be drained as needed for drinking water for washing.

I also maintain numerous 5-gallon water cooler jugs of water for easy access of ready-to-drink water. I keep multiple disinfection tools, like water filters and disinfection tablets, as well. I prefer two products from Katadyn and one from

Berkey for water disinfection. Katadyn MicroPur tablets are great for disinfecting water on the go. They take longer to work than iodine, but taste better (a key factor for keeping kids hydrated). Katadyn also makes a pump filter called the Pocket Filter, which even deals with tiny viral pathogens. For the household, we also have a Big Berkey filter. This gravity-fed filter is very effective and easy to use. Dump your raw water into the top and it filters down into a reservoir below. Even kids can use it with no problems.

Prep For The Long Game: Safety measures, first-aid, and water are needed right away, but soon enough we'd need to fall back on our supplies for the "long game." Defense, warmth, food, communication, transportation, and hygiene are the next orders of business. Researching weapons and home-hardening should happen well in advance of a scenario like this where civil unrest may soon follow. Have a plan for emergency warmth and cooking, too. We keep extra propane tanks for the outdoor grill, but never bring it inside for warmth, as the carbon monoxide it produces will kill. Keep an indoor heater on hand and numerous camping stoves with extra fuel for cooking.

When the budget will allow, I recommend home improvements that save or provide energy. Insulated or double-pane windows, blown insulation in the attic, solar heating and electric systems, wind power, and many other resources could be a Godsend in a crisis like this. As far as traditional supplies go, we stock plenty of batteries for flashlights, radios, and other equipment.

The bulkiest part of our stash is the food. We stock several months' worth of food, much of it in easy-to-cook staples like pasta and rice. Freeze-dried meals are even easier to cook. I like to keep Mountain House meals, a Jetboil stove, and plenty of fuel canisters on hand. With these, we can cook indoors by simply bringing the water to a quick boil. This way, we're not out in the yard cooking over a fire as much, which may advertise our preparedness to those who are becoming desperate.

We haven't forgotten about our pets. Dry cat food will feed both cats and dogs, and it can be stored in Mylar-lined buckets with oxygen absorbers. Store items sensitive to heat and sunlight in a cool, dark, dry place. Consider a satellite phone to communicate with people in areas unaffected by the crisis at hand.

One final issue is to make sure your kids are prepared for the earthquake itself. Teach them about the "triangle of life" and explain to them that their instinct to hide under a bed is dead wrong. When ceilings collapse on beds, the bed acts like a huge deadfall trap – crushing anyone hiding underneath. A safer, yet less intuitive, strategy is to lie beside the bed. So in the event that you are awoken in the night by an earthquake, roll off the bed and stay beside it. Don't crawl underneath!

On Site

Structural damage and dangerous leaks would be my biggest concerns in the initial aftermath of the earthquake and the beginning of the utility outage. If I were in a single-family home or townhouse, I'd look in the attic to see if there were any broken trusses. I'd also take a look through the basement, checking for damaged floor joists. If I weren't familiar with modern home construction, I'd try to find a neighbor who knew something and ask them to take a look. I'd also turn off all utilities. With a non-sparking wrench, I'd turn off the gas. I'd also turn off the water at the street (the same tool often does both jobs). I'd turn off the main breaker in the home's electrical panel as well.

If I, or any of my neighbors, have gas as a utility, there are some common practices that I'll want to avoid right after the quake. I'd limit (or better yet, avoid) all open flames until I'm certain that there are no gas leaks in and around the home and neighborhood. Lighting a cigar or firing up the propane grill could easily spark a natural gas or LP gas explosion. I wouldn't use candles for lighting, either.

So how can one get information in lieu of the Internet? The first thing I'd check is AM and FM radio signals and the NOAA weather bands. I could use one of our emergency radios (we keep two in our home) or hop in a vehicle and flip through the radio frequencies. There may be a station that could reach us, yet was unaffected by the quake or power outage. A CB radio may also provide contact with the outside world, if it was powered by a vehicle, or we had a back-up power source to run it. What am I trying to discover? I'd want to know the size of the impacted area, the extent of the damage, highway and road blockages, and the nearest area that still has power — just for starters.

The Crisis

Once the earthquake is over and we've put out the fires (literally and figuratively), it's time to rely on our preparations and get to work.

If a disaster knocked out the utilities for several hundred square miles, and you even suspected the outage might last a dangerously long time, get your spouse and kids the hell out of there. Leave as soon as you can. And in the event that you couldn't leave (for one or more very good reasons), then you'll have to defend and endure.

A scenario of this kind would undoubtedly inspire aid to flood into the area from the rest of the country, but the problem with that is standing in line to get supplies and possibly leaving your family undefended to do so. With your own food storage in place and the ability to disinfect water you collect near your home, you can focus on the protection of your property, family, and possessions. Collecting safe drinking water would be a frequent task in the grid-down setting, and collecting extra water for hygiene is important too.

Collect the rain and find small local waterways, as needed. In the city, we could turn a plastic bucket into a toilet. We could also use a separate bucket of soapy water to hand-wash clothing. We could even take sponge baths and wash our dishes too. Preventing illness begins with adequate hygiene, and this can be just as important as any of your other skills. And when the food runs out completely, you're going to have to get creative. Learn to forage for edible plants in urban and suburban environments. Learn to hunt and trap quietly in these same locales, though it's likely that there'd be nothing left after a few weeks, once every other family gets the same idea.

CONCLUSION

Natural disasters have been our natural enemy since the dawn of time. They try to lash us with wind, drown us with water, and shake our homes down to the ground. They're powerful and deadly to be sure, but there's one limiting factor that these mighty forces can't overcome. That factor is size. This is a big planet, and the average natural disaster can only affect a small part of it. Catastrophes like earthquakes can strike localities and regions, but they're not going to damage large nations or entire continents. And since the impact area is relatively small, this means that a mobile family, group, or individual may be able to escape the stricken area.

Ideally, you could load up your go-bags and drive to "greener pastures." Damaged roads and highways may prevent an exodus by vehicle, but unless there are great fissures in the earth, you may still be able to walk away from the affected area. And when bugging out isn't an option for your group, then you'd better be prepared. Stored food, water, and other supplies can get you through a crisis (if you're able to hide or defend these precious resources). ⠿

35

THE UNITED STATES HAS PLUNGED INTO ECONOMIC COLLAPSE?

By Tim MacWelch
Illustrations by Sarah Watanabe-Rocco

The filthy man had a knife at my daughter's throat, and his ragged friend had a gun to my boy's temple. "Give us what we want, and no one has to get hurt," he said. But were the supplies all that they wanted? The way they were looking at my wife and daughter made me think they'd like to stay a while, that food wasn't the only thing they wanted.

Suddenly, in an ill-timed burst of courage, my son started struggling with his captor and the man looked like he was ready to shoot. My boy screamed "Dad, do something!" but I was frozen in place down on my knees. He screamed again, "Daddy! Help me!" The gun fired – and I woke up.

My body was covered in a cold sweat, and all my muscles were as tense as steel cables. It was only a dream, but it seemed just as real as if those men had broken in again. As I lay there in the cold darkness, I realized that the waking world was not much friendlier than the world in the dream. We were still in danger. My family was at risk, every hour of the day. At any time, people could break into the house. Again. Maybe they'd kill my family this time. The situation was growing more desperate, and so were the criminals. Welcome to the end of the world as we know it, thanks to a total economic collapse.

In this edition of OFFGRID's "What If?" feature, we step into a gloomy scenario where our beloved U.S. dollar is worthless and the American way of life has degenerated into a hand-to-mouth fight for survival.

To delve into this bleak and brutal future, OFFGRID asked three different writers for their approach to living through these dark times. With us is Patrick McCarthy, a freelance journalist, lifelong outdoor enthusiast, and frequent OFFGRID contributor. Next is Erik Lund, a federal law enforcement agent with a vast array of tactical and survival experience. And myself, I have been a survival instructor for the past 19 years and am the author of books on survival and wild food, Prepare for Anything and The Hunting and Gathering Survival Manual. Here are our three different visions of a United States without money, utilities, or much of a future.

The Scenario

Situation type: Long-term and widespread bedlam
Your Crew: Your wife, a 16-year-old daughter, and a 10-year-old son
Location: Boulder, Colorado
Season: Spring (averaging 35 degrees Fahrenheit)
Weather: Snowfall still possible

The Setup

The U.S. dollar collapsed after more than a decade of multiple wars, skyrocketing energy prices, a faltering economy, and widespread corruption. Protests led to mass rioting and looting. Businesses close or were burnt down. Schools were shuttered for the safety of the kids. Police and fire departments stopped receiving paychecks and essentially disbanded. It was only a matter of time before utilities started to sputter and then completely stopped. Eventually, the only form of government was the military (which only operated to protect itself and an elite few).

The First Act

It's been two weeks after the massive rioting had stopped and given way to relative calm. Relative was the key term. Without reliable power and open businesses, you were running dangerously low on food, water, and supplies. You gathered with your neighbors and had a tentative bartering system established, hoping to survive until the National Guard arrives in three weeks to reestablish order...or so the rumor went. You didn't know how widespread the economic collapse and rioting had been. Had it hit all the major regions of the country, or just the greater Denver area?

The Complication

Realizing you wouldn't last long without new sources of food, water, and supplies, you ventured out of your trusted neighborhood to see who you could barter with safely. You trekked a few miles through the slush and mud and found a willing community. They seemed worse off than you, but they were open to a fair trade of toilet paper and toothpaste for some canned goods. But unbeknownst to you, you gave away too much information about yourself. A day later, gunmen burst through your front door. It was the same men you bartered with. They threatened to rape your wife and kill your son if you didn't give them everything. You complied and kept everyone safe, but you lost the weeks' worth of supplies you had been rationing.

The New Plan

What do you do now? How will you survive the freezing spring until the National Guard arrives in three weeks? Keep in mind you have only the following:

> Single-family home with attached garage and usual personal belongings
> Two cars with full tanks of gas
> Typical handtools in the garage
> No power or utilities
> No cash money
> Three mobile phones that work...if you can find a way to charge them
> One week's worth of food and water (which could freeze over) for each of you (that you secretly stashed)
> One loaded semi-automatic handgun (that you secretly stashed) with no extra ammo

AVERAGE JOE PATRICK MCCARTHY'S APPROACH

The day had finally come. The worst-case economic scenario I had heard about so many times — and always rolled my eyes at — had become our reality. After seeing footage of crowds storming the banks on TV, I knew we were actually in trouble, but I had no idea it would spread so far and so fast. I also couldn't have imagined the evil it would reveal in those around me. To think that I had actually tried to help those bastards who kicked in our door last night disgusts me. My foolish trust in strangers put my family at risk, and I refuse to be victimized like that again. Last night taught me that our safety is my responsibility, and when it really came down to it, we were on our own.

Speaking of which, we had all heard the rumors of the National Guard's arrival in about three weeks. The idea of rescue seemed to be giving Laura and the kids hope, but I knew not to be too optimistic. We had to get out of here, and get away from those who might do us harm. Fortunately, our cars were still in the garage and had plenty of gas, so we decided to take what we could and head for my parents' old cabin outside Granby. It was about 90 miles away, but the sizable plot of land, lack of nearby neighbors, and wood-burning stove would sure make life easier.

After scouring our house for supplies, I was able to find a few items the gunmen had overlooked. They barely checked the garage, so we still had the cases of canned food and bottled water I left in the closet out there – enough to last the four of us about a week, by my estimate. A few items from my toolbox could also come in handy, most importantly two utility knives, a claw hammer, nails, and some duct tape. Walking back inside, I grabbed the 9mm semi-auto I kept hidden upstairs – only 15 rounds. The rest of my supply walked out the door last night.

Finally, we had our cell phones, which I thought at first would be useless. Then I remembered that solar-powered battery charger Laura's brother gave me for Christmas last year. It seemed like a gimmick back then. Now, not so much.

The four of us loaded half the supplies (plus some warm blankets and clothes) into Laura's SUV, and the other half into my car. I figured since we had two cars, we'd be better off taking both. It might make us a slightly more noticeable target, but at least we wouldn't be stranded and helpless if one vehicle became disabled. Laura, Janine, and Johnny would take my car, while I would drive just ahead in the sturdier SUV. If we encountered a roadblock, the SUV's heavier weight might help clear it so the car could get by. Before we headed out, I handed Laura my gun, and reminded her not to stop for anything or anyone. If, God forbid, something happened to me, at least she could defend herself and the kids.

We left Boulder around midday. It was eerie seeing the streets so empty – no traffic lights, no cars, no pedestrians. I guess most people listened to the final TV broadcasts saying to remain in your homes until help arrives. I had hooked my cell phone up to the solar charger and set it on the dash before we left, and it wasn't long before it had enough juice to read "no signal." I hoped that we'd find a working cell tower at some point on the trip, so I could try checking the news or calling my dad. Unlikely, but at least worth a try.

I couldn't help but nervously check my rear-view mirror repeatedly, despite knowing Laura and the kids were right there behind me.

Though I had anticipated the highway to be a giant parking lot of abandoned cars, the roads leading up to the interstate were pretty clear, so I decided to check it out. After all, it was the faster way to get to the cabin. Other than a few dead cars on the shoulder, the highway remained surprisingly empty as we headed into the mountains.

The miles started to pass faster. About 30 miles in, we spotted a lone convenience store with no cars out front, so I motioned to Laura that we should stop. With the power out, the gas pumps wouldn't be working, but we could look for other supplies inside. Walking up to the front door, I noticed that it was locked, but the security shutters hadn't been drawn. I guess whoever worked here left in a hurry.

Desperate times called for desperate measures, so I wrapped my arm in a sheet for protection, shielded my face, and swung the hammer full-force at the door. Chunks of glass crunched under our feet as we stepped into the dark store. We needed to move fast, so each of us had a different objective – I picked through the limited medical supplies, Laura grabbed cigarettes and liquor for bartering currency, Janine looked for food that might provide some nutritional value, and Johnny started collecting water jugs. On our way out the door, I also picked up some magazines and playing cards – if we're going to be stuck in a cabin for weeks, we might as well enjoy it. Within 20 minutes, we were rolling again.

As the miles ticked away, I flipped through the radio channels – still nothing but static. It was 2:45 when we got to the cabin. No one had been here for months, and we wanted to keep that appearance, so we parked the cars around back. Dad had the keys, so I had to smash a window and awkwardly climb inside, but a little duct tape, nails, and wood scraps made for a solid patch against the elements. We also boarded up the other windows from the inside, just in case we're targeted again. With the supplies inside, we bolted the door and settled in for the long haul.

The first few days passed slowly. We stayed inside to keep a low profile, and only fired up the stove at night so the smoke wouldn't draw attention. Eventually, I decided to take my pistol and walk the property, and this soon became a daily occurrence. I also started collecting water from the stream to boil each night, firewood for the stove, and even tried fishing a few times (with limited success). After a week, I felt confident we were alone out here, so Laura and the kids started helping out. It was tough spinning this as a family adventure, especially to a teenager, but we made it work.

I still charged my cell phone and checked it periodically, more out of habit than anything. What did I expect, a stern email from my boss? Laughable. But, one day, there it was – signal. Almost refusing to believe it, I dialed my parents in San Diego. It rang and rang as my stomach sank. After two days of repeated calling, someone answered. "Dad?" I could hardly believe it.

Amazingly, he and mom were OK, and he told me things weren't so bad out there in California. Apparently the large Navy and Marine Corps presence there kept things in check, despite the federal government's near total collapse. There was still no word on the radio about the National Guard showing up in Boulder, or anywhere in Colorado for that matter, so we decided Laura and I should head for San Diego with the kids. It was going to be a difficult journey, but at least one thing had changed – the end was now in sight.

FEDERAL AGENT ERIK LUND'S APPROACH

Life is tough. It's tougher if you're stupid, and you're one stupid bastard. I stared into the man's eyes and concluded he was right. I wiped the trickle of blood away from my forehead and looked deeper into the eyes of the man in the bathroom mirror. The swelling from the pistol strike to my forehead wasn't too bad, but it definitely left a mark. Washing the blood from my fingers, I gazed back into the mirror. *Do not let this happen ever again! I promised myself.*

A gentle knock on the bathroom door broke the silence. I opened the door to see my concerned wife waiting for me. "I'll be alright," I said. "Get the kids. Family meeting time."

The situation was not good. We only had enough food and water for a week. Worse yet, the marauders from the other community could return at any time looking for more scraps. My initial primary concern was security. The threat of having my wife raped and my children killed in front of me would never happen again. I will never again feel that powerless and helpless. I remember my concealed-carry course instructor telling our class, "If you look like food, you will be eaten." At the time I didn't understand the reference, but now it's very clear. The strong will prey on the weak. It's time to harden up and face reality. People are starting to get desperate, and that desperation is justification enough to do terrible things to their fellow man.

I pulled the beat-up-looking SIG SAUER P226 9mm from its hidden location. Years ago a friend said a local gun store had several police trade-in P226s that looked rough, but were probably shot very few times. On his advice, I purchased the pistol, but it only came with one magazine. At the time it didn't matter to me, as I would purchase more magazines later; but later never seemed to happen. One pistol and one magazine of ammunition – it would have to do. I loaded the pistol, and put it in my waistband; never did find time to buy that holster either.

"OK, here's our situation," I started. It was a sobering conversation. We needed a long-term plan to survive until the situation changes. Our priorities were security, shelter, water, and food. Shelter wasn't an issue, and I already had plans to improve our security. Even though the power had gone out, we had plenty of firewood to burn to keep the house heated, to boil water for purification, and to cook our food on the wood-burning stove. The immediate concern was that all of the firewood was stacked in back of the house. It would have to be moved indoors immediately to be protected from thieves. We had enough holiday and decorative candles to last us for several months should we need light at night, and those could be supplemented with several flashlights that were available.

Fortunately, having solar-powered chargers for a few of our batteries and electronics proved one of our most valuable resources. We could turn on the phones and computers once a day to see if the cellular and Internet networks were on line, and the chargers provided all the recharging power we needed at the moment.

I asked my wife and daughter to bring every plastic bin and tote they could find down to the living room while my son and I started moving the firewood into the house. In short order, all of the firewood was secured inside. Stacked in the corner were around 15 plastic bins of various sizes and shapes. My plan was to cut all the rain gutters around the house and to place a bin underneath each drain to catch whatever rain water, snow, or morning dew that accumulated. We would collect up the bins at night to secure them and use the three bathtubs in the house as a place to store the water. If water ran critically short, I would drive to a running stream about 2 miles from the house and fill up the bins to bring back home.

I still needed to secure the ground floor of our home, but I had another task for my wife and daughter. "The neighbors need to know what happened to us and we need their help," I said. My wife wasn't thrilled with the idea of going outside, but we needed to warn the neighbors about the marauders and to see if any of them could spare some food. She finally agreed, and she and my daughter set out to warn the neighbors. "Hey, make a mental note of those homes who do help us, OK?" I asked. "We need to repay their generosity when we are able." My wife nodded in agreement and left. I looked down at my boy as I closed the door, "C'mon son, we got work to do."

Long ago I had built storage shelves in the garage; now I needed that wood for another purpose. After disassembling the shelves, everything was moved into the house. I was just about finished with the security preparations when my wife and daughter returned home. I was expecting some vigorous protests from my wife after she had seen how I had boarded up every first-floor window inside the home with sections of 2x4 wood bars. If anyone was going to force themselves into my home again, they would be funneled through the front or back door, making it easier to deal with them as a threat. Looking around, my wife quietly walked up and kissed me on the cheek with an approving look. I smiled and went back to work.

I mounted metal brackets into the frames around the front and rear doors. The brackets were just wide enough to lay two sections of wood flat into each bracket at the top and bottom of each door. The sections could easily be removed to allow the door to open. Nobody was getting through these doors without smashing down the entire façade of the house. Satisfied with my security preparations, I walked into the kitchen to check on my wife.

"Everyone I spoke with was grateful to know about the attack, and a few homes gave us some food. We now have enough food to get us through the next two weeks, maybe three if we ration it." While the news was good and it lifted my spirits some, I was still concerned. *This is a short-term fix*, I thought to myself. *I need better options*. Later that night, I discussed my plan with my wife. She was concerned, but understood and agreed with me.

Early the next morning, I grabbed my gear bag and backpack in the garage. I pulled out my hunting equipment and my compound bow. I hadn't been hunting in years, never seemed to have the time anymore, but now it wasn't for enjoyment. It was for survival. I gave the P226 to the wife. "Bar the door and shoot anyone trying to break in," I said. She nodded and was quite capable of doing it. "I'll be back tonight or sooner if I can find us some food."

I put my gear in the car and pulled out of the neighborhood. It was a short drive out of town to the mountains. Finding a secluded spot, I backed the car into some trees, doing my best to conceal it from view. I pulled out the dusty, old Club from the trunk and locked it onto the steering wheel. *Yeah, it's lame, but it's better than nothing*, I thought. Being the provider for my family had never taken on such a literal meaning, until now. I started walking into the woods — time to go shopping for dinner.

SURVIVAL EXPERT TIM MACWELCH'S APPROACH

Another frigid night had passed, and my family began to stir as the light came through the windows. It was too cold and too dangerous to sleep in separate rooms, so we all slept in a smaller upstairs bedroom. My wife and I had the little bed, and the kids slept on cots. We had discovered by chance that our guest room faced south and warmed up nicely in the sunlight each day, so this was where we spent much of our time.

The robbery yesterday still had the entire family rattled. My daughter was taking it the worst. Normally a chatty and upbeat girl, she was silent and slow moving, distracted, and depressed.

It was time to give the whole family a little bit of hope, to reveal what I had hidden: I led my wife and kids to the master bathroom. "Remember when we had that water leak, and I repaired the drywall myself?" My wife was quick to reply that she thought of oatmeal covered with copy paper every time she looked at my lumpy Harry Homeowner repair job. I smiled, and Johnny chuckled. It was good to hear that sound again. "Well, if the wall's so bad, I'll tear it down," I responded. A quick jab to the drywall and my arm was buried wrist-deep in the wall. My wife gasped and then stood shocked as I started ripping away chunks of the plasterboard. "Help me with this, Johnny" I asked. He was quick to oblige.

My son tore at the brittle sheetrock, shouting, "There's something in here!" Suddenly, my crazy idea to stash some food and supplies in the wall didn't seem so crazy anymore. "Oh my God," Janine said. I told them that there was one week's food for the four of us, bottled water, and a loaded handgun.

After being showered with kisses, even from the boy, I set us up with the first good meal we'd had in a while. The fuel tabs and folding stove I had stashed in the wall were handy for heating up some water, which quickly rehydrated our freeze-dried camping meals. Food in a pouch had never tasted so good. "We have to hide all of this, even hide the trash," I said. We didn't know if those men would be back, or if they told others about us. We decided to hide the trash back in the wall, and hide the food in the bottom of the Halloween decorations box in the attic. "Who'd ever think to look in there," we agreed. Now it was time to build a plan.

No one was going to work anymore. The kids weren't going to school either. I knew our food would be gone in a week. We had to find ways to get more, without exposing ourselves to so many risks. We had to restore some semblance of normalcy. And most of all, we had to be able to defend ourselves from another possible attack.

Since the power and water went out, life had drifted into a weird routine. In the morning, our family would collect snow in pots and pans, then bring it into the house and place it in the sunnier windows to melt. Our "bathroom" situation was a bucket for pee and a rectangular bin for the other business. The "shower" was a soapy washcloth wipe-down in the bathtub. Before the attack, when we weren't messing with water procurement, we spent the rest of the time sitting around bored. But that time was over. It was time to take our survival into our own hands.

We needed heat, water, food, and defense. The heat was tricky to come by, as so many people had scavenged all the deadfall sticks and wood around the neighborhood to burn in their fireplaces and stoves. But we did make a deal with a neighbor to help him split and carry firewood from a nearby strip of forest, in exchange for some of it. He had a chainsaw and the fuel, we had a splitting axe and labor to offer. Soon, we were able to burn wood for heat, cook by the fireplace, and melt our snow quickly and easily for drinking water. For food, we started making traps, like the ones they taught Johnny in Boy Scouts. We used all kinds of wire from the house and garage, and made some box traps too. Soon we were catching wild neighborhood rabbits in snares, and small birds in box traps. These became tolerable tasting soups and stews, allowing us to stretch our one-week supply of food into several weeks' worth.

The defense part was still the most pressing issue on my mind. We never went anywhere without all family members going together and the handgun tucked into my concealed holster. We boarded up the first-floor windows to make it harder for anyone to break in. We also made brackets behind the doors and set them up with 2x4 pieces to bar the doors from the inside. We finally felt a little safer in our own home.

Our self-reliant activity seemed to be catchy, as the neighborhood trade network was soon booming. Every afternoon, people met in the neighborhood playground and set out their trade goods on blankets, cardboard pieces, fold-out tables. We traded some of our skinned rabbits for candles and ammo. We also helped several neighbors fortify their houses in exchange for some precious canned goods. People traded goods, labor, security-guard services, and the like. And anyone who brought out paper money was generally laughed at, or occasionally run off. After a few weeks of trading, we finally had enough rounds of ammunition to feel like we could hold our own. Spring was coming to an end.

If the National Guard didn't show up soon, we planned to trade for seeds, use the tools in the garage to dig a garden, and grow some of our own food as soon as the danger of frost had passed. Maybe we could make it until the peace and utilities were established again, if our neighborhood could keep working together and fend off any possible robbers.

CONCLUSION

This type of scenario is a dismal one, with no easy exit strategy. We wouldn't wish this type of future on anyone, not even our worst enemy. And the scariest part is that this scenario has happened in recent years.

The economic collapse in Argentina left people without money, without utilities, and at the mercy of the rising tide of criminals between 1998 and 2002. People died from injuries during robberies, they died from dysentery due to a lack of clean water and basic sanitation, and they died from an inability to pay for the limited, overpriced medical care. If it can happen in a large, modernized country like Argentina, it can happen almost anywhere.

If this kind of scenario bothers you, then make some strides to be prepared for it. Stock up on some long-lived shelf-stable foods, water disinfection equipment, and tools for self-defense. You don't have to bury them in your walls, but it's a good idea to keep them in a secure, hidden location. And let's pray this bit of fiction never becomes reality. ⁞

36

YOU'RE CAPTURED BY MARAUDERS INTENT ON TAKING YOUR SUPPLIES?

By Tim MacWelch
Illustrations by Sarah Watanabe-Rocco

My head was still groggy from the last beating I received. It felt like my skull was packed full of cotton. Maybe it was — that would explain my difficulty in formulating a plan. All I knew right then was that my tight lips had kept me alive so far...but if I cracked — they'd probably kill me and kill my family when they got to my house. I knew that I had to escape, and very soon. Otherwise, they'd get bored with beating me and just finish me off. Or I might finally talk. I didn't like thinking about that one. It was nauseating to imagine being an active participant in my own family's demise.

Thank God I left my wallet at home. No driver's license meant no address. But it was time to make some more good luck happen. It was time to go. The escape plan began to clarify and take shape in my mind as I surveyed my surroundings. I was in an empty storage room, locked from the outside. I looked for something I could turn into a weapon, but the place was picked clean. I had to be the weapon.

This "what if?" scenario revolves around a person who must escape and evade a group of marauding thugs in the aftermath of a natural disaster. OFF-GRID asked two other subject matter experts to join me, as we look at man's inhumanity toward man in this unsettling scenario. Joining me is Ryan Lee Price, who is a journalist and self-taught jack-of-all-trades survivalist. Ryan contributes to the "SHTF" column in our sister publication, RECOIL. Kevin Reeve is a fellow survival school owner and instructor who has a long list of accolades and experience, specializing in tracking and urban survival. And as for me, I have been a survival instructor for the past 18 years and am the author of a new book on preparedness, Prepare For Anything. In my experience, man is the most unpredictable predator in nature.

The Scenario

You're in a dense urban area that hasn't seen a semblance of civility in at least a few weeks. A powerful and very destructive earthquake has taken the Northern California region by surprise, and government services have been excruciatingly slow to react. Roads are impassable, and even the major bridges have collapsed. Basic utilities are all but nonexistent, while food, drinking water, and other essentials are now being fought over by the survivors. It's a desperate situation and mob mentality is running rampant. You, being one with forethought, have prepared for the post-disaster survival of your family to the best of your abilities. You keep a low profile; your dwelling is dark and looks unoccupied. The situation being what it is and with an already sick 5-year-old on hand, you have little choice but to wait it out. Fortunately, no one has attempted to enter your dwelling thus far.

Situation type: Post-Disaster Urban Unrest
Your Crew: 2 Adults, 1 Child (age 5)
Location: San Francisco, CA (Dense Urban Area)
Season: Summer
Weather: Mild, temp range is 70 Highs to 50 Lows

Every few days, you slip out of your safe house to survey the situation first-hand and forage for supplies. Your child's health is improving. But then, on one of your runs, you stray farther away than usual and find yourself in an unfamiliar area. Tired and distracted, your guard slips just long enough to become cornered by a band of seven armed and desperate people looking to pillage your supplies. After stripping you of your gear, they notice that you look well fed and surmise that you have supplies stashed someplace. When you don't talk, they tie you up and forcibly take you back to a house they have occupied for further interrogation.

The bandits have stripped you of all your kit. Your gun, knife, flashlight – everything you had on your person – are now gone and in their possession. But you do realize that they took you to an area that is perhaps only 3 miles away from home so you are at least familiar with what direction home is. After beating you for your non-compliance, they throw you into a locked room with your hands and feet tightly bound with duct tape, where you wait for them to come "interrogate" you further.

You need to escape and then evade their pursuit so that you can get back to your home and family. You don't want to lead them back to your spouse and child, so you need to do this right. How are you going to do it?

AVERAGE JOE RYAN LEE PRICE'S APPROACH

Clearly, they would have killed me by now if that was their intention. I wasn't dealing with murderers – criminals, sure – but just hungry and desperate criminals. Of course, that didn't mean they wouldn't leave me here to starve to death when they decided to move on. It was their mistake not to blindfold me or leave the sack on my head that I wore for the trip to their temporary dwelling. Although duct tape is pretty strong, it tore easily when introduced to a sharp object. While the room was mostly empty (it looked like it used to be a bedroom), there was enough squatter's debris to sift through to find something to do the job. A discarded beer bottle would have worked, but I couldn't find a broken one (and breaking one would make too much noise). But I found a small screw that fell out of something which worked well enough. I wanted to hurry, but I kept dropping the screw. Instead of trying to cut the tape, I merely poked holes in it; a series of close perforations allowed me to break the tape.

My eye was swollen, and my head hurt from the beating. The big one had quite an arm on him, but I wasn't about to write down my address or lead them to my house. I'm just glad I stopped carrying my wallet a couple of weeks ago. I could tell some of the others in the group weren't really into it, but are hanging on for the prospect of some food. Hunger is a powerful force. I get it. But so are thoughts of freedom.

It took awhile, but finally I was able to free my hands. I left the tape on my wrists in case I had to feign restraint if one of them came in the room. They hadn't been back since they dumped me here, but muffled sounds of their conversations bled through the walls. Once free of the duct tape, it was only a matter of opening the window for my escape. However, I was on the second floor, and who knows what was down there. The second option was to wait until the door opened, surprise them and make a break for it. There were at least three guns that I saw, plus mine, and odds were good they'd come in here well prepared to deal with me. So window it was. After a few hours, the conversations filtering in from the other room died down to whispers and then disappeared altogether. I had no idea what time it was, but the change in temperature told me it might be a couple of hours before dawn. Perhaps they were sleeping, but the occasional noise made me wary somebody was still up.

The window slid open easily and quietly, but it was only about 10 feet to the ground. Although it looked far, it wasn't that bad. The key was to climb out feet first and shimmy your body over the edge of the sill until you're dangling out of the window by your hands. I'm guessing that my feet were only 3 or 4 feet off of the ground when I jumped. That was the good news. The bad news was that I couldn't see the dead bushes below me, nor did I expect to land in a pile of dry leaves. I couldn't have made more noise if I tried. A dog even started barking. I hopped to my feet and regained my bearings, while flashlights glared above me in the room and shouts of "he's getting away" filled the night air. I wasn't about to stick around.

Now, I've lived in San Francisco for a number of years, and if there's one thing I learned, real estate in this city is very expensive. Because of that, yards (if any) are very small. Standing in what was a small side yard – more like a planter with a walkway – of a three-story walkup in the middle of the night, I had three options: 1) Go out the front gate, which might be locked; 2) Go to the back of the house, where they might be coming from; or 3) Hop the neighbor's wall between the yards to get as far from this house as possible.

Two of them were now hanging out of the open window, with beams of light spilling all around me. They were yelling at me to stop, and I'm surprised they didn't shoot. After all, I know where they live. I know what they look like. That house was filled with supplies and equipment that would take them hours to move...and move where? If they were keeping me around and kept asking me where my house is, they must not have many options. And even though there's no working 911 system, and the police are too busy to come if I asked them, there's the National Guard. There's the Army. They've taken over what's left of the city. That's the law now, and if I could get to them before they get to me...

It was no problem bounding over the wall into the neighbor's yard; fear is a strong motivator. Since I wanted to stay off of the streets for a while – at least until I ran out of backyards – I continued north, perpendicular to the house and somewhat toward my own. I had to move fast. Their flashlights gave away their position, and every time I scrambled over another wall, I was able to look back and see that they were only a backyard's length behind me. My wrists hurt from the duct tape, but more noticeable now was a pain in my left ankle from the jump out of the window, or maybe from one of the walls. But a hurt ankle (or scraped up arms from the cinder blocks) is better than a bullet in the head. I could stop and fight, but I'd quickly be outnumbered. I could hide, but the odds of their finding me or stumbling into an uncomfortable situation with yet another group of survivors was high. My back wasn't to the wall, yet, and I was still able bodied.

So I kept going, but changed direction.

I had been in the Alamo Square District when they initially nabbed me on Scott Street near the park, and they hadn't dragged me too far before reaching their house — maybe four or five blocks at most. But I wasn't sure in what direction they took me. In the next backyard, I crouched down behind the wall and squeezed between two houses and through a gate to find myself on the street. It was the corner of McAllister and Lyon. The apartment building on that corner had slipped off of its foundation and most of it was in the street, as this was one street that hadn't been cleared yet. There was a Laundromat across from it and the church next to that. I ran. My captors had fanned out to the surrounding blocks, perhaps anticipating where I would be headed. I had counted 10 or 12 in the house, and maybe a couple more in other rooms (perhaps more like me in those rooms?), but in the quiet of the streets I could hear the voice of the big guy, shouting orders from a block away. They were organized and knew the area well.

They probably thought I would head back to Alamo Square Park where they caught me, but there was no way I was going near there. In fact, I was headed in the opposite direction, and I had a long way to go, over The Panhandle, through Haight-Ashbury District and Cole Valley to my house on Belgrave Avenue, near Mt. Sutro Greenbelt. I assumed that every person I saw from then on was one of them, so it was safest to avoid people altogether. I found a worn 2x2 that made for a nice club and kept a sharp eye out for strangers.

Despite the pain, I kept moving until the sun came up. Activity on the streets increased until, somewhere around Frederick and Clayton streets, I was able to blend in with other survivors on the street and disappear again, to finally make it home.

ESCAPE AND EVASION EXPERT KEVIN REEVE'S APPROACH

As I regained consciousness, I assessed my situation. My hands and feet were bound with duct tape. I was sore, and my nose was bleeding. Turns out it was broken. My ribs were hurting too. The bastard who kicked me had broken or cracked the ribs on my left side. My knuckles were bloody from having fought the gang who accosted me. In spite of my best efforts, six strong men subdued me and took my gear. They must have figured I was good for more food if they softened me up a bit, so there I sat.

Both the broken nose and hurt ribs were a problem. It was hard to breathe, and running would be an issue. But as my Marine Force Recon friend James always said, "Embrace the Suck."

I needed to get out of there. I looked down at the duct tape and smiled. Of all the restraints they could have used, duct tape was the easiest to defeat. It's funny how many people just give up when they get duct taped. I stood and straightened my body, trying to work out the kinks. Then I hopped over to the closet door. I raised my arms and rubbed the duct tape between my wrists up and down along the corner edge of the door. After about four passes, the duct tape tore. I bent down, placed my hands together, and slid them down between my knees. With a downward jerk, the duct tape tore and my legs were free too.

I had been thoroughly searched when they caught me, and the lock picks in my pocket were gone. They also took my belt, which had another set of picks and a handcuff key in a hidden pocket. However, on my jeans there's a leather patch on my right hip under my belt. It says Levi Strauss. Long ago, I began carrying a third set of picks, called Bogotás, in the pocket formed by that patch. Multiple backups paid off today. Also inside my hidden pocket were a cuff key, a diamond rod, and an auto jiggler. I pulled out the picks and checked the door. The double-sided deadbolt was a Schlage, medium difficulty. I put my ear to the door – no sound. I touched the door lightly with the back of my hand – no vibration indicating movement in the other room. I slid a lifter pick into the lock and began moving each pin individually. I started with the resistant pin and slowly lifted the break point to the shear line. One pin down. I repeated the process four more times, then slowly started to rotate the plug. It only went ¼ of a turn. Damn, I picked it in the wrong direction. I started over with the tension wrench applying torque in the other direction. A couple of minutes later, the tumbler began to rotate.

I was captured at around 8:30 p.m. An hour or two of pleasant conversation, then I was knocked out cold. I wasn't sure how long I was unconscious, perhaps a couple of hours, so I estimated the time to be around 3 a.m. I carefully peeked out the door. I was in an upstairs hall. It was very dark; the window showed no light outside. I moved very slowly and quietly down the hall, placing my lead foot down with no weight on it, slowly compressing the floor with my foot, then transferring my weight slowly. At the top of the stairs, I stopped and listened. No noise, so I started working down the stairs. I placed my feet on the sides of each stair tread where they are most supported, to reduce the chance of a creak. At the bottom of the stairs I heard noise; at least two people in the kitchen were talking. My heart jumped when I heard one say they were going to check on the prisoner. I quickly stepped to the door, unlocked it, and vanished into the dark of a new moon. Behind me, I heard the alarm being raised inside.

I had to go at least a mile and a half north on the road before I could turn east toward my neighborhood. I was just turning the corner when I was silhouetted by a flashlight beam. I dodged left and headed west. The pursuit was on, so I ran as best I could through the debris and cars. I was holding my ribs for support, allowing me to move a little faster. I passed an alley and ducked in. Moving along the side, I took advantage of the concealment from the dumpsters, then turned west again before my pursuers had caught up.

Up ahead I saw a parking structure. The top two floors were collapsed, but the bottom floors were intact. I ducked into the structure and cut across in near total darkness, coming out in another alley. Continuing west, I could see flashlights scanning the streets to the south and behind me. No time for rest. I turned north for a block, then back west, then back north. I zigzagged and used alleys to reduce the chances of being spotted. The faster I moved, the better.

I finally stopped in an alley behind a dumpster. My ribs were killing me. I was sucking air as hard as they would allow, but the pain kept my lungs from fully expanding. I had to stop and rest for a moment. Trying to remember where I was, I suspected I had at least another ¾ mile to go north. So I walked slowly, catching my breath and letting the adrenaline do its job. I soon started moving more quickly again, zigzagging north and east again.

There was a warehouse with a rollup door that was off its hinges. I squeezed in and was enveloped in darkness. Across the building, I could see another open door. I moved slowly toward it. As I crossed the floor, unable to see anything, I tripped on some pallets – add a skinned knee to the list. Once at the opposite door, I scanned the street. About 100 yards to the east, I could see a light, but it appeared to be a fire barrel, not a flashlight.

So far, I had avoided my pursuers – no time to get complacent. I peered around the warehouse, but couldn't make out many details. As I stumbled about in the dark, I found a door into another interior room. Complete darkness, no windows, no light whatsoever. It was a cavernous room, and I bumped into a forklift. A thought flickered in my mind. I closed the door, then shuffled back to the forklift. I turned the key and, sure enough, the dash lit up. I flicked on a working light, casting ominous shadows around the room.

There was a fridge in the far corner. Inside was rotting food, but also a couple of bottles of water. I gulped one down and put the other in my back pocket. I also found a roll of pallet stretch wrap, which I wrapped around my ribs – it helped a little. The warehouse had been looted, but there were many trays full of nuts, bolts, and other hardware. I grabbed an old rag and the largest bolt I could find; it would probably take a 1⅛ inch wrench to fit this monster. I slid the bolt down to the middle of the rag – now I had a close-range weapon. I tucked it into my back pocket, with the end of the rag hanging out, and looked around again. There were some cardboard boxes on one wall. After switching off the light and the key, I laid down on the cardboard to get some rest. With some water and a place to lie low, I decided to spend the day here. I could see the sun coming up beyond the outside door.

After a long day hiding in the warehouse, the sun finally set and darkness once again reigned. It was time to move. There was a sliver moon that night, so not much ambient light. I spent some time while resting sketching a map of my movements the night before as best as I could remember, trying to orient myself. While the first night was all about speed, the second would be about stealth and deception.

I moved to the north door and looked out. I sat for 15 minutes just watching and listening; I needed to be sure I was the only predator out there. As I crossed the street, and crawled about the rubble of a collapsed building, I found the unmistakable smell of decaying flesh. This building had obviously been inhabited. But next to the body was an 18-inch-long piece of ¾-inch rebar — another improvised weapon.

I slowly and carefully worked my way toward the cross street that would take me back home. I detoured around a group of about six men standing around a burning barrel. They were watching the fire, so they could not see anything, but I wanted to avoid any potential contact.

When I reached my cross street, I stopped again and waited for a full hour. From concealment, I watched my back trail for anyone who might be following me. Seeing no movement, I turned east and worked my way slowly along the alleys and streets toward home. About two blocks down, I saw flashlights dancing about like light sabers and slithered into an alley. I found a dumpster and climbed in. Ugghh, the stink of rotting food. I sat quietly and peered out of the crack of the lid. The flashlights went by, and I recognized one as from the gang that broke my nose. I resisted the urge to get some payback; I wasn't in the clear yet.

Fortunately, I was near one of my caches. There I would find a Glock 19, three mags, 100 loose rounds, two more bottles of water, a flashlight, a folding Hissatsu knife, and an MRE. These treasures were in a .50 cal ammo can that I had buried in a somewhat vacant lot.

After waiting another nauseating hour, I clambered out of the dumpster and headed east toward the field. It didn't look the same, but along the left side was my landmark, a telephone pole. I measured out 25 paces due east, then dug into the ground with my rebar. I was pretty exposed, so after a few false starts, I was relieved to hear the metal click of the box lid. Grabbing the handle, I tugged it out, then looked for some cover. There was a brick wall extending along the sidewalk. Crouching behind it, I opened the box. The Glock in my hand was one of the most reassuring feelings I had in two days. I grabbed the water, took a drink, and stuffed the rest of the gear in my pockets. There was an abandoned store nearby with a dark room, where I sat and rested. MREs never tasted so good. My ribs hurt, but this style of movement was much easier on them. I probed my nose and decided it was indeed broken. I really did want payback.

Another two hours and I was finally home. My wife was a bit of a mess with worry and turned her nose at my stench, but my son's fever had broken and he appeared on the mend.

SURVIVAL EXPERT TIM MACWELCH'S APPROACH

I must have looked like a huge rat, hunkered in the corner of that room, gnawing furiously at the duct tape. My lips and teeth were soon covered with adhesive, but I was finally able to start a tear in the tape. Soon my hands were free! I was able to quietly unwind the duct tape from my feet and ankles, which was still sticky. I saved some, pressing the top of the tape strip to the wall. I had ideas for that tape. This place had electricity; that must be why they picked it. There was just one bare light bulb hanging from the ceiling, but it was on. I listened to the activity in the house as best I could, and when it sounded like some of the group had left, I set my plans in motion.

Using part of my shirt to buffer the heat of the hot light bulb, I unscrewed the only illumination from the ceiling, pitch black descending on the room. I began scratching on the door and the wall. I wanted to arouse curiosity, not wrath, from my captors. Then, with a sticky strip of duct tape in my hands, I began tapping my foot against the door, standing there in the darkness. After a long while, I heard the door unlock and my muscles tensed. I only had one shot at this. As the light flooded the room, I hung back behind the door. As the man groped the wall to find the light switch, I kicked him in the groin as hard as I could. And as he doubled over in pain, I slapped the tape over his eyes, and kicked him again — this time in the throat. In a second, I was outside the room, shutting the door, locking it and turning the tables on my enemy. Then I ran. I ran like I've never run before. I ran past two very startled men, so quickly that I couldn't tell if I'd seen them before or not. Exploding out the door, I ran through the yard and into the street to get my bearings. Another bit of luck was in my favor — it was nighttime. But my luck turned quickly again when I heard shouting and running behind me. It was time to disappear.

On the darkened suburban street, I ran. I couldn't tell if they were catching up, or falling behind, so I just kept running. But I couldn't head straight home. That would take them exactly where they wanted to go. My home was north of this neighborhood, so I began heading west. I ran on the sidewalk when I could, heading west one block and north one block. I had to watch the ground carefully, as cracks and gaps from the earthquake might break my ankle and throw me down, but at least I was distancing myself from them. Quick glances back showed me that the heavier man was falling behind his fellow. Some of the blocks had power and streetlights, some did not. On the dark streets, I had to slow down to watch my footing. Garbage was strewn everywhere, and if I fell, they'd catch me.

After a few blocks of running, the adrenaline wore off and the pain set in. I felt my pattern of west, north, west, north, was getting predicable, so I turned east at an intersection and dove behind some bushes. I saw my pursuers stop, and look around hastily. Dawn was coming, and the darkness that hid me will be gone soon. The thinner man, who looked older and clearly exhausted, took out a cell phone and tried to call someone as his heavier companion gasped for breath, his hands on his knees. That phone was all I needed to see. "Phone Man" was looking at the street sign. He was calling the others.

I slunk away as quietly as I could to the backyard of that house, praying that this unknown family didn't have a barking dog back there. I wondered if anyone was in those houses who would help me. Would I let in a man who looked beaten, raving about being followed and captured? I probably wouldn't. And I hadn't seen a police car or officer anywhere. Getting home was the only thing that I could really count on. I continued east through the backyards of that block. The earthquake had toppled many of the fences that would normally have blocked my backyard trek through the subdivision. But periodically, I had to fight my way through debris and climb over fences to continue on my path.

At the end of the block, I was completely out of breath and had a tough decision to make – jump back out onto the street to move faster at the risk of being seen – or hide for a while. I chose the latter. I couldn't risk being run down by fresh reinforcements from this bunch of Mad Max wannabes. As I crouched in the shrubs, the sun crept above the horizon. Damaged vehicles were everywhere, so quickly rummaging through a nearby open car trunk, I found a tire iron. At last, I had a weapon. Settling back into the bushes, I carefully broke a few branches from nearby shrubs and thickened the area between me and the street. Soon, my pursuers appeared with larger numbers. Some of the faces belonged to people who had beaten me, and some were new. As I sat still in the bushes, I slowed my breathing and recalled all the hunts I had been on for deer and other wild game. If I could hide from an animal's sharp eyes and ears, these fools should miss me by a mile.

Two of the men broke off and headed toward the house. I stayed calm and ignored the ants starting to crawl on my skin. "He must live around here somewhere," said the first man to his cohort. "We'll find his ass and his food stash, if we have to go through every house around here," was the reply. They walked up to the door and began banging on it. A few moments later, a shotgun boomed from inside the home. No glass broke, and neither man fell. The homeowner must have fired a warning shot into the floor or walls, and it worked. Both men jogged away briskly. After canvassing the street, the gang moved off to the west, muttering obscenities and arguing about where I must have gone. I almost smiled, but my face hurt too much for that. After another few minutes of waiting, I stood up, brushed off the ants, and continued north and east, my new tire iron in hand. I borrowed some laundry drying on a line, which gave me a quick change of shirt, and I picked up some sunglasses through the broken window of a ransacked car. I hoped they did a good job of hiding my swollen eye. Would the predators recognize me, if our paths crossed? Maybe... But within the hour, I was home.

I did our secret knock on the door, which my wife hastily opened. I don't know if the sunglasses and strange shirt scared her, or my bloody lip and blackening eye, but she slammed the door in my face and re-locked it. Then I could actually smile. "Good girl, that's exactly what you were supposed to do." Then, after hearing my voice, she reopened the door and pulled me inside. After a long, silent hug, she asked what happened to me. I told her we'd talk about that later – right now, we needed to fortify the house and seal it up like a vault. I re-armed myself, and went to work. I practically beamed with pride at the way my wife was toting that shotgun in one hand and tools in the other.

As we noisily moved things around, my 5-year-old daughter emerged from her room. She looked like she was feeling better. She halfheartedly asked about the sunglasses, then got some Tylenol from her mother and went back to lay down. I asked where the bottle came from, and my wife sheepishly admitted to trading water to the neighbor for the medicine. That was, after all, the whole reason I went out in the first place. But neither one of us said any more about it.

After reinforcing the doors and windows, I cleaned up my face with a wash-cloth. It was time to get some information. Our block had no power, so the TV had been out since the quake. Instead, we gathered around the battery-oper-ated radio to scan through the channels, and used a battery-powered charger to make a few cell phone calls. I couldn't get through on 911 to report the peo-ple that had kidnapped and assaulted me, so I just settled for collecting some news. Help for the outlying towns and city of San Francisco was on its way. One radio announcer said that the National Guard would be moving in today, and another said that police patrols were being doubled in the wake of the rising crime. I could have used that last night...

During the long walk home, I had begun planning to bug out, but with the crime on the streets and increasing military presence, the choice soon shift-ed to bugging in. Now, more than ever, I thanked God for the foresight to stock water, weapons, food, batteries, lights, and a radio in the house. And I swore off solo supply runs for good.

CONCLUSION

This type of scenario is a dismal one, with no easy exit strategy. We wouldn't wish this type of future on anyone, not even our worst enemy. And the scariest part is that this scenario has happened in recent years.

The economic collapse in Argentina left people without money, without util-ities, and at the mercy of the rising tide of criminals between 1998 and 2002. People died from injuries during robberies, they died from dysentery due to a lack of clean water and basic sanitation, and they died from an inability to pay for the limited, overpriced medical care. If it can happen in a large, modernized country like Argentina, it can happen almost anywhere.

If this kind of scenario bothers you, then make some strides to be prepared for it. Stock up on some long-lived shelf-stable foods, water disinfection equip-ment, and tools for self-defense. You don't have to bury them in your walls, but it's a good idea to keep them in a secure, hidden location. And let's pray this bit of fiction never becomes reality. ❖

CONTRIBUTORS

Katheryn Basso is a U.S. Marine Corps veteran trained in identifying sources of instability in foreign countries. Proficient at navigating the complex civil-military terrain of foreign policy, she has advised and advocated for military and civilian leaders from multiple partner nations. She's currently the co-owner of TEAM TORN, a tactical training company based in Nevada that instructs U.S. military, government, and civilian personnel. She specializes in firearms instruction, conflict avoidance, and personal security strategies. www.teamtorn.com

Jacki Billings is a gun journalist and single mom of two. She holds a black belt in the Korean mixed martial art of Yongmoodo in addition to NRA Basic Pistol and Refuse to Be a Victim Instructor certification. She's put in 17 years as an American Heart Association Basic Life Support instructor, teaching CPR, first aid, and BLS classes. With a degree in journalism and a minor in criminology, she uses her experiences and knowledge to offer classes through her training site, Freelance Tactical. Check out more at jackibillings.com.

Hana L. Bilodeau has over 15 years of law enforcement experience, serving both locally and federally. Hana spent a large part of her local career in the detective unit investigating crimes against people, predominantly sex crimes. She was well known for her interview skills of both victims and suspects garnering multiple convictions. Hana has a wealth of knowledge in a number of different defensive modalities and presently serves as director of training and special events for SIG Sauer Inc. www.sigsauer.com / hana.bilodeau@sigsauer.com / Instagram: @hana.bilodeau

Jim Cobb is a recognized authority on disaster preparedness. He's studied, practiced, and taught survival strategies for about 30 years. Today, he resides in the upper Midwest with his beautiful and patient wife and their three adolescent weapons of mass destruction. His books include *Prepper's Home Defense*, *Countdown to Preparedness*, and *Prepper's Long-Term Survival Guide*. www.SurvivalWeekly.com

Patrick Diedrich owns and operates a one-man forestry business located in the remote north woods of Upper Michigan. Diedrich is the training officer for Superior Search and Rescue, an organization that responds to incidents within an area covering over 12,000 square miles of challenging terrain, hundreds of islands, and extreme cold weather. He has instructed domestic and foreign soldiers in close-quarters combat, small unit tactics, and vehicular operations. In a former life, Diedrich adventured across the globe conducting combat reconnaissance and providing humanitarian aid with the U.S. Army. You can learn more about his organizations and undertakings by visiting hemlockandbirchllc.com and superiorsar.org.

Kevin Estela is the Director of Training for Fieldcraft Survival and best-selling author of *101 Skills You Need To Survive In The Woods*. He's an Associate Level Sayoc Kali Instructor, Purple Belt in Brazilian jiujitsu, and graduate of numerous firearm schools. He's a lifelong outdoorsman who is an avid hunter, fisherman, and backpacker. When not teaching or writing about survival skills, he resides near the Wasatch Mountains in Utah.

Scott Finazzo has over 20 years of experience as a firefighter. He is a member of his department's technical rescue team and has served as an instructor since 2000. Scott has written five books, including the national bestselling *The Prepper's Workbook* and *The Neighborhood Emergency Response Handbook*, as well as his narrative of a kayak journey through the Virgin Islands called *Why Do All the Locals Think We're Crazy?* Follow Scott at www.scottfinazzo.com.

Sheena Green is a perpetual student, prior manager at CrossRoads Shooting Sports, and certified firearms instructor. She has attended many shooting, edged weapons, and self-defense classes by well-respected instructors such as Steve Fisher, Steve Tarani, Ed Calderon, and others. She co-leads the Des Moines, Iowa, chapter of The Well Armed Woman. In addition to defensive training, she also enjoys competitive pistol and shotgun sports.

Candice Horner has the heart of a prepper, but the traveling schedule of a gypsy. Ever resourceful, this U.S. Marine Corps veteran and emergency room/prison nurse has a honed and refined skillset, focusing on adaptability and utilizing the tools on-hand. As a competitive shooter, Horner is often on the road, so she's usually rolling with a go-bag, a survivalist mentality, and enough firepower to have your back in a SHTF scenario. www.candi323.com

Hakim Isler is a former psychological-operations sergeant with the U.S. Army, Hakim Isler is the designer of several wilderness survival products and the owner of Elevo Dynamics, the first "Dojym" (a 24-hour gym and martial-arts facility) in the United States. He is also the founder of the SOIL Foundation, a nonprofit that offers off-grid training and excursions to help veterans, law enforcement, and civilians recover from anxiety, depression, and PTSD. Moreover, Isler is a fourth-degree black belt in To-Shin Do. www.thesoilfoundation.org, www.blackmacgyver.com, www.elevodynamics.com

Erik Lund has more than 20 years of law enforcement experience – with much of that time spent as an instructor of firearms, defensive tactics, and use of force. He served as a Virginia State Trooper before accepting a position as a federal agent. Lund is also a senior instructor at Mike Seeklander's Shooting-Performance LLC, a tactical training company. As a champion competitive shooter, he's earned several regional, state, and national three-gun titles and is ranked as a grandmaster by the United States Practical Shooting Association.

Tim MacWelch has been a survival instructor for more than 20 years, training people from all walks of life, including members from all branches of U.S. Armed Forces, the State Department, DOD and DOJ personnel. He's a frequent public speaker for preparedness groups and events. He is also the author of three *New York Times* bestselling survival books, and the new *Ultimate Bushcraft Survival Manual*. When he's not teaching survival or writing about it, MacWelch lives a self-reliant lifestyle with his family in Virginia. Check out his wide range of hands-on training courses that are open to the public at www.advancedsurvivaltraining.com

David Howell Martin wears two hats, alternating between the fly-tying bench and the reloading bench, while dodging the occasional hurricane. From his Sarasota family home he serves as a light tackle/fly fishing guide-tour leader, paddling kayaks or poling canoes throughout Southwest Florida Gulf Coastal mangrove islands and river systems. Returning to dry land, Martin's serves as an NRA training counselor, chief range safety officer, and firearms instructor. The Houston native continuously seeks to improve his survival knowledge and capabilities through mentors, research, product consultation, prayer, and fresh kills over campfires. davidhmartin@me.com

The late Chad McBroom was a 24-year veteran law enforcement officer with most of his time spent in his agency's tactical unit. He's spent over 30 years studying various combative systems and focuses on the science of close combat. Chad was the founder of Comprehensive Fighting Systems, which offered training in empty-hand tactics, edged weapons, impact weapons, and firearms tactics. He was also a regular contributor to RECOIL and RECOIL OFFGRID.

Patrick McCarthy is a freelance writer, editor, and photographer with an avid interest in survival and the outdoors. After receiving his bachelor's degree in 2010, Patrick made his first foray into journalism as the associate editor of *Truckin* magazine. He later moved on to become a freelance contributor and photographed numerous magazine covers. Patrick currently resides in Tustin, California, and works in the marketing department at a classic car parts company.

"Muggs" McCoy is the owner of Team TORN (Technical Off Road Navigation) and is a retired, 24-year veteran of the military. With 18 years in special operations, Muggs' professional experience spans a broad range of technical and tactical skills essential for training the nation's elite forces. Throughout his career, he has trained hundreds of members of the special operations community in tactical mobility, as well as developed and utilized mobility tactics, training, and procedures in both Iraq and Afghanistan. Muggs began motorcycle and UTV racing during his military career, culminating in the country's longest off-road race: Vegas to Reno. He's also a reserve deputy sheriff, splitting his time serving his community and teaching defensive tactics and techniques. He's a CCW instructor, USCCA & NRA instructor.

Phillip Meeks is an agriculture and natural resources educator with a B.S. in Forestry and an M.S. in Community & Leadership Development. He, his wife, and three children live in the mountains of Southwest Virginia. Phillip and his family garden, keep bees, make maple syrup, and hunt mushrooms whenever they can.

Joey Nickischer is a retired detective with the New York City Police Department. He currently works as a lead technical rescue instructor with several different companies covering topics from wilderness search, high angle rope, mine rescue, and off-road operations. He serves as a team leader with the Westchester County Technical Rescue Team and is the commander of the Putnam County Technical Rescue Team, as well as serving as chief of department with the Patterson Fire Department.

Lt. John Nores is a life-long worldwide conservationist, outdoor adventurer and was a California game warden for 28 years. He spent the last 10 years of his career codeveloping the Marijuana Enforcement Team (MET) and Delta Team, the country's first wilderness special ops unit and sniper element, aimed at combatting the drug cartel's decimation of our nation's wildlife, wildlands, and waterways. Awarded the Governor's Medal of Valor for lifesaving and leadership efforts, Nores has written two books (*War in the Woods* and *Hidden War*). His work has been featured on popular podcasts including the Joe Rogan Experience, Cleared Hot, Mike Drop, Field Craft Survival, and Meateater. Contact him at www.johnnores.com and follow him on Instagram at @johnnores for speaking and training events.

Ryan Lee Price is a freelance journalist who specializes in outdoor adventuring, emergency preparedness, and the automotive industry. He has contributed to the *SHTF* survival column in our sister publication *RECOIL* and is a long-time hiking and camping enthusiast. He currently resides in Corona, California, with his wife Kara and their two children.

Danny Pritbor, director and owner of Firebase Combat Studies Group, currently serves as a Department of Defense contractor. Danny's career spans over 29 years with service as a U.S. Marine, law enforcement SWAT officer, Department of Energy and Department of State contractor, federal agent, and private security consultant. He's served worldwide in various war zones and high-threat areas. His company partnered with Panoplia to develop a nine-hour, online training program called Soft Skills and Tactics. It consists of three parts, nine lessons with 45 topics covered. In conjunction with the online course, Firebase offers a two-day security training program that consists of lecture, hands-on, and a field training exercise with stations that push participants to take charge, make decisions, and problem solve. For more information on the online SST program, please visit to panoplia.org. You can also reach Danny at firebasecsg.com.

Kevin Reeve is the founder and Director of onPoint Tactical, the leading provider of training in Urban Survival and Escape and Evasion. onPoint has trained many members of elite military groups such as U.S. Army Special Forces, U.S. Navy SEALs, MARSOC, AF Pararescue, Navy, and Air Force SERE Instructors, as well as members of the DEA, U.S. Marshal Service, ICE, Secret Service, and OGA. In addition to urban skills, Kevin teaches wilderness survival, tracking, SERE, point man training, scout, and related skills. He also provides training to executives and businessmen on counter and anti-kidnapping. Kevin has also been involved in scouting for over 35 years, including 25 years as a Scoutmaster. www.onpointtactical.com

Rudy Reyes is a former member of Force Reconnaissance, one of the U.S. Marine Corps' elite special-operations units. He ran combat missions in Afghanistan then, as part of the 1st Reconnaissance Battalion, helped lead the invasion of Iraq. This mission was documented in the book *Generation Kill* and the HBO adaptation of the same name, which he costarred in. Later, he served as a Defense Department contractor, trained African wildlife preserve rangers, and authored his book, *Hero Living*. For more information, go to www.rudyreyes.com.

Nila Rhoades is a U.S. Army paratrooper's wife and homeschooling mother of three ninja kiddos (10, 4, and 18 months). She has two master's degrees in Homeland Security and Emergency Disaster Management. She's currently obtaining a graduate certificate in counterterrorism. She's also a firearms instructor, workout enthusiast, and avid peanut butter ice cream lover. www.milspecmom.com

Morgan "Rogue" resides in Texas with her husband, daughter, and two dogs, with their second daughter on the way. Her family is always venturing into the wilderness and challenging themselves, as well as others, to love the outdoors. Through Rogue Preparedness, she works toward making the world a more prepared place, where people can feel confident in knowing that they possess the skills, knowledge, and items to get through any emergency or disaster. She educates and entertains on her YouTube channel, website, and social media platforms, as well as in-person events held in Texas. You can find Morgan at roguepreparedness.com.

Dennis Santiago is a global risk and financial analyst. His national policy expertise includes strategic warfare, asymmetric warfare, and global stability. He's a financial industry subject matter expert on systemic risks to the U.S. economy and the safety and soundness testing of U.S. banking institutions. www.dennissantiago.com

Jerry Saunders is a Marine Corps veteran, Scout Sniper, and former Staff NCO in charge of Survival for the United States Marine Corps, Mountain Warfare Training Center. He has trained U.S. and foreign military units across the globe and is internationally recognized for his work in cold weather survival. Saunders recently moved his company Corvus Survival up to the Upper Peninsula of Michigan where he holds private survival classes and operates a small custom knife shop all while rebuilding an old homestead. Learn more about him at corvussurvival.com.

Andrew Schrader is a structural engineer and an Urban Search and Rescue (USAR) specialist for the State of Florida's USAR Task Force. In his role as a Structures Specialist (StS), his job is to advise firefighters and technical rescue teams on the least hazardous means of search-ing for, locating, and extricating live victims in collapsed buildings. Trained by FEMA and the U.S. Army Corps of Engineers, he has been deployed in support of rescue operations for Hurricanes Hermine (2016), Irma (2017), Michael (2018), and Dorian (2019). www.reconresponse.com

Mike Seeklander is the owner of Shooting-Performance LLC, a full-service training company and co-hosts *The Best Defense*, the Out-door Channel's leading firearm instructional TV show. In addition to being a U.S. Marine Corps combat veteran, a former law enforcement officer, and a competitive shooting champion, he's an accomplished martial-arts instructor and holds multiple ranks. Learn more about him at: www.shooting-performance.com.

Kris Southards spent over 26 years with the Federal Bureau of Prisons (BOP). He started as a correctional officer and worked his way up to eventually retire as a management center administrator. During his early years with the BOP, he was selected to attend the first class of Hostage Negotiation Training. While much has changed in the years since then in technology and weapons, the art and science of hostage negotiation has remained fairly constant. The other things that have remained constant are the suggested behaviors hostages should follow. These skills were used on a routine basis during his work with prisoners.

Jason Squires has been an attorney in Arizona for over 21 years. He has an emphasis on self-defense and firearms cases. During his off-time, he's an avid three-gun competitor across the country. He's also a collector of military firearms and vehicles. You can check out his practice at squireslawaz.com.

Miles Vining spent his childhood and teenage years growing up in Thailand, Burma, and Malaysia, returning to the region after his service in the Marines to work with an international relief group that works in conflict zones in Iraq, Syria, and Sudan. He also worked in digital media with a local Afghan company in Kabul. Beyond RECOIL, his work has appeared in Small Arms Review, The Firearm Blog, the TFB TV YouTube channel, and Strife Blog. Currently, he's the editor of Silah Report, an online resource group focused on researching historical and contemporary small arms and light weapons from the Middle East and Central Asian regions. Learn more at www.silahreport.com.

Mel Ward is a husband, father, and combat veteran. He served in Afghanistan and Iraq with 2nd Ranger Battalion, 75th Ranger Regiment. Over the last 15 years, he has worked in the security industry. He's an advocate of preparedness and believes self-reliance isn't an option, but a duty.